THE LIVES AND TIMES
OF THE
PATRIOTS

THE
LIVES AND TIMES
OF THE
PATRIOTS

An Account of
the Rebellion in Upper Canada,
1837-1838
and of the Patriot Agitation
in the United States,
1837-1842

EDWIN C. GUILLET

Nothing extenuate, nor set down aught in malice: SHAKESPEARE

UNIVERSITY OF TORONTO PRESS

Originally published in 1938 by
Thomas Nelson and Sons, Ltd., and in
1963 by The Ontario Publishing Co. Ltd.

This edition
© University of Toronto Press 1968
Printed in U.S.A.
Reprinted 2015
ISBN 978-0-8020-6088-4 (paper)

FOREWORD, 1963

When *The Lives and Times of the Patriots* was published twenty-five years ago B. K. Sandwell said in a review in *Toronto Saturday Night*: 'To compile this work Mr. Guillet must have examined thousands of records in scores of different collections, and he has done his work so thoroughly that it seems improbable that any important addition to it can be made for a generation to come.' The generation has passed, and there are some additions which have been made in the interval.

In connection with Van Diemen's Land, W. D. Forsyth's *Governor Arthur's Convict System* (London, England, 1935), has been supplemented by M. C. Levy's *Governor George Arthur: A Colonial Benevolent Despot* (Melbourne, 1953). These volumes document an unfortunate period in British colonial history, and the Patriot narratives are obviously not exaggerated in their accounts of barbarous treatment.

Donald G. Creighton's *John A. Macdonald, The Young Politician* (Toronto, 1952) gives in detail for the first time Macdonald's part in the trials of the raiders captured at the Prescott invasion. Within the strict limitations of military courts-martial he acted behind the scenes of the trials of Daniel George and the leader, Von Schoultz, both of them lost causes from the start.

A good biography, *The Firebrand*, by William Kilbourne (Toronto, 1956), is the first modern treatment of Mackenzie's life. A recent study of the Patriot movement, particularly in its American aspects, is Oscar A. Kinchen's *The Rise and Fall of the Patriot Hunters* (New York, 1956). He makes the point that the Hunters' Lodges were probably named (as their counterparts in Lower Canada, Frères Chasseurs) to signify Patriots along the frontier carrying arms.

An authority on Patriot activities in the St. Lawrence region, George F. G. Stanley, has recently added details on two episodes. 'Invasion: 1838' (*Ontario History*, Vol. LIV, No. 4, December, 1962) describes the Battle of Windmill Point, Prescott; and 'William Johnston, Pirate or Patriot' (*Historic Kingston*, No. 6, 1956) pieces together the career of the buccaneer of the St. Lawrence. In particular, the author has added new materials from newspapers in Kingston and region contemporary with the events.

From time to time local histories add details to escapes or other experiences of Patriots. Though Esther Heyes' material on the Rebellion is largely from well-known secondary sources, her *The Story of Albion* (Bolton, 1961) records the location of a version of the experiences of John Stewart of Paisley as 'in a Toronto paper'. It turns out to be an account in the Toronto *Globe*, May 17, 1890, and bears strongly the imprint of all the other much earlier accounts of the famous escape from Fort Henry. A long letter from Randal Wixon, one of the nine *ex post facto* prisoners released in England (see *Patriots*, pp. 200-7) is in the possession of the Pickering Township Historical Society. It is printed in W. A. McKay, *The Pickering Story* (1961).

Fred Landon's *An Exile from Canada to Van Diemen's Land* (Toronto, 1960), to which is added on the title-page 'Being the story of Elijah Woodman transported overseas for participation in the Upper Canada troubles of 1837-38', is a study of the Woodman Papers. Though available in part during the writing of the *Patriots* (see bibliographical note, p. 208), the Papers have been amplified by correlative material from the printed Patriot narratives. Seventeen letters are about all that has survived, though the journal that Woodman wrote in Van Diemen's Land reached the State of Maine after he had died at sea in 1847 en route to America in the whaler *Young Eagle*. With skilful use of a wide range of supplementary material the author has made a valuable contribution to Patriots annals, and, as he says in his Preface, 'The story of Elijah Woodman is . . . the first of such accounts to appear in almost one hundred years, and is, probably, the last that will be added to the records of the Canadian exiles of 1837-38'.

One evening in the winter of 1938-39 the late Prime Minister W. L. Mackenzie King telephoned me with reference to the Clifton Memorial Arch at Niagara Falls, then but recently erected. Those responsible for its inscription had not only made several serious errors of fact but had also named upon it a number of executed American Patriot Hunters who have no greater claim to a memorial in their honour than have the Fenians of some thirty years later (who were, in fact, superior in personnel and conduct). Mr. King believed that the inclusion of American raiders with Canadian Patriots was unjustified, and detracted from proper appreciation of the merits of the Canadian Rebellion. A subsequent article in *Toronto Saturday Night* ('Memorials to the Patriots', February 18, 1939) expressed my views—but the inscription has not been altered! Named on the Arch is the Canadian Quaker, Joshua Doan, subject of a novel (Toronto, 1956) by Gladys F. Lewis.

It is, perhaps, worth adding that a school in North York has been named, by vote of the pupils, the William Lyon Mackenzie Collegiate Institute; and that the home of the leader of the Rebellion, whose return to Toronto in 1849 was greeted by 'a bloody riot', is now a historic site and museum under the authority of the Historical Board of what was for a century known as 'Tory Toronto'. Sir Wilfrid Laurier's statement is now pretty generally accepted: 'In 1837 Canadians were fighting for constitutional rights, not against the British Crown'.

Edwin C. Guillet

Toronto, March 1, 1963

PREFACE

There is no general agreement as to when the citizen may revolt against constituted authority, but it is universally admitted that with human nature as it is, rebellion is inevitable from time to time. A successful revolution alters the status of the rebel, who immediately becomes a patriot, and a halo is thrown about the actors in a drama that may have had but little to commend it. Failure, on the other hand, leads not only to the severe punishment and persecution of the participants, but frequently to a distortion of motives and actions on all sides.

A century has passed since the Upper Canadian Rebellion of 1837, and it should now be possible to view the struggle dispassionately and reach common ground. Only two histories worthy of the name have appeared in that time, the first seventy-six and the second fifty-three years ago. The earliest, by Charles Lindsey, son-in-law of William Lyon Mackenzie, can hardly be said to be unbiased, while that of John C. Dent, though generally of greater literary merit, is marred by excessive animus against Mackenzie and a determined effort to elevate Rolph to a pedestal altogether unwarranted by the evidence; nor can either work be considered a full history of the events and results of the Patriot agitation, though in general highly satisfactory in their detailed presentation of the causes.

The present work is designed to present the human side of the story, to bestow for the first time upon the rank and file of the agitation, as well as their loyalist opponents, the attention their lives and times merit. The revolt was not merely the crushing of one or two incipient risings of malcontents, but a condition of seething agitation extending over years. People felt strongly in those days, and loves and hates were exceedingly intense. Neighbour suspected neighbour, and otherwise decent people stooped to all sorts of petty meanness, vindictiveness, and persecution. American Patriot activities in sympathy had frequently much more behind them than appeared on the surface, for politics and personal antipathies were often much more prominent than a desire for Canadian constitutional freedom. There is, indeed, very little in that part of the movement that can be justified.

The causes of the failure of the Patriot agitation are obvious. The lack of support from the right wing of the Reform party, and the last-minute defection of leaders who had been influential in the earlier stages, demoralized the Upper Canadian movement, which suffered also from a lack of military leaders; while its continuance on the other side of the international border was entirely lacking in leadership and continuity, and received no serious support in

Upper Canada. Never was a movement so characterized by jealousy and disunion. In many respects it was every leader for himself and the devil take the deluded followers.

The writer is not an antagonist of or apologist for any person or group, nor interested in the controversies of the past except insofar as the weight of evidence indicates the truth. In general the documents are allowed to speak for themselves, and the author's judgment is given only on controversies of importance and after careful study of all evidence. Most of the progress of the world, as well as many of the mistakes, has been due to men who were called rebels and fanatics by their contemporaries; and the rise in recent years of repressive autocracies should further restrain unwarranted criticism of the motives of those who prevented the continuance of arbitrary rule in Canada, and who were criticized in their own day chiefly for advocating the type of democratic government that we, in common with other Anglo-Saxon nations, have long enjoyed.

The greater part of the material upon which this work is based is entirely new, or presented for the first time in its natural sequence. The writings of the period, whether memoirs, newspaper reports, or editorial comments, are commonly biased one way or the other and full of gossip and suspicion, but there is not much indication of deliberate misrepresentation except in certain items of undisguised propaganda. Materials have been gathered from every source, by research in the largest public and private collections of manuscript and printed materials, by personal contact and correspondence with descendants of participants, and by a careful collation of data from diaries and narratives, British, American, and Canadian newspapers, official reports and private letters, registers of prisoners and lists of recruits, obituary notices and tombstones. It will be apparent even to the casual reader that it has been no small task to bring some semblance of order and truth out of such a mass of conflicting data, but the writer has worked upon the principle that every detail, however trivial and inconsequential, is worthy of preservation. To assemble accurate lists of participants in the various Patriot concentrations and raids was particularly involved, for not a few passed under aliases and many were ignorant of or inconsistent in the spelling of their names; while even official records convey incomplete and erroneous information as to the eventual punishment meted out to those tried and convicted. That it was essentially a workingman's movement added to the difficulty, for the participants were consequently persons who quickly sank into the obscurity from which they had risen for a brief and painful interlude.

The illustrations, which have been assembled from various parts of the world, are as nearly as possible contemporary with the events described. It is unfortunate that with but few exceptions the likenesses of participants are available only in their old age, if at all; but primitive photography and the high cost of obtaining any type of portrait explain why most people of the period died without leaving any representation of their appearance.

Of great value in the search for material was the bibliography of sources compiled by Miss Frances Staton of the Toronto Public Library, and that by the late Frank H. Severance of the Buffalo Historical Society. In addition to documents in the public collections in Ottawa and Washington, many valuable items, both manuscript and printed, have been obtained from the Burton Historical Collection, Detroit, the Buffalo Historical Society, the Archives of Ontario, the Victoria College Library, the Legislative Library of Ontario, and the public libraries of Toronto, New York, Rochester, Buffalo, Syracuse, and Albany. Previously inaccessible to historians and still unorganized, the Lindsey Papers in the University of Toronto Library have provided Mackenzie's correspondence, his collections of clippings, the files of his newspapers, and fugitive writings of great interest; some of the more valuable of these are given to the public for the first time in the Appendix.

It is invidious to name a few persons where so many have contributed items without which the book would be much the poorer, but the author is particularly indebted to Dr. James F. Kenney, Public Archives of Canada, Ottawa; Dr. Robert Bingham, Director of the Buffalo Historical Society; Mr. W. S. Wallace, Librarian of the University of Toronto; Mr. Fred Landon, Librarian of the University of Western Ontario, London; Miss Leckie, Legislative Library of Ontario; Mr. Charles S. Buck, London, Ontario; Messrs. F. W. Hayden, Charles Lindsey, and T. Wilbur Best, Toronto; Mr. Sidney Watson, London, England; Mrs. Arthur Williams, Captain Henry Johnston, and Mr. J. Donald Garnsey, Clayton, N.Y.; Miss Loy Neads, Fort Frances; Mrs. Edna Barrowclough, Wesleyville; Mrs. Zoe Stevens, Toronto; Mr. James B. Scott, Oakland Township; the Reverend N. H. Noble, Thornhill; and Mr. Louis Blake Duff, Welland. My wife has not only aided in compiling the Index and putting the book through the press, but has continued to endure graciously a somewhat intensive preoccupation in historical research.

EDWIN C. GUILLET.

Toronto, Canada,
New Year's Day, 1938.

CONTENTS

CHAPTER		PAGE
I.	William Lyon Mackenzie and the Agitation for Reform	1
II.	The Siege of Toronto	15
III.	The Remarkable Escape of Mackenzie	29
IV.	With the Newcastle District Militia	34
V.	Charles Duncombe and the Concentration at Scotland	46
VI.	Among the Refugees	57
VII.	Navy Island and the *Caroline*	71
VIII.	The Schooner *Anne* and Bois Blanc Island	88
IX.	Donald McLeod and Fighting Island	94
X.	The Pelee Island Raid	99
XI.	The Short Hills and St. Clair Raids	104
XII.	John Montgomery and the Jail Delivery from Fort Henry	114
XIII.	Edward Theller and the Celebrated Escape from the Citadel of Quebec	121
XIV.	The Battle of the Windmill	132
XV.	The Battle of Windsor	143
XVI.	Bill Johnston and the Burning of the *Sir Robert Peel*	153
XVII.	Ben Lett and the Cobourg Conspiracy	163
XVIII.	The United States and the Patriot War	178
XIX.	Jails and Convict-Ships	191
XX.	Van Diemen's Land	209
XXI.	The Exiles' Return	221

Appendix—Select Documents and Collation of Data:

A	Resolution Declaring Mackenzie Unworthy of a Seat in the Legislative Assembly	243
B	The 'Family Compact'	244
C	(1) The Flag of Truce	245
	(2) Deposition of Samuel Lount	246
D	Proclamations of Sir Francis Bond Head	247
E	The Cobourg Rifles, 1837	248
F	The Deposition of Peter Coon	249

CONTENTS

G Upper Canadians Arrested and Imprisoned - - 250
H (1) The Navy Island Proclamation - - - 256
   (2) List of Recruits at Navy Island - - - 259
I Navy Island Correspondence - - - - - 263
J The Pelee Raid:
   (1) Statement of John McIntyre - - - - 266
   (2) The St. Thomas Cavalry, 1838 - - - 267
K Lount and Matthews:
   (1) The Reverend John Ryerson's Account of the Executions - - - - - - 267
   (2) The Graves and Monuments - - - - 268
   (3) Theller's Biographical Notice of Lount - - 269
   (4) Biography of Lount by Mackenzie - - - 270
   (5) Biography of Matthews by Mackenzie - - 270
   (6) Letter of Mrs. Lount to Mackenzie - - 270
   (7) Miscellaneous Items - - - - - 271
L The Short Hills Raid:
   (1) Disposition of the Prisoners - - - - 272
   (2) Letter of Warner to his Mother - - - 272
   (3) Letter of Maria Wait to Mrs. Warner - - 273
   (4) Warrant to Captain Morton of the *Captain Ross* - - - - - - - - 273
   (5) Letter of Fox Maule to Joseph Hume - - 275
M The St. Clair Raids - - - - - - 276
N Documents Relative to the Invasion at Prescott:
   (1) Daniel Heustis's List of Participants - - 276
   (2) Escape of N. Williams after the Battle - - 279
   (3) The Charge against Stephen S. Wright - - 281
   (4) The Trial of Von Schoultz - - - - 282
   (5) Biography of Von Schoultz by Warren Green 283
   (6) Disposition of the Prisoners - - - - 285
O Documents Relative to the Battle of Windsor:
   (1) Disposition of the Prisoners - - - - 286
   (2) Letter of Doan to his Wife - - - - 286
   (3) Address by Amos Perley from the Scaffold 287
   (4) The Executions - - - - - - 288
   (5) Epitaph on Surgeon Hume's Tombstone - 289
P Documents Relative to the Return of Prisoners from Van Diemen's Land:
   (1) Letter of Wright and Dresser to the New York *Tribune* - - - - - - 289
   (2) Letter of Edward Everett to Daniel Heustis 291
   (3) American Prisoners Pardoned on Application of Mr. Everett - - - - - - 294
   (4) The Pardon of Stephen Wright by Sir John Franklin - - - - - - - - 294
   (5) The Pardon of Orrin Smith by Sir Eardley Wilmot - - - - - - - - 295
   (6) Letter of Linus Miller to the New York *Express* - - - - - - - 296
Q Extension of Amnesty—The Pardon of David Gibson - - - - - - - 297

INDEX - - - - - - - - - 299

ILLUSTRATIONS

William Lyon Mackenzie		Frontispiece
		Facing Page
Gold Medal Presented to Mackenzie, 1832		2
Doel Home and Brewery, Toronto		2
Elliott's Tavern, Toronto		2
Sir Francis Bond Head		3
Dr. John Rolph		3
Forging Pikes for Rebellion		3
Toronto at the Time of the Rebellion of 1837		18
Bloor Toll-Gate, Toronto		19
Powell Escapes to Warn the Lieutenant-Governor		19
Battle of Montgomery's Farm		34
Death of Lieutenant-Colonel Moodie	*Adrian Sharp*	34
Isabel Baxter Mackenzie		35
Marshall S. Bidwell		35
Charles Durand		35
Dr. Thomas D. Morrison		35
Dr. Charles Duncombe		50
Sir Allan MacNab		50
Samuel Chandler		50
Eliakim Malcolm		50
Proclamation of Reward for Rebellion Leaders		51
American Patriot Handbill		51
Bringing Patriot Prisoners to Jail	*J. H. Lynch*	66
Navy Island, Niagara River	*W. H. Bartlett*	66
Daniel Conant		67
Joseph Gould		67
Refugees Escaping to Oswego	*E. S. Shrapnel*	67
Navy Island Note		76
Eagle Tavern, Buffalo		82
Burning of the *Caroline*		83
Admiral Andrew Drew		98
Alexander McLeod		98
The *Caroline's* Last Voyage	*W. R. Callington*	98
American Satire on the British Capture of Navy Island		99
Detroit from Windsor, 1837	*W. J. Bennett and F. K. Grain*	114

LIST OF ILLUSTRATIONS

	Facing Page
Anderson and Montgomery in 1875	115
Courtyard of Fort Henry, Kingston	115
Execution of Lount and Matthews	123
David Gibson	130
Chief Justice John Beverley Robinson	130
Mrs. Lount Petitioning Sir George Arthur — *William Bengough*	130
MS. Title Page of 'The Canadian Tragedy'	131
Patriot Commission	146
Citadel of Quebec — *W. H. Bartlett*	146
Title Page of *Narrative* of Robert Marsh	147
Title Page of *Narrative* of Daniel Heustis	147
Battle of the Windmill	162
Defeat of the Rebels at Dickinson Landing — *Coke Smyth*	162
Final Page of Von Schoultz Trial Record	163
William Johnston	178
Colonel John Prince	178
Engagement in the Thousand Islands — *Coke Smyth*	178
Figurehead of the *Caroline*	179
Brock's Monument after the Explosion	179
Cobourg in 1840 — *Lieutenant Philip Bainbrigge*	179
'Old French Prison', Liverpool — *W. Herdman*	194
View of the Inside of Newgate, London	194
Upper Canadian State Prisoners in England	195
Sir John Franklin	210
Benjamin Wait	210
York Hulk in Portsmouth Harbour — *William Carey*	210
Map of Van Diemen's Land	211
Embarking for Van Diemen's Land	226
Convict Labour on the Roads	226
Prisoners Carrying Timber	226
Hobart Town, Van Diemen's Land, from the Barracks	227
Hobart Town, Van Dieman's Land, from the Harbour	227
Edward Everett	242
Lord Durham — *Sir Thomas Laurence*	242
South Seas Whaler *Canton*	242
Pardon of Orrin Smith	243

CHAPTER I

WILLIAM LYON MACKENZIE AND THE AGITATION FOR REFORM

THE distinction between rebels and patriots is often very finely drawn, for the success of a revolution makes the difference between blood-thirsty insurgents and national heroes, and political or personal sympathy sometimes keeps alive for generations an allegiance or hatred out of all proportion to the causes of the conflict. Armed rebellion in Upper Canada came only after a long-sustained but unsuccessful effort to secure administrative reform, and it is evident that the struggle in the beginning was against the constitution, not the Queen. The issue was by no means clear to all. There were some among the rank and file of the Patriot agitation whose motives were no more lofty than hope of plunder or desire for excitement, and, on the other hand, there were in the loyalist militia many who had no understanding of the point at issue, but were actuated solely by animosity and a desire for revenge. But with these exceptions and limitations, both parties to the dispute played an honourable role, and even those who favoured independence or a union with the United States sincerely believed that such a solution was in the best interests of Canada.

Although there was an occasional flurry of opposition to the provincial administration prior to the War of 1812, the genesis of the Reform movement in Upper Canada was the early career of Robert Gourlay, a Scottish agitator who emigrated to the province in 1817. He was not long in the new land before he began to investigate and expose abuses. Particularly did he arouse opposition to the Clergy and Crown reserves, and very soon the oligarchy which ruled the province took steps to suppress him. A charge of libel was trumped up in August, 1818, but he conducted his own defence with consummate skill and was acquitted. After making one more futile effort his enemies changed their tactics and had him arrested under the Alien Act of 1804, which had been directed particularly against reputedly disloyal immigrants from Ireland and the United States, and on January 4, 1819, he was imprisoned at Niagara. A writ of *habeas corpus* availed him nothing, and he suffered greatly during the months prior to his trial, appearing in the prisoner's dock in an enfeebled and wasted condition and entirely unfit to defend himself. The sentence of the court was that he must leave the province within twenty-four hours or render himself liable to death as a felon, and in August, 1819, 'the banished Briton' crossed over to the United States.[1]

There were numerous other instances[2] of the same type of persecution, and with each success the Family Compact became firmer in its resolve to suppress opposition. However, the establishment of the *Colonial Advocate* by William Lyon Mackenzie in 1824 marked a turning-point in the fortunes of the Reform movement. Mackenzie was born in Dundee, Scotland, on March 12, 1795, of parents of the same clan. Both his grandfathers had been Jacobites, and one of them had accompanied Charles Edward, the Pretender, to Europe.[3] His father died when he was three weeks old, but he received a good common-school education, and was then set to work in a draper's shop. In his seventeenth year he opened a store at Alyth, near Dundee. He operated a circulating library in his shop, and this, no doubt, had much to do with the formation of his lifelong habit of wide reading. His first business venture was not successful, and he soon found himself £1,600 in debt, with assets of £1,150; but he records with pardonable pride that 'in law I was not responsible for sixpence—I was a minor, under twenty-two years,—but considering those I owed had an equitable demand I paid them in full at various periods when my circumstances afforded the means, and this without being in any one instance reminded of their claims.'[4]

After a short sojourn in Europe Mackenzie returned to Dundee, where he received further schooling; but in 1820 he set sail for Quebec. After being employed for a few weeks on the Lachine Canal, he proceeded to York and then to Dundas, in both of which he was associated in business with John Lesslie. He remained fifteen months in Dundas, during which, on July 1, 1822, he married Isabel Baxter.[5] The partnership with Lesslie having been dissolved, Mackenzie removed to Queenston, where on May 18, 1824, he commenced the publication of the *Colonial Advocate*.

The abuses of public administration, in opposition to which the *Advocate* quickly became the chief mouth-piece, were as characteristic of the United Kingdom as of the British provinces in

[1] After being banished Gourlay returned to Scotland, where he produced his *Statistical Account of Upper Canada* (1822). In 1836 he went to the United States, where he condemned the Rebellion and opposed American participation. In 1842 the sentence was declared null and void, and later he returned to Canada West. His eccentricity showed itself in his autobiography, *The Banished Briton and Neptunian* (1843), and in a scheme of land settlement which he projected, a summary of which is given in the author's *The Great Migration*, 30. He died in Edinburgh, Scotland, on August 1, 1863.

[2] Detailed accounts of the persecution of Wyatt, Willcocks, and Thorpe, and later of Fothergill and Collins, are given in Dent, I.

[3] 'I glory in my rebel blood', Mackenzie once said.

[4] 'Mackenzie's Account of Himself', reprinted from the New York *Sun* in the Toronto *Mirror*, April 21, 1838.

[5] She shared to the full her husband's vicissitudes, and died on January 12, 1873.

Gold Medal Presented to Mackenzie in 1832

Courtesy John Ross Robertson Collection
Doel Home and Brewery, Toronto
Prominent Reform meeting-place at Adelaide and Bay Streets

Courtesy John Ross Robertson Collection
Elliott's Tavern, Queen and Yonge Streets, Toronto
Known as 'the rebel corner' because Reform meetings were held there

Sir Francis Bond Head

Lieutenant-Governor of Upper Canada, 1836-1838, who was recalled after his obstinacy had resulted in rebellion

Dr. John Rolph

Prominent leader, who fled to the United States after acting as Bond Head's emissary to his fellow-Patriots at Montgomery's

From a contemporary print

Forging Pikes for Rebellion

For those without firearms, Lount and other blacksmiths provided hickory pikes eight or ten feet long, 'spear-shaped, sharply pointed, double-edged, and calculated for thrusting and ripping'

America. The great mass of citizens were governed by an aristocracy more or less benevolent, and only the few of family and influence had any appreciable share in government. In Upper Canada the lieutenant-governor held the supreme power, and the Church of England and the Executive Council exercised most influence, uniting with the governor to dispense patronage to their friends and supporters. Only those among the favoured class could find such a type of government to their liking, but many settlers, occupied in clearing their bush farms, had no time to voice their political grievances.

Those settlers who had come from the United States found the administration of public affairs particularly objectionable, for they had been used to a greater share of self-government. The Canada Act of 1791 quieted their murmurs for a time, giving them representative institutions, but it was apparent after the War of 1812 that opposition from those who were dubbed 'Americans' or 'Republicans' would not be tolerated. The system ensured that the spoils of office were all on one side—not even under a Reform government could Reformers hope to share to any appreciable extent. But, though it does not appear that Mackenzie and his followers had any exact comprehension of responsible government as the term was later understood, they had a very good knowledge of the causes and effects upon which their grievances were based.

In November, 1825, Mackenzie moved the *Colonial Advocate* to Toronto, so that he would be in the centre of political controversy; and at the same time he hoped to increase circulation and profits. He petitioned the Legislative Assembly to improve the administration of the Post Office, but quickly found that the elected House had little control over matters of importance and none at all over public policy. The Executive was not responsive to public opinion, and, as its attitude was usually sustained by the Legislative Council, the Assembly could be defied to do its worst. Restraint in speech or writing was not a characteristic of the time, and Mackenzie viciously attacked the system and the personal character of those in office. He imputed motives which did not exist, and no effort was made by him or his opponents to understand the point of view of the other. Vigour of speech characterized Mackenzie's attacks against the Family Compact. When he called the members of the Legislative Council 'tools of a servile power' he was accused of disloyalty, but he retorted that he would rather work for his bread than submit to 'the official fungi, more numerous and pestilential than the marshes and quagmires that encircle Toronto'.

His opponents naturally lost no opportunity to belittle him.

4   THE LIVES AND TIMES OF THE PATRIOTS

Sir Peregrine Maitland went out of his way to humiliate him on the occasion of the laying of the corner-stone of Brock's monument,[6] and he deleted from the public expenditure an item passed by a vote of the two Houses ordering payment of £37 16s. to Mackenzie for publishing debates. But it was the notorious attack on his printing-press[7] that swung public sympathy towards the Reform leader. The details of the incident have been told many times and need not be recounted here; but the outrage had results very different from what the perpetrators expected. While the young bloods of the Family Compact escaped adequate punishment, Mackenzie was able as a result of the damages of £625 to set up his *Advocate* on a more stable basis; and the publicity he received tended to make him a popular hero, though he was in no respect relieved of indignity and persecution.

In 1825 the Reformers were for the first time of appreciable strength in the Assembly, and in 1828, due largely to the attack on Mackenzie's printing-press, they secured a majority in the election. But the death of George IV put a sudden end to the life of that Parliament, and in the ensuing election the Reformers were defeated, the new House being 'more Tory than the Family Compact, more royalist than the King'. Mackenzie, however, had secured a seat, and he lost no time in resuming his attack upon the established order. His first offensive was directed against the custom of restricting the House chaplain to the clergy of the Church of England, but his motion suggesting that the various denominations officiate alternately was defeated, Attorney-General Boulton setting the key-note of the Tory majority by affirming that for the House to choose its own chaplain would be an example of brute force on a par with the right of an assassin to shoot down a man in the street. To attempt to argue the point with such opponents appeared entirely useless, but Mackenzie was persistent and he next moved for an inquiry into the state of representation in the House and its relation to office-holders and placemen of various types. This he followed up with a motion for an enquiry into pensions, fees, and salaries, and he then attacked the operation of the patronage-ridden Bank of Upper Canada. Consequently, before

---

6Mackenzie inserted a copy of the first issue of his *Colonial Advocate* in a hollowed portion of the foundation block of the monument. 'Many days afterwards', he wrote in his *New Almanack for the Canadian True Blues*, 'when the column was forty-eight feet high, Sir Peregrine Maitland . . ordered his courtier, Thomas Clark, to go and dig it out again. Clark obeyed, and after three days' excavation exhumed the record with the otter's skin in which it had been wrapped'.

7On January 2, 1828, the following took out an affidavit acknowledging the act but disclaiming any incitement: Samuel P. Jarvis, Henry Sherwood, James King, C. R. Heward, Charles Baby, Peter M'Dougall, John Lyons, and Charles Richardson. The £625 fine was paid, wrote Jarvis, 'not wholly by the Defendants, but by a tax . . . imposed upon Society'.

the session ended, he had aroused the antagonism of the Family Compact to fever heat.

During the recess Mackenzie organized public meetings throughout the province to support his campaign by resolutions, and at the same time he continued the agitation in the *Colonial Advocate,* with the result that, during the November session of the Assembly, he was charged with 'gross, scandalous, and malicious libel' calculated to bring the House into disrepute. By a vote of twenty-four to fifteen he was expelled from the Assembly, but he stood for re-election and on January 2, 1832, 'the People's Friend', as he was called, was almost unanimously chosen at a tumultuous poll at the Red Lion Tavern. The election was followed by an enthusiastic demonstration, and a parade of sleighs drove past Government House and other Tory strongholds. But when Mackenzie entered the House to take his seat he was again expelled, and this procedure was repeated several times in succeeding years. He was even declared incapable of being a member of the Assembly.

During the summer of 1832 he went to England and succeeded in obtaining sympathy from the Colonial Office. In 1834 he was chosen first mayor of Toronto. The persecution of the previous four years had had a characteristic reaction upon public opinion, and in the election of 1835 the Reformers obtained a majority.

The new Parliament lost no time in entering upon an investigation of political abuses, and Mackenzie had the satisfaction of having expunged from the journals of the House all proceedings relative to his expulsion. He also immediately moved for a committee on grievances, and was made its chairman. On April 10 the famous *Seventh Report on Grievances* was presented to the Assembly, and no stronger indictment of administrative government has ever been set forth. The report and its appendix of documentary material was widely distributed in the United Kingdom and the British provinces, wherever it was calculated to do most good. But apparently neither a majority in the Assembly nor an exposé of the system—not even the sympathy of the Imperial Government—could break the Family Compact, and the abuses continued without appreciable interruption. The Imperial administration was alive to the issue, however, and hoped to ameliorate conditions by the appointment of a tactful person to succeed Sir John Colborne as Lieutenant-Governor. It was not for some time generally known that religious grievances had been intensified by the endowment of fifty-seven rectories of the Church of England, a move which could hardly be interpreted otherwise than as an insult to public opinion.

Sir Francis Bond Head, the new Lieutenant-Governor, reached Toronto on January 23, 1836, carrying 'Mr. Mackenzie's heavy book of lamentations' in his portmanteau. The report that he was a thorough Liberal and 'a Tried Reformer'[8] had preceded him, but so much in error was it that his presence was to prove, more than any other circumstance, the cause of the Rebellion. Lord Glenelg's instructions to him showed a desire to be conciliatory, without in any sense suggesting that republican institutions might be imitated in Upper Canada, and there would have been no rebellion if Sir Francis had possessed even a small share of tact and common sense.

After a show of Liberal sympathy in the appointment of Baldwin, Rolph, and Dunn to the Executive Council, Sir Francis undermined their position by ignoring their advice, with the inevitable result that on March 4, after remonstrating without effect, they resigned. Under the influence of Chief Justice Robinson and the Reverend John Strachan, the 'Tried Reformer' was soon to be more Tory than any of them. As a result of a public meeting in Toronto an address was carried to Sir Francis by a deputation, to whom the remarkably tactless reply was made that he would comment upon it 'in plainer and more homely language' than he might have felt constrained to use if the address had not come 'principally from the industrial classes'. The implied insolence brought a rejoinder prepared by Rolph and O'Grady.[9] 'We are duly sensible of your great condescension in endeavouring to express yourself in plainer and more homely language, presumed by your Excellency to be thereby brought down to the lower level of our plainer and more homely understandings'. After outlining some of the major grievances and pressing for a responsible administration, the protest concluded in a menacing tone: 'If your Excellency will not govern us upon these principles you will exercise arbitrary sway, you will violate our charter, virtually abrogate our law, and justly forfeit our submission to your authority'. It was, as Mackenzie wrote, 'the first low murmur of insurrection'.

Meanwhile, the incident of the replacement of the executive councillors was arousing much public discussion and protest. The Reform attitude tended towards the theory of responsible govern-

---

[8] A placard on the streets thus welcomed the Lieutenant-Governor to Toronto. How far astray the report was is apparent from his own callous comment: 'I was no more connected with human politics than the horses which were drawing me'. It has been suggested that Sir Francis was appointed in error for Sir Edmund Head.

[9] The Reverend William John O'Grady, a Roman Catholic priest, came to Toronto in 1828. As a result of trouble with his religious superiors he was excommunicated, and in 1832 he founded the *Correspondent*. He continued Mackenzie's agitation when the *Advocate* merged with his newspaper in November, 1834.

ment, while the Tories believed such principles were but the first step to separation from Britain. The Assembly withheld supplies, and an Address to the King, signed by Marshall S. Bidwell, Speaker, minced no words in charging the Lieutenant-Governor with tyranny and deceit, and on April 20 Sir Francis prorogued Parliament amid the most intense excitement. But by imputing disloyalty to his opponents the Lieutenant-Governor capitalized on the dispute to gain supporters from the ranks of moderate Reformers, particularly in the rural districts. He also professed to believe that an invasion of American sympathizers was imminent, and called upon the loyal to rally around his leadership. Although noted more for obstinacy than sagacity, he apparently made a shrewder estimate of public opinion than the Reformers, and decided to trust the issue to a general election. The Tories were quick to respond. 'Victory or Death. The Rebels shall be defeated!!!' ran an election broadside. During the contest, which was held as soon as possible after dissolution, Sir Francis acted as party leader, and the conduct of both himself and his followers could hardly be interpreted other than as an open attempt to bribe and intimidate, for land patents were given out to electors at the time of polling, and Sir Francis, as well as gangs of ruffians, were at the polls in the Tory interest. The result left the Reformers an insignificant minority, and the more radical believed that nothing was to be gained by constitutional means.

There had, however, been a notable defection from Reform ranks which had much to do with the defeat. The Reverend Egerton Ryerson had previously withdrawn his support from Mackenzie, and, though he was not in Upper Canada during the election, his influence was exerted through the widely circulated and influential *Christian Guardian,* and large numbers of Methodists who had always voted Reform supported Bond Head's campaign in the supposed interests of loyalty to British connection. The election was fought, therefore, on an issue very different from the responsibility of the Executive Council, which had been the prime cause of the dispute with Sir Francis.

Mackenzie, bitter over his personal defeat and that of his party, once again established a political newspaper. The first number of the *Constitution* significantly appeared on the sixtieth anniversary of the American Declaration of Independence, July 4, 1836, while the results of the election were still coming in. It was more revolutionary in tone than the *Colonial Advocate,* but the administration, having learned by experience the futility of persecution, made no effort to suppress the publication. There was, too, more ephemeral political literature which, though often exaggerated in tone, frequently hit the nail on the head with annoying vehemence which was impossible of entire refutation:

'The backwoodsman, while he lays the axe to the root of the oak in the forests of Canada, should never forget that a base basswood is growing in this his native land, which, if not speedily girdled, will throw its dark shadows over the country and blast its best exertions. Look up, reader, and you will see the branches—the Robinson branch, the Powell branch, the Jones branch, the Strachan branch, the Boulton twig, etc. The farmer toils, the merchant toils, the labourer toils, and the Family Compact reap the fruit of their exertions.'[10]

Other publications were more frankly revolutionary. Samuel Hart, editor of the Cobourg *Plain Speaker*, was essentially a leveller, denouncing those who, 'wallowing in luxury, . . arrogate to themselves the right of *governing*, . . and are not the Producing Class in any other sense than this—they produce discord—engender strife—create rebellions—foster disease—and fatten upon the miseries of their fellow creatures'. His advocacy of a 'farmer Governor' indicates the agrarian protest.[11]

Meanwhile Dr. John Rolph, who had survived the election, carried on the Reform agitation in the House with his accustomed oratorical skill, though with but little effect on the majority of his auditors. Van Egmond, in the 'backwoods' Huron Tract, denounced the Canada Company and complained of the low status of farmers in Upper Canada. Mackenzie pressed the issue in various parts of the province, and at times narrowly escaped physical violence. During the early winter he was scheduled to speak at the Amherst Court House, near Cobourg, but a considerable group of Tories from Peterborough and vicinity determined to prevent the meeting. The ensuing events indicate the temper of the times. To effect their purpose secretly the Peterborough 'gentlemen' held a ball at 'Government House'—a large log structure which had been the Honourable Peter Robinson's headquarters during the Irish immigration—and in the early hours of the morning set off in sleighs for Cobourg, thirty-five miles distant. Upon arrival they found that the Tories of the locality had already seized the building and locked the doors, while Mackenzie and the Reformers were vainly seeking admittance and threatening violence if refused. The Peterborough sleighs lined up in front of the doors, and as it was useless to attempt to pass them the Reformers commenced an open-air meeting. Their opponents

[10]*Patrick Swift's Almanac* for 1834, quoted in Scadding, *Toronto of Old*, 105-6. The aptness of the term 'Family Compact' is apparent from Mackenzie's researches. See appendix B, and, for the resolution of the Assembly declaring him unworthy of a seat in Parliament, appendix A.

[11]See bibliography for sources on Hart, and chapter XVII for his subsequent activities. For a survey of the social status and aims of the Radicals see appendix G.

raised derisive shouts and stationed a bugler near by to play *The Rogues' March* and similar tunes. Finally Mackenzie had to secrete himself until he could make a safe retreat.

Events in the capital fanned the smouldering discontent, particularly Sir Francis's refusal of Lord Glenelg's suggestion that it would be good policy to elevate Marshall Spring Bidwell to the Bench. He had not forgotten when Bidwell was Speaker of the Assembly and signed the Address to the King criticizing his actions as lieutenant-governor, and he peremptorily refused to accede to the wishes of the Colonial Office in this respect. His obstinacy was to bring about his recall, but the lack of speedy means of communication left the matter in abeyance long enough to bring about rebellion. 'Of this I am perfectly assured,' wrote Egerton Ryerson, 'that had Bidwell been appointed to the Bench, Mackenzie never could have made an insurrection'.

During the early summer of 1837 armed resistance began to be regarded as the only means to effect a change. Among the first rural meetings to further such a policy was a secret gathering in Lloydtown on June thirtieth, at which it was resolved that, constitutional resistance having proved in vain, it behooved every Reformer to arm himself in defence of his rights. In other parts of the Home District there were similar meetings, though it does not appear that actual plans of rebellion were contemplated at that time. In Toronto, headquarters of the Reform party, the first measures taken were in sympathy with the aspirations of the French-Canadian *Patriotes*; but the number of those who favoured passive endurance in Upper Canada was becoming less and less, and the party of active and militant opposition more and more numerous. Elliott's Tavern, at the north-west corner of Yonge and Queen Streets, was a favourite Reform meeting-place, and there, during the last week of July, two meetings were held to formulate and discuss resolutions designed to support the Lower Canadian Reformers. On the twenty-eighth they were further considered at Doel's Brewery, were adopted on the thirty-first, and published in the *Constitution* on August 2. One of the resolutions[12] called for the holding of a convention in Toronto, and the furtherance of this object was left largely to Mackenzie, who was appointed agent and corresponding secretary. He set to work with characteristic energy and zeal, dividing Upper Canada into districts and arranging to address meetings and inaugurate branch societies. The Home District was particularly well organ-

[12] The 'Declaration of the Reformers of the City of Toronto to their Fellow Reformers in Upper Canada' may be found in C. Lindsey, II 334-342. It is signed by T. D. Morrison, Chairman, John Elliott, Secretary, and a committee of seventeen which included all the prominent Toronto Radicals except Rolph.

ized in this respect, which accounts for the large number of recruits who eventually rallied at Montgomery's; but Mackenzie travelled farther afield, wherever his presence and enthusiasm were calculated to do most good.

The precautions which had to be taken to prevent attacks upon Mackenzie as he passed through the province are indicative of the violence of party feeling. After the earliest meetings at Newmarket and Lloydtown on August 3 and 5, where banners inscribed 'Liberty or Death!' were carried, fifty men on horseback escorted him to Boltontown, where Orangemen prevented the continuance of the deliberations in public. A collision between the opposing factions, which had barely been prevented earlier, disturbed the peace of the neighbourhood:

'Twenty-six Mackenzie men, mounted, were crossing the bridge over the Humber when one of the opposite party seized the hindmost by the thigh, as if with the intention of forcing him into the river. Two others were attacked at the same time. All the twenty-six dismounted instantly and fell upon their assailants with whatever was within their reach. Blood flowed freely; and some of the assailing party, as they lay on the ground, were made to confess that they had only got their deserts.'

After the next meeting, which was at Caledon, Mackenzie was accompanied to Chingacousy by some twenty horsemen. There on August 10, partisans of both political groups made their way to John Campbell's house, armed with muskets, pistols, and heavy clubs; but to avoid bloodshed the Reformers gave up the open-air meeting and, leaving the Orangemen outside, proceeded to consider the resolutions within the house. It is not remarkable that a special resolution was then passed to the effect that independence would have some advantages over the state of government which obtained in Upper Canada. Thirty carriages and a hundred horsemen escorted Mackenzie and Gibson to a subsequent meeting, and the Orangemen were given to understand that disturbers of Reform activities would be met with the same violence. Referring to a meeting in Vaughan, 'One Who Saw and Heard' wrote to the *Constitution* that 'we all separated with the understanding that to produce good order there must be hickory sticks, pikes, and rifles at our future meetings, for Orange ruffians and Tory squires stand in need of such special constables as these, and with them are as meek as lambs'. At times there were threats to murder Mackenzie, and he was quick to observe the state of mind of the people. 'There is', he wrote, 'discontent, vengeance, and rage in men's minds. No one can have any idea of the public feeling who has not taken the same means that I have to ascertain it'. Some two hundred meetings are believed to have been held in the Reform interest during the summer and autumn of 1837.

Mackenzie was present at most of them, and the main item of the agenda was usually the adoption of the Toronto resolutions and the formation of a Vigilance Committee.

A Tory account of the meeting at Stouffville on Monday, September 18, indicates the attitude of mind of the Family Compact party. Written to the Toronto *Patriot* by 'A Spectator', with the express purpose of counteracting an 'exaggerated' description of the same meeting in the *Constitution,* the letter belittles both participants and proceedings. The chairman was Ludovick Wideman, but more prominent from the Tory viewpoint was W. Doyle, postmaster, at whose home Mackenzie had spent the previous night. Doyle, we are told, 'brought out a rifle tied upon a pole, and placed it over Mr. Mackenzie's head, and said he wished the Governor and the damned Tories were there to see it; and they would know by looking thereat what they had to depend on before the lapse of many months'. Mackenzie then delivered his oration, and the resolutions were passed one by one; but the Tory 'Spectator' observed that mere boys or entirely illiterate persons had to be got to move and second their adoption, and altogether he considered the proceedings pitifully ineffective yet 'treasonable'.[13]

Authorities strongly biased against Mackenzie have claimed that the great mass of Reformers who attended these meetings had no motive other than constitutional reform, but that the leader and only a few of his most radical friends, such as Hunter, Lloyd, Fletcher, Gorham, and Matthews, were bent on rebellion. It would certainly have been unwise to make every man a repository of the plans for revolt, but it is mere prejudice to suggest that these leaders were playing a lone hand and that all the rest were their dupes. There is good reason to believe, on the other hand, that a large number of Reformers who supported the resolutions did so in the belief that a monster concentration upon the capital—a demonstration rather than an armed attack—was to be the climax of the movement. This plan is thought to have originated with Lount, with Mackenzie opposed to it as unlikely to be efficacious; but an agreement appears to have been reached by the chief leaders, fixing the spring of 1838 for the combined convention and demonstration. The mere force of numbers in Toronto might, it was thought, be sufficient to wring concessions of importance; while, if not, there would be a ready opportunity to attempt the formation of a provisional government.

Such a plan necessitated military training, for an undisciplined

[13]The letters are, respectively, from the *Constitution*, August 23, 1837, and the *Patriot*, September 29, 1837. Wideman was fated to be killed at Montgomery's on December 7.

mob would be difficult to keep in order, nor could a mass of unarmed men effectively back up their demands. Various means were therefore adopted to acquire weapons and some discipline and skill in their use. Secret drill after nightfall supplemented such practice as might be obtained at turkey and pigeon matches, an occasional *feu de joie* in honour of Papineau, and other gatherings which provided a ready excuse for firearms; while old muskets, cutlasses, and pistols were put in order, and Lount and other blacksmiths entered into the wholesale manufacture of pikes to supplement whatever materials of war might be imported surreptitiously from the United States. It was all 'a very tragic reality', observed a contemporary commentator. 'Under the shadow of "Township Clubs" strange things had been ripening; an universal rising of Mackenzie's dupes was in a real state of progress. Meetings had been held by night in the solitude of the forest, in this quarter and that. Cart-loads of arms had been conveyed from post to post throughout the country'. Nor was there much attempt at secrecy. The last issues of the *Constitution* are full of references to military activities among Reformers, and Mackenzie publicly advised every man to provide himself with a musket. It was apparent that sedition was in the air and open rebellion brewing.

The government was kept informed of the main Reform activities but persisted in underestimating the danger. Among those who told the Lieutenant-Governor of the preparations for rebellion was the Reverend Egerton Ryerson, but as his efforts to induce Sir Francis to nip the revolt in the bud were unsuccessful, he concluded that the Governor's policy was to give the radicals rope enough to hang themselves.[14] The few troops in the capital were sent eastward, leaving six thousand stand of arms in the City Hall under the guard of but two constables, and Sir Francis even publicly drew attention to the dangerous situation in a letter to the mayor stating that he had 'cheerfully consented' to the withdrawal and had 'very great pleasure' in committing the protection of the city to the corporation. As for the radicals, 'I publicly promulgate', he said, 'Let them come if they dare!' It began to appear to the Reform leaders that under such circumstances it was foolish to delay the concentration until the spring of 1838.

In October Jesse Lloyd made several trips to Lower Canada for the purpose of co-ordinating the Reform movements in the

---

[14]The Lieutenant-Governor later wrote: 'The more I encouraged them to consider me defenceless the better'. Ryerson's attitude widened the breach between himself and Mackenzie, who never forgave him; and the *Christian Guardian* later referred frequently to the 'nefarious plot', 'blood-thirsty' Mackenzie, and the 'Navy Island pirates'. Ryerson believed that he was to be the 'first victim' of the rebels.

two provinces, and he returned with a cipher letter from Thomas Storrow Brown which, with verbal communications,[15] indicated that the Lower Canadians wished the first move to be made in the upper province. The situation in both provinces pointed, therefore, to the advisability of quick action, and Mackenzie called a secret meeting in Doel's Brewery, inviting some fifteen men to consider the matter. Neither J. H. Price nor Dr. Rolph accepted the invitation, but the other chief Toronto radicals were present.[16] From Mackenzie's own account of the proceedings we learn that a bold stroke was in contemplation but was defeated through the antagonism of Dr. Morrison and, apparently, the majority of those present. Mackenzie outlined the failure of the attempt to obtain redress by constitutional means and presented the choice between gradual organization for armed resistance and an immediate *coup d'état*, of which he preferred the latter:

'I said that the troops had left; that those who had persuaded Head to place four thousand stand of arms in the midst of an unarmed people seemed evidently not opposed to their being used; that Fort Henry was open and empty, and a steamer had only to sail down to the wharf and take possession; . . and that my judgment was that we should instantly send for Dutcher's foundrymen and Armstrong's axe-makers, all of whom could be depended on, and with them go promptly to the Government House, seize Sir Francis, carry him to the City Hall, a fortress in itself, seize the arms and ammunition there and the artillery, etc., in the old garrison; rouse our innumerable friends in town and country, proclaim a provisional government, send off the steamer of that evening to secure Fort Henry, and either induce Sir Francis to give the country an executive council responsible to a new and fairly chosen assembly to be forthwith elected after packing off the usurpers in the "Bread and Butter Parliament",[17] or, if he refused to comply, go at once for Independence and take the proper steps to obtain and secure it.'

But the hesitancy of the others to take such bold action forced Mackenzie to give way,[18] and about November 18 the alternative

15M. Dufort was another emissary from Lower Canada. He stopped at Toronto *en route* to Michigan, where he was to assist in the organization of a raid in sympathy with the Rebellion. A letter of Birge, his brother-in-law, in the Lindsey Papers, implicates Bidwell in the revolt.

16The following were present: Dr. Morrison, John Mackintosh, John Doel, Robert Mackay, John Armstrong, Timothy Parson, John Mills, Thomas Armstrong, John Elliott, and William Lesslie. Lindsey says the meeting was early in November, but several of those present stated at Morrison's trial that it was in October.

17So called from an allusion in Head's address to the electors of the Newcastle District: 'If you choose to dispute with me and live on bad terms with the mother country you will quarrel with your own bread and butter.'

18Several gave evidence at Morrison's trial that 'every individual put him down', and his scheme was 'ridiculed by all others'. The emphasis was undoubtedly prompted by the hope that they would thus divert suspicion from themselves, for a reign of terror was in full progress. In his reminiscences the Reverend John Doel states that as his father objected to Mackenzie's policy he would not allow his house to be used for subsequent meetings. Just as moderate Reformers like Bidwell, Perry, and the Baldwins had earlier dissociated themselves from the more radical element, so now, when the crisis was approaching, Mackenzie was deserted by others who were unprepared to take direct action. While a case might be made out to indicate the defection of several minor Toronto radicals, and possibly Morrison, there is no evidence that Rolph was not committed to armed revolt, though his subsequent course of action suggests that he seized every means to divert suspicion from himself.

plan, with the date of concentration fixed at December 7, was agreed to by Rolph and probably Morrison.[19] The scheme to subvert the government was apparently to proceed if Mackenzie found the Branch Reform units throughout the province favourable. On the evening of November 24 he set out from Dr. Rolph's house on the mission. There is some doubt as to his instructions and their implications, but he, at least, considered that the die was irrevocably cast.

[19] Mackenzie and Morrison are known to have told the proposed date to persons not directly concerned, and consequently it came to the knowledge of the authorities. In his deposition upon arrest, Morrison said: 'I solemnly deny any knowledge of, or participation in the revolt.' Several men, however, deposed that they had seen him in the vicinity of Montgomery's, or connected him with the supplying of arms to the rebels. See *Appendix to Journal of the House of Assembly of Upper Canada, 1837-8*, 406 et seq.

BIBLIOGRAPHY

The most detailed consideration of the causes of the Rebellion is given in Lindsey, *Life and Times of Wm. Lyon Mackenzie*, and in Dent, *Story of the Upper Canadian Rebellion*. Opposing versions of the destruction of Mackenzie's printing-press are given in Mackenzie's *History of the Destruction of the Colonial Advocate Press* (1827), and Samuel Jarvis's *Statement of Facts Relating to the Trespass on the Printing Press* (1828). The Jarvis pamphlet detracts from rather than enhances its author's reputation. Wallace, *The Family Compact*, is a valuable work on the ruling clique. Dent canvasses thoroughly the possibility that Sir Francis Head was appointed in error for Sir Edmund, in his *Story*, I 286-8, and *The Canadian Portrait Gallery*, IV 172. Sir Francis's impressions and prejudices are apparent in his *Narrative of the Canadian Rebellion*, and *The Emigrant*, as well as in his despatches. The issue of the *Plain Speaker* of August 28, 1838, appears to be the only survival of that publication. It was printed at the time in Cobourg, but was established in Belleville in 1836, and ended its existence there when loyalists destroyed Hart's office and assaulted him. In this connection see articles by Riddell and Gardiner in Ontario Historical Society, XIX and XX; and for Hart's subsequent Patriot activities, chapter XVII of the present work. The Reverend John Doel's reminiscences, taken November 1, 1896, are in the Archives of Ontario. The original record of Morrison's trial does not appear to have been preserved, but it is reported in the *Patriot* of May 4, 1838. The attitude of Egerton Ryerson and other Methodists towards the Rebellion is now more completely apparent in Sissons, *Egerton Ryerson, His Life and Letters*. Several election broadsides in the Toronto Public Library indicate the tension of feeling in 1836; while the loyal yet neutral attitude of the Reverend Anson Green (*Life and Times*, 214-6) represents that of moderate Tory and Reformer alike. Mackenzie's own files of his various newspapers are with the Lindsey Papers in the University of Toronto Library. The entire collection is, however, held in trust, is uncatalogued, and unorganized except insofar as it was arranged in packages by Mackenzie and Lindsey; and in the seventy-six years since Lindsey wrote, its use by an historian has not previously been authorized. The 'Declaration' of July 31 was printed in the *Constitution* of August 2, 1837, a draft of the proposed constitution, based on that of the United States, appeared *ibid.*, November 15, and a handbill entitled 'Independence!' was struck off 'secretly and anonymously' about the last week of November. These documents form appendices D, E, and F, respectively, to Lindsey II; while appendix G is the Navy Island proclamation of December 13. The Lieutenant-Governor's letter of October 29 to Mayor Gurnett of Toronto, and his reply, are in the *Patriot* of November 3; and in the same issue is a letter from Fitzgibbon to Head, offering the services of militiamen under his command, and Head's reply, both dated October 31. Aileen Dunham has made a careful study of political conditions leading up to the Rebellion in her *Political Unrest in Upper Canada, 1815-1836*. Stanley Ryerson's *1837—The Birth of Canadian Democracy* (1937) treats the causes of the Rebellion as social in essence, and relates it to similar movements before and since. The official documents for the period are available in *Imperial Blue Books on Affairs Relating to Canada*.

CHAPTER II

THE SIEGE OF TORONTO

MONTGOMERY'S TAVERN, a large frame building on the west side of Yonge Street, was the central rendezvous of the Patriots of Upper Canada. The hotel was a well-known stopping-place for travellers *en route* to Toronto, for at that time the city lay nearly four miles to the south, and Yonge Street was a country road along which the hemlock and pine forest still stood. When the Patriots marched southward they did not know whether Gibson's or Montgomery's would be the rendezvous, but Mackenzie chose the latter on account of its size. John Linfoot, a Tory, had rented the tavern from John Montgomery in July, 1837, and had taken possession on December 1, only a few days before the rebel concentration, but the Radical owner was living in one of the rooms.

In the absence of any statement from himself, the part taken by Dr. John Rolph remains less definite than that of the other leaders. His first move during the crisis was enough to disrupt the gathering of Patriots at Montgomery's. On Saturday, December 2, possibly in agreement with Dr. Morrison, Rolph, upon learning that a special session of the Executive Council had been held that afternoon, sent a verbal message by John Mantach to David Gibson, suggesting that the date of the rising be changed from the seventh to the fourth. His motive was apparently to save bloodshed and enhance the chances of success by staging the attack on Toronto while it was still undefended. Mackenzie was then at Stouffville, 'delivering sealed letters to the captains of townships for Thursday the 7th', but there is no reason to suppose that Rolph knew exactly where he was, and as a warrant had been issued for Mackenzie's arrest it was not unreasonable to act without his consent—assuming such action was necessary. It was dangerous to commit anything to writing, and Gibson relayed Rolph's message by sending William Edmondson to Samuel Lount at Holland Landing. Edmondson delivered it to Mrs. Lount, who communicated the news to her husband when he returned home. 'I'm afraid,' said Colonel Lount to his wife, 'that Dr. Rolph is going to be the ruin of us.' Lount immediately consulted Anthony Anderson, and they assembled one hundred men, divided them into squads to avoid suspicion, and proceeded unarmed by various routes to Montgomery's Tavern.

On Sunday, the third, Mackenzie reached Gibson's house, some four miles above Montgomery's, and was angry when he learned of the change of date which had been made in his absence. He sent a messenger to Lount countermanding Rolph's order, but Lount, who had proceeded by a circuitous route to collect recruits, replied that he was too far on his way to turn back. The first party to reach Montgomery's consisted of twenty Lloydtown men who arrived about seven o'clock in the evening. The next to come was Anderson's, and by morning about a hundred and fifty men were at the tavern. The change in date created a problem that would not otherwise have arisen—that of providing food for hundreds of men for several days. It was consequently no fault of Mackenzie's that neither arms nor supplies were found at the tavern. Dry bread, biscuits, cheese, and whisky did not go far to refresh men who had been marching all day, and there were many complaints that the commissariat had been neglected by those who had organized the concentration.

Meanwhile Mackenzie, Rolph, and Gibson had met at the home of Hervey Price, and the best was made of a bad situation by placing a guard at the tavern to intercept travellers to Toronto. At the same time it was suggested that about a hundred men be sent to attack the city that night, but this move was opposed by Gibson, who considered they would be too tired from their long march. Rolph seemed dispirited at the reported defeat of the Lower Canadian *Patriotes* at St. Charles and insisted upon an immediate attack, if at all, but the final decision was left to Lount, who had not yet arrived. Mackenzie and Gibson then went to Shepard's Mill, near the Humber, where a group was busy running bullets; and word shortly reached them that Lount had arrived at Montgomery's. On Tuesday morning men were sent out to seize arms from neighbouring homes, while other groups went foraging. A few loads of oats were obtained, and meat was taken from Thomas Nightengale, who was told he might be paid by an order on 'the new Constitution'! Later some cattle were seized on William Ketchum's farm, and they were brought to Nightengale to slaughter;[1] so that in one way or another the deficiency of food was made up.

In Toronto a peculiar condition of affairs existed. Sir Francis Bond Head obstinately refused to take the rebels seriously, and not only took no steps to protect the capital but discouraged those who had more foresight and common sense. When Colonel James Fitzgibbon protested he was told that if the militia could not

[1] These details are from evidence at the trial of Montgomery as given in the official record, State Book K, Public Archives of Canada.

defend the country the sooner it was lost the better!² Even the staunch loyalist who published *Mackenzie's Own Narrative* (with the sole purpose of discrediting it) wrote:

'We are clearly of the opinion that the city might have been captured, sacked, and destroyed at any hour during the nights of Sunday the 3rd, and Monday the 4th instant, in the total absence of all precaution on the part of the government,—even by a less force than 200 men, under dashing and spirited leaders.'

Such protective measures as were taken were due entirely to Fitzgibbon, who roused the people to their danger and warned many a citizen 'to go to bed every night with loaded arms near his bedside, and on hearing the College bell he should run to me to the Parliament House with his arms'.

On Monday night two incidents occurred which showed the authorities that the siege of Toronto had commenced in earnest. The loyal inhabitants of York County were quite aware of the concentration of rebels at Montgomery's during Monday, and a number of them met at the home of Lieutenant-Colonel Robert Moodie. They despatched one, Drew, to warn Toronto, and when news reached them that he had been captured Colonel Moodie and several others started out. They found that three lines of pickets had been posted at the tavern. Passing the first, Colonel Moodie drew his pistol and fired on the second row; but four rifles were discharged at him and he fell mortally wounded. One of the party, Brooke, got through and carried the news to the city.³ During the same night Captain Anthony Anderson, the rebels' most trusted military leader, was shot in the neck by Alderman John Powell. Anderson and Shepard had captured him while on a reconnoitring expedition, but Powell had retained two loaded pistols, and falling a little behind Anderson, suddenly fired at him with deadly effect and escaped during the ensuing confusion. Reaching Davenport Road he abandoned his horse and hid in the woods for awhile; then ran across Queen's Park and down College (University) Avenue to Government House, where

---

²Fitzgibbon was also worried by a move to supplant him by MacNab, who wished to attack the rebels in the middle of the night; while Head did not want to march against them at all. 'O no, sir!' cried he, 'I will not fight them on their ground; they must fight me on mine!' No wonder Fitzgibbon exclaimed (mentally): 'Good Lord! What an old woman I have here to deal with!' . . . 'Many an old woman,' observed Mackenzie, 'will feel insulted by the comparison!'

³Evidence of Captain Hugh Stewart at Montgomery's trial. Stewart was captured. Colonel Moodie, who had been wounded in the Revolutionary War, had a farm on Yonge Street, near Richmond Hill. He was buried in the Anglican churchyard at Thornhill on December 7, and the interment was a curious one. The Reverend George Mortimer, the rector, who believed he was marked for death as holder of the 'obnoxious rectories', was annoyed when everyone came to the funeral 'accoutred in their swords, daggers, pistols, and fowling pieces'; but he could not forbear a 'momentary smile' when he saw one man leaning on his pitchfork! Ryan, who is said to have shot Moodie, hid in thickets and cedar swamps in the vicinity of Goderich, and was almost worn to a skeleton when picked up by an American schooner.

he succeeded in arousing Sir Francis and communicated his news.[4] The Lieutenant-Governor, now 'completely terrified' and as panicky as he had been blusteringly over-confident, quickly placed his family and that of Chief Justice Robinson on board the steamer *Transit* for safety,[5] at the same time despatching messengers to call the militia of the province to Toronto; but there was something admirable as well as absurd in the sight of Sir Francis armed to the teeth and ready to die—if only given credit for doing his duty! William Copland, who lived on Yonge Street about a quarter of a mile north of the Bloor toll-gate, describes the alarm which spread through the region as the news of the death of Colonel Moodie passed from house to house:

'At about twelve o'clock I was awakened by the report of two guns fired in a wood in front of my house: I listened some time but could hear nothing more, and went to sleep. At about half-past one, however, I was called up by a neighbour, who said that the rebels had got into the city and had killed one gentleman on the road. . . I thought no time was to be lost; and as soon as we knew the road was clear we packed up our plate and such other things as we could carry on foot, buried my account-books in the garden, went off to town, and took refuge in my brother-in-law's house.'[6]

Meanwhile there was serious disagreement among the Patriots as to the tactics to be followed, with the result that the chances of success gradually became less and less. The plan eventually adopted, and put into partial execution about noon on Tuesday, called for a march upon the city. Some fifty or sixty prisoners were forced to go along in charge of Gibson, largely for the effect of making the invaders appear more formidable. At Gallows Hill, just south of the present St. Clair Avenue, the force was to be divided, Lount continuing down Yonge while Mackenzie was to lead his men down what is now Avenue Road, the two companies to meet at Osgoode Hall. But a delegation bearing a flag of truce met the invaders at Gallows Hill as they were preparing to advance on the city.

[4] Anderson broke his neck in falling from his horse; he was the father of eight children. William Copland, who lived near by, says: 'It is the opinion of myself and many others that it was this apparently trifling event which saved the city.'
[5] Sir Francis stated that Dr. Strachan made the suggestion. In a letter to Dr. Rolph, June 1, 1854, John Hawk, nephew of Lount, says that Mackenzie told his fellow-Reformers that the Robinsons favoured rebellion, but Mackenzie gives no reason for his belief. Possibly the following note in his handwriting in the Lindsey Papers alludes to John Beverley Robinson among others: 'Mr. Lount, when in concealment, stated to persons whose veracity is undoubted, that had he not known, from the best possible sources of inform.n that cert.n persons of high stand.g & respectability, men high in office, were parties to the proposed armed opposition, he never w'd have entered into it.'
[6] A woman's reminiscences of events in the early days of the revolt are given in Lizars, *Humours of '37*, 358-61. Cornelia De Grassi's visit to Montgomery's Tavern, her capture, and eventual escape on her pony, and her sister Charlotte's exciting adventures as a despatch-bearer on the Kingston Road, are described in the New York *Spirit of the Times*, October 13, 1838, quoting the New York *Albion*. The conduct of these 'high-spirited damsels', both of whom were under fifteen years of age, is praised as an example of 'the more sublime virtues'. Mackenzie refers to Cornelia as a spy employed by Dr. Horne.

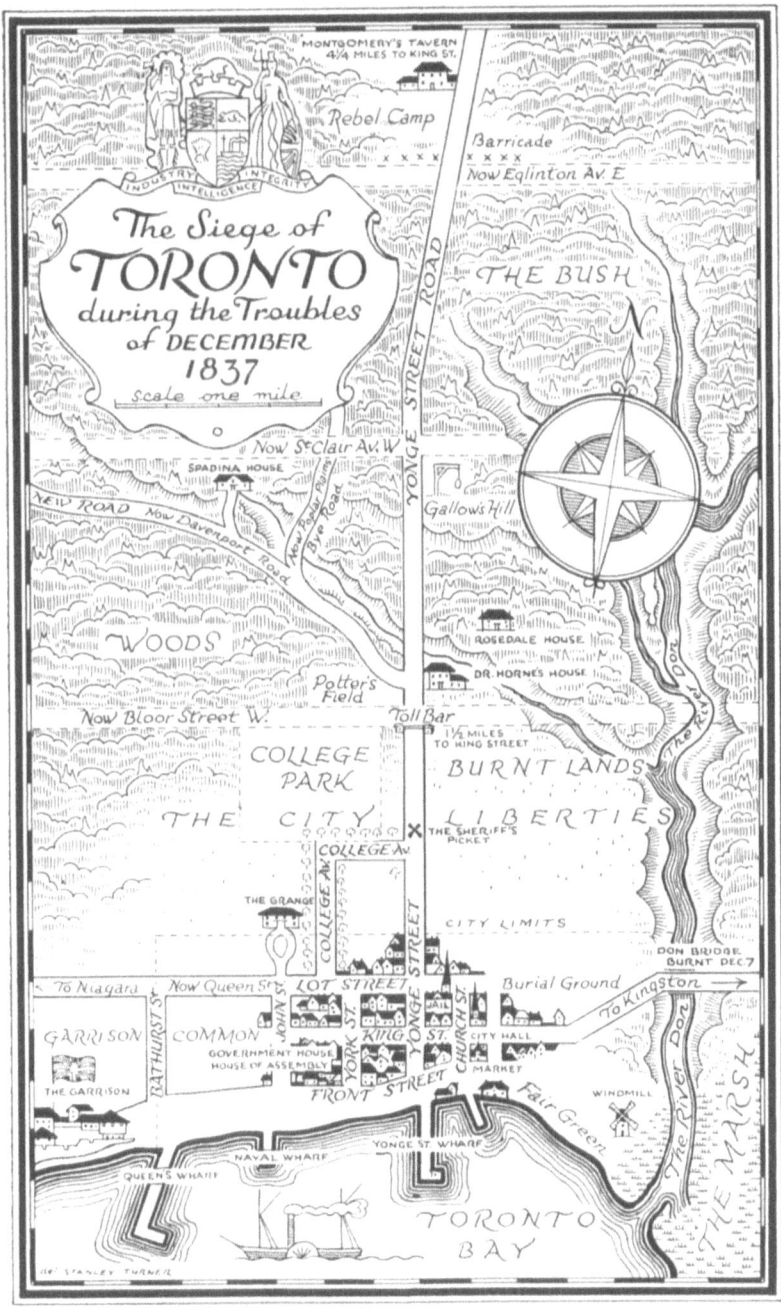

Courtesy Rous & Mann, Limited, Toronto

Toronto at the Time of the Rebellion of 1837

Courtesy John Ross Robertson Collection

Toll-Gate at Bloor and Yonge Streets, Toronto
The rebels had reached this point when stopped by the flag of truce

From Dent, *Upper Canadian Rebellion*, 1885

Powell Escapes to Warn the Lieutenant-Governor
'I suddenly drew my pistol and fired; he fell and I instantly set off full speed down the street.'—*Narrative of John Powell*

The main facts of this episode are clear. Sir Francis thought that if his emissaries were prominent Reformers the effect upon the rebels would be greater, and Hervey Price was asked to be a member of the party. He refused, but Robert Baldwin consented to be one and suggested Bidwell for the other. He refused, and Rolph, who was asked next, accepted only after he had been told that two had already aroused grave suspicions by refusal. Hugh Carmichael, a carpenter, carried the white flag as the party proceeded up Yonge Street. Upon reaching the rebel body they communicated Sir Francis's offer of a complete amnesty of all offences if they immediately dispersed. Mackenzie conferred with Lount before the final reply was given, demanded a national convention to consider his demands, and at the same time asked that Head's offer be put in writing.

During the course of the conference Rolph took Lount aside and said: 'Wend your way into the city as soon as possible, at my heels.' The delegation thereupon returned and communicated the rebel attitude to Bond Head, who decided to refuse any further parley. Rolph and Baldwin rode up Yonge Street to communicate the result to Mackenzie, and found that the rebel force had marched as far as the toll-gate and were lined up on Bloor Street. It is admitted by all concerned that, after communicating the Lieutenant-Governor's message, Rolph spoke privately to Mackenzie; but while Rolph claims it was then that he urged the march on the city, Mackenzie states that he suggested also the burning of the Horne and Jarvis homes to 'induce a speedy capitulation'. Rolph thereupon caught up with Baldwin and rode down College Avenue to report to the sheriff, while Mackenzie and some of his men burned Horne's house. A contemporary opinion was that Rolph 'did not desire to check the rebels, though too cautious or too cowardly to join their ranks'.[7] But his part was to organize Toronto Radicals in support of the attack from the north, and he certainly did his best to expedite matters. As for Bond Head, by refusing to place his proposal in writing he left himself open to the charge that he was merely gaining time in sending the embassy at all.

Apparently expecting that Mackenzie and Lount would at once lead their men against the city, Rolph proceeded to Elliott's Tavern at Queen and Yonge, where a number of Radicals were awaiting news of the situation. He told them to arm themselves at once, for Mackenzie would immediately bring his force into

[7]'The Rebellion!', *Cobourg Star*, December 13, 1837. The controversy over Dr. Rolph's conduct raged for more than half a century. The evidence, including items not previously available, is considered in appendix C(1). Lount's deposition is C(2).

Toronto.[8] Shortly afterwards another meeting was held, apparently at Doel's Brewery, to discuss means of aiding the expected attack. When nothing happened during the next hour or so a messenger, Henry Wright, rode northward to learn the reason. Gibson and Lount stated that Mackenzie was not ready, and when Wright located the leader himself he was told to inform Dr. Rolph that he would be in shortly, but it was apparent from the lateness of the hour that it would have to be a night attack.

Rolph's appearance with the flag of truce had increased their demoralization, but at six in the evening Lount led several hundred down Yonge Street, many of his men being only half-armed, and some cutting green cudgels for themselves on the way. Reaching the toll-gate at Bloor Street they were harangued by Mackenzie and pushed on three abreast towards the city. A loyalist picket of twenty-seven men under Sheriff William Jarvis had been stationed during the afternoon in the open country above the present McGill Street, and later removed to the garden of William Sharpe, near Maitland Street. As the Patriot force approached this body Lount's men, armed with muskets, were in front, a force with pikes came next, and a rabble of useless fellows carrying sticks and cudgels brought up the rear. The engagement which followed was a burlesque:

'After firing once, the loyalists under Sheriff Jarvis started back at full speed towards the city. The front rank of Lount's men, instead of stepping aside after firing to let those behind fire, fell down on their faces. Those in the rear, fancying that the front rank had been cut down by the muskets of the small force who had taken a random shot at them, being without arms were panic-stricken; and in a short time nearly the whole force was on the retreat. Many of the Llodytown pikemen raised the cry, "We shall all be killed!", threw down their rude weapons, and fled in great precipitation.'[9]

The loose discipline among the Patriots was no worse than in the average company of militia of the period; but their lack of confidence in their leaders was more pronounced, and the most innocent objects made them nervous. A farmer who lived on Yonge Street observed that

'while a detachment of rebels were marching southwards down the hill since known as Mount Pleasant they saw a wagon-load of cordwood standing on the opposite rise, and supposing it to be a piece of artillery loaded to the muzzle with grape or canister, these brave warriors leaped

[8] Dr. R. C. Horne says he saw Dr. Rolph and his companion 'at the rebel corner on their return from their pretended mission of mediation'. Some 150 'city lurkers' were 'eagerly swallowing the information' that he conveyed of the strength of the Patriot force and the fear they inspired in the government, while Horne remonstrated with him that he should have given them the opposite impression.

[9] James Henderson was killed during the action, and his body is said to have been given to surgeons for dissection. Two Patriots, Edgar Stiles and James Kavanagh, both of East Gwillimbury, were wounded and carried to Montgomery's. After the loyalist victory they were taken to the hospital, where they died.

the fences right and left like squirrels, and could by no effort of their officers be induced again to advance.'

Wednesday dawned, and still the Patriots remained in a state of indecision. The rout of the night before did not suggest another immediate attack, and there was also the hope that by the next morning Colonel Van Egmond would be present, as well as numerous others who had not heard of the change in the date of concentration. Shortly after despatching messages to Dr. Duncombe in the London District, Mackenzie, Lount, Alves, and a small body of men proceeded to Dundas Street to intercept the westbound mail. The object was effected at the Peacock Inn, about four miles west of the City Hall, where the stage was stopped and with its driver and passengers conveyed to Montgomery's, along with the possessions of certain persons who happened to be at the inn at the time. At the rebel headquarters the mail-bags were opened, their contents investigated, and in some instances appropriated to the cause of the Patriots. But more important information came from Toronto, which was that Dr. Morrison had been arrested and charged with high treason, while Dr. Rolph had fled westward. Upon this news leaking out, a few deserted the cause, but the rest put in the time in drill and preparation for the final episode of the morrow. Joseph Gould arrived at the tavern that evening and was not sanguine of success when he saw that valuable time was being wasted and ordinary precautions lacking:

'I found that there was no order or discipline; that there had been no picket-guards put out, and that the whole party were liable to be surprised at any moment, and that probably before morning they would be surrounded and cut off. Tired as I was after our long march I determined to set pickets at once. This I did, and had the guard relieved until morning.'[10]

During this time Toronto was in a highly excited state. Fitzgibbon had been appointed adjutant-general of the defending force, but even on the night of the abortive raid he had to spend half an hour of his valuable time in seeing that all the city's bells were rung to arouse the inhabitants to their danger. It was a rather motley group of men who mustered at the call, but reinforcements soon began to arrive. Captain McLean's Scarborough contingent of a hundred men was probably the first, to be followed shortly after by Mr. Speaker MacNab's sixty-five, who came by steamship from Hamilton on the afternoon of Tuesday, the fifth. By the next morning volunteers were 'pouring in from all directions',

[10]The rebel plans were no doubt the same as Mackenzie had projected at the November meeting, but rumours were current that they included the robbing of the banks, the firing of the city 'in sixteen different places', and 'a general massacre'.

and the city was 'a spectacle of uncommon grandeur, . . . one general camp, resplendent with dazzling steel and bristling with bayonets'. Under the circumstances it was pleasant enough to see 'a company of old Pensioners in quick march up King Street'— even though they were in the usual motley garb of militiamen. Samuel Thompson describes how 'the principal buildings—the City Hall, Upper Canada Bank, the Parliament Buildings, Osgoode Hall, Government House, the Canada Company's office—and many private dwellings and shops, were put in a state of defence by barricading the windows and doors with two-inch plank loopholed for musketry'. Almost every store closed its doors, and bread, potatoes, and meat rose to famine prices. Thrilling spectacles were a commonplace. On the night of the fifth a three-pounder cannon was seized at Norton's Foundry—'just dry from painting, and was to have been delivered [to the rebels] this morning'; between seven and eight a.m. on the sixth a force took possession of Mackenzie's printing office; an hour or so later arms were being moved from the City Hall to the Parliament House, which was easier to defend; and at three p.m. '400 athletic men' under Mac-Nab 'are now passing our office with traitor Morrison', who, with one Kennedy and 'Mr. Gibson, the carpenter', were captured at Mackenzie's dwelling. A loaded cannon preceded the prisoners as they were marched to jail, and it was everywhere apparent that events were fast approaching a climax.

At eight on Thursday morning, December 7, Colonel Van Egmond reached Montgomery's, and a council of war was held. Mackenzie, Lount, Gibson, and Fletcher participated actively with Van Egmond in this stormy meeting, while Montgomery, and at times Linfoot, heard what transpired but took no part in the deliberations. Gibson was apparently in opposition to the plans of Van Egmond and Mackenzie, who considered that it would be best to attempt to stave off the loyalist march against them by alarming the city with a feint attack from the east; while the rest of the armed men were apparently to be ready to march towards Toronto and 'to move either to the right or the left, or to retreat to a strong position as prudence might dictate'.

Captain Peter Matthews's company of sixty men proceeded towards the Don Bridge with the intention of burning it and intercepting the mail-stage from the east. The latter object was accomplished first, and the force marched across the bridge about noon, continuing along King Street until alarmed by the approach of a detachment of militia under George Ridout. As they beat a hasty retreat they tried to set fire to all the buildings in the vicinity. A tavern on the eastern bank of the Don, with the adjacent stable, driving-shed, and toll-gate, was totally destroyed, and during an interchange of bullets the hostler was fatally shot in the throat. The bridge itself was reported at the time to have been saved by a negro with a double-barrelled gun, while Mrs. Ross, who lived near, later claimed to have extinguished the fire at the cost of a bullet in her knee. But while these activities of Matthews's men were serving their purpose, the main body at Montgomery's remained inactive and disorganized, and they were still in the same state when a scout, William Asher, arrived from the head of College Avenue with the news that the loyalist force was approaching, their bayonets gleaming in the sun.

It had been a grand day in Toronto, for so many volunteers had arrived that all gloom and foreboding had been dispelled. Colonel Boulton's Durham cavalry, the forerunners of nearly two thousand men from the Newcastle District, reached the city early in the morning. Contingents had arrived from the Niagara district, and other companies, including 'Capt. McGrath and his Volunteer Cavalry', came from the western part of the Home District. Some fifteen hundred men were ready to advance against the rebels, and though it is quite probable that some of the volunteers might have joined the opposing force under other circumstances, there was no lack of enthusiasm in any quarter. 'If your Honour will but give us ARMS', shouted a voice from the ranks in a broad Irish brogue, 'the rebels will find LEGS'.

The personnel of the loyalist force is a matter of considerable interest. Mackenzie, and Patriot writers generally, contend that the army at Toronto consisted chiefly of 'Tory college boys,[11] lawyers, and judges', a statement true enough with respect to the nucleus of the force, for an eye-witness wrote:

'We saw the Lieutenant-Governor in his everyday suit, with one double-barrelled gun in his hand, another leaning against his breast, and a brace of pistols in his leathern belt. Also Chief Justice Robinson, Judges Macaulay, Jones, and McLean, the Attorney-General, and the Solicitor-General with their muskets, cartridge-boxes, and bayonets, all standing in the ranks as private soldiers under the command of Colonel Fitzgibbon.'

But when the loyal army was ready to march northward it was democratic enough. 'Judges, Crown Officers, and most of the other public functionaries', runs a contemporary report, 'the Merchants, Mechanics, and labourers, the White and Coloured population, mingled in the lines without distinction of rank, station

[11] Most of the students of Upper Canada College offered their services to the Lieutenant-Governor, but after entertaining them to refreshments he advised them to go home. William Hamilton Merritt, his brother, and James Ingersoll, all of St. Catharines, were 'not quite satisfied with playing so tame a part', and, venturing too close to the rebel camp, were shortly imprisoned in the Bloor toll-house; but they climbed out of a window and returned to town 'the heroes of the hour'. W. H. Merritt, sr., aided Maria Wait in 1839-40. See p. 206, and Wait, 338-9.

or colour'. They were drawn up in order of battle in the street and esplanade in front of Archdeacon Strachan's residence, and as even the Lieutenant-Governor recognized that his force was so 'overwhelming that there remained not the slightest reason for delay', at twelve noon the expedition got under way 'with an enthusiasm which it would be impossible to describe'. Many unarmed citizens, including the redoubtable Dr. Strachan, could not be prevented from marching along behind the militia, even to the scene of battle.

Though estimated unofficially as high as 2,000 men, the force consisted of 920, of which 600 led by Sir Francis, Fitzgibbon, and MacNab, marched up Yonge, supported by right and left wings of 200 and 120, respectively. The left column, nominally in command of Colonel William Chisholm but actually under Judge McLean and Colonel O'Hara, proceeded up College Avenue and onward through Queen's Park and by various side roads. The right wing under Colonel Jarvis marched to the east of Yonge Street.[12] Colonel Chisholm led a small force to the Peacock Inn, Dundas Street West, and the two guns which formed the battery of the main force were in command of Major Carfrae of the militia artillery. It was a remarkably fine day, and as the soldiers swung along to the tune of *Yankee Doodle* from two bands the enthusiasm of citizens and militia alike knew no bounds:

'The windows and housetops along the chief thoroughfares were crowded by men, women, and children, who waved miniature flags and lustily cheered the cavalcade as it passed along. The volunteers responded in kind, and the welkin rang again. Never had the streets of the little provincial capital presented so stirring an appearance—not even when the guns of the invader had thundered along the waterfront in 1813. To many who beheld the scene and participated in the enthusiasm which it was eminently calculated to arouse, this 7th of December was the most memorable day of their lives.'

In a contemporary political pamphlet there is a series of letters concerning the Rebellion, purporting to be written by a member of the loyal army but sounding more like Bond Head himself. In one of them 'William Steady' tells his brother in England of the advance northward: 'We found the rebels posted near "Gallows Hill" (a very proper place for them!). They fired; we advanced steadily, and soon drove them before us like chaff before the wind.'[13] The engagement was, however, somewhat more ex-

---

[12]John W. Hunt was a member of the right wing, and recalled that they marched in great disorder through ploughed fields. Stopped by a creek, and seeing the main force, 'a splendid sight', to their left on Yonge Street, they ran to join them at Gallows Hill.

[13]*The True Briton of the Nineteenth Century; Canadian Patriots and English Chartists*, 5. Gallows Hill was not the gentle rise near Montgomery's but the hill below the present St. Clair Avenue where the loyalists were first observed by the rebel sentinels near the tavern.

THE SIEGE OF TORONTO 25

tensive, lasting about twenty minutes. Mackenzie personally investigated the reported approach of the loyalist force, and having assured himself that the fatal hour was indeed at hand he asked his men if they wished to fight. Upon receiving an affirmative answer a hasty disposition of the Patriots was made. The main company of 150 men under Lount and Van Egmond was placed in a belt of woods about half a mile south of Montgomery's and 150 yards west of Yonge Street; some sixty took up a position behind rail fences in an open field across the road; a small force was in the Paul Pry Inn, on the east side of Yonge some distance south of Montgomery's; while Mackenzie states that 'about 200 of our friends stood at the tavern during the battle, being unarmed'.[14]

When Fitzgibbon's force reached the brow of the hill just north of the present Mount Pleasant Cemetery the two nine-pounders were placed on the west side of the road and fired northwesterly upon the rebel body in the woods. Joseph Gould gives interesting details of the first actual contact with the loyalist left wing:

'We soon got under arms and started down Yonge Street to meet them. The troops, however, turned to the west and made as though they wanted to get round the west side to our rear. We hastened through the woods, climbing over dead hemlock trees and through the underbrush, and rushed to head them off. We had no arms but our rifles, and some had only rude pikes and pitchforks. The troops, besides their muskets and plenty of ammunition, had two small field pieces—one controlled by a friend of ours, and the other by an enemy. The friend fired grape-shot, and fired over us into the tops of the trees, cutting off the dead and dry limbs of the hemlocks, which, falling thickly amongst us, scared the boys as much as if cannon-balls had been rattling around us. The other gun was fired low, and so *careless* that I did not like it. One of the balls struck a sandbank by my feet and filled my eyes with sand, nearly blinding me. Another struck one of those dry hemlocks, scattering the bark and splinters about, and into my face. Captain Wideman was killed on my left side, and F. Shell was shot through the shoulder to the left of the fallen captain. But we got to the west of the troops. They then turned and crossed to Yonge Street behind us.'[15]

Observing that the left wing was in contact with the enemy, the main loyalist body advanced up Yonge at the double. Stopping again, the artillery fired a shot under the eaves and through the roof of the Paul Pry Inn, and the rebels posted there fled at once.

[14] William Gymer, Linfoot's hostler, stated at Montgomery's trial that when the loyalists were seen approaching, Montgomery shouted: 'Turn out! turn out! all you who have guns, and do your best, for the Tories are coming!' Captain Hugh Stewart said that Montgomery was not armed nor did he wear a white badge like the 'lower classes', but seemed to act as commissary-general.

[15] Gould and his companions from Brock, Scott, and Uxbridge townships were on the wrong side of Yonge Street to get back home readily, and were captured a few days later when they built a camp-fire in a swamp. He narrowly escaped transportation and remained in prison until the following October. Gould, who was born in 1808, represented North Ontario in the Legislative Assembly, 1854-61. He died at Uxbridge on June 29, 1886.

26   THE LIVES AND TIMES OF THE PATRIOTS

'As the militia advanced', writes Samuel Thompson, 'their opponents melted away. Parties of volunteers dashed over the fences and into the woods, shouting and firing as they ran'. A couple of cannon-balls passed right through Montgomery's Tavern, and the Patriots within poured out 'like bees from a hive, . . flying in all directions into the deep, welcome recesses of the forest'. The militia captured a considerable number of them, but Bond Head magnanimously freed all but the leaders and ordered them to go home. Some eleven Patriots were wounded, and at least four of them afterwards died in hospital; while Ludovick (Ludwig) Wideman was killed in action.[16] The loyalist force suffered a loss of five wounded, none of them seriously.

Before ordering the burning of Montgomery's Tavern Sir Francis looked about for relics of its occupation by the rebels. The flag of which he made most use was that inscribed 'Bidwell, and the Glorious Minority! 1837, and a Good Beginning!'[17] But there was also a white flag, a banner inscribed 'Victoria the 1st and Reform!', and another—which was to become the usual Patriot standard—bearing twin stars and the word LIBERTY, and in this instance an eagle as well. Much more important was the discovery of Mackenzie's carpet-bag, 'the Devil's snuff-box', as Bond Head called it. Among the papers in it were lists of those who had adhered to the Patriot cause, and many were consequently arrested who would not otherwise have been suspected of complicity. Mackenzie could hardly have been expected to return to the tavern for incriminating papers during his flight, but some arrangement whereby they might have been secreted elsewhere or destroyed could have been effected without much forethought.

The loyalist troops, meanwhile, had penetrated a mile or two beyond the tavern, and a few were sent two miles farther to set fire to David Gibson's house at Willowdale. Bond Head ordered the burning of the hotel, and in the face of some disposition on the part of Fitzgibbon to save the building, he stayed on the spot to see it done, gloating over the sight with satisfaction:

'Volume after volume of deep black smoke rolling and rising from the windows of Montgomery's Tavern now attracted my attention. This great and lofty building, entirely constructed of timber and planks, was soon a

[16] As the hospital apparently kept no records, the names of those who died are not known. Wideman was a lieutenant in the militia, a veteran of 1812, and became a Patriot because of indignities at the election of 1836. Details of his life, his descendants, and of a pilgrimage to his grave in Ringwood Union Cemetery are given in the *Wiarton Echo*, December 11, 1930, under the caption 'This Man Was Grandfather of Aaron Spragge'.

[17] The Bidwell flag was an old one used in the election contest of 1832, the figure 7 having been substituted. Bond Head was only too glad to use it as evidence of Bidwell's complicity in the Rebellion, though he had retired from active political life in 1836.

THE SIEGE OF TORONTO 27

mass of flames, whose long red tongues sometimes darted horizontally, as if revengefully to consume those who had created them, and then flared high above the roof.

'As we sat on our horses the heat was intense; and while the conflagration was the subject of joy and triumph to the gallant spirits that immediately surrounded it, it was a lurid telegraph which intimated to many an anxious and aching heart at Toronto the joyful intelligence that the yeomen and farmers of Upper Canada had triumphed over their perfidious enemy, "responsible government".'

There was soon nothing to be done but return to Toronto. The wounded were sent to hospital in wagons, while the militia, and a considerable number of citizens who had come out to view the battle, passed triumphantly down Yonge Street. 'The march back', says Samuel Thompson, 'was very leisurely executed, several of the mounted officers carrying dead pigs and geese slung across their saddle-bows as trophies of victory'. Upon reaching the Parliament Buildings they formed a solid square and were addressed by the Lieutenant-Governor.

As for the scattered Patriots,[18] it can hardly be contended that 'never did men fight more courageously'; but neither can it be said that they were basically much different from the militia. Both forces were primarily composed of farm rustics and small tradesmen, though the loyalist force was obviously better officered and better armed, and—which makes a big difference in both appearance and discipline—many of them wore uniforms. The Patriots 'were not Spartans; Montgomery's farm was not Thermopylae; and assuredly Leonidas was not there'. But considering all the circumstances it is improbable that any other soldiers with the same leaders and arms—or lack of them—could have done any better. Nor did their effort lack appreciation:

'They have met—that small band, resolved to be free
As the fierce winds of Heaven that course o'er the sea—
They have met, in bright hope, with no presage of fear,
Though the bugle and drum of the foemen they hear.
Some seize the dread rifle, some wield the tall pike,
For God and their country—for Freedom they strike;
No proud ensign of glory bespeaks their renown,
Yet the scorn of defiance now darkens their frown.
See the foemen advancing! And now sounds afar
The clang and the shout of disastrous war.

[18] The Toronto *Patriot* extra of December 6 describes the rebels as from 400 to 600, 'generally young ruffians, with some scattering hoary villains among them'. Mackenzie, presumably for purposes of propaganda, greatly exaggerates the number by stating that 'about 3,500 persons joined us during the three days on which we were behind Toronto'. The Reverend George Mortimer states that 500 men passed southward through Thornhill on December 4. There is evidence that many who set out for Montgomery's never arrived, while others deserted after a few hours. See appendix G for the names of those arrested throughout the province.

Yes! Onward they come like the mountain's wild flood,
And the Lion's dark talons are dappled in blood'.[19]

[19] *Mackenzie's Gazette*, quoted Lindsey, II 95. Among other verse are two long Tory descriptions of the Rebellion. 'New Words to an Old Song; or John Gilpin Travestied' appeared in the *Cobourg Star*, February 7, 1838. A similar effusion, 'A True History', by 'The Patriot Boy', appeared in the Toronto *Patriot*, January 2, 1838. Typical of both, and illustrative of the sentiment expressed, is the last stanza of the former:

'And now to Mac there's still one step
To end his life of evil;
Soon may he take the last long leap
From gibbet to the ——.'

With more literary merit was a poem, 'Suggested by the Lamented Death of the Late Col. Moody', which was reprinted from the *Church* in the *Patriot* of January 5, 1838.

BIBLIOGRAPHY

The available source material is quite voluminous. Besides those which it has been considered preferable to mention in the notes, various issues of contemporary newspapers, and particularly the *Cobourg Star*, the Toronto *Patriot* extra of December 6, and the *Mirror* of December 16, contain accounts of the events in and around the capital. Mackenzie's *Caroline Almanack*, though obviously propagandist in nature, contains much reliable information not found elsewhere. Mackenzie's *Own Narrative*, edited unsympathetically by the loyalist, Fothergill, has recently been handsomely reprinted with notes by W. S. Wallace. The letter in which Sir Francis Head describes the sending of families aboard ships in the harbour is given in Robinson, *Life of Sir John Beverley Robinson*, appendix VII, 425-6. William Hamilton Merritt's diary is quoted in the *Upper Canada College Times*, Easter, 1907. A. M. Howard's narrative describing the rebel occupation of James S. Howard's house, a mile south of Montgomery's, is appended to chapter XXIV of Thompson's *Reminiscences*. Lount stated after his capture that he had saved the Jarvis home from being fired like Horne's. 'Dr. Horne's Narrative of the Burning of His House', *Patriot*, January 2, 1838, and 'Escape of Mr. Powell, and Death of the Rebel Anderson', *Cobourg Star*, February 21, 1838, give details of the incidents. An interesting account of Lieutenant-Colonel Moodie's interment is found in Armstrong, *Life and Letters of the Rev. George Mortimer* (London, England, 1847). In spite of the Lieutenant-Governor's apparent leniency in allowing many captured rebels to return to their homes, they were largely imprisoned in succeeding weeks, as may be seen in the 'Register of Prisoners Committed to the Home District Gaol', recently discovered and in the Ontario Archives; while many others, of whom we have no list, were taken to the Legislative Council Chamber. The *Appendix to the Journal of the Legislative Assembly, 1837-8*, 409-10, gives details of awards to owners and tenants of buildings burned near the Don bridge, and to John Linfoot for the loss of furniture in the tavern. Bond Head's books give details of interest, such as the appearance before him at Montgomery's of 'a raving maniac' who had lost her reason as a result of anxiety over the fate of her rebel husband; but in general the historical value of his writing is restricted because of the predominance of prejudice over truth. Lindsey and Dent incorporate in their accounts the reminiscences of participants who were still living when they wrote. Colonel Fitzgibbon described his campaign, and the difficulties under which he carried it out, in his *Appeal to the People of Upper Canada*. Higgins, *Life and Times of Joseph Gould*, describes his Rebellion activities. Among the rarest items is Copland's *Narrative of the Early Events of the Rebellion in Upper Canada*, published in London, England, in 1838, of which the only copy the author has seen is in the New York Public Library. Duncan Campbell's MS. letter, and W. W. Street's, which is in the Legislative Library of Ontario, give, respectively, reports of the rebel plans, and a detailed account of the excitement in Toronto during the rebel concentration, though the information varies but little from that in contemporary newspapers. Of some interest is Colonel William Dunlop's novel *Two and Twenty Years Ago, a Tale of the Canadian Rebellion* (1859), which its author says is based on actual events 'in danger of being lost to the rising and future generations'. *The Forging of the Pikes*, by 'Anison North' (May Wilson), is a more recent novel of considerable dramatic intensity; while a number of plays have recently been written on the Rebellion.

CHAPTER III

The Remarkable Escape of Mackenzie

DURING the brief engagement with the loyalist force Mackenzie was near the belt of woods below the tavern and to the west of Yonge Street. When he saw that the day was irretrievably lost, he ran northward over a ploughed field to the rear of Price's house. The main loyalist force did not proceed more than a mile or two above the tavern, for the road beyond had not been macadamized and was almost impassable. One of Fitzgibbon's men saw Mackenzie abandon his horse and run into the forest but dared not follow further, 'for we were without muskets or rifles and were two or three miles in advance of our men, while rebels were flying through the woods in every direction'. Mackenzie obtained a horse from the first man he met, a friendly farmer, paused for a few minutes near Hogg's Hollow, where Fletcher, Van Egmond, and a few others were discussing their prospects, and then turned westward at the Golden Lion Inn.[1] With Van Egmond and John Reid he fled towards Joseph Shepard's farm. His stay at Shepard's was not long. When the soldiers appeared Mrs. Shepard managed to keep them engaged in conversation until Mackenzie escaped, but Van Egmond was too exhausted to get away and was taken as a prisoner to Toronto.

Soon afterwards Mackenzie caught up with Lount and ninety men. The force broke up then, and Mackenzie, accompanied by sixteen partially-armed men, continued on foot through Vaughan Township towards the Humber Bridge. When a scout brought back word that the bridge was strongly guarded, they followed the shore of the river some distance northward, had supper at a farmer's, and crossed the Humber on a small foot-bridge. Finally, in an exhausted condition, they reached the home of Absalom Wilcox, near Dixie, several of whose sons took part in the revolt; it was then two o'clock Friday morning, and precautions were immediately taken to divert searchers.

'Blankets were hung over the windows to avoid suspicion', wrote Mackenzie, 'food and beds prepared, and while the Tories were carefully searching for us we were sleeping soundly. Next morning (Friday) those who had arms buried them, and after sending to inquire whether a friend a mile below had been dangerously wounded, we agreed to separate and make for the frontier two and two together'.

[1] The Golden Lion, Lansing, remained until September, 1933, when it was demolished. The Lion is preserved in Sharon Temple Museum.

Mackenzie and Allan Wilcox hurried to Comfort's Mills, near Streetsville, where they had dinner. Comfort had not heard of the revolt, but when they told him he offered Mackenzie money to assist him to escape, but the leader would accept only a horse. A young Irishman employed in Comfort's mill, the son of Bernard Doherty, drove the two fugitives westward in a wagon. As they proceeded along Dundas Street through the Credit Village (Springfield) they noticed the Lieutenant-Governor's proclamation posted at many points, offering £1,000 reward for Mackenzie's capture and £500 for the apprehension of David Gibson, Samuel Lount, Jesse Lloyd, and Silas Fletcher. A few minutes after they had passed, mounted troops rode up, hot in pursuit, and Mackenzie took the reins when the driver became frightened. They found the bridge over Sixteen-Mile Creek[2] guarded by a party under Colonel Chalmers, so they were practically surrounded. Jumping from the wagon and asking a labourer the road to Esquesing, to throw their pursuers off the track, the fugitives made for the woods and hid in the thickets while the soldiers combed the district. Mackenzie said that they owed their escape to a friendly militiaman who saw them but did not divulge their hiding-place. Capture was avoided here only at the cost of intense suffering:

'There was but one chance for escape, surrounded as we were, and that was to stem the stream and cross the swollen creek. We accordingly stripped ourselves naked, and with the surface ice beating against us, and holding our garments over our heads, in a bitter cold December night buffeted the current and were soon up to our necks... In an hour and a half we were under the hospitable roof of one of the innumerable agricultural friends I could then count on in the country'.[3]

At this house they were provided with dry clothes[4] and took a short rest. The help Mackenzie everywhere received made him feel that his sufferings were not in vain.

They then continued their flight, crossing Twelve-Mile Creek on a fallen tree about midnight. Once more they were pursued, and again escaped into the woods. When the soldiers had gone by, the fugitives continued westward, and passed through Wellington Square, finally reaching, half an hour before dawn, the home of a magistrate whom Mackenzie knew. He told them that his premises had been twice searched on the previous day by troops

[2]The creeks were early named according to their distance from Burlington if on the north shore of Lake Ontario, and from Niagara if on the south. See appendix D for the proclamations offering rewards for the capture of the leaders.

[3]Mrs. Clinton P. Lawrence, née Doherty, Palermo, aged ninety-three, recalls hearing her father's part in aiding Mackenzie. After 'helping him from a tiny attic with a rope ladder' and escorting him across the creek, he guided him to the home of David Ghent, where he hid in a pea-stack.

[4]It is probable that women's clothes were supplied to Mackenzie at Ghent's home. Mrs. Lawrence so states, though Mackenzie makes no reference to it. William Copland and Samuel Thompson refer to the women's clothes in which he escaped.

THE REMARKABLE ESCAPE OF MACKENZIE   31

who were scouring the whole country-side, and he warned them that it would be unsafe to proceed towards Burlington Bay. Consequently, Mackenzie and Wilcox separated,[5] believing they would have a better chance to escape if they travelled singly.

At day-break it began to snow, and rather than leave tracks, the rebel leader called at the home of another farmer, who offered to hide him in his barn. He chose, instead, to conceal himself in a peas-rick on a high knoll, from which he could see all that went on in the vicinity. From this hiding-place he saw the Sheriff, Colonel McDonell, and his posse searching the neighbourhood.

When they had gone on to the next house the excited farmer brought Mackenzie some food and two bottles of hot water to bathe his feet, at the same time expressing the hope that he would leave before another visitation of the soldiery. During the night Mackenzie, with the help of a small boy who acted as guide, reached the home of a friend named King, whose farm was located immediately next to Colonel John Chisholm's, the headquarters of his pursuers.

King provided him with a good supper and he set out on foot towards Dundas, passing a few armed men on the road. His guide left him at a friend's house, and here he obtained a horse and travelled onward into the mountain country above Hamilton. Some Dutch friends warned him to avoid the well-travelled roads, and this advice probably saved him from capture.

Near Ancaster he procured a fresh horse from an old friend, Jacob Rymal, and proceeded along a concession road until it appeared safer to take to the woods. With great difficulty he led his horse through several miles of dense forest and tangled underbrush, eventually reaching the solitary hut of a negro, who directed him on his way. He soon came to a small hamlet where he was called by name, and this caused him to gallop away at great speed. When he had gone ten miles he stopped again, and this time he was suspected, not of being an escaped rebel but a horse thief, and a farmer by the name of Waters insisted on conducting him to one McIntyre, the nearest magistrate.

Mackenzie might have shot Waters, but instead he decided to reveal his identity. He began a discussion on the grievances of the people of Upper Canada and learned that the man was rather favourable to reform, so he said: 'I am an old magistrate but at present in a situation of some difficulty. If I can satisfy you as to who I am and why I am here, would you desire to gain the

[5]Wilcox, aged twenty, also reached the United States, but was in frail health for four months. It is said that friends arranged for Mackenzie to spend that night with Barney Collins, 'a rabid Tory' whom no one would suspect.

price of any man's blood?' Waters naturally answered in the negative, and Mackenzie then showed him his pocket-book and the initials on his watch, with the result that he guided the fugitive for some distance on the road to the frontier.

It was Sunday morning, and after Waters had left him he met people on the way to church. He spoke to them, asking them to direct him on his road, and while in their sight travelled in a leisurely fashion. He crossed Twenty-Mile Creek a second time and once more went along the mountain path. He saw that a military guard was stationed above him, so he was cautious:

'I moved on very slowly as if going to meeting, but afterwards used the rowels to some advantage in the way of propellers. . . Many whom I met evidently knew me, and well was it for me that day that I had a good name. I could have been arrested fifty times before I reached Smithville had the Governor's person and proclamation been generally respected'.

His troubles were not yet over, however, for unfriendly people put soldiers on his track, and he avoided his pursuers only by putting his horse into the stable of a friend at Smithville. A few minutes afterward he saw militiamen dash along the road he had just left. Mackenzie remained several hours at this farm and had rest and food. With a companion, Samuel Chandler,[6] he then continued, crossing the Welland Canal and the Chippewa River, and reaching Crowland before daylight. From here they went on foot towards the Niagara River, reaching the farm of Captain Samuel McAfee about nine Monday morning. Before sitting down to breakfast Mackenzie thought it best to look about outside, for he realized that every effort would be made to stop him at the border:

'It was well for me that I did so. Old Colonel Kirby, the Custom House officer opposite Black Rock, and his troop of mounted dragoons in their green uniforms and with their carbines ready, were so close upon me riding up by the bank of the river, that had I not then observed their approach they would have caught me at breakfast. . . Mr. McAfee lost not a moment—his boat was hauled across the road and launched in the stream with all possible speed—and he and Chandler and I were scarcely afloat in it and out a little way below the bank when the old Tory Colonel and his green-coated troop of horse with their waving plumes were parading in front of Mr. McAfee's dwelling.

'How we escaped here is to me almost a miracle. I had resided long in the district and was known by everybody.[7] A boat was in the river against official orders; it was near the shore, and the carbines of the military, controlled by the collector, would have compelled us to return or

[6]Chandler, wagon-maker at St. Johns, was forty-six years old and the father of ten children. After serving on Navy Island he was captured during the Short Hills raid and transported to Van Diemen's Land.

[7]'Mackenzie safely reached the United States', says Emily Weaver, 'and one cannot help thinking (with him) that it is something to be proud of that no Canadian was base enough to try to sell him for Head's thousand pounds'. (*The Story of the Counties of Ontario*, 73.)

THE REMARKABLE ESCAPE OF MACKENZIE 33

have killed me for disobedience... Not a few must have seen the whole movement, and yet we were allowed to steer for the head of Grand Island with all the expedition in our power. In an hour we were safe on the American shore'.

So ended the perilous escape of William Lyon Mackenzie. Through ingenuity and dogged perseverance he had saved his life. For sheer melodrama his adventures are unparalleled in Canadian history.

BIBLIOGRAPHY

Mackenzie's account of his escape, 'Winter Wanderings Ten Years Since', was published in the Toronto *Examiner*, October 6, 1847. It was later reprinted in the *Globe* and in various British and American periodicals, and is quoted in Lindsey, II 102-22. Mackenzie says his flight occupied five days, but in his earlier *Narrative* gives it as three days, though as a matter of fact it was four. Supplementary information is inevitably fragmentary and contradictory, and in some instances entirely unreliable. Mrs. Lawrence's reminiscences appeared in the Toronto *Globe and Mail*, April 23, 1937. Betty Duffield, later Mrs. Dew, quoted in Lizars, *Humours of '37*, 361-3, saw Mackenzie fling away his cloak as he fled, and it was returned to him anonymously two years later when he was in Monroe County Prison, Rochester. Mrs. Zoe Stevens, Toronto, grand-daughter of Henry Sanders, states that his brother Andrew, who had been at Montgomery's, later took a democrat full of provisions to help feed the fugitives at Shepard's Mill, but was intercepted *en route* and the food confiscated. Reported incidents in the early portion of the escape indicating that Mackenzie was hard pressed near Coomber's Mills, are given in John Hunt's reminiscences in the Ontario Archives; while material in E. E. Ball's 'Landmarks of 1837', *Acta Victoriana*, 1904-5, 265, illustrates how the truth was distorted when memories began to weaken and hearsay and imagination were substituted. The Lieutenant-Governor's proclamations offering rewards for Mackenzie, Lount, Gibson, Fletcher, and Lloyd, and giving unique descriptions, are printed herewith in appendix D. The reminiscences of Anson H. Wilson, as recorded in 1904 in the *Jackson Republican*, Maquoketa, Iowa, point out alleged discrepancies in Mackenzie's account of the last stages of his escape. Wilson states that his father (John Wilson), William Current, and Mahlon Brookfield helped him reach McAfee's in a sleigh, and that Mackenzie fainted from sheer exhaustion when he entered the rowboat. The Wilsons, Current, and Brookfield left Upper Canada and, with other refugees from the Niagara District, settled in Maquoketa.

CHAPTER IV

WITH THE NEWCASTLE DISTRICT MILITIA

THE inhabitants of Upper Canada never exemplified their loyalty more emphatically than at the commencement of the Rebellion of 1837. The response to the Lieutenant-Governor's frantic appeal was magnificent. He estimated that from 10,000 to 12,000 men hastened to the defence of the capital within a few days of the beginning of the 'Siege of Toronto' on December 4.

The shooting of Colonel Robert Moodie early in the evening of Monday, and the escape to Toronto of John Powell after he had killed Captain Anthony Anderson, brought home to Sir Francis Bond Head the danger which threatened the city. For the first time he realized that Mackenzie's Patriots were in the act of cutting off Toronto's communication with the rest of Upper Canada. 'The city has been in an uproar all night,' wrote William Weller, stage proprietor.

Couriers were despatched in all directions, and the order was to march to Toronto with all possible speed. Subsequent activities in Cobourg may be taken as typical of central Upper Canada generally. One of Bond Head's messengers[1] rode into town late in the night of the fifth, and couriers were instantly sent throughout the district to direct an immediate muster and report of companies. Units already organized were put 'under orders to march early to-morrow morning for Toronto. . . God save the Queen and protect the unity of the Empire!' A consultation of officers was called, and they assembled at Sheriff Ruttan's home two hours after the arrival of the courier. The most prominent of those present were the Honourable Zacheus Burnham and the Honourable George S. Boulton, members of the Legislative Council. The inhabitants of the entire region were aroused, and by ten o'clock in the morning of the seventh some 2,000 men were on their way to the meeting-places designated.[2]

---

[1]The General Order of December 4, of which there is a copy in the Ontario Archives, is Enclosure 1 in Head to Glenelg, December 19, 1887. The messenger who carried the news as far as Kingston was waylaid by 'two fellows' a few miles out of Toronto 'and forced to shoot one of them in order to escape'.

[2]In a poster calling for recruits for the Queen's Royal Borderers, Brockville, each man was offered '8 dollars bounty, a new suit of clothes, and a great coat & pair of Boots, also a free Gift of sixty days pay when discharged'; to which inducements was added an implied threat: 'Let no Man pretending to LOYALTY HANG BACK!' A valuable sidelight on the rise of the militia is in a letter of Egerton Ryerson's, who was in Cobourg and heard 'that Rolph and Bidwell were under arms in defence of the city against Mackenzie'; and adds that the report doubled the number of volunteers who rose to the support of Bond Head.

34

From Lindsey, *Life of Mackenzie*, 1862

The Battle of Montgomery's Farm, December 7, 1837

Montgomery's Tavern was burned by order of the Lieutenant-Governor after the skirmish with the rebels. 'The yeomen and farmers of Upper Canada had triumphed over their perfidious enemy, "responsible government".'—*Sir Francis Bond Head*

From Lindsey, *Life of Mackenzie*, 1862   Adrian Sharp

The Death of Lieutenant-Colonel Moodie

Shot near Montgomery's Tavern while attempting to ride through the rebel lines to warn Toronto of the concentration, he was buried at Thornhill on the day of the battle, and his neighbours came to the funeral armed with muskets, pistols, bowie-knives, and pitchforks

Isabel Baxter Mackenzie
A staunch Patriot

Marshall S. Bidwell
Forced into exile

Charles Durand
His sentence of death was commuted to banishment

Dr. Thomas D. Morrison
Acquitted of high treason, he fled to the United States

From references in contemporary letters and other records we are able to visualize the excitement and alarm that flew from house to house as the news reached the rear townships. Copies of the Lieutenant-Governor's proclamation were carried to Peterborough on Wednesday morning, and the word was speedily relayed farther into 'the backwoods'. To Bond Head's appeal every wild report that the mind could invent was added. One rumour had it that Toronto was besieged by 60,000 men, another that 400 Indians had descended upon the city and slaughtered many of the inhabitants. Indeed, the only item of truth which came through was that Colonel Moodie had been shot.

The answer to the call of the government was immediate. James Caddy took a copy of the proclamation to Samuel Strickland's home in Douro Township, and Strickland at once set to work cleaning up his double-barrelled gun and running a quantity of balls. At ten o'clock at night, in a blinding snow-storm, he set out for Peterborough, stopping at the home of his father-in-law, Robert Reid, for a few hours' sleep. The Traills were told by Strickland, and, writes Mrs. Traill at midnight on Thursday, 'My beloved husband goes at daybreak.' The Moodies, further northward, received the news Friday evening, and Mr. Moodie insisted on setting off at dawn in spite of having broken a bone in his leg. An aged pensioner, shouting that 'the Nankees [Yankees] wounded me at New Orleans, and I'll never die until I have a shot at them,' could not be kept from the march.

On Thursday morning a force of nearly 400 well-armed and well-equipped men mustered in the town and set off southwards at eleven o'clock. Captain Cowall, formerly of the 1st Royals, was in command of the company, and they appear to have marched seventeen miles the first day, halting for the night at Joseph Graham's Tavern, now Bailieboro. On Friday they reached Bletcher's Tavern, three miles from Port Hope, where they remained for the night as Port Hope was crowded with militia companies. On Saturday, after they had arrived at Port Hope, they were joined by the 2nd battalion of Northumberland militia under Colonel Alexander McDonnell, and the 4th under Colonel Brown. The latter force had taken along two supposed spies whom they placed in jail at Amherst, just north of Cobourg. They then waited a few hours in the expectation that a steamship would call, but when she failed to do so they marched to Port Hope. In that town were then about 1,000 men, including 170 Indians under Colonel Anderson, trader at Rice Lake. It was expected that the steamer *Traveller* would stop in on her downward trip and return to Toronto with the militia; but she passed by, ignoring their gunfire and other signals. While they were preparing to proceed a courier from Bond Head arrived bearing an order that countermanded their march and announced 'that there existed no further occasion for the resort of militia to Toronto.'³ Sir Francis subsequently wrote to Lord Glenelg that 'from the Newcastle District alone, 2,600 men, with nothing but the clothes in which they stood, marched in the depth of winter towards the capital, although nearly 100 miles from their homes.'⁴

One of the most radical of Reform newspapers—the *Reformer* —was published in Cobourg, so it was expected that many would support Mackenzie; but the Tory *Cobourg Star*, which would have been the first to impute disloyalty to Reformers if there had been any grounds, was quick to emphasize their co-operation in support of the government. 'We are proud and gratified to say,' wrote the editor, 'that all the leading Reformers in the town of Cobourg have to a man denounced the present measures of Mackenzie, and are to a man actively aiding the arrangements to oppose him.'

The arrangements were not restricted to the despatch of volunteers. At a meeting in the Albion Hotel a large sum was subscribed to take care of families unprovided for when their men suddenly joined the militia. 'The men were all gone,' wrote Frances Stewart, 'and women and children had to attend to the stock and procure firewood, etc. The fear and uncertainty about the enemy kept those who were at home in a state of great anxiety.' To add to the difficulties of the situation, some of the officers, 'drest in a little brief authority,' tyranically refused their men permission to go home for a few hours, under threat of imprisonment and confiscation of their property. It was decidedly not a time of unadulterated enthusiasm and patriotism.

The company of some forty men which took the name Cobourg Rifles was organized a few days before the arrival of Bond Head's courier, and consequently they were able to set out with greater expedition than most other units. Thirty-six officers and men⁵ of the Rifles marched to Toronto, and it was claimed that, in spite of its youth, the company was better organized than any other volunteer corps in the country, the credit being given to Captain Warren and Lieutenant McDonald, both of whom had served in regiments of regulars.

³Head to Glenelg, December 19, 1837. The Peterborough contingent returned home, but hearing that Mackenzie was in hiding in the Township of Ops, proceeded to invade Purdy's Mills (Lindsay). Rather than leave empty-handed they arrested William Purdy and took him and one or two others to jail.

⁴With the various units on duty, and 'parties arriving constantly from the back townships', there were probably 4,000 militiamen ready to answer the call.

⁵See appendix E for the list of 'young gentlemen of this town' who composed the Cobourg Rifles.

The more extensive information available about the Cobourg Rifles must not be allowed to dim the exploits of other units, for it is quite evident that the experiences of all who proceeded to Toronto were drawn on for the narrative that has come down to us. From Cobourg there were also in the first flight three companies under Captains Clark, Calcutt, and Conger, which followed in that order behind the Rifles. Colonel Burnham led the volunteer cavalry westward on Friday, and another company of infantry, under Captain McKyes, was in readiness to leave on short notice. Then there were from Port Hope Colonel Williams with thirty cavalry, and Lieutenant-Colonel Boulton and Major Smart with some 200 men. Further east along the front were several forces which, like those from Peterborough, were too remote to be in the first line of march. Within the limits of the Newcastle District alone there were the Haldimand Volunteers, thirty-six in number, under Captain Williams, who reached Port Hope on Saturday, the ninth; and the Cramahe militia, under Colonel Ruttan, who assembled 600 at Brighton on the same day, and were divided into two companies, one being placed on duty at the River Trent and the other at Colborne. All these units were eager to proceed to 'the front'.

Meanwhile the Cobourg contingent which had left on Thursday morning, the seventh, 'amidst the cheers of the inhabitants', was well on its way to Toronto. They were in high spirits and trudged on manfully, proud of their position as the advance guard of the volunteer army that was gathering from the side lines and bush roads far in the interior of the region. The day was fine, and it was by no means unpleasant to march even over mud roads when the 'nods, winks, and wreathed smiles of the country girls' enlivened still further the jubilant spirits of the adventurous militiamen. They did not stop at Port Hope, but continued to De la Rey's Tavern,[6] six miles beyond, which they reached a little after dark.

Upon arrival there the more youthful and unsuspicious immediately sought such comforts as might be obtained in the bar and kitchen of rural inns, while 'the old and knowing' were looking ahead and reserving 'the best bedrooms, taking the precaution to put the keys in their pockets.' Apparently fourteen of the thirty-six in the Cobourg Rifles secured the choice beds, the others having to make the best of the one that remained. It broke down

[6] In Robert Rogers's diary it is called Delaree's Inn. It was probably located at the crossroads in the village now called Morrish. Marsh's Tavern, which still stands, has been suggested as the stopping-place, but it is two miles east, and Thomas Marsh, grandson of the builder, says the tavern was never in charge of De la Rey.

when eight threw themselves upon it, and after a friendly struggle for the bedclothes, it was decided that the mattress should be placed in the centre of the floor, and that no one should lay more than his head upon it. The story-teller of the party now related 'The Red Whale', a tale of the Sioux Indians; but the circumstances were not conducive to sleep, and at three o'clock they decided to while away the time around a bowl of punch until it should be the hour of marching. A youth of seventeen, who although in the last stages of tuberculosis had bought a pony to enable him to accompany the force, read a poem, 'The Time to Die', of his own composition and bearing upon his condition. As he was reading the last verse a stranger entered the room and observed, 'The time to die may be nearer than some of you young jokers imagine'.

Within a few moments the whole company was aroused. The newcomer had escaped, he said, from a large party who were sent by Mackenzie to hold the pass at Rouge Hill.[7] Captain Warren ordered his men to get breakfast and fall in, and after they had eaten a large platter of cold fat pork and boiled potatoes the Rifles shouldered arms and with three cheers for the Queen set off westwards. The excitement was now increased by the possibility of an engagement with the enemy, and every turn in the road, every clump of trees, was carefully scanned for signs of an ambush. They felt, however, that they were 'an overmatch for four times their number of rebels; for they had in them enthusiasm and bravery, and that spirit of patriotism which regards danger and death as unworthy a thought when duty calls'. The pale youth on the pony struck the key-note for the whole army as he rode along murmuring the lines of Ossian—'Happy are they who die in their youth while their renown is around them!'

The force marched in one division and had gone about five miles when a scout brought word that eight or nine suspicious characters were approaching. Drawing back his company and placing some men in ambush on either side of the road, Captain Warren awaited their arrival; but another scout brought news that they had entered a wayside tavern, and a party of five was thereupon sent to take them prisoners. By making a detour and descending suddenly upon the group, Lieutenant McDonald, Corporal Armour, and Privates Buck, Perry, and Allan captured them all. A search yielded balls, percussion caps, and pistols, and the men, all of whom had passed the prime of life and were

[7] These men were apparently part of Peter Matthews's company who had retreated eastward after burning buildings near the Don Bridge.

apparently well-to-do in the world, were placed in the midst of the rear-guard.[8]

It might have been supposed that a longer march than fourteen miles would have been attempted the second day; but the health of the men and their accommodations for the night were all-important considerations, which could be best met by a stop at Bowmanville, leaving the heavier days' marching for the last, when the troops were more hardened. Colonel Ham wrote that night that some 600 men, still in good health and excellent spirits, were spending the night there after having been accorded a loyal reception along the route of march. 'A True Briton', also writing from Bowmanville, describes how upwards of 800 men, including Captain Warren and his company, were quartered upon the inhabitants. Many of the Old Country villagers, he states, asked that the volunteers be sent to their homes, and good order and quietness prevailed everywhere. It would appear certain that the Port Hope companies did not leave home until Friday morning, marching the twenty miles to Bowmanville that day and overtaking the Cobourg units which reached that village earlier in the evening.

As the Cobourg Rifles plodded along next morning between Bowmanville and Oshawa they were intrigued by the appearance of a young Irishman and two fine-looking girls, his sisters, who were travelling by cart to Toronto to secure work as servants. 'Full of laughter and spirit and their healthy and hardy frames elegantly shaped,' the group provided a pleasing diversion as they kept pace for a time with the militia. In their bundles were bread and cheese which they offered to share with the men.

An order had reached the force at Bowmanville to arrest Dr. Hunter of Whitby. Four of the Rifles—Buck, Perry, Armour, and Rogers—were accordingly sent ahead as scouts, with orders to station themselves near his dwelling and allow no one to leave it. This move prevented the doctor from escaping, which he attempted to do upon the approach of the main body. A resident of the neighbourhood stated that there were twelve well-armed men inside the house, so it was surrounded and the troops were ordered to effect the arrest without loss of life, if possible. This movement, which threatened to have serious consequences, became a humorous interlude:

'The writer of this, being the thinnest of the number, was assisted through the window of a cellar by Sergeant Meredith, as he went through backward in order to present his front to the enemy. The cellar being as

[8] Rogers's diary, December 8, and Colonel Ham's letter from Darlington (Bowmanville), dated December 8, 11 p.m., to Colonel the Honourable Z. Burnham, Cobourg, (*Cobourg Star*, December 13, 1837), corroborate the capture of seven of 'Mackenzie's principal men'. This method of seizing suspected rebels was general throughout Upper Canada, though entirely contrary to law.

dark as night, the seat of his inexpressibles caught in a confounded meat hook, and he remained like Mahomet's Coffin, suspended between Heaven and earth. The Rifles, always alive to the ludicrous, gathered round the hole and laughed as if their hearts would break; at last Corporal S—— extricated him from his corporeal sufferings.'

A pistol shot rang out, suggesting that a life had been taken, but it was only Lieutenant Chatterton firing in the attic to see by the flash whether anyone was there. Half an hour's search finally brought Dr. Hunter from his hiding-place, and he was marched along towards Toronto with the other prisoners.[9] The troops conducted their search in 'a quiet, gentlemanly manner and with every respect towards the family'—consideration which was frequently lacking in similar circumstances.

It was dark when, after a march of about eighteen miles, the force halted for the night at Lee's Tavern,[10] three miles west of Whitby. Here the Cobourg Rifles took up their lodging on the floor, with their arms and accoutrements as pillows. The long march had begun to tell on them, and they were asleep almost immediately, but there were numerous interruptions. The rest of the Newcastle District force came up shortly afterwards and were quartered in a Methodist chapel. An hour or so later, at midnight, the sentry fired off his musket at a horseman who refused to stop, and five minutes later the Rifles were drawn up ready to repel any attack that might be made. But he who had caused the alarm escaped, and after standing under arms for half an hour the troops retired once more—but only to the kitchen fire, in order to be in readiness at short notice. Several members of Captain Evans's company were there too, and Roe Buck, 'ever foremost in fun and danger', suggested that as there was no grog to be had someone should provide a song or story. A sergeant warned the group against singing, but Pat O'Neill had a reputation as a storyteller, and, fortified by the promise of a drink, 'if we arn't all kilt at the Rouge to-morrow,' produced a suitable Irish yarn. A few hours later the shout of the sentry, 'Guard turn out!', brought the company face to face with realities, and they were out of doors in the twinkling of an eye.

As the column lined up on Sunday morning for the day's march it was seen that several companies of the Cavan Volunteers

[9]Mackenzie describes Dr. James Hunter as 'a native of Yorkshire and a sincere Patriot'. Charles Fothergill considered him to be, 'next to Mackenzie himself, the most active traitor of them all' (*Mackenzie's Own Narrative*, 7 fn.). The official record of the disposition of his case reads: 'James Hunter, physician, arrested December 10th, discharged December 21st by Commission after examination'. At his trial Thomas Henry supported an alibi for Dr. Hunter, but Hunter heard during the winter that another charge was being prepared against him. 'Elder' Henry hid him in a shack and then took him to Jesse Trull's schooner, upon which he escaped to Rochester. For his Patriot activities in the United States see page 132.

[10]Lee's Tavern, in Pickering Township, was a few years later operated by Hiram Post. The red-brick building still stands, and 'H. POST'S HOTEL' may still be deciphered across the front.

had overtaken the leaders during the night. Like most militia units of the period, they were armed with 'sticks, bayonets, muskets without locks, and in short with whatever came first to hand'.[11] In the line of march there were now no less than 1,750 men, and the sight must have been impressive. The Rifles were still honoured with the foremost position, and Captain Warren, Roe Buck, and Robert Armour formed the first file of the advance guard, and Lieutenant McDonald and Henry Ruttan the second; while Lieutenants Chatterton and Covert marched respectively at the front and rear of the company. Captain James Rogers's cavalry came next, being described as a 'fine troop whose Sabres, playing artful dodges with the struggling rays of the morning sun, gave them a very martial appearance'. There followed the Port Hope Rifles, a well-armed, gallant body commanded by Colonel Kingsmill, and 'the Boys of Cavan' brought up the rear.

As the loyalist army approached the Rouge River, it was remarked how excellent a defence it would afford. It requires but little imagination to picture the road of 1837, 'between almost perpendicular hills, leading over a river broad and deep, and spanned by a miserable plank bridge'.[12] As it was expected that the rebels would make a stand there to prevent the militia from reaching Toronto, scouts had been sent ahead to reconnoitre, but no ambush was discovered, and the force continued its march. The hill at Highland Creek provided a sharp descent, and a shout was suddenly raised that the buildings at its foot were occupied by the enemy. An engagement unrecorded in military annals followed as the militia advanced at the double to disperse the rebels:

'Immediately Captain Rogers' troop galloped forward to cut off the retreat of any force that might be there, while the Cobourg Rifles, with muskets at the trail, in extended order gallantly dashed forward to engage the enemy hand to hand; immediately the doors of the houses were forced or thrown open, and the place was captured without a struggle. The prisoners which fell to the share of our section consisted of one old woman, one old fur cap, and a bushel of apples. The last of our prisoners we devoured on the spot. Amidst much laughter and many jokes we hastened to re-form, and then proceeded on our march.'

The roads had been bad all the way, and 'one mass of mud about 18 inches deep of the consistence of putty' had thenceforth to be

[11]The appearance and conduct of those who turned out on militia parade-day is the best evidence of their equipment for battle. See the author's *Early Life in Upper Canada*, 345-8.

[12]When Captain Basil Hall passed that way in 1827 a boy carried passengers across by canoe, and one's horse or carriage was yanked through the stream by whatever means presented itself. (Hall, *Travels in America*, I 267-72.) A glance at the remains of the early roadway and bridge enables the traveller to appreciate something of the tortuous course.

negotiated. A heavy snowstorm added to the difficulties of the march, and as it melted upon them everyone was soaking wet and covered with mud:

'Instead of making a soldierly appearance, our hose or stockings, dragging in the mizzle, and our iron pipes sticking out from under our coats, gave us much more the appearance of *Portable Engines* going out to exercise. As for the Dragoons, they were so covered with mud and so disguised in the storm that they looked like a grove of horse chestnuts gone to seed. Alas, could our fair townswomen have seen us on that eventful day we fear that their weeping would have been changed into laughter.'

After the mud and hills of Highland Creek and the Rouge, the column found the open country beyond Gates's Inn[13] a little easier going. Everyone was tired but happy as the end of the long trek was in sight. Roe Buck broke into *Old King Cole,* the regimental song of the Cobourg Rifles, and a moment later it was being thundered out by the whole column. About five miles from Toronto a halt was called, the captain announcing that they had marched twenty miles in seven and a half hours, which, considering the state of the roads, was 'better than I ever knew soldiers of the line to do'. Corporal Saunders expressed the general sentiment when he exclaimed that 'if our feet hadn't been kept in perpetual motion we should have been pillars of mud by this time!' A 'quart pocket pistol' revived as many as could get a sip out of it; while a teamster who had been hired to follow along with baggage caused a laugh when he sat down to eat a lunch he was carrying under his hat—for his head, alas, was 'one mass of melted bread and butter'!

The column had proceeded about two miles farther when a scout brought back news that some red-coated horsemen were advancing towards them. Captain Warren so disposed his forces that these men might be captured if they proved to be rebels, but everyone was pleased when Colonel the Honourable G. S. Boulton, who had earlier led the Durham Cavalry to Toronto, brought a group of Toronto men into their midst to welcome them to the city. 'Of course we gave them three hearty cheers,' says our informant; but when they attempted a salute, 'only 8 of nearly 40 firearms would go off!' An hour later the militia were marching along King Street.

The citizens were out in force to cheer the Newcastle District Volunteers as they crossed the bridge over the Don which Peter Matthews and his men had tried to burn a few days before.

---

[13]Gates's Inn was about ten miles east of Toronto. A few days earlier Dr. Hunter had fled there after the battle at Montgomery's Tavern. The landlord had permitted him to hide in an old oven, where he remained until Colonel Boulton's cavalry and other militia units had passed by. The story is told by Read in his *Canadian Rebellion of 1837*, 352.

Particulars of the 'Siege of Toronto' were conveyed to them as they trudged along, and they were still able, in spite of blistered and bleeding feet,[14] to get some fun out of life. The force marched on towards Government House, taking in the state of the city and the many evidences of the panic of a few days earlier:

'Everything bore the appearance of a seized city. Houses barricaded, civilians in arms, sentries in all directions, and bustle everywhere. The pigs in the gutter were stalking about with set up bristles, and the tom cats with set up backs; the dogs looked as if they had been crunching dead men's bones, and the cows as if each had devoured her "Paddy the Piper".'

'Celebrated for intemperance houses', Toronto appeared on that day a perfect groggery. 'Pipes, Tobacco, and Whiskey Sold Here' ornamented every second door; and when there was no sign, two pipes laid crosswise and flanked by a plug of tobacco answered the purpose. 'So bewildered did the imagination become that I mistook an old mop set out to dry for a scalp on a pole, and an owl in a cage hung out for sale I thought

"That even he took up the loyal cause,
And made a bat cry murder in his jaws."'

Although it was late Sunday afternoon Sir Francis Bond Head was ready to receive them as they approached Government House, King and Simcoe Streets. The column was admittedly 'very extended and not very stately, and except as far as numbers went was not calculated to impress a military man with much enthusiasm as to the value of our services in the field'; but they were brave and loyal men who had marched seventy-two miles at his call, and the Lieutenant-Governor was pleased to review them when they had been drawn up in a hollow square in Government House Yard:

'Sir Francis did not inspect us very minutely, which was very kind of him, considering the state of our wardrobe. He knew that the seat of honour and loyalty, the heart, was sound, and made us a speech accordingly, which we acknowledged by giving him three hearty British cheers, three more for the Queen, and three more for the British flag which from the summit of Government House waved proudly over our heads. Oh! we forgot in that moment all our weariness and fasting and raggedness. We

[14]Similar suffering was the price of loyalty throughout the province. When news of the revolt reached Goderich on December 10 a battalion was raised. Early in January they learned of the activities of filibusters along the Detroit, and on January 6 a company set off 'through the woods for Port Sarnia'. Other detachments followed, and the sufferings of all were very great. They had to 'plough, dig, swim, and wade' through several townships, and after marching 120 miles they remained on duty for ten weeks. An eye-witness of the commencement of the homeward trek notes: 'The last of the brave and loyal 1st Regiment of Huron Militia have just marched from this place for their ain firesides, under a heavy shower and through a muddy road.' See 'Bravery and Sufferings of the Loyal Militia', New York *Albion*, June 16, 1838, quoting letter of 'A Freeholder', Port Sarnia, March 13, to the Toronto *British Colonist*.

44   THE LIVES AND TIMES OF THE PATRIOTS

thought only of our Fatherland, and many a sun-burnt and sun-dried cheek were wet with tears—the overflowings of truly honest, upright, and loyal hearts.'

With three more cheers for Sir Francis the militia set out for such accommodation as could be provided; for the population was then only some 12,000, and almost as many volunteers had entered the city within two or three days. The Cobourg Rifles were among those assigned to 'Lawyers' Hall' (Osgoode), and were inclined to question the hospitality of the citizens when they found that their quarters consisted of 'two large damp rooms without stoves or fireplaces,—nay, they were not even provided with seats'. While they were bitterly complaining of such accommodations, Messrs. W. Boulton and J. Robinson came in and insisted that the Rifles take up quarters in their homes; but not being 'in drawing room trim' they refused, and marched instead to the North American House, where they 'fortunately secured a room each in the excellent Hotel'. The prospect of a bath and the best dinner that could be got did much to restore their spirits. At six o'clock, with several senior officers and other guests, the Rifles sat down to a repast which was good enough under any circumstances, but the most sumptuous of banquets after such a march. Turkeys, geese, ducks, chickens, and meat of all kinds disappeared in quick succession, and the substantials were succeeded by generous quantities of sherry. 'I, for one, drank everybody's health at least three times over, and I believe I was the most remiss of the company in paying this questionable kind of compliment. After the removal of the cloth and the due dressing of a formidable line of bottles, our captain gave The Queen. After the grand display of lungs which this toast called forth, others followed in quick succession', —and so ended this grand climax to the celebrated march of the Newcastle District Volunteers.[15]

[15] A considerable number of the Newcastle District men, including the Cobourg Rifles, were sent to Chippewa, and eight of the Rifles participated in the cutting-out of the *Caroline*. On January 19 Robert Rogers, and probably the other members of the unit, returned to Cobourg on the steamer *St. George*, the early winter being very mild. Their activities at Toronto and Chippewa are also described in letters to the *Cobourg Star*; while the Reverend N. Bethune indicated something of the high regard in which they were held when he wrote: 'The Cobourg Volunteers, under the command of the Chief Justice, have been ordered to Niagara, as a demonstration of their loyal spirit might have a good effect in that district'. (Archives of Ontario). There was a second march of volunteers from the Newcastle District early in January, 1838, and it was similarly characterised by bad roads and rebel-hunting. In the evening of the fifth day from Peterborough they reached Toronto, where they were warmly complimented by the Lieutenant-Governor.

BIBLIOGRAPHY

An outline of the settlement and political background of the old Newcastle District (Northumberland, Durham, Peterborough, and Victoria counties) is given in the author's 'The Cobourg Conspiracy', *Canadian Historical Review*, March, 1937. The description of the rising of the militia in the back townships is based upon Frances Stewart, *Our Forest Home*, 95; Susanna Moodie, *Roughing It in the Bush*, II 186-93; Catharine Traill, *The Backwoods of Canada*, 1929 Edition, 325-35;

WITH THE NEWCASTLE DISTRICT MILITIA 45

Samuel Strickland, *Twenty-seven Years in Canada West*, II 259-67; Thomas Poole, *Early Settlement of Peterborough*, 177; and the *Cobourg Star*, December 13, 1837. The account of the march to Toronto is based upon 'The Adventures of the Cobourg Rifles during the Campaign of 1837', by 'One of Themselves', which appeared in the *Cobourg Star* of October 27, November 3 and 17, 1847, and April 19 and 26, 1848. The only known file for the period is in the possession of the author. Supplementary information has been gleaned from letters appearing in the *Cobourg Star* and elsewhere, as indicated in the notes, and from Robert Rogers's short diary in the Peterborough Public Library which is printed in the *Canadian Historical Review*, December, 1932, 429-30. The escape of Dr. Hunter to the United States is described in Snider, 'Schooner Days', Toronto *Evening Telegram*, February 27, 1937. The Kingston *Upper Canada Herald* of December 12, 1837, gives details of the progress of the messenger who carried eastwards the Lieutenant-Governor's General Order calling out the militia, and the Misses Lizars's *Humours of '37* contains a valuable account of the Upper Canadian militia of the period. Egerton Ryerson's comment on the rise of the volunteers is in Sissons, I 427. The second march of the Newcastle District militia to Toronto is recorded in Poole, 32-6, where the names of a small number of those who participated are given. Among poetical efforts inspired by the times were several widely circulated 'loyal staves' from the pen of Susanna Moodie, *Roughing It in the Bush*, II 191-209.

CHAPTER V

CHARLES DUNCOMBE AND THE CONCENTRATION AT SCOTLAND

DR. CHARLES DUNCOMBE, who was born at Stratford, Connecticut, on July 28, 1791, was descended from a distinguished English family. He came to Upper Canada in 1820, settling first at St. Thomas and later moving to Bishopsgate, Burford Township, where he became one of the largest landowners in the county. He was highly esteemed in his profession, and to him and Dr. Rolph was granted the first charter for a medical college in Canada. He was prominent among the founders of Masonry in Upper Canada, and was the first to go to England to receive the thirty-second degree. A tall, handsome man of dignified appearance, his abilities were such that, had he chosen the opposite politics, he might well have been among the favoured members of the Family Compact. It was his political philosophy that 'a Nation never can rebel: those only are Rebels who resist the will of the people'; and he envisioned a Canada free from 'the dynasty of a foreign governor and an Orange Oligarchy'.

In 1830, and again in 1834 and 1836, he was elected Member of Parliament for Oxford, though William Lyon Mackenzie did not support him in his second contest. While a member of the Assembly he was appointed to a commission to investigate the need of a lunatic asylum, as well as 'the system and management of schools and colleges'. In carrying out these duties he travelled widely in the United States and obtained documentary material from Europe, issuing three valuable reports as a result. His work upon the committee on finance in 1836 shows still further his high qualifications and public spirit. After the election of that year he visited England to present charges against Sir Francis Bond Head, but he was not accorded a proper hearing, and the only results were the exoneration of the Lieutenant-Governor and his own embitterment.

It is believed, however, that Duncombe was not easily persuaded to support Mackenzie's plan of rebellion, preferring instead an impressive political demonstration. He had just returned from England when the Montgomery's Tavern concentration occurred, but he agreed to support the revolt even though he lost the backing of the moderate Reformers of his district by doing so. The depositions of those subsequently arrested indicate a course of

THE CONCENTRATION AT SCOTLAND 47

events which characterized every district where disaffection was rife. Abraham Sackrider said on oath that early in the second week of December he found Duncombe's men collected at the meeting-house near Sodom (Norwich). A few days later he heard 'a Methodist preacher of the name of Bird . . . encourage the people to take up arms and fight for their freedom'. Such 'Ryersonian strolling demagogues', as the redoubtable Colonel Talbot[1] called them, were not, however, the only religious body charged with seditious utterances. Among others were 'Hickory Quakers', particularly in Yarmouth Township, and that their religious tenets[2] did not prevent their taking up arms shows the intensity of political feeling.

Peter Coon, a blacksmith in Burford Township, adds to our knowledge of the preparations for the outbreak. In a deposition sworn at Hamilton on December 17, 1837, he stated that frequent meetings had taken place in Burford Township for about a fortnight, and he named Isaac and Eliakim Malcolm,[3] Charles Duncombe, and William McGuire as particularly active in calling meetings and drilling recruits. He swore also that two of these leaders made him manufacture pikes for the purpose of arming some of the rebels, and that he was forced to billet men in his house. Among other incidental information, he said that Eliakim Malcolm and others let it be known 'that they had pills for the Lieut. Gov., Sir F. B. Head, and that they would shoot him if they could get a chance'.[4]

The assembling of the Patriots could hardly be effected secretly, nor does there appear to have been much effort to do so. John Kelly, who was one of them, swore that on Thursday, December 7, the day of the rout of Mackenzie's men at Mont-

[1]For an account of the Reform activities of those whom Colonel Talbot called 'diabolical wretches' and 'sheep with the rot', and of a famous St. Thomas meeting which 'Tommy Tough' (the colonel) changed into a demonstration of loyalty, see the author's *Early Life in Upper Canada*, 131-3.

[2]In a letter to the Toronto *Globe*, September 6, 1890, Frank Hunt wrote: 'The petty officials who did the dirty work for the Family Compact took special delight in annoying the inoffensive Quakers. . . The Friends were warned out to drill contrary to all precedent and laws of the realm, and when they would not respond their houses were pillaged.'

[3]Probably no family had as many representatives among the Patriots as the Malcolms. While only six of that name appear in the official list of those jailed, there were at least eleven implicated. Eliakim and James fled the country; Peter was sentenced to death, but his punishment was commuted to transportation, and later he was bound over to keep the peace for three years; Finlay, sr., late Member of Parliament, was acquitted after three months in jail; Finlay, jr., was in jail in London for six months, then tried in Toronto and sentenced to fourteen years' transportation, and finally released in England on a writ of *habeas corpus*; Charles and George spent a period in Niagara jail; Norman was three months in prison, but was found not guilty; Isaac Brock Malcolm was similarly indicted, but bailed on providing security to keep the peace; Edy was dismissed after a week in jail; while no bill was found against John, and he was discharged after three months in prison.

[4]Coon's deposition is given in appendix F. No bill was found against him but he spent three months in jail. William McGuire, a schoolmaster, was later a lieutenant on Navy Island.

gomery's, there was a public meeting at Joseph Beemer's Inn at Scotland, and that Malcolm and McGuire asked for recruits to assist Mackenzie in Toronto. About half of those present volunteered, and they 'remained under arms and kept their headquarters there and were on duty as soldiers'. It would appear to have been at this meeting that a Provisional Committee was formed to co-operate with Mackenzie's projected Provisional Government; and officers were also appointed to collect arms and make other necessary arrangements for a rising. John Tufford of Bishopsgate, son-in-law of Duncombe, was among those detailed to assemble firearms, and, although in general it was hoped to obtain them from known sympathizers, it is evident that they were secured by force from some who would not voluntarily support the cause. John Finlay deposed that Adam Yeigh and George Rouse came to his house 'and there demanded of him that he should deliver up to them the possession of any firearms he might have; . . and the said Adam Yeigh and Geo. Rouse were armed with guns and were attended by several other armed men'.

Apart from small groups, the actual gathering of the Patriots did not commence until December 10. Charles Perley swore that on that day Dr. Duncombe had a force of from 100 to 200 men in Norwich, 'and that there is also another body in Oakland, in the village of Scotland, under the command of Eliakim Malcolm, in number from sixty to seventy men'. Peter Coon stated that on Tuesday, the twelfth, the rebels began to assemble in his neighbourhood (Burford), and on Wednesday evening they left 'in a body and in tolerably good order', amounting in all to some 400 men. Perhaps others of the recruits were like Abraham Sackrider, who claimed that after a gathering in the Methodist meetinghouse at Sodom Dr. Duncombe and James Dennis endeavoured to persuade him to enter the Patriot service; but not succeeding readily they 'took him to the Inn and gave him something to drink, and when the deponent was in liquor they got him into a baggage waggon and took him to Oakland'. There he was guarded, and his property was threatened if he refused to take the part assigned him. On the other hand he may not have been such a lukewarm Reformer, for Lewis Jacques swore that he had heard Sackrider several times 'shout for Jackson' and 'damn the King'; and, what was possibly still worse, he heard him shout, 'Damn the Tories, we will make an end of them!'[5]

Neighbouring townships were meanwhile assembling their

[5]Sackrider was dismissed from custody after three months in jail. In the *History of Toronto and the County of York*, I 175, it is stated that 'Colonel Sackrider', a veteran of 1812, was strongly against Duncombe's decision to disperse without a fight. If this is the same man he was capable of a remarkable volte-face.

quota of Patriots. In Dumfries the chief centre was near Mudge's Mills, as the village of Ayr was then called. The place of meeting was McBain's Mills, one mile beyond the village, and when the disaffected assembled to join General Duncombe's army at Oakland Plains, 'such a mustering of old rusty rifles and melting of bullets was never previously witnessed in that quiet neighbourhood'.

The statement of Caleb Tompkins of Norwich indicates other activities which compromised many persons, who in some instances did not actually enlist in the Patriot force. Elias Snider 'was sent messenger to Yarmouth'; King Emigh 'gave the Rebels fourteen or fifteen fat hogs'; Orsimus Clark 'gave powder and lead to the Rebels, was commissary, and pressed Caleb Tompkins' waggon and took their names down'; Albert Delong 'was sent on express by Duncombe'; Jacob Kelley 'went with his team to Scotland to convey Duncombe's men and provisions'; while Garret Delaney, London innkeeper, wanted Tompkins 'to take all the provisions he could to the rebels'. Through some such support of the cause large numbers of persons were soon to find their locality too hot to hold them, though not a few sought to cover their tracks by joining one or other of the militia units called out by Colonel MacNab.

The actual movements of the Patriot force were complicated not only by defective organization but by the slowness of communication. On December 6, the day before the battle at Montgomery's Tavern, Mackenzie sent Nelson Gorham and John Hawk to inform Duncombe of the concentration on Yonge Street and asking immediate support. But even the mails were delayed by the almost impassable condition of the roads, and it was several days before these couriers arrived. Upon receipt of the news General Duncombe hurried his men, though by that time Mackenzie's force had been routed, and their leader had fled to the United States. The original intention was apparently to assemble at the village of Scotland, march through Oakland Plains to Brantford, and thence descend upon Hamilton, consolidating these towns under Patriot control and eventually effecting a junction with Mackenzie; just as, a few days later, it was Mackenzie's plan in occupying Navy Island to cross the Niagara and join Duncombe's rising in Brant County.

Duncombe, whose headquarters were in Joseph Beemer's Tavern, Scotland, instructed Captain Jacob Yeigh, a distinguished officer in the War of 1812, to call out his men, secure as many arms as possible, and march to that village, where he would be joined by a detachment under the Malcolms. He himself hastened to Norwich and sent out express riders to assemble his followers.

A force under James Malcolm marched to Waterford and back on Tuesday, probably to recruit other men; and the same night Duncombe arrived from Norwich with a company of 100. The Patriots from a distance were on the march to Scotland on December 12 and 13. Some fifty men set out from St. Thomas, and a similar group, largely from the vicinity of Sparta, left Yarmouth Township on the twelfth under David Anderson, while a third under Robert Anderson and Henry Fisher marched from Bayham Township the same day. The Yarmouth men included Joshua Gillam Doan, after whom the company was called 'Doan's Spartan Rangers'. Marching north and east they reached Eagle's Tavern, near Delhi, that night, and tramped through eleven miles of thick woods to Scotland on the thirteenth. When the St. Thomas militia passed Eagle's the following day they were told that the Yarmouth men were well armed and resolved 'to conquer or die'.

The whole Patriot force at Scotland intended to march along the main road to Brantford, but they were still at Scotland Wednesday evening when news arrived which dampened their enthusiasm and very considerably altered their plans. Not only did they hear of Mackenzie's defeat, but also of the arrival in Brantford of MacNab's force, as well as word of the approach of some 250 loyal troops from London, Woodstock, and St. Thomas under Colonels Askin and Bostwick, and of still another company of militia from Simcoe. James Oswald, a member of the Patriot force, describes what happened at Scotland on the receipt of this news:

> 'About eight o'clock in the evening a despatch was received; the men were about four hundred, and drawn up in a line, Duncombe, addressing them on horseback with a drawn sword in his hand, said, fellow soldiers, we will retreat to Norwich—news have arrived that Mackenzie is wholly defeated—that they would retreat and conquer into Norwich, where the cannon could not reach them, they then marched towards Norwich.'

Not all agreed with Duncombe in his decision to disperse without making a stand. Some were of the opinion that strong defences might have been erected in the Pine Woods south of Burford village; but the great majority accepted the decision as inevitable. The loyalist forces were meanwhile approaching the rebel position from all sides. After the skirmish at Montgomery's, Sir Francis Bond Head had ordered Colonel MacNab to lead some 400 men to the centre of trouble in the London District. On December 13 they reached Brantford, where the force was augmented by 250 men, including 100 Indians under Captain Kerr. Messengers were immediately sent in all directions to raise other companies and order a concentration upon Oakland Township, for

Dr. Charles Duncombe
Leader of the London District Patriots, he escaped to the United States and remained there the rest of his life

Sir Allan MacNab
Commander of the Militia who suppressed the rising, he was knighted after the cutting-out of the *Caroline*

Courtesy Louis Blake Duff, Esq., Welland

Samuel Chandler
Prominent at Navy Island and the Short Hills, he escaped from Van Diemen's Land in 1842

From Reville, *History of the County of Brant*

Eliakim Malcolm
A leader with Duncombe in the London District, he fled to the United States

Courtesy Buffalo Historical Society
An American Patriot Handbill

Courtesy Public Archives of Canada
Proclamation of Reward for Rebellion Leaders

THE CONCENTRATION AT SCOTLAND

it was well known that the Patriots had chosen a piece of ground near 'Little Scotland' as suitable for their stand against the loyalist forces.

At one o'clock on the fourteenth MacNab moved off from Brantford to Scotland. Major Thompson and 100 men were ordered to march down the Back-Settlement Road while the main body proceeded by the Main Road. The two forces were to attack the rebel position simultaneously, while the Indians were sent to take possession of the Pine Woods south of Burford. 'I regret to say,' wrote MacNab, 'that the rebels became alarmed and moved off during the night'. The fact was that a doctor in advance of the Patriot army had been taken prisoner at the bridge entering Brantford. He, however, feigned that he was visiting a sick person in the town, but upon being released rode back at full speed to warn Duncombe's force—a few shots from the militia speeding him on his way.

When MacNab's army reached Scotland some fifteen Patriots were captured, and three others were shot down as they attempted to reach the woods. One thousand militiamen arrived that afternoon, and the total was soon swelled to 1,900, each company being greeted on arrival by a salute of firing which some people at a distance took to be evidence of a battle in progress. Among others who made a forced march towards Oakland were the St. Thomas volunteers, both horse and foot, who approached by way of the Talbot Road. From Delhi they passed through eleven miles of unbroken forest, and as they reached the open plains near Scotland they formed into military order in the expectation of a hot encounter; but instead of a pitched battle with Duncombe's Patriots they received a hearty welcome from MacNab's men. A large number of the assembled militia were forthwith billeted upon the inhabitants of Burford Township, 'a rebel hold';[6] while a welcome more sincere and lavish was bestowed upon the officers at the mansion of Colonel Charles Perley, an uncompromising partisan of the Family Compact.

The militia were disappointed that the rebels had dispersed, and MacNab decided to please them and put fear into the Patriots by marching through Norwich, 'the most disaffected part of this district'. A force was left in occupation of Scotland, while 1,600 men set out next morning on a march which was to prove no pleasure trip. Apart from the excitement of the work it was a cheerless task, for night overtook them in the woods. Fires were

[6]'I enjoyed eating my roast goose at a rebel's fireside,' wrote R. S. Woods. The goose was given to him by Mrs. (Colonel) Racey as the militia marched through Mount Pleasant.

lit, but there was neither food for men or horses nor proper equipment to protect them from the cold and dampness of a winter campaign.

William Copland, whose son John joined MacNab's force at Hamilton, observed that a winter march in Canada was 'no joke, particularly as no beds were to be had. They lodged in churches, meeting-houses, or any house, stable, or barn that could be met with'. This was putting it mildly, for another militiaman stated that the only good meal he had throughout the march was the pork and bread that was served out as they encamped on the streets of Ancaster, where they were attempting to sleep on the frozen ground.

'For the ensuing two weeks of our expedition,' he writes, 'we looked back in raptures to that meal, for we got hardly another bite except an occasional one stolen from the farmers... Lane, the commissary, was all the time a three-days' journey behind us. Generally our meals consisted in sucking a corner of a blanket; we kept our mouths moist that way, and averted faintness and reeling.'

The sojourn of the militia in Norwich was most terrifying, for the property of Reformers was appropriated or destroyed and some 500 men were apprehended[7] during the march. Of these about 200 were placed in the centre of a square of militiamen and given a lecture. Bond Head amplified the incident considerably:

'Sir Allan read to them papers written by many of them, showing that it had been their intention to pillage the banks, rob and destroy the property of the loyalists, "tie Sir Allan MacNab to a tree, fire a volley into him", and carry into effect many other *"reforms"*... "Yet", said he, "I will allow you all to return to your homes except you, Solomon Lossing, a justice of the peace, whose oath of office required you to communicate all treasonable attempts; and as it appears from the papers I hold in my hand that you have been present at all Dr. Duncombe's meetings to get up this rebellion, that as an extensive miller you have supplied pork and flour for the maintenance of the rebels,.. I shall deal differently with *you*".'[8]

MacNab and his men proceeded thence to Ingersoll, which they reached on the nineteenth after a very severe march through ice and snow. In his despatch to Bond Head, MacNab mentions the capture of Robert Alway, M.P.P., near Simcoe, and of Finlay Malcolm, on the way to Ingersoll. On December 24 the punitive force was reported back in Hamilton, from which they were

[7] A petition of 104 Norwich men acknowledging their 'great error and wickedness' and asking mercy and pardon was presented to MacNab. They stated that they had been 'led away by Charles Duncombe, Eliakim Malcolm & other wicked & designing leaders' and acknowledged themselves to be 'completely subdued'. This 'Humble Petition' was enclosed in Head to Glenelg, December 28, 1837.

[8] Head, *The Emigrant*, 339 *et seq.* In his address to the Legislature on December 28 the Lieutenant-Governor similarly described how 'upwards of three hundred misguided men laid down arms—craving pardon for their guilt—asking permission to assist the loyal militia in capturing the fugitive leaders'. Lossing was taken to Hamilton jail, where he was found not guilty. Head bitterly describes his restoration to the office of justice of the peace by the first parliament after the Union.

shortly to proceed to Chippewa to join the militia opposite Navy Island.

The hunting-down of fugitives was largely left to the force of Indians which had been sent to the Pine Woods to attack the rebels in the rear if they should flee before MacNab's force. A correspondent of the *Rochester Daily Democrat* was on the field and saw the Indians 'bearing the royal standard, with faces painted in a most frightful manner'. The orders were to make prisoners of all 'who had not in their caps a badge of red flannel, which was worn by all the loyalists, and to shoot every one who attempted to escape'.[9] Among those who avoided capture was Benjamin Wait, who fled towards the Niagara frontier. In his narrative he states that he was

'twice intercepted—once by Indians, whose chief, a particular friend, let me go, having been attracted by a red rose, the badge of loyalty, which I had providentially picked up and pinned on my cap; and once by a band of drunken volunteer guards, from whom, by a daring manouver, I made a happy escape. On Christmas eve, *gallantly assisted by patriotic ladies,* I launched an old canoe upon the Niagara and crossed to the Land of Freedom, from whence I soon found my way to Navy Island, where I partook a cheerful Christmas dinner beneath the banner of the sister stars.'[10]

The seizure of the papers of Duncombe and Eliakim Malcolm at Scotland made the identification of their followers easy. They had made an effort to hide them, but a militiaman, noticing the earth newly turned over, thrust his sword into the ground and discovered a box which contained a muster roll of all the leaders, as well as the names of many Reformers who could be depended upon throughout the province.[11] A large group of Bayham and Yarmouth men retreating from Scotland were captured at Otter Creek (now Richmond) by the St. Thomas volunteers on their way home. The forty men taken at this point offered no resistance, for they had suffered very severely; fearing that fires would aid in their detection they had lain concealed in the woods without heat or food, and were only too glad to be confined in warm quarters—even the Simcoe jail, where most of them were taken.

Many of the Patriots immediately apprehended were sent home after being relieved of their arms, although subject to later arrest at the discretion of the magistrates; while a very considerable number at Scotland and elsewhere felt constrained to acknowledge

[9]As the militiamen had no uniforms, strips of red flannel were sewed on their fur caps. Lord Glenelg protested to Sir George Arthur against his severity in general and his use of Indians in particular. (Public Archives of Canada, Q 425A, *passim.*)

[10]Wait was born in Markham, September 7, 1813, but removed to Haldimand County and in the early 'thirties conducted a sawmill near York on the Grand River. He was captured on June 24, 1838, after the Short Hills raid.

[11]The various lists and other papers captured here and elsewhere were apparently saved only long enough to serve in the prosecution of suspects, for in no instance have they come down to us.

their error and join the militia when MacNab's forces arrived. Notices were speedily printed offering substantial rewards for the capture of several of the ringleaders, the largest, £500, being for Duncombe; but most of them succeeded in evading arrest. Joshua Doan was for a time concealed in a log granary on the farm of Ephraim Haight, who enabled him to escape capture. Samuel Mills was hidden by his father-in-law, Abner Chase, a recess between the staircase and the chimney providing a retreat. One refugee adopted a novel means of preventing his footprints in the snow from being followed, for he walked backwards to his hiding-place in the woods.

Some refugees suffered severely. Henry Fisher and Jesse Paulding are said to have been 'sixty-four days in the woods, the snow knee-deep, before they effected their escape; during five of which they subsisted on one small cracker each'. Joel Doan, George Lawton, Jacob Yeigh, David Anderson, Eliakim Malcolm, and Walter Chase were among other leaders who escaped.[12] Anderson and Chase were in a small group which reached William Norton's Tavern in Westminster the day of the dispersal of Duncombe's force; and on the following day they paid the innkeeper to drive them eight miles beyond Delaware.[13] Dr. John T. Wilson of Sparta, who was to figure prominently in later Patriot activities, fled eastward, and, like Wait, escaped over the Niagara frontier.[14]

Elisha Hall, the seizure of whose papers led to his arrest, was apprehended and placed in Ingersoll jail at the end of December. Early in January, however, he escaped, but as he was ill, it was thought that he would not get far away from the Township of Norwich. A justice of the peace suggested that a reward equal to that for Duncombe should be offered for his capture, and that an announcement be made emphasizing the punishment awaiting those convicted of harbouring refugees. Hall made good his escape, however, and his name is found in a proclamation outlawing twenty-one leaders in the London District who had fled the country.

Dr. Duncombe was able to escape apprehension because he was held in high regard by most of the inhabitants of the district. He accompanied the main body of his men to Norwich,

---

12Joel Doan returned to Sparta after his brother Joshua's execution for participation in the Windsor raid, and married his widow. He finally settled in California. Jacob Yeigh died in Burford in 1863. Eliakim Malcolm also returned, was Warden of Brant County, 1853-54, and died on September 26, 1874.

13Both men figured in the raid under Theller in the *Anne*. See chapter VIII.

14Other refugees were being sought in the same region. G. Creighton, J.P., Queenston, wrote to Alexander Hamilton, Sheriff of Niagara: 'Jack Green has this instant brought advice that he has pudsued 2 Malcolms, Alway, and Duncomb, from Oaklands to within a few miles of the Frontier, that his party and another are still in pursuit. He supposes they will be at the ferries this morning or today.'

where they assembled in the Quaker meeting-house and were advised by their leader to disperse to their homes. Some, it is said, were disposed to impute cowardice to Duncombe, who rejoined that in this instance it was the better part of valour, for they had insufficient equipment to withstand a winter attack. His experiences after dismissing his followers form a thrilling narrative. He left Norwich attired in Quaker dress, fell through the ice of the mill-pond, but got out and, mounting his white horse, made for the woods. His daughter says that he slept the first night with a friendly couple who placed him between them to avoid possible detection. For three days he lay concealed in the woods, his faithful horse browsing near by in daylight while his master subsisted on such berries, herbs, and roots as he could find. As starvation threatened, he was forced to approach more settled districts. He entered Nilestown and knocked at the door of one Putnam, a political friend, whose wife admitted him and asked his business. Laying his revolver on the table he replied: 'I am Charles Duncombe and I must have food!' Mrs. Putnam was not as enthusiastic a Reformer as her husband, but she agreed to conceal him in her house. He was put to bed as 'grandmother', and his appearance in a night cap was sufficient to fool a posse of loyalists who, recognizing his white horse,[15] actually searched the house and gazed upon him in bed without suspecting the disguise. Another friend named Douglas sheltered him the next night, his house being burned to the ground a few hours later.

Duncombe, avoiding guards at the crossroads, now sought the home of his sister, Mrs. Shenich, near London. When she came to the door in response to his knock she did not recognize him. 'Is it possible you do not know me, sister?' asked the doctor; and by way of reply she led him to a mirror, which showed that his hair had turned gray from the anxieties and hardships he had undergone. Here he remained in a hay-loft several weeks, until Charles Tilden, who had been visiting a sister, suggested a disguise which might enable his escape across the border. He was to pass as 'Aunt Nancy', and certainly looked the part when his sister had finished dressing him—including in his make-up a curl of her own hair as a *pièce de résistance*. Thus attired he set out in a sleigh for the western part of the province, and was not stopped as he made his way towards the frontier. From Sarnia, Duncombe crossed over on the ice to the United States; and it is said that members of the militia, who gallantly offered to escort the 'lady' across, were astonished at a masculine shout from 'her' lips as the

[15] His horse was subsequently found tied to a tree near Bear Creek, according to a letter of Lieutenant Woodward to Edward Ermatinger, January 10, 1838. It was believed at the time that Duncombe had been drowned.

American shore was reached: 'Go back and tell your commander you have just piloted Dr. Duncombe across the river!'

In September, 1838, Duncombe took part in a convention of Hunters' Lodges in Cleveland, at which a republican government was formed for Upper Canada. Innumerable officials and ranking officers were appointed, and a Republican Bank of Canada, capitalized at $7,500,000 in $50 shares, was organized—largely, it is said, by Duncombe.[16]

In 1843 he received a pardon under the terms of the earlier amnesty, which permitted his return to Upper Canada, but after a short visit he resumed residence in the United States. His extensive holdings of property, which had been forfeited, were restored to him, and he showed his gratitude to Charles Tilden[17] by deeding a 200-acre farm in the name of his infant son, who subsequently occupied it. Dr. Duncombe spent the rest of his life in Sacramento, California, where he died in October, 1867, at seventy-six years of age. His friends erected a handsome monument over his grave, and upon it was placed the inscription: 'A FRIEND OF LIBERTY'.

[16]The proposed bills were to carry the heads of Lount, Matthews, and Morreau, and in addition to their names the expressions 'The Murdered', 'Death or Victory!', and 'Liberty, Equality, Fraternity' were to be inscribed upon them. Dr. Duncombe also aided in assembling arms for the Fighting Island raid, and is said to have urged men to join the expedition against Windsor.

[17]Tilden was arrested on February 15. After being held until May 10 he was discharged.

BIBLIOGRAPHY

Head's despatches to Glenelg, and the enclosures of MacNab to Head from Scotland, Sodom, Ingersoll, and Hamilton are in the *Imperial Blue Books*, 1838. Head gives a less reliable account of the events in *The Emigrant*. Glenelg's despatches to Sir George Arthur are in the Public Archives of Canada, Q 425A. The Hamilton Correspondence is also in the Archives, as are most of the prisoners' depositions, 'Papers re Examination before Magistrates of Persons Taken up for Treasonable and Seditious Practices'. A few depositions, including Oswald's, are in *Appendix to Journal of the House of Assembly, 1837-8*, 404-9. Several of Duncombe's letters are given in Muir, *Burford*, 157 et seq. Various local histories contain valuable information, particularly Muir, *Ermatinger*, *The Talbot Regime*, Young, *Reminiscences of Galt and Dumfries*, and Charles S. Buck's unprinted 'Old Sparta and Its Neighbourhood'. D. M'Leod's *A Brief Review*, though unreliable in general, contains some material of value. R. S. Woods's 'The Cutting Out of the *Caroline*, and Other Reminiscences of 1837-8' appeared in the *Chatham Planet*, from which a small reprint was struck off. George Kerr's reminiscences are in Ermatinger, 203-4. William Copland describes the experiences of his son in his *Narrative*, while the reminiscences of another militiaman are given in Lizars, *Humours of '37*, 122-30. The enthusiasm in London during the assembling of the militia is described in the Harris Papers in the Library of the University of Western Ontario, quoted in Landon, 'London and Its Vicinity, 1837-38', Ontario Historical Society, XXIV. The reminiscences of Mrs. Tufford and Mrs. Shenich's daughter relative to Duncombe's escape are given in Muir, 124-30, and Ermatinger, 205-6. Letters and proclamations quoted in Muir, 146-55, describe Hall's escape from prison. Details of the Doans who participated in the Rebellion may be found in A. A. Doane, *The Doane Family*. Wait's experiences are described in his *Letters from Van Dieman's Land*, 35-6. The most valuable newspaper account of the events is that of the correspondent of the *Rochester Daily Democrat*, which was reprinted in the Toronto *Palladium* extra of January 8, 1838. A recent valuable study of conditions during the Rebellion, and particularly in the London District, is Landon's 'The Common Man in the Era of the Rebellion in Upper Canada', Canadian Historical Association, 1937.

CHAPTER VI

AMONG THE REFUGEES

ACCORDING to the returns furnished by the sheriffs, less than 900 men were actually arrested in Upper Canada and charged with complicity in the Rebellion; but the list furnishes only a basis upon which may be built up the whole superstructure of revolt. Thousands had been enrolled by Mackenzie and his lieutenants, but their participation in the rising was prevented by mismanagement and indecision. There is evidence that the official list does not even include all who were apprehended; and there were besides, large numbers who voluntarily left the country and whose names cannot now be traced. Thousands of less active Reformers escaped arrest, though frequently subjected to indignity and plunder.

The intensity of political feeling in the province may be gauged by the condition of affairs in parts of the Newcastle District, which may be considered a loyal section, furnishing many soldiers at Bond Head's call. In a letter from Cobourg to Egerton Ryerson the Reverend Anson Green said: 'I believe that in Haldimand and Cramahe Townships there are twenty rebels to one sincere loyalist. Brother Wilson (son of old Father Wilson) says that his life has been threatened for circulating the petition you sent down, and others are in a similar condition'.[1]

Mackenzie and his followers had many friends throughout the province, which is best attested by the escape of hundreds of Patriots who were tracked by the authorities; for, in spite of the fact that their names were learned from the lists which Mackenzie and other leaders left behind them, and that great rewards were offered for the apprehension of many, most of the refugees eventually reached the United States and safety.

After the suppression of the two main Patriot risings it took very little to induce a whole countryside to go rebel-hunting. A rumour from Peterborough that Mackenzie was in hiding near Purdy's Mills (Lindsay) led to an armed invasion of the Township of Ops:

'A number of farmers who were with their ox-teams at Purdy's Mill one clear cool evening were startled to hear a volley of muskets and to see

[1] In Hastings County there were 482 'sworn Patriots', a list of whom was sent to Mackenzie. C. H. McCollom, who was one of many who fled across the border, wrote Mackenzie from Montgomery County, N.Y., giving details of the situation.

a column of about 300 armed men with a large flag descending the steep river-bank to the north. When the advance guard got on the bridge cheers were raised, trumpets sounded, kettle-drums rattled, the flag waved, and another mighty salvo of musket-fire let off into the upper air. The villagers, some thirty men, women, and children in all, rushed from their cabins to see what was happening, and found that their visitors were a detachment of Peterborough militia under Colonel Alexander McDonnell, searching for Mackenzie. . . .

'William Purdy had been speaking rather plainly against the Family Compact, and Major Murphy took this opportunity of laying information against him. The miller was accordingly arrested and taken to Cobourg jail. Here he lay without trial for some time, but was at last liberated and told to go home and mind his own business.'

Indignities of the type of modern college initiations were sometimes perpetrated by ultra-loyal mobs upon citizens whose political activities were disapproved. A Mackenzie sympathizer named Mallory was somewhat more candid than discreet, and as a result nearly lost his life. Some citizens of Cobourg decided that they would ship him off to the United States, for whose government he had often expressed admiration. They packed him in a crate and threw him into the lake. He was not allowed to die, however, for they hauled him out before he suffocated or drowned.

Persecution of this type was common in all disaffected localities, but the London District was systematically plundered by the militia after the Duncombe rising had been suppressed. Colonel Allan MacNab, who led the punitive expedition into the disaffected townships, does not appear to have been vindictive, but the same could not be said for the militia in general. For some weeks they were quartered here and there upon the people, and their vengeance was felt by all who were suspected of having Reform leanings. Perhaps Norwich Township was most harshly treated, for a three-day occupation was definitely for the purpose of 'scowering the very hot bed of treason', and the press reported that the visit would not soon be forgotten by those who had supported the cause of reform.

The thieving and destruction which characterized the military occupation is now traditional in the entire region, and the third and fourth generations of the descendants of those who suffered still recount the events of that trying time. In many instances the soldiery drove away cattle and sold them cheap to their friends, so that Reformers thought it best to hide them in the bush until the militia had gone; farm implements and wagons were similarly concealed in swamps; wheat was seized in large quantities, and whatever was not worth stealing was wantonly destroyed; jars of preserves were emptied out, barrels of flour ruined by the addition of filth, and every other species of villainy practised by the ultra-loyal gangs. There was some excuse for a general seizure of firearms, but the worst of it was the high-handed methods used in the search. When horses were requisitioned it was always the Reformers who were made to bear the brunt, and the animals, if returned at all, were so worn out as to be almost useless. Even writers with staunch Tory sympathies admitted that Reformers had been roughly handled and shamefully robbed;[2] while a contemporary newspaper correspondent who followed MacNab's force observed that the region 'bears the marks of the ravages of war... The blight of the destroying angel is visible wherever you go'.

Many people, believing with this correspondent that 'the progress of free principle' had been permanently crushed, left the country. Elijah Woodman wrote in his diary: 'Many farmers have sold farms worth three thousand dollars for five hundred or a like proportion. West of the Mississippi there has been a large company formed of Canadians for the purchase of lands, and large numbers have been flocking in'. The Detroit *Free Press* observed that on one day 'twelve covered wagons, well filled and drawn by fine horses', had crossed the frontier at that point, and similar emigrations were reported over many months at various other border localities. It is believed that at least 25,000 Upper Canadians forsook their homes at this time.

Another unfortunate feature of the repression was the encouragement it offered to tale-bearers. The frightened turned loyalist and informed upon their erstwhile friends. 'What a system of tell-taling there has been!', wrote the Reverend William Proudfoot in his diary. The experience of Elijah Leonard of St. Thomas, who was arrested four times, is typical:

'One charge against me was lodged by one of my most intimate friends, who laid information with Squire Ermatinger that I had cannon balls on my premises. Squires Acklyn (a great big tyrant of a Scotchman) and Chrysler were associated with him on the bench. I was summoned to appear, and made my statement as follows: "I had bought a sloop-load of these cannon balls from Captain Mallory, who had purchased them at Amherstburg from the condemned military stores at that point. The balls had accumulated there during the war of 1812." After hearing me the magistrates retired. To judge from the length of time they took to decide the case I had a narrow escape from jail. Squire Chrysler was favourable to my discharge, and I overheard him say, "Let the boy off. There is nothing in the charges. He is only fulfilling the scripture by beating swords into pruning hooks, or cannon balls into plow points"; so I was finally let go, but I never forgave my friend for the trouble and injustice he meted out to me. I was using these balls up as fast as I could. They were hard enough to melt without being arrested for the task.'

[2]See, for example, Edward Ermatinger, *Life of Colonel Talbot*, 156. There was frequently more fear of mobs of Orangemen and loyalist militia than of rebel attacks, Indian massacres, or American raids, and many people were too busy protecting their property to take part on either side. 'Guns taken by order of the magistrate' and 'teams pressed in the public service' were among the chief claims under the Rebellion Losses Act.

Even women were not immune from loyalist raids, but they frequently resisted the search of their homes with considerable spirit. One young woman in Pickering Township, wielding a hardwood sapling poker in her hand, threatened to smash the skulls of those who were attempting to enter her house. In the vicinity of Mudge's Mills (now Ayr) an attempt by James Fraser to arrest Mrs. Kenny was anything but satisfactory, for she was lithe and active, and bounding fences and brush heaps at a leap, she quickly out-distanced her pursuer and sped on towards her clearing to warn her husband; 'and before Captain Rich could reach Kenny's place the bird and his brave wife had flown and escaped capture'—though apparently at the cost of sacrificing their home.

Probably no woman suffered more severely than Mrs. Charles Durand. Her husband, who was a young Hamilton lawyer, had been in the mail stage when it was stopped at the Peacock Inn by Mackenzie on December 6, and it was stated at his trial that he 'jumped out and shook Mackenzie by the hand, led him on one side, and talked with him'. Still more serious, he was overheard to remark that the Patriots should not be afraid to go into Toronto, 'for they were most damnably scared; they have only one field piece, that is in the middle of the street near the City Hall'.[3] Durand then continued his journey; but before he could reach home he was arrested and conveyed to Toronto jail. The fears he had had for his wife were fully justified, as events showed:

'The Sheriff and his gang went to my house and searched for me, and after alarming the females with armed men insisted on searching the house for papers... In the morning a gang of twenty armed men with muskets and bayonets again came rushing into the house and took possession of it, using the most foul and threatening language. They were headed by a notorious Captain Wilson, a low black-guard. After filling the house with confusion and destroying my cellar and the vegetables in it—and after having threatened to burn the house and barn down—they left, only the same night to repeat their barbarities... They rushed into my wife's bedroom where she and her sister were sleeping, looked under the bed, ordered candles and water, and drew pistols at my wife's sister... They repeated their visit a third time the same night.'

The following day a guard was placed in and about the house, but on Saturday, the ninth, the militia departed, and Mrs. Durand and her sister attempted to go to a friend's house, only to be caught two miles from Hamilton and marched back. Guards were

[3] Evidence of James Patridge, stage-driver, at the trial of Durand on May 7. Some incriminating letters signed 'John Hampden' were also attributed to him. In an address to the Court he pleaded 'youth and inexperience', but was found guilty, sentenced to death, and eventually banished. His conviction of 'constructive treason' by Chief Justice Robinson and a jury on such evidence is a reflection upon the times, and an indication of the severity of the prosecution under Attorney-General Hagerman. Durand went to Buffalo, and a year later to Chicago.

AMONG THE REFUGEES 61

again placed about the house, but when they were removed on Tuesday Mrs. Durand set out for Toronto to see her husband. Once more armed men followed and ordered her return, but she was finally permitted to proceed. 'I could hardly have expected', says Durand, 'that any woman even in Russia would have been treated as my wife was'.

Many other Reformers in and about Toronto were immediately jailed, and in many instances their property was confiscated or plundered. The shop of James and William Lesslie was seized and placed under the guard of militia. When the soldiers left two weeks later it was found that much had been stolen and all the family preserves used or removed; while the owners were meanwhile languishing in jail without any charge having been laid against them. The callous unconcern with which many suspects were still being treated months later is typified by the experiences of William Comfort, who was arrested for harbouring Mackenzie during his escape:

'The magistrates so brutally treated his wife in the hope of obtaining information she did not possess, to implicate her husband, by telling her among other things he would be hanged the next day, that premature labour was brought on and she and her babe before that day's sun was set were in their graves. . . Unhappy man! What could he do but make an effort to brace his nerves and stay the bursting of his heart-strings for the sake of his other four motherless children.

'The brutality exercised in this case roused the indignation of even some of the Orange tory party; and when he begged the authorities to allow him to go out on bail, only to the funeral and to provide some place for his children, he was refused. The most unexceptionable bail was offered for one day, with the condition that he might be accompanied by a guard and returned immediately to his cell. They laughed in very derision at the request. . . His poor children came to Toronto and besought admittance to their father. Their tears and entreaties softened the heart of the jailer and he took them to the chancellor, Jamieson, whose office it was to grant passes, and begged permission to let the father see them; but it was against the orders of the Governor and could not be permitted.'

In Toronto were several men who, although not present at Montgomery's Tavern, were for one reason or another subject to suspicion, and narrowly avoided death or imprisonment. Prominent among them was Dr. John Rolph, who became the earliest refugee of importance. When Dr. Thomas Morrison was arrested on the Wednesday morning previous to the battle at Montgomery's, a medical student who resided with Rolph rushed to him with the news, and the doctor immediately decided to escape while there was a chance. He showed excellent judgment in effecting his departure from Toronto. The student who had told him of the danger rode westward on Lot (Queen) Street, while Rolph followed leisurely on foot, meeting Chief Justice Robinson on the way. When he reached the point where Dundas Street turns northward his friend awaited him, and without delay Rolph mounted the horse and rode for about twelve miles without molestation.

As he approached the River Credit he encountered a company of loyalist volunteers *en route* to the capital. The commander of the troop demanded his destination, and once more the doctor was equal to the emergency, for he produced a letter which he had received only the day before requesting his presence at the bedside of his sister, who was seriously ill. This was deemed satisfactory and Rolph was allowed to proceed; but soon the officer became suspicious and sent two men in pursuit. When they overtook him they forced him to return to Port Credit. But luck was with Rolph, for a former student of his, Dr. James Mitchell of Dundas, succeeded in persuading the authorities that it was absurd to suppose that Rolph would support Mackenzie, and soon he was on his way westward again. Mitchell, who was a loyalist, conferred a further benefit by exchanging horses with him, and he was shortly at the house of Asa Davis, near Wellington Square. With one of Davis's sons, Rolph rode all night, reaching Queenston soon after daybreak and crossing the frontier.[4]

Another resident of Toronto who became an exile was Marshall S. Bidwell. The most important ground for suspicion against him was the finding of an old banner at Montgomery's inscribed with his name, though it would have required but little investigation to determine its origin; but he had been singled out for official displeasure, and Bond Head, who claimed to have incriminating letters as well, lost no time in forcing him out of the country. Realizing that justice was not to be expected in such inflamed times and being of a nervous disposition, Bidwell accepted Sir Francis's offer to retire without interference, left Toronto on the steamer *Transit*, and crossed the border at Niagara on December 10. His persecution and banishment robbed the province of a clever lawyer, who became an ornament to his profession in Albany.[5]

[4]On December 11 the Lieutenant-Governor offered a reward of £500 for Rolph's apprehension. The intention was probably to stigmatize him and keep him out of the province. That Head was vindictive is apparent enough from his contemptuous reference to Rolph as 'a practising midwife'.

[5]The controversy over Bidwell's part in the Rebellion is second only to that of Rolph. The Lieutenant-Governor wrote Lord Glenelg on December 19 that 'Mr. Bidwell, who took no part in the affray, has amicably agreed with me to quit, and has quitted the province for ever'. Head, however, had just been dismissed and was trying to justify his past conduct at the expense of Bidwell, who later wrote complaining of his treatment. It is now generally considered that he played little or no part in the actual plans for revolt, though there are certainly grounds for the contemporary comment of S. S. Junkin, official reporter in the Assembly, that 'his present condition is morally speaking a just punishment for his past conduct, his double dealing, and want of political sincerity'. Sir John Macdonald was among men of influence who sought his return to Canada, but he made only a short visit to Toronto a few weeks before his death in Albany, October 26, 1872.

AMONG THE REFUGEES

Dr. Thomas D. Morrison's case was somewhat similar, though he appeared in court on a charge of high treason. There was no doubt that he was a leading Reformer, but his complicity in the Rebellion was not definitely proven. It was brought out in the evidence that while he was present at the last meeting of Reformers prior to the Rebellion, he consistently opposed armed force, and after lengthy consideration the jury returned a verdict of not guilty.[6] Morrison had narrowly escaped hanging, however, and, receiving a hint that another charge was being prepared against him, he hastened to the United States, joining his friend Dr. Rolph in Rochester.

After the disastrous rout at Montgomery's hundreds of men endeavoured to return home as quickly as possible, while the leaders knew their only hope lay in flight to the United States. Colonel Anthony Van Egmond made his way northward when the flight commenced. Some four miles beyond Montgomery's he was joined by Mackenzie and other refugees, but was too fatigued to proceed farther and sought shelter on the Shepard farm. He thought he was safe, but a detachment of militia discovered his hiding-place and conveyed him to Toronto; where, Mackenzie says, he was placed 'in a cell so cold that they had very soon to take him to the hospital—on his way to the grave'.[7] Silas Fletcher, Jesse Lloyd, and Nelson Gorham succeeded in reaching the United States a short time after the collapse of the Rebellion.

A very different fate awaited Samuel Lount, in every respect one of the most public-spirited men in the rebel ranks. After the skirmish he fled northward on horseback, and by following the second fence behind Price's house reached a side-line a mile farther north. He then proceeded eastward to Yonge Street, encountering fleeing rebels everywhere. Some who had horses joined

[6]The prosecution early abandoned its effort to prove Morrison's presence at or near Montgomery's, and concentrated upon his knowledge of Mackenzie's treasonable designs; but the defence countered with a clever contention that if it was treason to neglect to inform upon others, Bond Head was the 'greatest traitor in Upper Canada', for he bragged that he had known all about it for months! 'O! how Sir Francis *stunk* in the estimation of every man', wrote the Reverend John Ryerson, a strong Tory. The case was under consideration for seven hours, and it was reported afterwards that 'G. Spenser was a great means of getting a verdict in his favour', for there were several strong Tories on the jury. When the verdict of not guilty was returned there was 'great cheering which could not be suppressed for some time'; after which Mr. Justice Jones said: 'Doctor Morrison, you have been acquitted; but the length of time the Jury have taken to consider their verdict must convince you of the danger in which you have been. I hope it will be a warning to you during the remainder of your life.'

[7]Van Egmond was with Napoleon at Moscow, and was wounded while serving under Blucher at Waterloo. After living eight years in the United States he settled in the Huron Tract about December, 1828, keeping tavern some fifteen miles from Goderich, and holding 13,000 acres of land near the present Clinton. At the hospital he was identified by one of the fatally wounded Patriots. He died on January 5, 1838, aged sixty-seven, and his death was possibly caused by poison provided by one of his sons. While friends were taking the coffin to his home it was twice broken into by militia searching for hidden weapons. A plain slab marks his grave in Egmondville cemetery. His son Edouard found it impossible to avoid service during the Rebellion in Captain Lizars's company of the Huron militia,

him, but when they saw dense masses of smoke rising from the burning tavern they scattered in all directions, most of them going north on Yonge Street. Lount and Edward Kennedy reached Shepard's Mill first, to be followed soon after by Mackenzie and John Reid. 'Jacob Shepard's people', says Kennedy, 'gave us an oven full of bread, and milk, cream, &c.'

It was deemed advisable, however, not to attempt to escape in large groups, and each fugitive used his own judgment as to the best means of avoiding capture. Lount fled to the northern part of the Township of King, where he had to spend two nights in the woods without shelter. A basket of provisions brought to him by Elizabeth Dickson, a child of thirteen, relieved the pangs of hunger. His sole companion was Kennedy, and the two made their way westward from one place of hiding to another. Several times they were almost captured, and they continually suffered untold miseries. On the night of the ninth they took refuge in the home of David Oliphant, in Eramosa Township; thence they travelled to the vicinity of Guelph and on through Dumfries, being secreted several days in an almost impenetrable swamp near Galt. They continued their flight to a farm-house near Glenmorris, where Lount narrowly escaped capture, running out of the back door as a local magistrate entered at the front. 'Lount expressed great regret', wrote Kennedy, 'that he had parted from Mackenzie, toward whom he had the most friendly feelings. When sick in the woods he said, "I would not care if I was dead if I had Mac along with me".'[8]

The fugitives proceeded through Burford and Oakland townships to the village of Waterford, hiding for a time in a hay-mow near Grover's Tavern. Militia were watching for them everywhere, and they would probably have been captured on several occasions had not the law imposed the penalties of treason upon those convicted of harbouring felons, for even loyalists refused to inform under the circumstances. After having remained hidden for two days near Grover's they stole away by night to Mount Pleasant, where they were for over thirty hours concealed in a straw-stack. They next entered West Flamborough, where they separated for a time, Kennedy taking shelter with his children near Dundas while Lount was secreted in the houses of Obed Everett, Squire Hyslop, John Hathaway, and others. Only the loyalty of their friends and their own unceasing vigilance kept them from capture on numerous occasions.

They were soon forced to flee westward again, being hidden

[8] Mackenzie was familiarly called 'Mac', though after the Rebellion his enemies more often derisively referred to him, because of his stature, as 'the little rebel'.

for a time in the house of one Latshaw, near Paris, who also assisted in their conveyance by night to the vicinity of Simcoe. Exhausted by fatigue, anxiety, and exposure they determined to attempt to cross Lake Erie. Proceeding to Long Point they looked about for a vessel in which to sail to an American port for a cargo of salt for the Queen's forces, but were finally forced to embark in a small boat owned by one Deas, a French-Canadian sympathizer who lived near by. Deas and a boy accompanied them in the frail craft, perhaps for the purpose of bringing the boat back after landing the refugees on the Pennsylvania shore. For two days and two nights they buffeted the waves in a vain endeavour to reach the opposite coast. The bitter blast seemed to penetrate their very marrow, and they had but little clothing to protect them from its fury. Sleep was out of the question, for their united efforts were required to manage the boat and keep it clear of water. Nor were they spared the pangs of hunger, for their only provision was a piece of pork which was soon frozen. When it seemed as if they had not suffered in vain, for the welcome southern shore was near at hand, a strong southerly wind suddenly arose, and though they fought against it with vigour born of desperation they were gradually forced backward into the lake. 'We drifted to the mouth of the Grand River,' says Kennedy, 'where we would have froze to death if a farmer who had watched us drifting on the lake had not taken us prisoners with the aid of a party'.

The farmer who effected the capture was named Overtrott, and he received the £500 reward that had been offered—as well as the everlasting dislike of his neighbours. At the time, however, it was suspected that the men were smugglers, and they were consequently conveyed to William Orderley's Tavern, Dunnville, where they were examined by David Thompson, M.P.P., and Squire Miln, and sent on to Colonel MacNab at Chippewa. They would not have had much difficulty in clearing themselves of the charge of smuggling salt, but William Nelles of Grimsby identified Lount.

Kennedy was sent to Hamilton jail, while Lount was shortly forwarded to the capital. A few glimpses of the Patriot leader during his progress to Toronto have been preserved. A Galt militiaman saw him near Chippewa as he was being led along the road. 'The day being gusty his cap blew off into the river, when an old red nightcap was put upon his head. This was an indignity but quite in harmony with the bitter state of feeling which prevailed at the time.' But there were others like George Menzies, who, loyalist and Tory though he was, could not but feel pity for the prisoner. 'I met Lount on his way to Toronto,' he wrote. 'He is miserably emaciated; and I could scarcely help half forgetting his guilt when I beheld the poor old man pinioned and on his way to captivity for life or an ignominious death on the gibbet.'[9]

After his raid upon the eastern section of Toronto, Peter Matthews and his men retreated eastward. Early in the afternoon the news of the defeat at Montgomery's reached them, and they took to the woods in various directions. Matthews and some of his Pickering neighbours spent that night, as well as Friday and early Saturday, hiding behind logs and in clumps of bushes in the ravines of Rosedale and the valley of the Don, gradually working their way north-eastward.

'On Saturday evening a little before six o'clock they reached the house occupied by John Duncan in the third concession of East York. They were eleven in number, including their leader. They would have been sure of a warm welcome from Mr. Duncan under any circumstances, for he was a Radical of the Radicals; but their welcome was none the less warm from the circumstances that they were well-nigh starved, and stood greatly in need of his assistance. A supper was speedily prepared for them, whereof they heartily partook. "I know my doom if I am taken", remarked Matthews upon rising from the table, at the same time drawing his hand significantly across his throat.'

After a few hours' sleep they hoped to reach Pickering, where they planned to secrete themselves until they could cross the lake. Beds were laid out on the floor, but a small bedroom adjoining was assigned to Matthews, who slept soundly almost as soon as his head touched the pillow. The members of the family sat up, but without keeping any light except such as was afforded by the burning logs in the fireplace. But the suspicions of loyalist neighbours had been aroused. Matthews and his companions had taken a short-cut by a good road through the farm of an English settler named Johnson, and as snow had fallen their tracks were observed. Hoping to confirm his suspicions before taking action Johnson sent his little daughter to the Duncan home to borrow a darning needle. When she returned with news that there were strangers in the house Johnson set off on horseback for Toronto to inform the authorities. On the way he met a troop of about fifty militia, and the party proceeded to Duncan's, where they arrived a little before midnight. The watchers inside were aroused by voices, and saw at once that the house was surrounded by armed men. Those sleeping in the large room were awakened as a loud

---

[9] William R. Lount wrote that his father had been 'stripped of his money & watch & boots & hat & coat, and thus driven 12 miles in the cold'. The Toronto *Patriot* of January 19 reported that 'yesterday GENERAL Lount, . . we are happy to say, was brought a prisoner to Toronto, where he is safely lodged in jail to commune with some hundred and fifty of his brother traitors'. On the advice of Robert Baldwin, Lount and Matthews pleaded guilty, and they were sentenced to death. See p. 122 and appendix K for documents relative to the execution.

Courtesy Public Archives of Canada J. H. Lynch

Bringing Patriot Prisoners to Jail

'Like so many slaves driven to market. . . Some never saw their homes again, but perished thro' privation and neglect.'—*Reverend John Doel*

From Willis, *Canadian Scenery*, 1842 W. H. Bartlett

Navy Island, Niagara River

Many refugees who succeeded in reaching the United States joined Mackenzie and American sympathizers on Navy Island, where a Provisional Government was established and preparations made to invade the mainland of Upper Canada

Daniel Conant
Owner of the schooner *Industry*

Joseph Gould
Who narrowly escaped transportation

Courtesy Honourable Gordon Conant   E. S. Shrapnel

Patriot Refugees from the *Industry* Escaping Over the Ice to Oswego in December, 1837

knock at the door showed that the posse had no intention of remaining outside. The more impetuous of Matthews's companions were inclined to fight, and shooting followed the entrance of the militia, several persons being slightly wounded.

Matthews was awakened only by the entrance of a militiaman into his room and the pressure of the muzzle of a rifle against his breast; but the rebel leader was a large and powerful man, and pushed away his armed assailant as one might brush a fly from his sleeve, the man striking the opposite wall as though he had been hurled from a catapult. But others rushed in and threw themselves upon him, and further resistance was useless. The prisoners were handcuffed and marched out into the night, one of them who had been wounded in the leg being forced to tramp with the others over twelve miles of rough road to Toronto jail.[10]

David Gibson underwent his share of suffering but eventually was fortunate enough to escape. He was in charge of some fifty loyalist prisoners who had been detained in or near Montgomery's Tavern, and when it was apparent that the battle was lost he decided to release them. 'Gentlemen', said he, 'I shall not detain you: you may go'. He thereupon separated from other fugitives and struck eastward by devious ways through Scarborough and Pickering townships. After several days of hardship he reached the home of a friend near Oshawa, and there he remained between four and five weeks, most of the time in a straw-stack. A number of refugees were concealed in the vicinity, and arrangements having been made by their friends, Gibson and several others crossed in January from the mouth of the Rouge to Rochester in a schooner.

The most extensive escape of refugees is that described by Thomas Conant, whose father owned several schooners on Lake Ontario. One of his ships, the *Industry*, was laid up for the winter near Oshawa. During December the owner was approached by many refugees and their friends, who begged him to convey them across the lake. Although a Reformer he at first refused, as he did not wish to involve his family in trouble. Moreover, he felt that winter sailing was very risky. One man paddled a canoe across Lake Ontario, leaving the vicinity of Oshawa about ten o'clock in the evening and arriving on the American shore near Orchard Beach at four o'clock the next

[10]The Duncan reminiscences, which form the basis of this account, appear to be in error both as to the number of prisoners and the date of the capture, unless the men were taken elsewhere before entering Toronto jail; for the 'Register of Prisoners' states that they were brought in Thursday, December 14. Of the nine men who entered the jail on the same day as Matthews it is known that at least one or two were not captured with him. It is remarkable that the Duncans were not imprisoned with the men they were harbouring.

afternoon.[11] This eighteen-hour trip was the more remarkable because the bow of the canoe was entirely rotted away and had to be kept high in the air by placing a heavy stone in the stern. When the other refugees heard of this, they renewed their entreaties, and finally Daniel Conant was persuaded to encounter the dangers of navigating a schooner in winter. The commencement of the adventurous voyage presaged success:

'On the night of the 27th of December, 1837, the little vessel of 100 feet in length quietly slipped from her moorings and sailed close along the shore of Lake Ontario. It was a bright moonlight night, still but very cold. Every mile or so she would back her mainsail and lay to at a signal of a light upon shore that a canoe might put off to the vessel, bearing a Patriot from his hiding in the forest to the side of the boat... Some forty stops, and forty different canoes were paddled out to the vessel and forty Patriots transferred, panting for the land of liberty across Lake Ontario, to the south of them sixty miles or so.

'A fine sailing breeze blew off shore, and hoisting sail and winging out mainsail and foresail, nothing could bid fairer for a quick and prosperous voyage; and the land of liberty seemed almost gained. Lying upon blankets in the bottom of the vessel were the Patriots, with the hatches closed down tight on account of the intense cold. Quickly and gaily the little vessel sped on, with anxious hearts beating below.'

In the morning the mouth of the river at Oswego could be seen in the distance. But despair succeeded joy in the hearts of all when it was seen that a large mass of floating ice had been driven into the bay by the same wind which had carried them across the lake. The men worked valiantly to force a passage through the three miles of ice in front of the harbour; but their exertions were in vain, for when darkness forced them to stop, they had proceeded only a quarter of a mile towards the American shore.

During the night the wind fell and the cold increased, so that by morning the ship was firmly frozen in. When they saw what had happened, their only hope was that the lower temperature would also make the ice thick enough to enable them to walk to shore. It was found, however, that it was hardly sufficient to bear a man's weight. Nevertheless, as they feared that the icefloe might break up at any time, they decided to make the attempt to gain the shore.

Each man took a spar or pole from the ship to aid him in his hazardous journey. Before they had proceeded far one man broke through the ice; the others helped him out and the grim procession continued. Overcoats, gripsacks, and other valuables were thrown away as they became too exhausted to carry them.

[11]The Honourable Mr. Justice Riddell states in a letter to the author that he recalls hearing his father tell of several escapes across the lake by rowboat from the mouth of the Factory Creek, near Cobourg.

A man fell through every few minutes, and he was encrusted with ice soon after he was hauled out by his companions. It was not long before the entire group were human icicles. Many were on the verge of collapse, but the hope of freedom enabled them to continue. At last as they approached the shore from which hundreds of Americans were shouting encouragement the pack ice started to move out into the lake:

'Already it had parted from the shore streak of ice and left a space of open water now seven feet wide. Jump it they could not, because their clothes were frozen so hard that they could not spring, and besides, the ice on the other side of the open space was not thick enough to hold one alighting after the jump. Their last hope sank within them; death stared them in the face; their wives and friends in Canada would see them no more. Every minute added to the gulf of water between them and the shore ice.'

Fortunately one of the sailors had carried with him a plank instead of a spar. Bridging the open space with his board he called upon all to follow him for their lives, and with a last effort they gained the shore and freedom. The ship *Industry* was lost and became a wreck. The refugees she had carried across the lake remained for some time in the United States; but after the violent feelings roused by the Rebellion had subsided, all returned to Upper Canada, where many of them occupied prominent positions in later years.[12]

[12] See Thomas Conant, *Upper Canada Sketches*, 68-76. Even after the lapse of sixty-one years he considered it imprudent to divulge the names of these Patriots. In a letter to the author the Honourable Gordon Conant states that no list was found in his father's papers.

BIBLIOGRAPHY

The list of those arrested in Upper Canada is given in appendix G. Considerable material is available upon the experiences of many who fled the country. The documentary evidence implicating Bidwell in the plans of rebellion is slight, but it is implied in Mackenzie's publications that he was not inclined to free Bidwell of complicity. Egerton Ryerson came strongly to his defence in powerful letters to the Kingston *Upper Canada Herald* of May 8 and 29, 1838, and it is now generally considered that his worst offence was his attempt to be non-committal. Contemporary comment on his banishment may be found in Sissons, *Egerton Ryerson*, I 462-3. The chief source as to Rolph's escape is Dent, II 112-14. C. P. Mulvany wrote, *History of Toronto and the County of York*, I 175, that he had learned new particulars, but he died without making them public. Durand's trial is reported in the *Patriot*, May 15, 1838, and additional details are given in Mackenzie's *Caroline Almanack*, 50. Durand's letters to the *Buffalonian* describe the harsh treatment of his family, and are reprinted in the *Mirror*, September 14, 1838. His *Reminiscences* (1897) contains rambling and incoherent memories of his part in the Rebellion. A letter of James Lesslie describing his treatment during the Rebellion is given in Dent, II 150 fn.; while Comfort's experiences are recorded in Theller, *Canada in 1837-8*, I 164-6. The record of Morrison's trial does not appear to have been preserved, but it is reported in the *Patriot*, May 4, 1838. Details are added by 'A letter from a respectable gentleman in Toronto who was present', *Cobourg Star*, May 9, while other sidelights are given in Sissons, I 450-3. For information on Van Egmond see Kerr, 'Colonel Anthony Van Egmond and the Rebellion of 1837', Seaforth *Huron Expositor*, October 2 and December 11, 1931; and 'Van Egmond Noted Figure', by M.V.W., *London Free Press*, January 20, 1935. The experiences of Lount and Kennedy are given in some detail in Kennedy's letter, December 10, 1849, to *Mackenzie's Gazette*, a clipping from which is in the Lindsey Papers; a similar statement appears in Mackenzie, *Head's Flag of Truce*, 13-14. J. C. Dent gathered supplementary information from persons concerned, and Lount's son, William R., adds details in his letter to Mackenzie, June

70 THE LIVES AND TIMES OF THE PATRIOTS

12, 1838, Lindsey Papers, but he appears to have been mistaken in saying that Samuel Jarvis identified his father. Glimpses of Lount *en route* to Toronto are from Young, *Galt and Dumfries*, 163-4, and 'Navy Island As It Is Now', by the editor of the *Niagara Reporter*, in the *Cobourg Star*, January 31, 1838.

The reminiscences of William Duncan, brother of John, as recorded in Dent, II 145-6, form the basis of the account of the capture of Matthews. The incident of the darning needle, as well as the account of Johnson's part in effecting the capture has been obtained by the writer from Mrs. Zoe Stevens, Toronto, who says that the reward paid off the mortgage on the Johnson farm. Edward Kirkpatrick, Toronto harness-maker, whose mother was a Duncan and who recalls seeing bullet marks over the door of the log house, says that he always understood that a neighbour named Sellers was the informer. Edward J. Mellen, son of a labourer on the Duncan farm at the time of the capture, claims in a letter to the *Toronto Daily Star*, December 2, 1936, to have Lount's rifle, 'left by him back of Duncan's barn'. He may have Matthews's rifle, but he certainly has not Lount's.

The extensive escape on the schooner *Industry* is described in Conant, *Upper Canada Sketches*, 68-76. The capture of Purdy is described in Kirkconnell, *Victoria County Centennial History*, 94-5, and is also referred to in the *Cobourg Star*, December 20, 1837. The experiences of other refugees, as well as the general background of the subject, are based upon such local histories as Young, *Galt and Dumfries*, E. Ermatinger, *Life of Colonel Talbot*, C. O. Ermatinger, *The Talbot Regime*, Buck's unpublished 'Old Sparta and Its Neighbourhood', and Wood, *Past Years in Pickering*. Ryerson, *The Story of My Life*, and Sissons, *Egerton Ryerson*, and the letters of William R. Lount and C. H. McCollum, in the Lindsey Papers, have also been of value. The Woodman diary is quoted in Landon, 'The Duncombe Uprising', Royal Society of Canada, XXV 420; and the same writer has edited large sections of the Proudfoot diary. The diary of Joseph R. Thompson, in Stacey, 'The Crisis of 1837 in a Back Township of Upper Canada', *Canadian Historical Review*, September, 1930, is valuable as an example of the attitude of those who took no part on either side but were greatly disturbed by the excitement; see also Landon, 'The Common Man in the Era of the Rebellion in Upper Canada'. The most valuable newspaper accounts of the repression and its results are in the St. Thomas *Table of Events*, December 30, 1837, the Detroit *Free Press*, June 7, 1838, and the *Rochester Daily Democrat*, December 17, 1837. The last-named publication had a correspondent at 'the front', and his letters were reprinted in the Toronto *Palladium of British America* extra, January 8, 1838, of which a copy is in the Ontario Archives.

CHAPTER VII

Navy Island and the Caroline

THE United States began to pay a prominent part in the Rebellion when the refugees crossed the border. The first of importance was Dr. Rolph, who had fled from Toronto on December 6, and by riding all night reached Queenston and passed over the frontier to Lewiston early the following morning. There he was received as a distinguished visitor—even as a martyr. Individuals and crowds pestered him with their attentions, and when he addressed them he was vociferously applauded. A few days later Buffalo similarly received William Lyon Mackenzie. He had, perhaps not unwittingly, prepared the way for his coming by writing the *Buffalo Whig and Journal* from Montgomery's Tavern, asking support for the Patriots; though such a request was unnecessary, for a large section of the American press was only too glad to attack British institutions in Canada or elsewhere. The spirit of '76 was speedily revived along the border, and the numbers of those who were sympathetic were greatly augmented by unemployed Erie Canal boatmen and numerous other drifters, who were pleased to join the Patriot Army or any other organization which promised employment and adventure.

Mackenzie reached Buffalo on December 11 and was immediately in the limelight. A public meeting in the Patriot interest was held that night at a theatre, but he was too fatigued to attend. His arrival in Buffalo was announced, however, and amid great enthusiasm it was stated that he would address a meeting the following evening. On that occasion he spoke for an hour, emphasizing the parallel between the revolts of '76 and '37, and asking for 'arms, ammunition, and volunteers to assist the Reformers in Canada'. Several Americans also spoke, among them Thomas Jefferson Sutherland, later a Patriot general, with the result that several recruits were enrolled in the army of invasion which, it was announced, would proceed at once into Upper Canada. Rensselaer Van Rensselaer, described by one writer as 'a degenerate scion of an old Dutch family, . . a young man of more ambition than brains', offered himself and was acceptable to Mackenzie and Rolph as military commander, and the Eagle Tavern was made the headquarters for gifts of money, ammunition, and supplies.

Early on December 13, Sutherland was brazenly violating the

neutrality laws by leading a fife and drum band through the streets of Buffalo, followed by a number of recruits who have been described as 'friends of Liberty' and 'half-drunken vagabonds, roughs, and scallawags'.[1] These were thrilling times. One might have seen Mackenzie on a barrel making a speech to American militiamen, or Sutherland waving his Patriot flag on the American shore, to be answered from across the river by the Union Jack, each banner being loudly huzzaed by its respective partisans as they shook their fists at each other. 'The very women are inciting the men to proceed to the frontier', wrote a Canadian officer from Chippewa.

No time was lost in setting the invasion on foot. Whitehaven, a village on Grand Island, was chosen as the first rendezvous of the recruits, who were conveyed thither by night. Van Rensselaer and Mackenzie, who may have hastened the enterprise upon hearing the rumour that Bond Head was demanding his surrender, took them across on a scow to Navy Island in the early hours of the fourteenth. It has usually been stated that twenty-six men made up the initial army of occupation, but Van Rensselaer says they numbered twenty-four including himself and Mackenzie.

Navy Island[2] was well chosen for defence, being heavily wooded and surrounded by a treacherous current. It was sufficiently close to Chippewa for effective opposition to a force there, and yet near enough to American territory in two directions—Grand Island and Fort Schlosser—to enable foraging for daily supplies or to make possible a quick retreat. Mackenzie is believed to have suggested instead an invasion of Upper Canada at Fort Erie in the expectation of a successful rising under Duncombe, with whom a junction might be effected; but he was overruled by Van Rensselaer, who appears to have traded upon the military experience of his father, a gallant general during the War of 1812. Both the military and the civilian leader were disappointed at the smallness of the original force and the general lack

---

[1] A note in the Lindsey Papers defends the reputation of the recruits: 'One would naturally expect that volunteers for Navy Island would frequently be men of desperate fortunes, reckless of what they did, carried away by excitement; men with no character to lose, and ready for any desperate venture in favor of which a plausible case could be made'. But to consider all such, the statement continues, would be a calumny on men of good family, of whom two examples, both youths of twenty, are given—George Clinton and N. Beakes—whose fathers were, respectively, Secretary of State for New Jersey, and Clerk of the Supreme Court in the same state. A document signed by forty-eight men raised in Buffalo by Sutherland indicates a motive higher than adventure:

'We the young men residents of the city of Buffalo, whose names are hereto subscribed, pledge to each other our mutual support and co-operation for the commendable purpose of aiding and assisting our Canadian brethren in their present struggle for liberty and those principals which have given the world that asylum which we have the honor of calling our homes and built up that fabrick of human might which pronounces to mankind the sacred dogma of equality.'

[2] The name originated in the French regime, when it was called Isle-la-Marine because of its use for naval purposes. The Indians named it 'the big canoe island', in allusion to the large canoes constructed there by the French.

of supplies and arms; but Mackenzie, nevertheless, issued the proclamation he had had printed the day before in Buffalo.

Some seven or eight refugees from the Home and London districts were on the island, and the more important of these—Gorham, Hawk, Fletcher, and Lloyd—together with Jacob Rymal, who aided him to escape, were included by Mackenzie as members of his Provincial Government of the State of Upper Canada. The others present were Adam Graham and William H. Doyle, while the absentees, who could have had no knowledge of the use of their names, were Lount, then in hiding in the woods, Duncombe, in concealment disguised as a woman, Van Egmond, dying in Toronto jail, and Thomas Darling, who shortly denounced Mackenzie for using his name. Rolph was still playing a cautious game and would not join the group, but he was referred to in the proclamation as 'that universally beloved and well-tried eminent patriot'. It is probable that Dr. Morrison and Marshall Bidwell were meant in the reference to the 'two other distinguished gentlemen whose names there are powerful reasons for withholding from the public view'. There was misrepresentation, perhaps unintentional, in the statement that General Van Rensselaer of Albany, Colonel Sutherland, and Colonel Van Egmond would aid in the military direction of the expedition, the first-named being but the rather hare-brained son of a general, the last in jail, and the second having no military rank except what he chose to assume. Mackenzie himself was 'Chairman *pro tem.*' of his government.

The proclamation set forth the undoubted grievances of Upper Canada, and outlined the more important reforms which had long formed planks in the political platform of the Reform party. Equal rights to all were to be guaranteed by a written constitution; there was to be civil and religious liberty and the abolition of all hereditary honours; and a governor and legislature publicly elected by ballot, the members of which were to choose the judiciary. It is apparent that the law and custom of the constitution of the United States was in Mackenzie's mind when he drafted these terms; but, considering the abuses of the Upper Canadian government at the time, the suggested changes were radical only in comparison with the special privileges then granted to the ruling clique.

When they landed on Navy Island, the only inhabitants were a widow named Chambers, her two daughters, and a son-in-law, E. H. Learned. It was arranged that this family[3] remove themselves

[3] Upon evacuation of the island a number of articles were left to recompense the widow for the use of her property, but E. G. Lindsey says that the 'generous bloods' (the Canadians) destroyed it all. A letter in the Lindsey Papers asking settlement of the widow's account is given in appendix I (9). A notation by Mackenzie indicates that the claim was settled by part payment.

to Grand Island; and after raising the revolutionary flag over the house the Patriots built a breastwork of fence rails around their headquarters. Half worked and half watched during the next three days, at the end of which the force had increased to sixty men. A yawl belonging to the steamer *Constitution*, a small sailboat, and a few skiffs were used to communicate with the American shore.

Recruits gradually began to come to the island, attracted, no doubt, more by the 300 acres of land that was offered to each than by abstractions of political theory. A few days later a supplementary announcement described the lands as 'most valuable', and added as an extra inducement a hundred dollars in silver, 'payable on or before the 1st of May next'. In imitation of Bond Head, Mackenzie offered £500 reward for the apprehension of the Lieutenant-Governor, who did not fail to take due cognizance of the announcement.

Mackenzie was engaged in writing most of the time, for there were innumerable letters from all sorts of people. The original ammunition of the force was inconsequential, consisting largely of boiler punchings and other refuse of which some use was to be made as a substitute for grape-shot; but plenty of sympathizers, and others who were just cranks, wrote offering much better. The motives of the actual recruits were various. Many, like Van Rensselaer himself, sought the extension of republican institutions, or accepted the opportunity to vent their spite against all things British. German refugees, as well as others of British origin, wished to further the cause of 'American freedom', while some men wrote announcing themselves as on the march but never arrived. A few public-spirited citizens of the Republic indicated how sentries at arsenals might be circumvented, or suggested ingenious schemes by which the spirit of the neutrality laws might be broken—but not the letter.[4]

Meanwhile popular sentiment along the border was becoming increasingly favourable to the Patriots. While meetings of sympathizers had been held prior to the skirmish at Montgomery's, it was later in the month before the agitation got well under way. 'There is much excitement here', wrote Marshal Garron from Rochester. 'Forty soldiers marching the streets of Rochester today under drum and fife; two pieces of cannon went off this morning, and three-fourths of the people are encouraging and promoting the thing'. A local historian of the same town recorded that 'our market house was stacked full of arms for the Patriots,

[4] In appendix I is given a representative selection from a large number of Navy Island letters in the Lindsey Papers. Mackenzie's proclamation is given in appendix H(1). Thomas Darling, mentioned in the proclamation, settled in Iowa.

NAVY ISLAND AND THE CAROLINE   75

provisions poured in from the country, and old inhabitants on the Ridge Road tell us how the heavy wagons could be heard hurrying westward all night long'. The orders of the Federal Government as to the duties of neutrality were said to be but little regarded— 'as elsewhere along the line'. At Sackett's Harbor Silas Fletcher, Patriot organizer, was led into town 'by a procession, colors flying, guns roaring, and shouts of "God prosper the Patriots!" '

The Upper Canadian militia had in the meantime risen overwhelmingly to the Government's support. A force of 1,800 men was encamped along the Canadian shore near Chippewa shortly after the occupation of Navy Island, and they were steadily augmented. On December 24 Colonel MacNab was back in Hamilton after having put down the abortive rising of Duncombe. The inhabitants between Paris and Dundas took out their sleighs and drove the militia so fast that some of the horses died. Everyone, in fact, wanted to be of assistance. On Christmas day MacNab's force left for the Niagara frontier, and on their arrival at Chippewa there were some 2,500 white and Indian militiamen on the Canadian shore of the Niagara.

Much to their disgust, however, the orders were to be strictly on the defensive and not to fire upon the island. The danger of complications with the United States was one deterrent. 'It is annoying in theory,' wrote Bond Head, 'that these ruffians should be allowed to hold possession of our territory'; but he considered quite rightly that the risks attendant upon an attack were too great for the advantage which might accrue. The chance of defeat was considerable, and still greater was the possibility that many of the attacking force might be carried over the Falls. Assuming the capture of the island, a force would have to be left in occupation or the island abandoned—in which latter case the Patriots might at once re-occupy it.[5]

At first it was considered that a demonstration of strength and numerous military reviews might overawe the Patriots and cause the evacuation of the island. As this did not happen, a number of gunboats were fitted out as a start towards a naval expeditionary force. Sir Francis reached Chippewa on December 19 and remained several days with the militia, whose activities he described in a lively paragraph:

'Occasionally the armed guard, their bayonets glittering in the sunshine, were observed marching along the shore to relieve the sentries; and while their appearance was drawing upon them the fire of the American artillery from Navy Island, a number of young militiamen were to be seen in the

[5]Enclosure 3 in Head to Glenelg, December 28, 1837. The Lieutenant-Governor's decision in this matter would appear to be one of the few to his credit, but an American historian, Tiffany, attributes the inactivity to fear or cowardice 'entirely out of keeping with the usual skill and daring of Canadian soldiers'.

background of the picture running after the round shot that were bounding along the ground, with the same joy and eagerness that as school boys they had run after their football. Sometimes a laugh, like a roar of musketry, would re-echo through the dark forest, and sometimes there would be a cheer that for a moment seemed to silence the unceasing roar of the Falls.'

As Mackenzie's proclamation was distributed in the border towns the number of recruits passing over to Navy Island gradually increased. Captain Nelson Gorham, who personally enrolled each one, states that in the last week of December the Patriots numbered about 150. It was very difficult, however, to estimate the exact number of men on the island, for many came merely out of curiosity, or becoming dissatisfied with conditions, departed for the mainland. Charles Lindsey says that those who enrolled 'were inspired with such a desperate determination that, far from having provided any boats for their escape, they had taken the pins out of the screws of the scows and burnt the oars, resolved if attacked to conquer their assailants or die in the attempt'. But considering the course of events in most other Patriot concentrations, it is more likely that this action was taken to prevent the desertion of recruits.

Those who composed the force lived in large huts hurriedly erected of rough pine boards, while their food was similarly defective, and they were uncertain of its supply. The largest building formed the headquarters of the provisional government, and over it flew the Patriot flag with two stars, representing Upper and Lower Canada. Supplies being short and money lacking, Mackenzie issued scrip in denominations of one and ten dollars, payable four months later at the City Hall, Toronto, and signed by himself, by Timothy Parson[6] as secretary, and supposedly by

Navy Island Note

[6]Parson spent the rest of his life in the United States. He was active in American politics for many years, and lived latterly in Chicago. In September, 1883, he visited Toronto.

David Gibson as comptroller; but the signature of Gibson must have been forged, for he was at the time hiding in a straw-stack near Oshawa, and the evidence of himself and his family, which is corroborated by Gorham, is that he was not on the island during its occupation. The scrip was apparently accepted by several Buffalo merchants in payment of supplies which could not be secured otherwise. Ammunition and arms, however, were more generally obtained by a combination of nerve, sympathy, and the lax control of American arsenals; for the initial supply of seventy muskets was stolen from the Buffalo Court House, while a cannon was permitted to leave an arsenal for Navy Island 'to shoot wild ducks'!

Among the visitors to Navy Island were a number of spies[7] of various allegiance, and their reports, while not necessarily accurate, tell much of life among the Patriots. From some such informant the *Cobourg Star* described 'the true position of Navy Island', observing that among 'from seven to eight hundred men, 350 of whom are armed with muskets and bayonets stolen from the Arsenals', there were 150 or 200 'constantly prowling along the American shore, begging arms and provisions, money and ammunition, for the holy cause of "making the oppressed free" by cutting their throats and seizing their property'. On the island were 'nine pieces of brass cannon', 'abundance of shot cast by one Wilkinson', 'two large iron guns with the trunions broken off, marked G. R., mounted on logs, which can be fired *once* at an assailing force', and 'four days provisions', to which is added each day 'what their scouts can beg, borrow, or steal, which we guess is everything that is not too hot or too heavy to be conveniently portable'. Among other equipment, they had 'four scows, one worked by steam, a few stolen boats, and a schooner at their service, either hired or lent'. Eleven shanties served as barracks, and 'Buffalo bakers supply the daily bread'.

The inactivity which was so objectionable to the militia was just as monotonous to the Patriots, but they had more to occupy their attention. Trees were felled along the west and north

---

[7]The names and activities of several are recorded by Charles Lindsey. Sir Richard Bonnycastle wrote that 'the spies and informers, paid on both sides, kept up a very constant stream of intelligence'. One of these was Seth Conklin, who visited the island, escaped to the American shore, and was taken back. His deposition is decreased in value by his opinion that 'from 100 to 120 were killed on the island'. When passing through Kingston in 1842 Charles Dickens was intrigued by 'a beautiful girl of twenty, who had been there [in jail] nearly three years. She acted as bearer of secret dispatches for the self-styled Patriots on Navy Island during the Canadian Insurrection: sometimes dressing as a girl, and carrying them in her stays; and sometimes attiring herself as a boy, and secreting them in the lining of her hat'. But as she once stole a horse to use on one of her missions she was captured and jailed. 'She had quite a lovely face', says Dickens, 'though there was a lurking devil in her bright eye, which looked out pretty sharply from between her prison bars'. Penitentiary records (courtesy J. Alex Edmison, Ottawa) show that the lady was auburn-haired Eunice Whiting, alias Emma Whitney.

shores to increase the difficulties of a landing force; embankments were thrown up, and cannon mounted at strategic points kept up a desultory fire on the militia six or seven hundred yards distant, doing some damage to houses and killing one horse; while a rough roadway was constructed around the island to enable guns to be driven from one point to another by ox-sled. But if both forces were tired of inaction it was shortly to be broken by an event which caused excitement enough on all sides, and very nearly embroiled the United States and Great Britain in war.

On December 28 the steamship *Caroline*, of forty-six tons, commenced to operate a ferry service between Fort Schlosser and Navy Island. She had not been purchased by the Patriots, but seventeen men had bonded themselves to prevent the owner from suffering loss in case of trouble; and on the twenty-eighth she was cut out of the ice where she had been laid up for the winter, and taken down the American channel, commencing her trips immediately. The Patriot support along the frontier had become more general, and there were numerous passengers at twenty-five cents a head, as well as a cannon and quantities of supplies to be ferried over. Alexander McLeod had learned in Buffalo on Christmas Eve that the *Caroline* would be used, and MacNab, becoming suspicious that something was going on, sent him and Captain Andrew Drew in a skiff to investigate. They observed that the *Caroline* was tied up to a temporary wharf on the east shore of Navy Island, were fired at and their boat hit several times by the Patriots, and returned without mishap, although they had entered upon their hazardous enterprise with but one pair of oars.

The same night a group of officers of the Naval Brigade, their enthusiasm inflamed by a late dinner and plenty of wine at MacNab's headquarters, decided to engage in an unofficial raid upon the island, the intention being to seize one of the sentries, or possibly Mackenzie. Lieutenant Graham was the leader of the party, which, however, started too late to attempt their object, but rowed entirely around Navy Island. They were fired at by cannon both from Schlosser wharf and the island, and were very nearly carried down the rapids through what one of the men termed the 'incompetence and drunken bluster' of the leader. A Patriot description of the incident states that a sentinel challenged the boat at the head of the island but they answered him 'Go to hell!' Van Rensselaer thereupon

'elevated one of the guns about four rods ahead of the bows of the boat, which was then near half a mile distant, touched the match—the livid glare of the flash—the smoke—and the whizzing messenger, passing within

NAVY ISLAND AND THE CAROLINE 79

a few feet of them and spattering them with water, acted like magic to bleach their phizes and remind them that they stood a fair chance of being immediately where they had just bidden the sentinels to go'.

It was 10 a.m. before this reckless party was back at Chippewa. Throughout the twenty-ninth the *Caroline* continued to pass back and forth, and MacNab, after a conference with Drew, determined that she should be destroyed that night, a decision which was probably hastened by the increased firing and derisive shouts which came from the island and rendered the militia exceedingly restless and critical at the enforced inaction. Preparations for the daring exploit were speedily under way. Captain Drew was made commander, and with a number of other 'Elegant Extracts' for officers, fifty or sixty men armed with cutlasses and pistols made ready to follow their leader 'to the Devil' if need be.[8] Shortly after nine o'clock seven boats set out in the expectation that the *Caroline* would be found at or near the island. At the commencement the current proved strong and the men towed their boats upstream by their painters, two boats dropping out because of faulty equipment. Reaching a position above Whiskey Point they proceeded through the channel separating Grand and Navy islands, where they could see the *Caroline* well lighted up but at Schlosser. Stopping a moment, the commander, having been ordered to take the vessel wherever he should find her, said to his men: 'The steamboat is our object—follow me!' They rowed quietly along in the pitch dark and were not observed by the sentry until they had ascended the creek and were within twenty yards of the ship. A challenge, an evasive reply, a musket-shot, and a call to the crew occupied the few moments before grappling-pikes had seized the *Caroline* at several points and the raiders had climbed aboard. Doors were kicked in, and the crew of ten, together with twenty-three roomers who could not get accommodation at the inn, were herded together and driven at sword point from the deck to the wharf. 'There was the loudest hullabaloo I ever heard in all my life', recalled Richard Arnold. 'You would have thought that two mighty hosts were contending for the victory.' . . 'Up they came thick and fast,' says another participant. 'Then came the slashing of the cutlass and the sharp bang of the pistol', and one officer, Captain Warren of the Cobourg Rifles, was wounded as he fought his man: 'Being engaged hand to hand he did not perceive a coward come behind the man he was fighting with and level a pistol at him; luckily it only passed through his pocket and grazed his hip joint, but being

[8] Head to Glenelg, February 9, 1838. The 'Elegant Extracts' were so called by MacNab on account of their family connection and implied 'respectability'. Colonel J. B. Askin called them 'the Boy Volunteers from London & Woodstock'.

put off guard his antagonist managed to wound him on the left arm with a cutlass'. A young sailor named Reynolds was also wounded, but he grasped his assailant with one hand, and throwing him down, 'knocked his brains out with the butt end of his pistol'. Lieutenant McCormick was seriously wounded,[9] but he is credited with splitting at least one man's skull open.

The intention appears to have been to get up steam at once and run the ship to Chippewa under her own power. Arnold was consequently sent below to light a fire under the boiler, while others went ashore to untie the vessel and were fired at from the tavern and yelled at from all sides. An effort was made to see that everyone had been driven off the boat; whereupon, as Arnold had found it impossible to get up steam quickly enough, the word was given to set her afire, 'which they effected in the ladies' cabin, taking the bed clothes and throwing a jar of oil which was found on board over all'. The boats meanwhile towed her a short distance out to avoid firing the dock. Edward Zealand cut her loose, and she drifted down the river close to the eastern shore. For a moment she became entangled in a bed of rushes, then broke away and continued on her last voyage, the woodwork being rapidly consumed. A militiaman who had participated in the cutting-out gives a vivid description:

'It was a splendid sight which shed a light for many miles around,— the rippling of the water made it appear as if gold dust had been sprinkled on its surface, and the gleam of light was so great that the sentinels upon the island perceived some of the boats, fired, but the balls fell short. . . Her pipe got red hot and stood upright till the last. At the commencement of the rapids she appeared as if hesitating a moment, when plunge she went, rose once, then a sea struck her, she heeled over, sunk in the falls, and disappeared forever. It was a sight that made the boldest hold his breath.'

Such was the firing of the *Caroline*,[10] which 'nearly fired the continent as well'. A great many wildly exaggerated stories were immediately circulated, in the United States particularly, and many a violent resolution was adopted at public meetings along the border. Even in Congress the facts were distorted, and Governor Marcy stated in a message to the New York State

[9]McCormick was shortly made customs agent in Cobourg. Referring to the appointment Mackenzie wrote in his *Caroline Almanack* under date of March 15, 1839: 'Arthur rewards Shepard McCormick for his share in the midnight assassination of the Americans at Schlosser.' McCormick was shortly granted a life pension of £100 on account of the severity of his injury, and it was generously continued to his widow.

[10]MacNab was knighted as a result of the exploit and a distinct impetus given to his political career. He died on August 8, 1862. As for those who composed the expedition, R. S. Woods wrote that they were 'all marked men' and 'in constant danger of being shot', though he lived until 1906! Arnold died in 1884, and Drew, who was promoted to the rank of admiral in 1862, died in England in 1878. Zealand, a lake captain born in Yorkshire on July 23, 1793, was killed in Hamilton by an infuriated cow on December 21, 1869.

Legislature that 'probably more than one-third' of the thirty-three persons on board the *Caroline* were 'wantonly massacred'. As a matter of fact Drew reported five or six men killed, and the narratives of the exploit bear out the likelihood of his estimate being correct. But the only body found, either at Schlosser or in the Niagara, was that of Amos Durfee of Buffalo. It is stated that he 'had been shot in the back of the head, and his brains were scattered around'; while certain other evidence indicated that he had been killed at close range with a pistol, or by a musket-shot from the tavern, presumably intended for one of the attacking party.[11] The citizens of Buffalo proceeded to make a martyr of Durfee, whose body was displayed in front of the City Hall; and it is quite apparent that he received greater honours after his death than had ever been bestowed upon him in his lifetime. It is significant that no other deaths were actually proven, and there is some ground for the suggestion that many of those on the *Caroline* were mere 'strolling vagabonds' who would not be missed.[12] S. F. Wrigley and Alfred Luce, refugees who had been with Duncombe, were captured by Drew's party, but Luce's nationality was in question and he was deported.

There were many inaccurate statements about the last voyage of the *Caroline,* and a controversy long continued as to the facts. Mackenzie employed his inventive genius to make the most of the incident as Patriot propaganda, stating not only that the boat went over the Falls but that several people could be readily imagined (if not seen) stretching out their arms in supplication that some aid might save them from their awful fate. Bond Head was similarly careless in describing the boat's end, though the truth that the Goat Island bridge would have prevented any such final leap should have been common knowledge. The fact was that the greater part of the *Caroline* sank in the rapids, where her engine could be seen for years afterwards; but parts of the ship went over the Falls, and the figurehead was picked up near Lewiston.[13]

11E. G. Lindsey states that Durfee had been on the boat, where he was shot and stabbed several times. At McLeod's trial Lieutenant Elmsley of Toronto stated he killed Durfee.

12Evidence of their previous existence is almost entirely lacking. American sources state that of thirty-three on board only twenty-one could be accounted for. Perhaps the most exaggerated account appeared in the *Lewiston Telegraph* of December 30, where under the caption 'Horrible! Most Horrible!!' it is stated that 'every individual was butchered except four, and three of these severely wounded'.

13It was salvaged by Jack Jewett and is in the Museum of the Buffalo Historical Society. C. S. Finlaison of Cobourg captured the *Caroline's* flag, and it was presented to Lieutenant McCormick in recognition of his courageous part in the expedition. He gave it to Captain Drew, who presented it to the United Service Museum, Whitehall. Many years later it was obtained by Dr. Bain of the Toronto Public Library, where it is a treasured relic. In a letter written in 1905 Finlaison described the capture of the flag.

82   THE LIVES AND TIMES OF THE PATRIOTS

But if there was uncertainty as to the course of events there was none as to the result. Not only did the Patriot agitation receive a great impetus, but the raid did far more to strain Anglo-American relations[14] than any other incident since the War of 1812. Opinions differ as to the legality of the cutting-out of the *Caroline*, but the general view is that it was in accord with international law, though rash under the circumstances. Other nations, the United States among them, had acted similarly,[15] and the American Government could not consistently complain if Canada was inclined to follow the same reasoning under circumstances equally aggravating.

The number of Patriots on Navy Island, however, was greatly increased as a result of the cutting-out of the *Caroline*, and the recruits, which before contained a considerable percentage of Canadian refugees, now consisted chiefly of American citizens; while at times it appears to have been difficult to keep the American militia from going over to the followers of Mackenzie and Van Rensselaer. Nelson Gorham stated that at no time did the force number more than 450, and this statement is partially corroborated by Van Rensselaer, who said that the numbers were trebled after the cutting-out of the *Caroline*.[16]

The state of mind engendered by the act is exemplified by its reaction upon Robert Marsh. Although he claimed to be an American citizen, he was in Upper Canada in 1837. As delivery boy for his brother, a Chippewa baker, he drove a cart laden with bread and crackers and dispensed his goods in the various villages between St. Catharines and Fort Erie. His contact with the inhabitants led him to believe that the cause of liberty was about to triumph in Upper Canada. 'I began to think that I must soon become an actor on one side or the other,' he says. But it took the burning of the *Caroline* to rouse him to action. The following day, December 30, he and a companion procured a boat, apparently from Mrs. McAfee, and passed across to Grand Island. Proceeding some miles over forest, swamp, and creek, they reached the small village of Whitehaven, where some American militiamen detained them for a time. They were not long held, however, and

[14]In British eyes it served at least to balance the books when so many American raids upon Canada were later being made. For the McLeod trial and the political repercussions in general see pp. 87 and 189-90.
[15]In 1818 American troops pursued Indian raiders across the frontier into Florida, although at that time at peace with Spain. 'We had a right by the laws of nations', maintained President Monroe, 'to follow the enemy and subdue him there'. (Message to Congress, November 17, 1818.)
[16]Mackenzie exaggerated when he wrote in his *Caroline Almanack* that they numbered 'not many more than 600', for the official list as preserved in the Lindsey Papers totals about 350, printed herewith for the first time in appendix H(2). Contemporary American publications, however, estimated the Navy Island recruits at from 500 to 1700.

The Eagle Tavern, Buffalo
A prominent rallying-point for Canadian refugees and American sympathizers

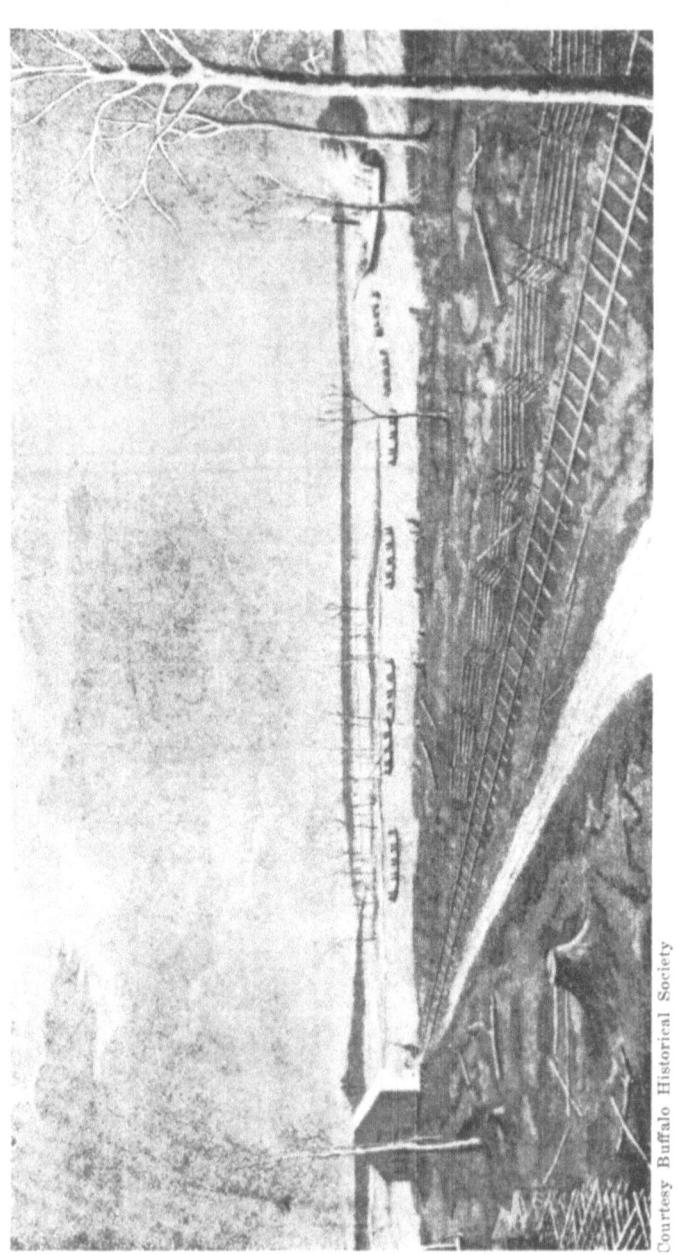

BURNING OF THE CAROLINE ON THE NIGHT OF THE 29TH. DECEM. 1833.
From Field's Tavern, near Schlosser.

proceeded to the American shore of the Niagara. Marsh, his resolution fired by blood-stains on the wharf at Fort Schlosser, crossed over to Navy Island and enrolled under Mackenzie's Provisional Government for 'seven years or during the war'.[17] Like many another, he was fated to pay roundly for his service in the Patriot cause.

After the *Caroline* episode there was no lack of firing on the part of the Canadian militia, though the protection of the forest prevented extensive damage, only one man, Nelson Beebe, formerly a gunner in the American Army, being killed during the entire occupation. The militia, on the other hand, had no such protection from gunfire, and three were killed.[18] But, though they had a slight advantage in this respect, there were other difficulties facing the Patriots. Winter was not the most favourable season for life in pine shanties, even though the early weeks of 1838 were unprecedentedly mild. Van Rensselaer and Mackenzie were finding it increasingly difficult to tolerate one another, the former apparently living up to his reputation as the black sheep of the family. Mackenzie reported that his military leader spent most of his time 'drinking brandy and writing love-letters', but Van Rensselaer tells how overworked he was—'Nor did I undress myself once during the whole period of my stay.' Eventually he is said to have apologized for his malevolent bitterness towards Mackenzie, but there is no evidence that either his conduct or his ability was ever more than mediocre.

Details of military activities on Navy Island are given by Robert Marsh with considerable candour and no little humour, and as they are to be found nowhere else they have the merit of freshness:

'After my informing the General of their preparations and intention of attacking the Island, breastworks were hastily thrown up and all necessary arrangements made to give them a warm reception. There were twenty-five cannon, mostly well mounted, which could easily be concentrated at any point required, and manned by men that knew how to handle them. Besides other preparations, tops of trees and underbrush were thrown over the bank at different places to prevent them landing... It was hoped and much regretted by all on the island that the attempt was not made; for if they had done so it would have thinned their ranks and made it more easy for us to have entered Canada at that place. They finally concluded to bring all their artillery to bear upon us and thus exterminate all within

[17] Marsh, *Seven Years of My Life*, 6-14. Possibly he enrolled under an alias, for his name is not found on the official list of recruits. The list is, however, obviously not the original, and the copyist may have inadvertently omitted a few names or have been unable to decipher them.
[18] Sir Richard Bonnycastle records as 'the most melancholy result' of the siege of Navy Island, the death of 'a fine young man, Mr. Smith of Hamilton, who was lying in a barn on some hay when a red-hot shot from the island struck him'. One Millar, a naval gunner at Chippewa, was hit in the leg by a cannonball and died shortly after it was cut off. 'He desired to see it, gave three cheers for the Queen, and after a few hours expired.'

their reach. Now the work of destruction commences; the balls and bombs fly in all directions... I felt a sudden jar at my back, and the other three that set near me did the same; we rose up and discovered that a cannon ball had found its way through our breastwork, but was kind enough to stop after just stirring the dirt at our backs. I had only moved about an inch of dirt when I picked up a six-pound ball.

'As it happened, our gun was a six-pounder. We concluded, as that was the only ball that had as yet been willing to pay us a visit, we would send it back as quick as it come. We immediately put it into our gun and wheeled around the corner of the breastwork... We were about to give them another shot when the officer of the day came up and told us the orders from headquarters were not to fire unless it was absolutely necessary, that we must be saving of our ammunition. I told him that it was their own ball that we had just sent back. When he saw the execution it had done he smiled.'

Lett and Johnston were among the notorious Patriots who had some part in the Navy Island campaign; while Sutherland left the island on December 28, being sent by Van Rensselaer towards Detroit and picking up 200 recruits at Cleveland to aid him in the projected activities of the 'Patriot Army of the North-west'. Of a different character was Dr. Rolph, who spent but an hour on Navy Island, his extreme caution or his distrust of Mackenzie preventing whole-hearted support of the enterprise. Mrs. Mackenzie bravely came to her husband's side, and remained about two weeks on the island,—'the only female who spent any length of time' there. She arrived just before the destruction of the *Caroline,* and occupied herself in making flannel cartridge-bags; but ill-health forced her to retire to the American shore before the general evacuation.

The practicability of an invasion of Upper Canadian territory by the Navy Island force was never a reality, but after MacNab's large force had assembled it became tactically impossible. Samuel Chandler, who had escaped with Mackenzie, was, however, busy stirring up the inhabitants of the Niagara peninsula, and it is said that an invasion was once decided upon, but that in an effort to obtain the steamer *Barcelona* the Patriots were outbid by $500 by General Scott of the American Army. 'We stood under arms from sunset to midnight,' wrote Van Rensselaer. It was intended that the steamer should tow the Patriots to Chippewa in yawl-boats and flats, and that after defeating the defenders they would seize a government steamer and proceed to Toronto. The British force at Chippewa continued to the end to maintain a heavy fire upon the island, for on the twelfth of January 283 rounds were fired from guns and mortars, and on the thirteenth 130 more. But the sensible decision of evacuation was made by the Buffalo Committee of Thirteen and Van Rensselaer, for Mackenzie appears to have had little or no influence in the matter. On January 13 the military command announced the decision, and the movement was effected on the following day. The original plan was to remove the expedition to some rendezvous along the shore of Lake Erie, probably opposite Detroit, but once more Federal troops under General Scott upset their plans by detaining the steamship *New England*, which was supposed to have been engaged to aid the evacuation. As a result some went to Grand Island, others direct to the mainland, while the cannon and arms which had been taken or borrowed from American arsenals were seized, the rest being removed by wagon to the cellars and barns of friendly farmers along the south shore of Lake Erie. Many of the men proceeded to the vicinity of Detroit, where they were shortly to participate in a series of futile raids upon Canadian territory.

Two incidents informed the militia of the evacuation. A man bearing a white flag suddenly appeared on the west shore of the island, which was the first intimation. Just prior to the general exodus Matthew Hayes, high bailiff of Toronto when Mackenzie was mayor, surrendered at Chippewa. He had formerly been a sergeant in the Fifteenth Regiment of Foot, but drilled the Navy Island Patriots during the occupation.[19] When it was learned that the evacuation was under way, Captain Drew was ordered to prevent any effort to proceed by steamship to some other point of entry into Upper Canada, and in so doing he anchored two schooners in American waters, producing another tense situation, which, fortunately, was of short duration.

On the morning of January 15 the Canadian militia occupied Navy Island, and Sir Francis Bond Head paid it a visit two days later. The account written by George Menzies, editor of the *Niagara Reporter*, not only describes the actual condition of affairs but enables some deductions as to life there during the occupation. He found the shanties miserable—'not fit for pigs'; their walls were of pine branches, with beds of the same material. 'Mrs. McKenzie's *bed-room* is a recess of a wretched log-house at the upper end of the island. On a shelf in this recess the unhappy woman is said to have nestled her misery among filthy straw'. As a whole the island provided 'a disgusting scene'. Scattered about were 'Temperance newspapers, ragged shirts, old boots and shoes and dilapidated trowsers'; while among the straw were bones and pieces of meat and bread, as well as beans and peas, which seem to have been the staple of their food, as they were scattered all over the island.

The island as a defensive position appeared to this observer a

[19] For some reason he was not severely punished. He accompanied Lount to Toronto jail, but on July 25, 1838, was admitted to bail.

mere bugbear. Brushwood had been cut down and thrown into the water, and a few breastworks raised; but it was 'entirely defenceless' and 'could have been taken without difficulty'—though at the expense of lives. Evidences of exploding shells showed that considerable damage had been done, and some boots lying about appeared to have been cut off dead or wounded men. One body was exhumed, supposed to have been that of a Lockport man who had been shot by the Patriots themselves, for 'his arms were pinioned and he had been killed by a rifle ball'.[20]

It is difficult to agree with the American assertion that the Navy Island invasion was the most successful of any in the history of the Rebellion—unless the implication is that the other activities were such great failures that it was a success in comparison. The occupation had, of course, attracted a considerable number to the Patriot cause, but on evacuation the force broke up and no considerable number could continue as a unit in the various activities which appear to have been planned as simultaneous raids along the border from Michigan to Vermont on George Washington's birthday. In spite of the impetus to the Patriot agitation through the cutting-out of the *Caroline,* the administration of President Van Buren stood firm for peace and strict neutrality, warning American citizens that they forfeited all claims to the protection of their country if they engaged in armed invasions. The issue, consequently, was clear cut, and could not be misinterpreted.

[20]Elsewhere this is referred to as Beebe's grave. In any case when the news reached the 'backwoods' the grave had grown into a huge pit containing 'nearly a hundred bodies'. (Traill, *The Backwoods of Canada,* 340.)

BIBLIOGRAPHY

A large amount of manuscript material in the Lindsey Papers has been used here for the first time. Of particular importance is the list of recruits (see appendix H(2)), and the letters to Van Rensselaer and Mackenzie, a representative selection from which is given in appendix I. Head's despatches to Glenelg, and enclosures therewith, are supplemented by his two books. The Messages to Congress and Proclamations referred to are in the public collections in Washington. Van Rensselaer's side of the story is presented largely in 'A Voice from Albany Jail', and 'Narration of Facts Connected with the Frontier Movements of the Patriot Army of Upper Canada', Toronto *Patriot,* April 10, 1838; and in his letter to his father, January 4, 1838, in Bonney, *Legacy of Historical Gleanings,* II. A large amount of documentary material relative to the campaign is in print, though widely scattered. Bonnycastle's *Canada As It Is,* II 61-127, contains much of Van Rensselaer's correspondence. Gorham's letter relative to the number of recruits is in Dent, II 193 fn. The Navy Island proclamation is given in appendix H(1). Marsh's account of the campaign is given in his *Seven Years of My Life.* Among the rarest printed items is E. G. Lindsey, *A History of the Events which Transpired during the Navy Island Campaign; to which is added the Correspondence of Different Public Officers, with the Affidavits of Individuals in the United States and Canada.* This pamphlet was published in Lewiston in 1838, and the only copy which the author has seen is in the library of the Buffalo Historical Society. The excitement in and about Rochester is described in Parker, *Rochester, a Story Historical.* The letters of Captain Battersby, in Lizars, *Humours of '37,* 213-16, describe the life of the militia at Chippewa. George Coventry's narrative, in Riddell, 'A Contemporary Account of the Rebellion in Upper Canada, 1837', Ontario Historical Society, XVII, is also of value in this connection, while sidelights are found in Head's *Emigrant,* chapter X, and in E. G. Lindsey, 9 *et seq.* Tiffany's 'The Relations of the United States to the Canadian Rebellion of 1837-1838', Buffalo Historical Society, VIII, is a scholarly and valuable account, though frequently erroneous in references to Can-

NAVY ISLAND AND THE CAROLINE

adian events. The activities of spies are described in O. Lindsey, II 140 fn., Bonnycastle, *Canada As It Is*, II 75, Dickens, *American Notes*, chapter XV, and Alexander, *L'Acadie*, I 55. The deposition of one of the spies, Seth Conklin, is Enclosure 20, Head to Glenelg, February 7, 1838, and is given also in the contemporary press. The *Caroline* episode is well covered in narratives published by Drew and Woods, while George T. Dennison's is in the *Canadian Monthly*, April, 1873, 289-92, Richard Arnold's in Dent, II 214-18, a letter on the subject is in the *Cobourg Star* of January 3, 1838, and a copy of Finlaison's letter is in the Toronto Public Library. Other information, including documents in some cases, may be found in O. Lindsey, E. G. Lindsey, Bonney, and Mackenzie's *Caroline Almanack*. McLeod's trial, which is referred to more fully in chapter XVIII, is outlined in Colquhoun, 'Famous Canadian Trials', *Canadian Magazine*, January, 1915, 201-4, and more fully in several contemporary printed accounts of the case. Among poetical efforts inspired by the *Caroline* incident was one by Susanna Moodie, in *Roughing It in the Bush*, II 206-9, another in the *Cobourg Star*, February 7, 1838, and a third by a prisoner in Toronto jail is in the Lindsey Papers. Numerous accounts of the Navy Island campaign are found in the contemporary press, and particularly in the *Buffalo Commercial Advertiser*, the *Lewiston Telegraph*, the *Albany Daily Advertiser*, the *Cobourg Star*, and the Toronto *Patriot*. For a biography of Edward Zealand see Fred Williams, ' "Caroline Zealand" Killed by a Cow,' Toronto *Globe and Mail*, January 7, 1938.

CHAPTER VIII

THE SCHOONER ANNE AND BOIS BLANC ISLAND

THE first of a series of disjointed invasions along the western border of Upper Canada occurred early in January, 1838, when Dr. Edward Alexander Theller of Detroit led an expedition in the schooner *Anne* against Fort Malden, Amherstburg. Theller was a native of County Kerry, Ireland, and never lost an opportunity to show his feelings against Britain for the wrongs she had heaped on his country. For a year or two enthusiasm for the Patriot cause monopolized his attention. When he undertook to lead an armed force into Upper Canada he was an apothecary, grocer, and whisky dealer, but in the Patriot movement held the imposing if meaningless title of 'Brigadier-General to command the first Brigade of French and Irish troops to be raised in Canada'. He says he went over to Windsor a short time before his cruise in the *Anne,* apparently in the expectation that a rising of Canadians would enable him to make good his high-sounding title; but he was known thereabouts, and after an unpleasant chance meeting with the redoubtable Colonel Prince he considered himself fortunate to get back across the river alive.

Preparations for a descent upon Upper Canada in support of the Navy Island occupation had been under way in Detroit for some time, and were aided by an exceedingly mild winter. A theatre devoted its proceeds to the Patriot cause, and funds and arms were subscribed at a public meeting on New Year's Day. Gibraltar, a village some twenty miles below Detroit, was the rendezvous of the Patriots, and to this point the *Anne,* which had been seized, (or, as General Handy stated, contributed to the cause by Captain Gillet), was moved from Detroit after a series of complicated manoeuvres. She was laden with arms and ammunition, most of which had been taken when the jail was broken into on the fifth of the month. The American forces were supposedly on the watch for expeditions, but the cutting-out of the *Caroline* had intensified anti-British feeling, and although Governor Stevens Mason and two steamer-loads of militiamen set out for Gibraltar to intercept the *Anne,* all they did, it is said, was 'hob-nob and drink wine with the Patriot leaders'. The attitude of the Michigan authorities was certainly complacent enough, but Federal troops accomplished something to the purpose when they seized the

THE SCHOONER ANNE AND BOIS BLANC ISLAND 89

steamer *McComb,* in which General Henry Handy had set out; for the 'Commander-in-Chief of the Patriot Army of the Northwest', though not detained, made no effort to cross the border. Theller, meanwhile, had proceeded by other means to Gibraltar, where he came into collision with another would-be commander, General Sutherland, who reported that he had been placed in control by Mackenzie's Provisional Government on Navy Island. After much wrangling[1] it appears that Sutherland ordered Theller to take charge of that part of the expedition which was to proceed in the schooner, while he was to support him by leading a force on sloops, scows, yawl-boats, and canoes to Bois Blanc Island, some 500 yards from Amherstburg, but for some unexplained reason he stopped in American territory on Sugar Island.

Upon learning of the projected attack, 300 Canadian infantry and cavalry were carried by steamship to Bois Blanc Island on January 8. This force, under Colonel Thomas Radcliff, was stationed at three strategic points.; but, although they could hear the fife and drum band of the Patriots almost continuously, no effort was made to land on Bois Blanc. Towards evening the invaders were observed moving by boat in the direction of the Canadian shore, and Colonel Prince suggested that the militia return to Amherstburg. The *Anne* proceeded to Malden, and without first demanding a surrender fired upon the militia as they stood upon Gordon's Wharf—an act which was considered piratical even by the Patriots. The canister shot from the *Anne* was returned by the muskets of the militia, the bullets resounding on the canvas and smoke-pipe of the schooner. Part of Radcliff's force gave chase in the steamer *Alliance,* and the *Anne* thereupon withdrew to Sugar Island. From the pen of Theller we have an interesting description of the scene which met his eyes as the *Anne* approached the island in moonlight:

'The encampment was shelterless and comfortless. The general had his headquarters in a log shanty, but the men, with their arms piled up around, were gathered about the fires; some stretched upon the earth, others warming themselves, and a few cooking provisions, but all in the open air. The night was extremely cold; and yet, though destitute of blankets and the necessary camp equipage, mirth and merriment prevailed and the spirit of the expedition was unsubdued. After formally reporting myself, there being no accommodation on shore, I was ordered again on board and to keep watch for the enemy. Bad as were the quarters on board the schooner, still the encampment was worse; and after discharging her

[1]Among the outstanding characteristics of the American Patriot movement was jealousy among the leaders. Van Rensselaer described Sutherland as 'a tall hawk-eyed looking personage', but Theller called him 'a plumed popinjay and blustering Bobadil'. A curious commentary on his character is from his own hand. 'In the struggle should you fall and I survive', he wrote Van Rensselaer upon setting out for Detroit, 'you may rest assured I will see justice done to you—and if I fall and you survive I think ah—I know you will see the same kind service rendered my name'.

freight of barrels of provisions and boxes of arms and leaving on shore the greater part of the men, we again weighed anchor and gently cruised in the neighbourhood of the detachment on the island.'

On the morning of the ninth Theller advised Sutherland that the militia had evacuated Bois Blanc Island; whereupon Sutherland took some sixty men there and read a bombastic proclamation to 'the Patriotic Citizens of Upper Canada':

'You are called upon by the voice of your bleeding country to join the Patriot forces and free your land from tyranny. Hordes of worthless parasites of the British Crown are quartered upon you to devour your substance—to outrage your rights—to let loose upon your defenceless wives and daughters a brutal soldiery.

'Rally, then, around the standard of Liberty, and victory and a glorious future of independence will be yours.'

The island being uninhabited,—for even Captain and Mrs. Hackett, keepers of the lighthouse, had left with the militia,—the Canadian people received no benefit from this oratorical effort. The invaders did no damage to the lighthouse or the home of its keeper, although they carried off Mrs. Hackett's clothing and a gold ring. Theller and his men of the *Anne* were meanwhile cruising about, as was also the small sloop *Geo. Strong*, which appeared from the opposite end of Bois Blanc. The cannonading recommenced, and trees, houses, stables, and the windmill were damaged by the fire. At seven o'clock the schooner attempted to return to the island, but she suddenly grounded on Elliott's Point. The militia at Malden had kept up a continual fire, and the bullets had disabled the helmsman and cut the halyards, letting down the mainsail. In the expectation that a landing would be attempted the troopers ran around the bend of the river to the point and waded into the icy water to their armpits to board the vessel. Colonel Radcliff stated in his report to Colonel Strachan that Theller 'was at that moment in the act of reloading the six-pounder, but Captain Lang took the cartridge out of the mouth of the gun, and Ironside captured the flag'. Without further ado the occupants of the schooner were brought out and marched ashore. Twenty-one men were found on board—one of them dead and eight wounded. The commander reported the capture of 'all descriptions of useful equipment, muskets & Bayonets, Pouches, Knapsacks, ammunition, 3 pieces of cannon, &c, which I will detail more accurately when I am in possession of the Returns'. The muskets and bayonets are said elsewhere to have numbered from 200 to 300, indicating that a large force might have been equipped had a landing been effected. Cash to the total of six hundred and thirty dollars was also taken from the vessel.

The prisoners included David Anderson, formerly a tavern-

THE SCHOONER ANNE AND BOIS BLANC ISLAND 91

keeper in Selborne (Suckertown), near Port Stanley, and Walter Chase, merchant of the same village; both were wounded, and Anderson, who had earlier served under Duncombe and for whose apprehension £250 had been offered, died a few days later. Colonel W. W. Dodge was described as by far the most respectable of the prisoners. Theller also had been wounded and was carried ashore on the back of Lieutenant W. L. Bâby of the Kent militia. He was the only Patriot in uniform, being resplendent with a gilt star on his left breast. He appreciated Bâby's kindness, and wrote that Colonel Radcliff[2] had protected him from insult, 'saying in my hearing that we were prisoners of war, had conducted like brave men, and must not be abused but be handed over to the proper authorities for judicial treatment'. Colonel Prince, however, kicked and insulted him, and by his order the prisoners were tied to a rope and fastened to a cart; and so, 'tied to a cart's tail', they were ignominiously marched to the Amherstburg guard-house[3] and crowded into cramped quarters.

Dr. Theller, who did not lack spirit, removed a bullet from his own eye; and although Trooper Samuel Williams, who talked with him, thought the eye was 'in a dreadful condition, he entirely recovered his sight. One of his companions on the *Anne*, however, had no such estimate either of Theller's wounds or his courage. Angered at the leader's implication that he alone was brave while the others had cowered in the hold of the *Anne*, Chauncey Parker wrote that Theller was another Falstaff. His wounds, which supposedly caused him to fall down the hatchway into the hold, appeared to have hardly broken the skin: 'Poor man, he has seven balls through his hat, but unfortunately he could never shew them. His sword was shot off at the hilt while he held it drawn in his hand; but, bad luck to him, I happened to see him break it himself by striking it on the wheel of the cannon.'

[2]Colonel Thomas Radcliff, a Peninsular veteran of twelve engagements, had settled a few years before in Adelaide Township. When a courier arrived with the news of Theller's attack, he led his regiment westward, but bad roads necessitated the descent of the Thames in an open boat, and through Lake St. Clair and the Detroit to Sandwich. Colonel John Prince later moved in the Legislative Assembly to present a sword to him for gallantry, but the motion was not adopted. Colonel Radcliff was appointed to the Legislative Council, and later became Collector of Customs in Toronto. He died on June 9, 1841, aged forty-seven, his early death being attributed to his arduous experiences in January, 1838.

[3]The following were taken when the *Anne* was captured: Edward Theller, Stephen Brophy, Abram Partridge, Theron Culver, Benjamin Pew, Walter Chase, Squire Thayer, Henry Hull, Nathaniel Smith, W. W. Dodge, Chauncey Parker, all of whom remained in custody (see also chapters XII and XIII); and Claude Campeau, Augustus Berdeneau, Francis St. Augustin, Henry Johnston, Louis Lenoux, Francis Clutier, and George Davis, who were shortly pardoned and deported to the United States. The Patriots were very indignant that former negro slaves were to be found fighting against them, and it was suggested that if the movement proved successful they would 'send every coloured man in the Province back into southern bondage'. Many details of the panic in Amherstburg, compiled by David B. Botsford, may be found in the *Amherstburg Echo*, January 7, 1938. A cannon and two swords from the *Anne*, and one of three blockhouses erected on Bois Blanc just after the raid, have been preserved.

On Bois Blanc Island, meanwhile, General Sutherland and his men were marching about with banners and music. But hearing the firing and becoming curious as to the activities of the *Anne,* the leader, according to General Handy's report, was rowed in a yawl-boat to a point from which he could see what had happened to the *Anne;* whereupon, in the face of some desire on the part of his men to go to the rescue of their fellow-Patriots, he cried out in alarm, 'Away to Sugar Island! Fly! Fly! Fly! All is lost!' When the island was evacuated the sloop *Geo. Strong* was left behind and was captured by the militia. The Patriot force, safe from pursuit, remained on Sugar Island for some time, apparently in the expectation that another expedition would be organized. General Handy came there on the tenth of January and was chosen leader over Sutherland, who returned to Detroit. Some days later the Governor of Michigan consented to aid in bringing the Patriots back in the steamer *Erie,* and the evacuation was apparently effected to everyone's satisfaction. 'Thus ended,' observed the Toronto *Patriot* in vehement indignation, 'an attack to which the annals of civilized nations can probably furnish no parallel for unprovoked and wanton aggression'.

The subsequent fortunes of Sutherland were varied. He got into difficulty with the authorities soon after his return to Detroit, for he published his proclamation and took every opportunity to boast of his prowess. He continued, moreover, to take part in Patriot activities, exhorting men to march to Fighting Island on February 24—though he himself did not proceed with the expedition. Early in March he was taken prisoner[4] on the ice near the frontier line. It appears that Colonel Prince and two or three companions were driving in a sleigh, and having a keen eye for Patriots, the colonel arrested Sutherland on sight and had him taken to Fort Malden. General Handy believed that he was both a traitor and a coward, but the insinuation is probably but one more example of the personal spite and jealousy which was to be found throughout the Patriot army, and particularly among the generals. In any case Sutherland was soon imprisoned in Toronto, where his stay was quite eventful:

'On my arrival at that place I was directly taken to the Government House, where I had an interview with Sir Francis Bond Head, then Lieutenant-Governor of the Province, who informed me it was the intention of "the Government" to subject me to a speedy trial; and he advised me to prepare my mind for an execution, as he assured me nothing could save me from such a fate! From the Government House I was conveyed to the

[4] The *Cobourg Star* reported the capture on March 14, 1838, under the caption 'Glorious News from the West'; while on the sixteenth the Toronto *Patriot* recorded the arrest of a 'brace of knaves' under the head 'Capture of the Brigands Sutherland and Spencer'.

THE SCHOONER ANNE AND BOIS BLANC ISLAND 93

garrison, and on the next day at ten o'clock I was arraigned before a Court Martial... I was confined in a room of a magazine whose walls were four or five feet thick, with treble-locked doors and massive grates at the windows. This of itself would have forbidden all idea of getting out, if I had been left there alone; but the security against my escape was made doubly so by a chain of five sentinels posted on the outside of the building, with another who walked by the side of my bed. Then to these there were added three Irish Orangemen sworn in as special constables, who remained in the room near my person to ensure the fidelity of the soldiers, who are always distrusted by their officers'.[5]

Though he does not mention it himself, Sutherland, after having been sentenced and removed to Toronto jail, tried to commit suicide by opening his veins; but he recovered and was sent to Quebec. There he spent his time writing a long, scholarly, and carefully documented letter to Lord Durham, which he very appropriately dated July 4. His sentence had been transportation for life, but his trial, besides being in some respects irregular, was in others hardly fair; and more important still, he was probably not on Canadian territory when arrested by Colonel Prince. In August, 1838, the British Government ordered his discharge, but lack of proper security for future good conduct, and other pretexts, led to his detention in the citadel for some months longer. He did not participate in the escape planned by Theller and Dodge but was placed in the 'black hole' for safety after his compatriots had got away. Finally, he was taken to Upper Canada and deported to the United States.

[5]Sutherland had been a solicitor and the editor of several New York newspapers. His writings, both prose and poetry, have considerable merit.

BIBLIOGRAPHY

Theller's version is given in his *Canada in 1837-8*, which is reliable as far as concerns the main trend of his own experiences, but not in respect to events in which he took no part. Other descriptions based largely on Patriot sources are Ross, 'The Patriot War', Michigan Pioneer and Historical Society, XXI 529 *et seq.*, and C. Lindsey, II, where the confusing reports of General Handy and other documents not now available have been unravelled with considerable success. Sutherland's letter to Van Rensselaer is in the Lindsey Papers. The proclamations of the Patriots are Enclosures 2, 3, and 4 in Head to Glenelg, February 7, 1838; and Enclosure 3 in the despatch of March 12 outlines the capture of the *Anne*. Chauncey Parker's letter to his father is in the *Cobourg Star*, February 20, 1839. An excellent and very fair account of the occupation of Bois Blanc is reprinted from the Sandwich *Herald* in the Toronto *Patriot*, February 2, 1838. In addition to Head's despatches and their enclosures, a letter of Colonel Radcliff in Ermatinger's *Talbot Regime*, 358-9, reports the *Anne's* capture in detail; while the reminiscences of Trooper Samuel Williams, in Ermatinger, 213, and more fully in the Elgin Historical Society's *Reminiscences of Early Settlers and Other Records*, 64-9, describe the treatment of the prisoners, with sidelights on Theller. Patriot protests at the presence of negroes in the militia are in 'The Canada Crusade', *Michigan Observer*, January 17, 1838. Sutherland's *Loose Leaves from the Port Folio of a Late Patriot Prisoner in Canada* describes his stay in Toronto, while the *Christian Guardian* of March 21 gives the details of his attempt to commit suicide. A short estimate of Sutherland's life and letters, with comments on the legality of his capture and trial, is given by the Honourable Mr. Justice Riddell in 'A Patriot General', *Canadian Magazine*, November, 1914, 32-6.

CHAPTER IX

Donald McLeod and Fighting Island

THE raids of Theller and Sutherland resulted in increased vigilance at Detroit, and there was a lull in Patriot activity for a few weeks. But 'the town guard patrolled the city and river bank every night, and it was proclaimed that if any exigency should arise, the civic soldiery would be notified by the ringing of the bell of the Presbyterian Church. . . It was rung several times at night, but they proved to be false alarms'. But at midnight on February 23 the loud clanging of the bell brought a few adventurous spirits to the wharves to find that military activities were again under way. The *Erie* had steam up and was about to leave the harbour. Blankets and other equipment could be seen in the dim light piled on her deck, while an ammunition wagon stood on the dock. Apparently fearful that her departure would be prevented, the *Erie* left in haste without the wagon, which was immediately hauled away.

The Rising Sun Tavern in Springwells Township was a well known Patriot rendezvous, and a considerable number of them were then asleep on the floor of the inn. The ammunition wagon soon reached the same point, and the *Erie* had already arrived. With all possible speed both men and wagon were taken aboard; and the *Erie* proceeded down the river to Fighting Island, a long, narrow strip of marshy ground a short distance below Sandwich, and there the expedition landed.

On the following day General Sutherland was active in Detroit exhorting some thirty Patriots to join their fellows on Fighting Island. He promised them land and glory, and they set out for a point seven miles below the town and opposite the island. Here they were joined by several hundred who had marched from Cleveland during the night under General Donald McLeod, a Canadian refugee, formerly a sergeant in the British Army and a teacher in Prescott.[1] These men were almost entirely unarmed, the expectation being that equipment from Navy Island, which had been stored in barns and attics of sympathizers along the Erie shore, would be assembled by General Vreeland. But

[1] McLeod's career had been most varied. Born in Scotland on January 1, 1779, he was educated at Aberdeen University for the church. In 1803 he entered the navy, and in 1808 the army. He fought in the Peninsular War at Corunna, in several battles of the War of 1812 in Canada, and at Waterloo. He returned to Upper Canada in 1816 and opened a classical school in Prescott. At the outbreak of the Rebellion he held the rank of major in the Grenville militia.

the plans miscarried, and only about fifty muskets, many of them stolen from American armouries, had been collected; while one six-pound cannon, 'borrowed by the citizens of Ypsilanti from the Dearborn Arsenal'—ostensibly for a Fourth of July celebration—comprised the artillery, which it proved necessary to mount on a rough platform of fence rails. It was learned also that American troops were on the march from Detroit to disperse the expedition and arrest the leaders. The ensuing episode formed the one big moment in the life of 'the General', as McLeod always called himself, and he gives a detailed description of the disposition and experiences of his force:

'Col. Wilcox was immediately ordered to parade the men on the ice. All the arms in their possession were barely six rifles and one musket, a few swords and some pistols. The General addressed them in a very animated speech, and at the conclusion asked them whether to avoid the U. S. troops and marshals they would march with him and occupy Fighting Island until the arms arrived. All responded in the affirmative, gave three cheers, and marched off under the command of Col. Wilcox. Through the treachery of Vreeland[2] these brave men were thus unavoidably placed between two fires, having their enemy, the British, in front, without the means of defending themselves in the event of an attack; the U. S. troops in their rear, to starve them out and prevent any succor reaching them. . .

'After they marched for the Island, the General remained for a short time to consult with Dr. Duncombe on matters relating to the expedition, and if possible to prevail with Vreeland to give up the arms or inform where they could be found. . . But Dr. Duncombe, having lost all further confidence in him, mounted his horse and rode to Detroit to collect and forward all the arms he could.'

Short scrubby oaks covered Fighting Island, and there was but little other protection from the biting wind. Posting pickets to prevent a surprise attack, McLeod inspected the disposition of his army 'and returned very much fatigued to his camp, the snow being considerably deep'. Adjutant Jones was ordered to arouse the men half an hour before daybreak. During the night thirty-five serviceable muskets, procured through the exertions of Dr. Duncombe, arrived from the mainland, and Captain Dodd was placed in command of the armed men. Having had experience in the American army, Dodd directed his company during the night in making cartridges.

Meanwhile General Brady of the American Army advised the Canadian authorities of the expedition, and then ordered the boundary line to be marked on the ice with small red flags. During

[2]Vreeland's reputation was not high among his contemporaries. The Detroit *Free Press* of July 12, 1838, describes him as 'five feet four inches in his shoes—that is, when he is fortunate enough to have a pair that can be so called—not lacking in impudence by any means, and a miserable drunken vagabond, as his appearance plainly indicates'. The Patriots in general are described as 'an unspeakable set of vagabonds; . . a more miserable set of beings never existed in any country'.

this time a force had been gathering on the Canadian shore opposite the island, and soon after daylight on the twenty-fifth they bridged a large air-hole with planks and marched against the Patriots. McLeod describes, with pardonable if exaggerated pride, the short defence of the island:

'At day-break the British appeared on the ice and fired on the Island, wounding one man. Captain Dodd was immediately ordered to march a few yards on the ice with twelve men, three paces apart, take deliberate aim, and fire among them. This had the desired effect—the British dispersed in rather a hurry; the men gave three cheers, and after remaining some time on the ice and seeing nothing more of the enemy, they were ordered to finish their breakfast with their arms in hand, so as to be ready to turn out in case of another alarm. About half an hour afterwards the enemy opened their batteries pouring round shot, grape, and canister on the Island in fine style. The men with arms were ordered to form line under Captain Dodd; those without to keep in the rear and not expose themselves unnecessarily.

'Colonels Wilcox and Bacon contrived the evening previous to get a three-pounder on the Island, which they mounted on rails and gave in charge of Adjutant Jones; but, having neither cartridges nor balls, they broke open a keg of rifle powder, and loaded her in the following manner: Colonel Bacon held the muzzle up between his legs; Jones poured in the powder with his hands and rammed the wad home with a piece of broken rail, and in lieu of a ball filled her up with boiler puncheons, Colonel McKinney firing her off. This they repeated two or three times.'

The report of Major H. D. Townshend to Colonel the Hon. John Maitland indicates the strategy of the British. He directed the 32nd Regiment 'to keep the outskirts of the Island, facing the American shore, with a view of intercepting the retreat of the rebels'; while the 83rd 'moved at extended order through the brushwood, flanked and supported by the Militia and Volunteers'. The defenders fired off their cannon two or three times, and at each discharge it tumbled from its rude carriage and had to be remounted. The riflemen kept themselves out of sight as far as possible, taking an odd shot at the advancing redcoats as the opportunity offered. General McLeod sought the protection of the largest tree on the island, but a six-pound shot struck a branch a few inches above his head, wounding Wilcox.

'The patriots,' he says, 'maintained their ground until reduced to one round of cartridges apiece, and even until they were nearly surrounded. Seeing that any further resistance would only be a wanton and unpardonable waste of human life, and satisfied that all was done that brave men could do placed in similar circumstances, the General ordered a retreat and directed Captain Dodd with his armed men to cover the rear of the unarmed and by no means to allow them to run or break the line, which order was punctually obeyed. Previous to this, as the General was ordering the men without arms to retreat to the American shore, a grape shot carried away the front of his cap, severely wounded a man on his left, and destroyed a musket in the hand of another.

'The General, on leaving the Island, remarked to Colonel Bacon that the three-pounder would fall into the enemy's hand. This gallant son of Mars picked up an axe, and in the face of a heavy fire returned to the piece, broke its axis, and assisted Lieutenant Lett and some others to bring off one of the wounded men.'

The Patriot casualties were four slightly and one severely wounded. Some of them stated that the British force lost five killed and fifteen wounded, but the truth, as McLeod recognized, was that they suffered no losses. During the occupation of the island many Detroiters came out on the ice in sleighs 'to see the fun', but all they saw was the ignominious rout of the Patriots. Perhaps the small boys enjoyed the affair most, for they were to be seen along the river bank gathering stray round-shot which had rolled over the ice.

When the Patriots reached the Michigan shore they 'formed themselves into Platoons and fired several rounds' at the British force, but without effect; whereupon they were dispersed by American troops. They had left on the island a considerable number of muskets, their one gun, and some supplies which, consisting of 'crackers in barrels' and 'boxes of smoked herrings', appeared to have been contributed by 'a *sympathizing* public rather than by a Commissariat'. John McCrae relates that he was one of a party that 'obtained a sleigh and dragged the six-pounder over the treacherous ice to the mainland. . . We soon had our prize mounted in front of our quarters at Windsor'. This relic, nicknamed 'the Rebel Pup', was taken to Chatham in the following May, and after some years at the bottom of the Thames it was placed in front of the McCrae residence.

The United States Government had begun to be more active in apprehending border raiders, and McLeod gives a lengthy circumstantial account of the means by which he avoided arrest for breaking the neutrality laws. When he learned that General Scott's forces were hot on his trail, he exchanged clothes with a junior officer and set out for Monroe in a small sleigh. Hide-and-seek now became an exciting pastime for him, 'the ladies, the patriot soldier's true friend', aiding him at every move. Mrs. Spaulding dressed him in female apparel and furnished him with knitting, later putting him in bed with her husband; so that when searchers entered the room they were sternly reproved for their inexcusable intrusion. Next morning he got out of town, and Mrs. Hale disguised him in 'ragged clothes and an old furless cap'; and 'being naturally of a coarse rough countenance', McLeod was transformed into 'a hideous spectre' and escaped from the district, finally reaching Lower Sandusky. Shortly afterwards he proceeded with some volunteers to the Lake Erie

98 THE LIVES AND TIMES OF THE PATRIOTS

shore with the intention of reinforcing the filibusters who had raided Pelee Island, only to receive a despatch from the colonel in charge that the Patriots had been forced to retreat. He was shortly tried in Detroit for breaking the neutrality laws, but was acquitted. In May he participated with Bill Johnston in the burning of the steamer *Sir Robert Peel*.

McLeod returned to Canada some years later, at the suggestion, it is said, of Dr. Rolph, who secured him a position in the Bureau of Agriculture. In his later life he enjoyed a retiring allowance from the government against which he had been so active during the Patriot War. His pension continued until he died in Cleveland on July 22, 1879, at the age of one hundred years.

BIBLIOGRAPHY

McLeod's version is given in his *A Brief Review*, 212-6. While the book is in general unreliable, his account of his own experiences is, except for an occasional lapse, as authentic as the general run of memoirs. Ross, 'The Patriot War', 529 *et seq.*, contains other material from the Patriot point of view. Major Townshend's report and a number of other documents are printed in the Toronto *Patriot* of March 2, 1838. Reminiscences of loyalist participants form the basis of McCrae, 'The Battle of Fighting Island, February, 1838', Essex Historical Society, I 28-30.

Courtesy Public Archives of Canada

Admiral Andrew Drew
Captain of the force which fired the steamship *Caroline*

From Lindsey, *Life of Mackenzie*

Alexander McLeod
Loyalist who was tried in 1842 for the murder of Durfee

SCHLOSSER   NAVY ISLAND   CHIPPEWA

Courtesy Public Archives of Canada   W. R. Callington

The *Caroline's* Last Voyage
The ship, however, broke up in the rapids above the Falls

Courtesy Buffalo Historical Society 'Hogarth'!
American Satire on the British Capture of Navy Island
'All hearts were nerved for the contest. . ; An immense porker, surrounded by her infant family, came fiercely bristling up to dispute our passage.'—*Alleged extract from 'Col. McNab's dispatches to Gov. Head'!*

CHAPTER X

THE BATTLE OF PELEE ISLAND

PELEE ISLAND, some eighteen miles from the Canadian shore of Lake Erie between Kingsville and Leamington, was the scene of the next Patriot raid, and a sharp engagement with British regulars occurred there on March 3, 1838. At that time the island, which contains about 11,000 acres, was largely the property of William McCormack, but ten families lived there. It has usually been supposed that the Patriot occupation of Pelee began on March 1, but a field officer of the British force learned that they came on February 26.

The original invading force numbered some 450 men under Colonels Seward and Bradley. Having established a rendezvous at Sandusky Bay, they marched across on the ice, which is said to have been fifteen inches thick[1] from shore to shore, and occupied all the buildings on the island; and later detachments which arrived from time to time swelled the total to well over 1,000 men. It was, therefore, the greatest of the raids in point of numbers. Such persons as were then on the island were made prisoners, and several others who approached from the mainland in sleighs or on foot were captured or fired upon, including Messrs. Wright and James, who reconnoitred the situation for the British force when news of the occupation had reached the village of Colchester. They helped themselves to stock and provisions, sending what they did not need to the American shore. One farmer estimated that he had been robbed of £1,000 in property, and in addition to these depredations the invaders dismantled the lighthouse and carried off whatever they considered of use.

When Colonel Maitland at Amherstburg learned of the raid he sent a scout to test the ice. He reported that it was strong enough to support artillery, so the commander made ready his force, which consisted of four companies of the 32nd Regiment, one of the 83rd, two six-pounders, twenty-one men of the St.

[1] After exceptionally mild weather it had become very cold. A curious raid which occurred about the same time at the other end of Lake Erie exemplifies the futility of Patriot movements. Some thirty-five Americans had established an encampment on the ice near the middle of the lake, off Hamburg, Erie County. Shanties were built, hemlock boughs prepared as beds, and the force settled down to await reinforcements 'to liberate Canada!' They planted a row of branches almost to the Canadian shore, to guide the army. A few had firearms, but most had pikes. This Patriot effort was broken up by the Buffalo City Guard and Captain Clapp's Volunteers. See Johnson, *Centennial History of Erie County, New York*, 419-20.

99

Thomas cavalry, and a few mounted men from Essex. In the afternoon of March 2, a bright, cold day, the men moved off from Amherstburg, proceeding on the ice of the river, and thence similarly along the frozen shore of the lake. About 11 p.m. a halt was called at a Colchester tavern to enable a short rest before proceeding to Pelee.

At one o'clock in the morning they again moved off, crossing a stretch of some twenty miles of Pigeon Bay and the channel to Pelee Island. The cavalry rode their mounts, but not all of them were properly equipped; the artillery also had their horses and hauled along two six-pounders; while the infantry were in sleighs, Captain Fox of the Essex troop acting as pilot for the whole expedition. By sunrise they were within half a mile of the island, and when their sentry gave the alarm the Patriots were seen to turn out in full force, their bayonets glittering in the sun; but they almost immediately retired across the clearing into the woods, where they debated what they should do. The majority clamoured for war: they had come to fight and wanted 'to have the fun of it'. Sleighloads of Americans from Sandusky and vicinity had also come 'to view the invasion of Canada'.

The disposition of the British force showed some attention to strategy. Captain Browne with two companies of the 32nd was ordered to intercept the retreat of the invaders by stationing his men on the west and south shores, and he was to be aided by the cavalry to the east of the island while Colonel Maitland and the rest of the troops proceeded to drive the invaders out of the woods from the north. But all that Maitland's men found on the shore was an abandoned camp, with potatoes still boiling over the fires; while the thickness of the forest and the depth of the snow prevented a pursuit by land.

Captain Browne's force, meanwhile, had reached the track over which the Patriots had crossed from the United States and by which it was expected they would return. Eye-witnesses saw the regulars get out of their sleighs and form in open order one and a half paces apart. The Patriot force, led by Henry Van Rensselaer,

'emerged from the cedars on the shore and forming a long line three paces apart advanced upon the British force—at the same time pouring a converging fire upon the little band... Van Rensselaer, with the courage of his ancient race, led on his men fearlessly in this ignoble cause, while Captain Brown, an old Waterloo veteran, kept steadily advancing. But the rapid fire of the Patriots beginning to tell, Captain Brown shortly gave the command to fire. Then came the command "Fix bayonets! Charge!" The line of steel at double-quick, with the half cheer, half roar of British troops, bore down to the long line of Patriots near the shore.'

THE BATTLE OF PELEE ISLAND 101

The St. Thomas cavalry were for a time in a dangerous situation, for they were only partially armed and no reinforcements were available. Trooper Samuel Williams gives the most reliable account of the engagement, and particularly of the activities of his unit:

'The Captain, after scanning our arms, ordered us to remount, and having given up hope of reinforcement, led us towards Captain Browne's detachment, whom the enemy were approaching. As we proceeded we saw the sleighs retreat, and the soldiers were strung out in a long line across the ice like fence posts. The enemy were approaching them at a quick march. We could not see them just at first. They approached Captain Browne's force in solid column, and then spread out in a line about the same length as that of the British infantry. There were about 500 of the enemy. Captain Browne had ninety men, and our troop then numbered but twenty-one. Both sides fired simultaneously. We got none of this volley. We were approaching at a gallop. We heard the enemy call out, "There comes the cavalry! Fire on them!" They did so and the bullets whistled around us. We were coming on their flank. We halted and fired. The infantry charged with fixed bayonets at that moment, in face of a heavy fire from the enemy. When the infantry were within about six rods of the enemy the latter retreated in disorder, running like wild turkeys every way, leaving five killed; while we had one soldier and one trooper, Thomas Parish, slain on the spot.

'The enemy retreated to the island, staining the snow for a quarter of a mile in width with blood. I saw Parish, as I supposed, loading. He was on his knees and was shot. The Captain put him on his horse and held him there, and brought him up and called for help to take him off his horse, saying, "He's a dead man." William McCormack, who had gone out as a teamster, helped take him from his horse. An alarm was just then raised that the enemy was crossing further down towards three other islands there. Captain Browne said to Captain Ermatinger, "Captain, take your men and chase them!" He did so, flourishing his sword and leading us until his horse's foot broke through the ice, when he called to us to wheel to the right and left. We did so. We knew we were getting on thin ice. The enemy appeared to be crossing on this and so made their escape, though it is said that many went through the ice and perished. We went back and followed their trail on the island and found a great many of their wounded having their wounds dressed at Fox's house.'

Colonel Maitland's report of the battle does not enter into much detail. He states that the leaders of the Patriots were Bradley and Howdley, and that both were killed. Eleven prisoners, some of them badly wounded, were taken, as well as some forty muskets and 'a large tri-coloured flag with two stars and the word "Liberty" worked upon it.' The British loss is given as two killed and twenty-eight wounded, who fell before the fire of 'a desperate gang of murderers and marauders', all of the 'banditti' being reported as American citizens.

Unofficial sources are very contradictory, and particularly with respect to the number of Patriot casualties. While one account indicated that eleven were killed, Dr. McCormack said that fourteen were buried at Fishing Point. General Donald McLeod stated in a letter written three days after the battle that two officers, Major Hoadley and Captain Van Rensselaer,[2] and eleven privates were killed, one drowned, and eighteen wounded. One Canadian, Major Benjamin Wait, claimed he was not only present at the engagement but was second-in-command; and that when Colonel Seward advised an immediate retreat he became commander. Spreading the 150 men with muskets throughout the force, Wait flashed his sword in the air, 'a death-dealing volley' poured into the British, and 'it was one of the few times that British troops recoiled from a charge of bayonets'. Having broken through the British line, the Patriots are said to have reloaded and kept on their way to the American mainland.[3] There they were taken in charge by General Hugh Brady of the Ohio militia, though they were not long held.

Many of the British force had had no food since the night before, and it was nearly midnight when they reached the mainland, where they remained over night. Early on the morning of the fourth, after a scanty meal, they set out for Amherstburg, which they reached in the evening, completely fagged out, having had but four hours' sleep in the forty-eight since they had left the barracks. Three of the wounded died soon afterwards, the stone erected to their memory in Amherstburg carrying this inscription:

'This monument is erected by the inhabitants of Amherstburg in memory of Thomas McCartan, Samuel Holmes, Edwin Miller, and Thomas Symonds, of H. M. 32nd Reg. of Foot, and of Thomas Parish of the St. Thomas Volunteer Cavalry,[4] who gloriously fell in repelling a band of brigands from Pelee Island on the Third of March, MDCCCXXXVIII.'

The enthusiasm of the Patriots was greatly dampened by their reception at Pelee, and the agitation noticeably diminished in importance during the next few months. Mackenzie busied himself in newspaper work, while General Van Rensselaer, after the Hickory Island fiasco[5] of a few days earlier, shortly found himself in prison. For more than a year the Pelee captives were held in jail without trial. Finally in June, 1839, five of them—Philip Jackson, Diogenes Mackenzie, Benjamin Warner, Isaac Mace, and John McIntyre—were brought to trial in Toronto. Two others, James Wood and William Carroll, a boy of eighteen, turned

[2]Henry Van Rensselaer was a relative of the Navy Island commander. General Donald McLeod wrote to his mother informing her of his death and stating that a monument would be erected to his memory in Canada when that country became free.

[3]Wait's reminiscences were given in his seventy-seventh year. He liked nothing better than to tell a good yarn, and as no other source mentions his presence, there is good reason to disbelieve that he was in any way prominent.

[4]A list of the members of the St. Thomas Cavalry is given in appendix J(2).

[5]See chapter XVI.

Queen's evidence. While obviously as guilty as any other raiders, it was reported that 'owing to a point of law reserved' the Pelee prisoners 'could not be convicted of high treason, as being treated as prisoners of war', and that consequently they would likely be released or deported to the United States. These, as well as the others who had not been tried, were discharged at various times during the ensuing eight months.[6]

[6] Presumably one of the eleven prisoners died of wounds, for only three others—Isaac Myers, Philip Brady, and William McCarrick—are listed in the 'Register of Prisoners'. Carroll was not brought to Toronto jail, while Wood was sent back to Kingston by the Lieutenant-Governor's order, probably because he was an informer. McIntyre stated that they were saved from transportation because the only 'slave of Victoria' (i.e., British subject) who was proved to be with them at Pelee was William Carl, 'Chandler's servant, New Brunswick'. See appendix J(1). Jackson, Wood, McIntyre, and Mackenzie had served at Navy Island. The first names of two of the prisoners, Mace and Wood, are elsewhere given as James and Samuel, respectively.

BIBLIOGRAPHY

The official record of the engagement, dated at Amherstburg, March 4, 1838, was obtained from the War Office Records, London, England. Supplementary information from the loyalist point of view is found in 'Notes of a Field Officer', *Patriot*, March 27, 1838, and in the reminiscences of two troopers, Samuel Williams and Roswell Tomlinson, as narrated to Judge C. O. Ermatinger and printed in his *Talbot Regime*, 216-18. The event is described from the Patriot point of view in Ross, 'The Patriot War', 534-41, including Wait's reminiscences relative to his alleged prominence in the engagement. Some light is thrown upon the raid by letters of McLeod, appended to Tiffany, Buffalo Historical Society, VIII. The trial and disposition of the prisoners is based upon 'Trial and Conviction of Five American Prisoners Taken at the Battle of Point au Pelee, Upper Canada', *Mackenzie's Gazette*, August 17, 1839, the Toronto *Mirror*, July 26, 1839, and the 'Register of Prisoners' in the Archives of Ontario.

CHAPTER XI

THE SHORT HILLS AND ST. CLAIR RAIDS

THE incursion of Patriots across the Niagara frontier in June, 1838, was unique in one respect, for they remained some ten days in Upper Canada before their presence was generally known. The genesis of the raid was apparently the report received at Navy Island, probably from Samuel Chandler, that 'Moses Brady has 100 equipped men, ready to join us. Mr. Cutting G. Stevens [is] at Mr. Price's Tavern, Short Hills, three miles south of St. John's, with Brady, and is to get twelve hours notice to join us'. On June 8 some 200 men, presumably instigated by the Canadian Refugee Association, gathered at Clark's Point, near Lewiston, under the leadership of Colonel George Washington Case, a refugee from Hamilton who had been in the Duncombe rising, and Colonel James Morreau. A scow and an open boat lay moored to the shore, and Case claimed a steamboat would soon appear to tow them across the river; but for some reason only twenty-three responded to the call for volunteers, and Case left in disgust. Morreau, an Irish Roman Catholic from Girard, Pennsylvania, stood by those who agreed to go, though the Lewiston crossing was abandoned and the force temporarily dispersed upon hearing that American troops were marching against them.

The excited state of Upper Canada at that time led to highly exaggerated accounts of the invasion when it first became known, and this was apparent even in official reports. Sir George Arthur wrote Lord Glenelg on June 30 that at least 1,000 men[1] had crossed the Niagara, though he subsequently indicated that less than 100 had entered the province, and that many of these did not remain long. As a matter of fact it is unlikely that more than thirty-four actually crossed the frontier, but they were joined by some fifteen inhabitants of Pelham and neighbouring townships. The main party of twenty-six men gathered two or three miles above Fort Schlosser on Sunday, June 10, and passed over to Grand Island, where they received arms. They remained in the woods until Monday night, when they crossed the Niagara in the

---

[1] The Toronto *Patriot* of June 26 and the *Cobourg Star* of July 4 had most of the main facts, probably obtained from the *Niagara Chronicle*; though it was stated in earlier issues that several prisoners had been immediately tried by court-martial 'and executed on Table Rock!'

steamer *Red Jacket,* landed near the head of Navy Island, and marched three miles into the woods, carrying from fifty to sixty stand of arms in the expectation that their number would speedily be increased.

The object of the expedition was believed to have been to induce a rising of the Grand River Indians, and the Lieutenant-Governor consequently ordered detachments of militia to guard the bridges at Paris, Brantford, and Cayuga. The raiders were largely Canadian refugees, some of whom had been prominent at Montgomery's Tavern or under Charles Duncombe, and they led the five or six Americans to believe that many oppressed Canadians would rise to their support. Samuel Chandler was particularly prominent in this respect, showing a list of 526 residents of Pelham Township who had promised to aid an invasion; he also arranged the food supply. Morreau issued a proclamation headed 'State of Upper Canada, June 7, 1838'. Upon Chandler's person was later found a similar document announcing the capture of Fort George and Fort Mississauga and calling upon Canadians 'to rally round the standard of liberty'.

After lying concealed two days and a night in the woods, the invaders proceeded further into Crowland Township, Chandler obtaining food for them. The party continued to the Quaker Settlement, near the Short Hills, stopping on the farm of Lewis Wilson, a refugee in Buffalo, to whose barn they were led by Dr. J. T. Wilson, a relative who had escaped from Upper Canada the previous winter. Two young women from this household aided in the supply of food, while several men joined the party there. About this time Magistrate James Cummings of Chippewa, hearing that suspicious characters were about, sent men out to reconnoitre. They discovered one of the deserted camps, but while they were able to estimate the approximate number in the party they could not locate the raiders, for the ridged and wooded country offered many excellent hide-outs.

On June 15 the expedition left Wilson's and encamped in the woods near Beckett's for two days. At this point Linus W. Miller, James Waggoner, and David Deal joined them, having been despatched from the United States, as Solicitor-General Draper was told, to learn how the expedition was getting along; or—as Miller[2] claimed—to urge them to withdraw from the country, since their presence would prejudice the chances of success of the rising planned for July 4. Miller did not intend to remain, but finding

[2]Miller was supposed to hold the rank of colonel and aide-de-camp to General Donald McLeod. One of his companions, Deal, changed his name to William Reynolds to avoid recognition as one of Bill Johnston's gang who burned the *Sir Robert Peel.*

the frontier too well guarded to permit his return to Lockport he rejoined the party, making an ineffectual attempt to persuade them to wait at least until the fourth of July.

The expedition now removed to Solomon Kemp's tannery, in a tamarack swamp; but some arrangement had been made between Chandler and Eber Rice, and during part of the time many of the men slept in Rice's Tavern. A few Canadians and five men from across the border joined the invaders here. Edward Seymour, formerly of Vaughan Township, later stated at Morreau's trial that he had been forced, while at Manchester, N.Y., to accompany four armed men who were bound for Upper Canada. This group went to Cayuga Creek, crossed to Buckhorn Island, and then rowed over above Chippewa. Proceeding into the woods they removed the next night to a barn a mile south of Rice's Tavern, and thence to Winchester's Woods, where they came upon the main expedition, which was then being provisioned by Aaron Winchester. Word was brought by these men that General Donald McLeod was on Navy Island and would soon bring over 300 reinforcements.

The Patriots, or as Sir George Arthur termed them, 'these atrocious banditti', had now been nine days in Upper Canada without having committed any serious act of violence, but the decisive hour had come. Morreau and a few others wanted to give up the invasion as useless, but Jacob Beemer and Dr. Wilson led a majority in favour of action,—'having come to Canada to fight, they would not return without striking a blow',—and it was decided to attack a party of Lancers who had been posted in the village of St. Johns to be on the look-out for them. Morreau thereupon resigned the leadership but accompanied the raiders as a private, and the three detachments were placed under Beemer, Alexander McLeod, and Lalor (or Lalande). Beemer's party proceeded to rob Abraham Overholt, a man of ninety years, of $1,000, and his son Martin of $300, the family being obnoxious not only as Tories but because the elder Overholt had served in the Revolutionary War in the Hessian contingent of Burgoyne's army, and later in Butler's Rangers.

After this outrage Beemer's detachment joined the other two at the school-house a mile from the village. The third division was then posted in a hollow near Davis's, while the other two attacked Osterhout's Tavern, where seven Lancers were stationed. The invaders opened fire on the building; then they brought straw and set fire to it, thus smoking out the occupants and forcing them to surrender. It is suggested that a large number of Canadian citizens were engaged in this attack and then left the party, but

THE SHORT HILLS AND ST. CLAIR RAIDS 107

this impression probably arose from the confusion of a night attack. Linus Miller says that they numbered forty-nine at the time, so that only fifteen joined after they entered the province.

Accompanied by their prisoners the Patriot force returned to the woods, where a dispute arose over what treatment should be accorded the captives. Beemer appears to have been the greatest villain[3] in the party, and was bent on hanging them. Morreau and Miller, however, interfered in their behalf. The latter says that he acted under the authority conferred upon him by General McLeod and placed Beemer under arrest, at the same time delivering a lengthy oration condemning his actions. Some of the plunder was then returned and the lancers freed 'on parole' upon taking an oath of Miller's composition. The party was once more placed in charge of Beemer, for Miller now considered it advisable to 'resign' his command and make every effort to get out of the country—as, indeed, they all did.

As the raiders had thus attracted attention to themselves they were soon being pursued. The first to be captured was Chandler, who had left the rest to obtain a supply of food. An officer of the Lancers states that he saw him running in the valley and sent three men after him. Cornet Heath was mounted, but when his horse became mired he leapt off and followed Chandler on foot into the swamp.

'He was armed with a rifle when Mr. Heath rushed in on him and threw him down, when he proved to be the notorious Chandler, colonel and commissary-general to the rebels, who had arrived the night before from the States, fulfilling the saying of his family, to whom he wrote stating that he would "arrive with Lord Durham, when they would have everything their own way". Unfortunately Mr. Heath lost both his pistols (and one of his scales) where his horse swamped, else I would not have had the trouble of bringing him in a prisoner to you.'[4]

Chandler is said to have been defiant and to have expressed regret that he did not shoot Heath—as well as all the Lancers.

The rest of the invaders immediately retreated. Edward Seymour stated that they went up Canborough Road to the Narrows of the Chippewa, and thence through the woods to about three miles above Smithville, where they separated. It was then every man for himself, and unnecessary arms were abandoned. James W. Doan said that a considerable number of muskets were

[3]'That is the man who brought me to this situation', said Morreau as Beemer entered Niagara jail.
[4]Report of James Magrath from Battle-ground Inn, June 21, 1838, to Colonel Townshend. Chandler, however, had been in the raid from the start and informed the members that 800 Canadians would rise to their support. The Toronto *Patriot* of June 26 reported that Heath had killed Chandler, but the wish was father to the thought. In the same issue the hope was expressed that all prisoners would be treated 'like mad dogs', and that none would escape 'the halter, the rifle, or the tomahawk'.

left near Bucklin's Tavern, Grimsby, the rest being thrown away as the fugitives hurried along.

Seymour and Grant, who were Canadians, McNulty, a Scotchman, and Kemp and Van Camp, described in the press as Americans, the latter of whom wore a Lancer's cloak, were captured in Gainsborough Township. Others were found lurking farther away from the scene of battle, some even on Gull Island in Mohawk Bay, near the mouth of the Grand River, where they were vainly awaiting a chance to escape across Lake Erie. Benjamin Wait, described in the Toronto *Patriot* as 'a Yankee Dandy, quite young', (although he was a Canadian), was captured with Mallory on the Philips farm, near Welland, and on his person were found muster rolls, letters, and maps of the Niagara district, as well as a blue and white silk banner upon which were two stars and the word LIBERTY.[5] Five others were reported taken in Hamilton dressed in Lancers' cloaks. Altogether thirty-nine men and two women were captured, five being Americans, and the rest either British by birth or naturalization or resident aliens; so that very few of the original force could have escaped[6] across the border. It was only with difficulty, wrote Sir George Arthur, that the militia were prevented from shooting the prisoners as bandits; and particularly some who defiantly threw down the Lancers' caps and said 'they would not wear the damned things'.

Linus Miller gives a long account of his experiences prior to capture. His narrative is characterized by long interludes of pious and philosophical reflection upon the beauties of nature, his own misfortunes, and the depressed state of liberty in general. These serve but to confuse the issue and obscure the realities of the situation. As he hid in the forest, for example, he was soon overtaken—not by the militia—but by sleep, sweet and refreshing, which 'soon bound my spirit in her silken chain, and its tabernacle of clay feasted upon the luxury of rest'. In the morning he milked a cow to obtain a little refreshment and called upon a friend in a neighbouring village. As the place was full of militia he swaggered about,[7] asking how many 'scoundrel rebels' had been taken.

[5]Letters addressed to the 'Patriot Camp' were also found in the woods. Some were evidently forged to get certain inhabitants into trouble. Many years later Wait called upon William Bunce, one of his captors, and got his rifle back.

[6]Among those implicated in supporting the invaders were Alonzo Merriman, Aaron Winchester, David Jennings, Chester Jillet, and Thomas Lambert, all of Pelham Township. They reached the United States and were included in the list of those attainted of high treason. A letter of William R. Lount to Mackenzie shows that he was a member of the expedition and was successful in evading capture. His information about the battle does not agree with other accounts, particularly where he says that several Lancers were shot to death and one hanged to a tree.

[7]Compare his alleged earlier activities in Hamilton, page 182. At his trial it was stated that Miller tried to escape dressed as a Lancer and mounted on one of their horses.

The friend to whom he went for shelter was a magistrate, but as he was under suspicion he could do nothing for him; so 'whistling *God Save the Queen'*, Miller again passed through the soldiery and hid in a hole under some large logs.

When, driven by hunger, he crawled out and sought refuge at a farm-house, the sentries of the militia had been called in. In the absence of their elders the children gave him a meal and permitted him to shave. He returned to the forest, where he was seen and pursued by cavalrymen. In the morning he secured food at another house, but lost no time in once more taking to the woods:

'Finding it difficult to get through a large swamp which lay in my way, I was foolish enough to risk travelling about three miles in the road. I had passed the swamp and in five minutes more should have entered the forest again which extended to the house of my friend, when a lieutenant and subaltern officer belonging to the enemy's cavalry suddenly made their appearance from a hill in the road. . . I turned carelessly aside, got over the fence into an adjoining field, and waited for the two gents to pass. . . They rode slowly along until within twenty-five yards and then charged upon me with as much energy as would have served to rout a host of the enemy—shouting, "Surrender or die!" Not intending to do either I ran across the field to the bush.'

Miller says he was well ahead of his pursuers when his strength failed, and he could not climb the last fence between himself and the swamp, so he felt for his pistols, thinking to sell his life dearly, but they had fallen through a hole in his breeches! There was nothing left but surrender, but it is suggested that his swashbuckling attitude almost saved him. He said that he was an American traveller, and no less than three sets of magistrates in as many villages refused to interfere with such an important personage! Finally, word came to St. Catharines to forward all suspects to Drummondville, and so by a mere thread was Linus Miller reserved for the vengeance of the Canadian Government. And in spite of his pretended unconcern he does admit that 'my neck began to feel somewhat uncomfortable'.

At the Pavilion Hotel lancers and others who supposedly owed their lives to Miller besieged him with 'protestations of sorrow', 'tortured' his hands with 'warm squeezes and shakes', and 'inundated' his ears with 'eternal gratitude'. But Miller was soon locked up in jail at Niagara, with every indication of a speedy trial and execution.

Morreau, thirty-five years old and 'of a fine, commanding figure and gentlemanly manners', made a determined effort to escape but was captured by a farmer named Farr:

'In the hope of escape Moreau swam Black Creek, and was found in a state of great exhaustion by a lone loyal Scotsman, who bound him and brought him in his waggon to the Pavillion at the Falls, where to his surprise and doubtless joy, he found he was entitled to £500, which we heartily hope may prove the foundation of the future opulence of his family.'

He seems to have been a man of some spirit, for when he was given a glass of wine as he was being conducted through Queenston he drank it off to the toast, 'May Canada never become quiet until the American eagle floats on the Heights of Queenston!' He was sentenced to death,[8] and his execution was carried out by Sheriff Alexander Hamilton. The *Quebec Gazette* gave a flippant account of the event:

'Moreau, the Yankee Land-Pirate, was executed at Niagara on Monday last. Owing to a want of the necessary precaution in securing Mr. Ketch, who was a coloured man, beforehand, that sensitive functionary bolted; and, it is said, narrowly escaped with his life; and what is very unusual, Mr. Sheriff Hamilton was obliged to *execute* his own duty in *propria persona*—and it is said that duty was WELL DONE!'

Seventeen others, including Miller, whose lawyer put in a defence of insanity,[9] were also found guilty and sentenced to death, which in all cases but one was commuted to transportation to Van Diemen's Land. Sir George Arthur wrote to Lord Glenelg after Morreau's execution that the Executive Council considered Beemer's case quite the worst, and planned to leave him for execution while commuting the death sentences of the others to transportation for life; but the intervention of Lord Durham saved him, and probably also Wait, Chandler, and Miller. Erastus Warner, sentenced to death, received a commutation to fourteen years' transportation but was subsequently released, probably because of ill-health resulting from a severe wound.[10]

The suggested plan of invading the western counties, together with an expected escape to that region of certain of the Short Hills raiders who had lived there, led to a careful watch in those districts. Jacob Beemer was captured in the vicinity of Brantford, placed in jail in London, and thence forwarded to Niagara for trial. Dr. Wilson, a tall, thin man with a large

[8]Before the prisoners were tried they were taken to Toronto on the steamer *Experiment* and kept in jail there over the Fourth of July, apparently in the expectation that there might be a border raid to release them. See appendix L(1) for a list of prisoners and their disposition.

[9]Evidence was given at his trial by his brother, William G. Miller, that his 'mind was affected from childhood'; while his companions stated that he was continually talking to himself and making 'absurd gestures'. Miller himself states that he had had a mental derangement a few months earlier.

[10]Several letters written by Warner to his mother are in the possession of descendants in Fort Frances, Ontario. In one, dated at Fort Henry, February 12, 1839, he stated that he and John Brown were the only Short Hills prisoners remaining there. A letter written from Kingston to Mrs. Permelia Warner, November 9, 1838, by Maria Wait, and a copy of one from Lord Durham's secretary informing Mrs. Warner that her son's death sentence 'will not be put into execution,' are in the same collection. Warner had contracted tuberculosis, and died soon after his release from Fort Henry. He was buried in the Soper family burying-ground, four and a half miles west of Port Hope. See also letters, appendix L(2) and (3).

THE SHORT HILLS AND ST. CLAIR RAIDS 111

Roman nose, also got away from the Niagara district, and it was expected that he would make for the vicinity of his old home. A contemporary letter indicates that the authorities were making every effort to apprehend Wilson:

'He was last seen in the Grand River Swamp and is supposed to be somewhere in this District. I have sent to Norwich in search of him, & the Bearer Mr. R. Warren Dy. Shff. has a warrant to apprehend him—as he may probably be lurking about Sparta... It is also suspected that many of the others may flee in this direction... Wilson is supposed to have a good deal of money with him. About $1,000 were stolen by the rebels from two persons in the Niagara District.'

The expectation proved correct, for Dr. Wilson was shortly arrested in Norwich. He was taken to Doyle's Tavern, Burford, and the next day placed in a one-horse wagon which was to carry him to London jail, two bailiffs, Sumner and Bennett, accompanying on horseback. Near the Caufield farm, ten miles from Burford, the party was fired upon from an ambuscade, and after a sudden attack the prisoner had to be released to a group of men and with them made for the woods. Two of the ringleaders, Enos and John (Job) Scott, were later captured, and they confessed that nineteen persons had pledged themselves to rescue Wilson, but as he drew near under the escort of the Sheriff's officers twelve of the party fled. John Scott further confessed that he shot one of the horses and took the pistols from Bennett and gave them to Wilson. Shortly afterwards the doctor was retaken in the home of Richard McKenny, Malahide Township, and with the two Scotts was soon held under close guard in Toronto.[11]

Thoroughly aroused by these activities, the militia of the region were quick to rise to the occasion. Colonel Whitehead of Burford led one group of sixty-five volunteers and eighty Indians, while other companies swelled the total to some 500. From enforcing law and order these loyalists soon developed into an army of rebel-hunters, claiming to have discovered secret societies everywhere, and 'a most desperate and bloody plot for a general rising and massacre to take place on the night of the 3rd of July'. When they closed their hunt the indications are that everyone had a thoroughly enjoyable time:

'The Village of Otterville, known as Cromwell's Mills, a most Radical nest, was taken possession of in the name of Her Majesty Queen Victoria,

[11] There was an epidemic of white horses among leaders in the Rebellion. Wilson is said to have been traced through his, while both Mackenzie and Van Egmond rode white horses at Montgomery's, and Dr. Duncombe fled from Norwich on his favourite, 'White Pigeon'. Dr. Wilson must have been taken to the Garrison or the Legislative Council Chamber, for he is not recorded in the 'Register of Prisoners'; though Enos and John Scott, Ebenezer Wilcox, Robert Cook, and Alvan Leader entered Toronto jail at the time. The Scotts were taken back to London jail on September 13, while the others were bailed the same month. There is no indication of Wilson's disposition, nor information as to his later life.

the Union Jack raised high in the air, three hearty cheers given, and the ceremony of consecrating the ground as British territory gone through; after which the officers accompanying the expedition sat down to a sumptuous dinner, where the greatest hilarity and good cheer presided, and many a loyal toast was given on the occasion—much to the astonishment of the village *natives*, many of them having never before seen a British flag.'

There is considerable corroboratory evidence that an elaborate scheme of revolt had been set on foot by Henry S. Handy, 'Commander-in-Chief of the Sons of Liberty', and that it was expected to include some 20,000 Canadians from the Gulf of St. Lawrence to the western boundary. Agents commissioned by Handy were sent out to initiate members, and the general plan in centres of population was to have a person stationed in each square mile of territory with power to confer the rank of captain upon those in his locality whom he considered suitable for the purposes of the secret army of revolt. The members who composed the lodges elected their colonels, and Handy was to be kept in constant communication with the entire system by one hundred spies and couriers, each of whom had a beat of ten miles which he was to cover daily, communicating with the next man on either side and so indirectly with the commander-in-chief in Michigan. The revolution was to be initiated by the capture of Windsor, upon which the couriers were to spread the news of the uprising as speedily as possible, and the members in each locality were to seize all available arms and supplies and attack and fortify some place of strategic importance.

These well-laid plans, if they were actually as elaborate as projected, were upset by the Short Hills raid and by two attacks in the St. Clair region. A raider named Baker gathered a band of some forty freebooters along the Black River and entered Upper Canada at Sarnia, pillaging a store and a house or two before being driven out. George Henry wrote from the St. Clair Mission that a few Indians 'drove the unfortunate fellows over again, and chased them on the other side'. The incident figured also in official despatches, being referred to in exaggerated terms by Sir George Arthur, who wrote that about 300 men had raided Nugent's Inn, River St. Clair, attacking Mr. Govin's store; but ten days later he reported that not more than a hundred had crossed, that twelve or thirteen had been arrested by the American authorities on their return, and that he would protest to Washington if they were not punished. Another group of 'pirates' crossed to Bear Creek, marching towards Delaware and releasing several Patriots from jail, while a third detachment sailed a sloop to Goderich and robbed stores before leaving. It was feared that an attack upon

THE SHORT HILLS AND ST. CLAIR RAIDS   113

Penetanguishene was planned, but nothing came of it, the empty sloop being later captured by the American steamer *Gratiot*, while six of the men were taken by another steamship, the *Governor Marcy*. Lieutenant Elmsley of the Royal Navy captured six of the Bear Creek force on Lake Erie, and several of those who crossed at Sarnia were taken prisoners by Indians, one of them, Spencer, being released after informing upon his fellows. Horace Cooley, described in the Toronto *Patriot* as a resident of Upper Canada who was found to be the 'bearer of despatches from the pirates in Michigan to those in Canada', was transported to Van Diemen's Land for his part in the disturbance.[12]

The result of these raids, as was anticipated by McLeod when he sent Linus Miller to the Short Hills, was the defeat of the plan for a widespread rising on July 4. The St. Clair invasion led to the arousing of General Brady's American forces, the placing of a new and stronger guard at the Detroit arsenal, from which, with the connivance of guards, was to have been obtained a large supply of arms for the Windsor invasion, and the collapse of the entire scheme on the day previous to its inception. Similarly the Short Hills raid, for which Chandler and Alexander McLeod are blamed in Patriot correspondence, rendered futile the exertions of two months.

12See appendix M for a list of prisoners and their disposition.

BIBLIOGRAPHY

The official sources on the Short Hills and St. Clair raids consist of the despatches of Sir George Arthur to Lord Glenelg, June 30, July 1 and 10, 1838, with enclosures, which include an excellent account of the Short Hills raid compiled by the Honourable W. H. Draper. The report of James Magrath to Colonel Townshend, dated at Battle-ground Inn, June 21, gives many details of value. Lount's and Chandler's (?) letters are in the Lindsey Papers, while other correspondence relative to the raid is found in the Alexander Hamilton Papers, Public Archives of Canada. The letters of Warner and Maria Wait, referred to in note 10, are in possession of Miss Loy Neads, Fort Frances, Ontario. Many documents are appended to Tiffany, as above, and to Ermatinger's *Talbot Regime*, appendix F; while still others, as well as newspaper accounts, are found in General Cruikshank's two articles, 'The Insurrection in the Short Hills', and 'A Twice-Told Tale', Ontario Historical Society, VIII and XXIII, respectively. The records of the trials, and particularly those of Morreau and Miller, *Imperial Blue Books*, X 329 *et seq.*, are illuminating. Miller's account in his *Notes of an Exile* is in general corroborated by other sources, though he was frequently subject to flights of imagination. The execution of Morreau is reported in detail in the *Quebec Gazette*, August 10, and the *Niagara Reporter* of the third. General Handy's plans are outlined in Arthur's despatches, while Handy's private papers are the basis of a similar account in Lindsey, II 192-5. The following newspapers contain material of some value: New York *Journal of Commerce*, New York *Commercial Advertiser*, Lewiston *Telegraph*, Toronto *Patriot*, *Cobourg Star*, *Niagara Chronicle*, and *Quebec Gazette*. Many details of the excitement in the Western District are given in 'Pirate Doings on the River St. Clair', Toronto *Patriot*, July 13, 1838. 'Incidents of the Short Hills Affair', and other articles by Harvey Reid, published in the *Jackson Republican*, Maquoketa, Iowa, 1902-04, are of value particularly for their information relative to refugees from the Short Hills region, many of whom went to Iowa when the 'Black Hawk Purchase' was opened for settlement. After his escape from Van Diemen's Land in 1842, Chandler also settled in Maquoketa, where he was long called 'the General'.

CHAPTER XII

JOHN MONTGOMERY AND THE JAIL DELIVERY FROM FORT HENRY

'JOHN MONTGOMERY, you have been found guilty of high treason,' said Chief Justice John Beverley Robinson. 'Have you anything to say before the judgment of the court is passed upon you?'
'I have,' replied Montgomery bitterly. 'I have not had a fair trial. There are witnesses here who have sworn my life away. The perjured evidence of William Gymer, William Crew, and David Bridgeford will haunt them in after years. These perjurers will never die a natural death; and when you, sir, and the jury shall have died and perished in hell's flames, John Montgomery will yet be living on Yonge Street.'[1]

Montgomery had been a prominent Reformer; he had signed most of the Patriot declarations, and supported Mackenzie until a few weeks before the outbreak. Then, according to his relatives, he disagreed with him when Mackenzie advocated direct action at the meeting in Doel's Brewery in November. His tavern was presumably chosen as a place of concentration on account of its size and proximity to Toronto, rather than because of its owner. There is evidence that he quarrelled with Mackenzie during the occupation, but he took some share in the provisioning of the men at the tavern.

A short time prior to the loyalist attack, Montgomery's wife and six children took refuge at the Murray home, where they were subsequently protected from the militia by a detachment sent there on the Lieutenant-Governor's order. Montgomery had meanwhile spent most of his time carrying furnishings from the tavern to his new home, and at no time was he in arms or drilling men, or participating actively in the rebel arrangements. During the battle he went to William Snider's, but he found that he was nevertheless included among the leaders.

The evidence at his trial was generally corroborative of his claim that he took no active part. Linfoot, his tenant and a Tory, was somewhat non-committal but generally favourable. Amelia Gray, housemaid, said that Mackenzie used abusive language towards him, and she was corroborated by many others in her belief that he was not a party to the revolt. The most remarkable evidence was given by William Ketchum, who owned a farm near Montgomery's and described a visit to the tavern on December 5.

[1] An obituary notice in the Picton *Times* of January 29, 1880, is the basis of the alleged address to the court, which had been one of his favourite stories as an old man. The prophecy was partially fulfilled, for one man shot himself and another cut his throat, and Montgomery outlived judge, jurors, witnesses, and prosecutors.

Courtesy Burton Historical Collection, Detroit   W. J. Bennett, after a sketch by F. K. Grain
Detroit from The Ferry (Windsor) in 1837
Several Patriot invasions against Windsor and Amherstburg were organized in Detroit

Courtesy Mrs. Ida Sinclair, Toronto
Colonel John Anderson and John Montgomery in 1875
Two of the twelve Patriots who escaped from Fort Henry

Courtesy University of Toronto
Courtyard of Fort Henry, Kingston

He had a talk with Montgomery about various aspects of the rebel occupation and plans, but he gave no information to the authorities when he returned to the city. Because of this he was severely criticized by the Chief Justice, who said it was sufficient to convict him of high treason. Ketchum excused his conduct by saying he was friendly to the Reformers but had decided to take no part on either side.[2]

It was brought out in Montgomery's favour that he had served in the militia in the War of 1812, and that a brother was on the loyalist side during the revolt. The jury, consequently, added a recommendation of mercy to their verdict of guilty. On April 10 he was sentenced to be executed fourteen days later. The Reverend John Doel recalled that when he was in Toronto jail, 'poor Montgomery would sit for hours sying and brooding over his troubles—he was often heard to exclaim, they will surely hang me as they did poor Lount and Mathews'. But his sentence was commuted to transportation for life, and on May 25 he was among some twenty-five prisoners who were removed to Fort Henry on the *Commodore Barrie*.

When Montgomery first arrived at Fort Henry he had some hope of clemency, but later, with a large group of the prisoners, turned his thoughts to the possibility of escape. A committee was formed to investigate and make arrangements. They had learned from a friendly Orangeman, John Orgen, who was employed about the fort, that there was a subterranean passage under the adjoining casement, and that if they could get into the next room they might easily climb over the inner wall into the ditch. Orgen explored the passage and found that all they had to do was to cut a hole through the wall and then a like passage through a door into the gun-room. By a code of signs he gave them the news daily and furnished them with a pointed piece of flat bar-iron about a foot in length and a large spike-nail.[3]

The stage was well set, for the mortar loosened during the work was burned in the stove or carried outside in the pockets of the men and buried in a wood-pile, while the stones were carefully numbered and hidden under the bed. Some of the furniture was placed in front of the aperture, and the noise of the work was

[2] Apparently frightened by the judge's remarks, Ketchum, who was a son of Jesse Ketchum and had in February been bailed after a day in jail, fled the country, but he was later pardoned.

[3] Stephen Brophy, one of those who escaped, was careful to state that there was 'no assistance from any person', and that both implements were picked up on the parade ground. Other sources indicate, however, that a workman had been furnished with a plan 'drawn by someone who had access to the Engineer department'; and that the setting-bar used 'had been recently pointed by a blacksmith in the works'. John Orgen was arrested after the break; while the keeper, 'Br. Ashley', is referred to as 'much sensured' and 'in confinement', in a letter from James Rorison to Egerton Ryerson, July 30, 1838.

smothered by two men, who, says Montgomery, 'apparently for their amusement were with shovel and tongs beating the stove with all their might, and eliciting thereby roars of laughter from their companions'. Montgomery, meanwhile, was reading the Bible and exhorting his fellow-prisoners to give over their unseasonable mirth and reflect upon their serious situation.

Between Tuesday and Saturday a hole large enough to crawl through was made, and that night, August 4, three men examined the passage. One of them, Stephen Brophy, describes it in considerable detail:

'At six o'clock, a dark lantern being prepared, I had the pleasure of passing through, followed by two others of our party, entering the trap door and descending a narrow subterraneous passage by a ladder of some eight or ten steps placed under the trap door; following this passage we ascended to the level of the room we left by a ladder placed at the opposite end of the passage, and entered the works in the outer wall; thence through a narrow passage, and four small rooms, all studded in front with port holes for musketry—thence by a short passage turning at right angles and ascending a few steps into the gun rooms, from whence we were enabled to survey the ditch and low point referred to in the outer wall... On raising the shutter an entrenchment fifteen feet deep was perceptible on the outside... Not having the means of descending into this entrenchment we returned and reported progress.'

The prisoners were satisfied that the scheme was practicable, and on Sunday they urged the keeper, Ashley, who had been married only two or three days before, to accompany his wife to church instead of giving them their daily airing. When he was gone they hung up blankets, ostensibly to keep out mosquitoes but in reality to screen the final preparations, and set to work enlarging the passage and making a scaling ladder from the boards of their bedsteads. At half-past ten at night all was ready for the jail delivery. When the guard beat the evening tattoo and descended from the ramparts the prisoners commenced their escape, all in their stocking feet. When they reached the sally-port they lay down in the ditch until an advance guard located the most suitable place to scale the twenty-eight foot wall. Picking a spot about forty feet from one of the sentries, they huddled together in silence and waited for the moon to go down.

An unfortunate accident to Montgomery greatly increased the difficulties of escape. Being in the lead he fell head foremost into one of the pits which were cut to a depth of ten feet out of solid rock; but a flash of lightning showed the others his predicament and saved them from following him. They helped him out, and with difficulty he mounted the ladder and crossed the wall. Fearful that in their attempt to aid him the others would be retaken, he begged of them to leave him to his fate and save them-

MONTGOMERY AND THE JAIL DELIVERY 117

selves. 'We will escape or die together' was the answer. Edward Theller describes what followed:

'As Mr. Parker was ascending, the sentinel cried out "Who comes there?" in a loud sharp voice; at which he, doubtless imagining it to be him that the sentinel challenged when it was the advancing relief-guard, became somewhat frightened. He placed himself beside Montgomery and the others on the top of the wall; and from that time he was seen no more by his comrades, who could not know how or where he had gone.

'From the glacis where they then were is a gradual descent towards the water; and when they gained the beach they called over their number and found all but Mr. Parker present. Fearful that some accident had happened—that he had fallen into the ditch—Colonel Brophy and Mr. Morden went back and examined over the ground they had passed, but could not find him. This was regretted the more, as from his long residence in Kingston he knew the country and its inhabitants, while the others were strangers.'

A point about 100 rods north of the fort had been reached at the time, and the party moved off rapidly on the return of Brophy and Morden, though Montgomery had to be carried most of the way. The river road to Gananoque was reached just as the guards were crying out 'All's well!' at half-past twelve. At daylight they found they had covered eight miles, but as they knew that patrols would immediately be sent in pursuit they kept to the woods. They divided into two groups of five and one of four, Brophy, Chase, and Morden volunteering to remain with Montgomery in his crippled and almost helpless condition. Yet, as it happened, this group first reached the American shore. That evening they approached the shore of the St. Lawrence. Morden and Chase discovered a canoe, but they lay low all the next day, and Wednesday night they set out for Long Island. Rails from a fence served as oars, and they were soon investigating the possibilities of a portage, for they feared capture by armed boats if they continued further by water.

At first they believed they were on American territory, but their mistake was soon apparent and they had also reason to believe that the inhabitants could not be trusted. With great pain and in a state of exhaustion, they at length succeeded in launching their boat on the south shore of the island and proceeded towards what they thought was the mainland. But they were on Carleton Island in Canadian territory, and had once more to embark. Almost famished, for they had had but two biscuits a day since leaving the fort, the men were too weak to row their craft against the wind to Cape Vincent, and were forced to put ashore again. This time they were overjoyed to learn that they were in the United States; and for a dollar and a half they obtained conveyance to Farren's Tavern. 'Great sympathy and attention were shown us,' says Montgomery. 'A public dinner, largely attended, was given in our honour'—a very different reception from that accorded their fellow-Patriots when they arrived in Van Diemen's Land.

The other parties[4] reached the United States within a day or so, joining Montgomery's group at Watertown; but three men, John G. Parker, Leonard Watson, and William Stockdale, had been captured. Parker had reached a point six miles below Kingston; Watson was three or four miles beyond, while Stogdill, as Mackenzie calls him, was first reported to have crossed the frontier. The Kingston *Herald* learned that a corporal of the 83rd Regiment was Parker's[5] captor; that he had been offered $900 to let him go but 'nobly refused the bribe'; and that consequently a subscription was being taken up to reward him. His arrival at the fort is said to have been 'the first intelligence that the garrison received of the escape'. Watson remained in the woods with the others for two days; but, becoming exhausted from hunger and fatigue, he wandered away and was captured by a farmer who thought he looked suspicious. On being asked if he was not one of the escaped prisoners from the fort, the old man, in a strong Yorkshire accent and with the wild and reckless daring of a man who had made up his mind to something desperate, cried: 'Give me something to eat; and when I am refreshed I will tell you all about myself'. This was done, and when his appetite was appeased he told them his name, but would say nothing of his companions.[6]

Those who had succeeded in gaining American soil[7] were kept

---

[4]*Mackenzie's Gazette* of August 11 indicates that the last group—Wilson Read, and Thomas and Michael Shepard—were expected to reach Watertown on the evening of the sixth. John Stewart stated that his group were rowed across the river at Brockville by a landlord who took them for smugglers.

[5]Born at Westchester, New Hampshire, Parker was a merchant in Kingston and Hamilton and was the first prominent rebel suspect apprehended. His capture is described in the *Patriot* extra of December 6, 1837. Some of his letters were intercepted and showed treasonable designs, while others were seized after a 'prodigious struggle' with his wife, who was trying to burn them. The *Quebec Gazette* of August 13 states that he was treasurer of the group which escaped, and rewarded generously those who aided. Parker was later removed to England with others who had petitioned to escape trial, and he was released by British courts. (See chapter XIX). Upon returning to America he became a grocer in Rochester, where he died in 1879, aged eighty-three years. A local historian refers to him as 'one of our most honored and valuable citizens'. (Jenny Parker, *Rochester*, 250.)

[6]Leonard Watson had lived near Montgomery's Tavern. In the reminiscences of Betty Duffield the riddling and plundering of the Watson home is described. Peter Watson fled to Darlington, and Betty took money there to facilitate his escape. He shortly reached the United States. Leonard Watson was taken to England with Parker and others and released at the same time.

[7]Those who escaped with Montgomery were Edward Kennedy of West Gwillimbury, John Anderson of Toronto, Thomas and Michael Shepard, Yonge Street, John Marr of Brock, Walter Chase and Stephen Brophy, captured on the *Anne*, Gilbert Morden and Thomas Tracy, Lloydtown, Wilson Read of Hope Township, and John Stewart of Esquesing. Stewart was captain of a force of sixty which started for Montgomery's, but most deserted and only five were left when they reached the Green Bush Hotel. Stewart was later arrested at Richmond Hill. He spent his later life as joint owner of a foundry in Paisley, where he died in 1899.

MONTGOMERY AND THE JAIL DELIVERY 119

in hiding by well-wishers until it was known that the Governor of New York State refused to surrender them to the Canadian Government. Thereupon they went on their way rejoicing, and had their brief moment of prominence in the public gaze. Montgomery settled in Rochester, where he was knocked down by a team of horses and his skull fractured. He fully recovered and opened a boarding-house,[8] which became a rendezvous for Patriot refugees and sympathizers. In 1843 he was pardoned and returned to Toronto, where he again became a tavern-keeper, at first in the central part of the city, and then in later years on the site of the old tavern on upper Yonge Street. Some years later he was appointed postmaster of Davidtown. Eventually he received partial compensation under the terms of the Rebellion Losses Act for the burning of his old hotel. The latter part of his long life was spent at the home of his son in Barrie, and we catch a glimpse of him on the occasion of a visit from Colonel John Anderson of Florida, his companion through many vicissitudes:

'There are very few Canadians but who have heard of John Montgomery, a hero of Canada's troublous times in 1837, who has been for several years past a resident of Barrie. The old man is now in his 92nd year, and though physically decrepit he is mentally as active as ever, and upon the theme of the "Rebellion" he discourses with an enthusiasm that seems to kindle in him new life, lifting the mantle of his old age and reproducing the active man of forty years ago. A few days since he was visited by Colonel John Anderson, now a resident of Florida, and who after an absence of forty years came back to grasp the hand of his old compatriot. Colonel Anderson is about ten years younger than his old friend and is hale and hearty as a man of fifty. He is a well-to-do farmer and owns broad acres in both Florida and Wisconsin. The meeting between these two old "companions in arms" was as affecting as might be expected between men so identified with each other in the history of their country, and day after day was spent in reviving, amid tears, the incidents of their arrest, trial, sentence to death, imprisonment, escape, flight, and final pardon. On Thursday morning parting took place, probably the last on this earth between these two, and Colonel John Anderson started for his southern home; while Mr. John Montgomery resumed his favourite easy chair in the quietude of his son's domicile—to dream over the re-furbished associations of his former life.'[9]

John Montgomery died on October 31, 1879, within a few weeks of his ninety-sixth birthday.

[8]The Rochester directory for 1838 indicates that Montgomery was boarding at the North American hotel. A few months later he opened an establishment of his own, for Mackenzie's *Caroline Almanack*, 124, carries the following notice: 'John Montgomery, Boarding House and Grocery and Provision Store, Main Street, Rochester'. In 1841 he was listed as a grocer at 85 Main Street.

[9]From a clipping from a Barrie newspaper, 1875, on the back of a photograph of the two men. Montgomery eventually received under the terms of the Rebellion Losses Act $3,500 compensation for materials taken and used by the government—not for the loss of his building. Postal Station K is now on the site, and until 1936 included parts of Montgomery's second tavern.

BIBLIOGRAPHY

The official record of the trial of Montgomery is in State Book K, Public Archives of Canada. The trial was reported at length in the *Christian Guardian* of April 11 and the *Patriot* of the thirteenth. Mackenzie comments upon the jurors and informers in his *Caroline Almanack*, 37; while Mrs. O. B. Sheppard, granddaughter of Montgomery, records the family traditions in her 'Incidents in the Life of John Montgomery during the Rebellion of 1837-38', York Pioneer and Historical Society, 1927. Doel's 'Recollections' is in the Archives of Ontario. The escape from Fort Henry is recorded in three accounts: (1) that of Stephen B. Brophy, 'Colonel of Engineers in the Patriot Service of Canada', whose 'Narrative of the Escape of the State Prisoners from Fort Henry' is much the best. It is reprinted from the Watertown *North American* in the Toronto *Patriot* of August 21, 1838; (2) E. A. Theller's account in his *Canada in 1837-8*, which is apparently based upon conversation with Brophy as well as his narrative; (3) Montgomery's shorter description appended to Lindsey, II 369-73. Supplementary comment, and information gleaned from participants or accomplices, appears in the *Quebec Gazette*, *Quebec Mercury*, Kingston *Upper Canada Herald*, *Mackenzie's Gazette*, Toronto *Patriot*, and Toronto *Mirror*. Rorison's letter is in the Victoria College Library, Toronto. The Duffield reminiscences are in Lizars, 361-3. Supplementary information about John Stewart is from his reminiscences as recorded by A. E. Byerly in 1899 in the London *Free Press*, and quoted in the *Paisley Advocate*, July 24, 1935. The account of the meeting of Anderson and Montgomery in 1875 is from a clipping from a Barrie newspaper, pasted on the back of the photograph of the men taken on that occasion.

CHAPTER XIII

EDWARD THELLER AND THE CELEBRATED ESCAPE FROM THE
CITADEL OF QUEBEC

THE second notable escape which served to keep the Patriot agitation in the public eye during the lull between the Short Hills raid and the extensive invasions by the Hunters' Lodges was a remarkable break from the Citadel of Quebec. When Dr. Theller was captured in the armed schooner *Anne* he was imprisoned in Fort Malden over night, and thence removed to London. Ten wagon-loads comprised this cavalcade, six of them containing two Patriots each and one three, together with four militiamen with loaded muskets and fixed bayonets. Three wagons were filled with soldiers, and in addition twelve of the St. Thomas volunteer cavalry rode ahead as scouts. The prisoners were not only fastened together but secured with ropes.

It took five days to reach London, where the prisoners were placed in small cells similar to those of Malden. Ten days later they were conveyed to Toronto by way of Brantford and Hamilton, avoiding the Dundas Road, which, says Theller,[1] 'lay through a thickly settled country of reformers'. Crowds of people were in the streets to see the curious procession enter the capital, and the captives were soon in the old jail at Toronto and Court Streets.

Theller was not indicted until he reached Toronto, whereupon he was supplied with a copy which domiciled him in Malden Township and recounted that, 'not having the fear of God before his eyes and instigated by the devil', he did 'traitorously assemble with wicked and evil designing men to the number of five hundred and upwards, armed with swords, pistols, muskets, cannon, dirks, bowie-knives, and other warlike weapons, and traitorously devised the death of Her Majesty the Queen'. Taking this document literally, Theller was highly amused. His trial took place on April 6, 1838, and his main plea was that, being an American citizen, he owed no allegiance to the throne, and that if he had committed any offence it 'was against the laws of nations' or contrary to those of the United States, in which case he should be tried either in England or the Republic. He records a lengthy

[1] Theller has been well described as 'a blustering, mendacious, yet withal courageous fellow, full of loquacity but greatly wanting in discretion'. He is said to have been prominent in a Free Love Association, but his wife came to Toronto jail to visit him, her expenses being paid by Buffalo sympathizers who also looked after their four children. His book, *Canada in 1837-8*, is neither well written nor reliable, but in general there is corroboration of his account of his own experiences.

and impassioned address which he made before the court, and states that the jury declared him guilty of treason 'if he is a British subject'; whereupon he was sentenced, according to his version, to be 'hanged and quartered and given to the surgeon for dissection'.

Theller describes in considerable detail the execution of Lount and Matthews, which he saw from his cell window; for the scaffold had been removed from the usual place and erected in the full gaze of the other prisoners to give them a foretaste of their punishment:

'At length the morning dawned, the hammering ceased, and there it stood, a finished work[2]—the two fatal nooses suspended from the beam which crossed the platform—and the executioner, having adjusted the ropes, fixing the drops, and eyeing the whole with the air of a connoisseur, preparatory to his departure to give the intelligence that the stage was ready, the actors in waiting, and the audience growing impatient.

'We were surprised by a knock at the door and by the voice of Lount calling me. . . He appeared firm and perfectly prepared for his doom, saying that this would be our last interview; . . and then, requesting us to look at him through the window when he should ascend the scaffold, bid us farewell forever! . . A few minutes afterwards we saw him and Matthews walk out with the white cap upon their heads and their arms pinioned, preceded by the sheriff and his deputy dressed in the official robes and with drawn swords, followed by two clergymen and a few of our prison guard. . . Lount looked up and bowed to us; then kneeling upon the trap underneath one of the nooses, the cord was placed about their necks by the executioner, and the cap pulled over their faces. One of the clergymen, Mr. Richardson, made a prayer, the signal was given by the sheriff, and in an instant these two heroic souls, the first martyrs to Canadian liberty, were ushered into eternity.'[3]

Theller received a respite on the day before his execution was to take place. He attributed his good fortune to the intervention of numerous fellow-Irishmen, but it was due more to a technical dispute over his citizenship, upon which it was considered that the authorities in England should adjudicate;[4] there was also a reaction after the execution of Lount and Matthews, leading to the commutation of several death sentences and the release of numer-

[2]Mackenzie says that Wardsworth's men refused to erect the scaffold, but Ritchie and Hill's carpenters 'very willingly did so', and he records the names of eight of them in his *Caroline Almanack*, 77. The gallows' yard and two cells adjoining the guardroom in the basement may still be seen in the remodelled building.

[3]Several well-signed petitions had been presented to secure commutation of their sentence, but without effect. It cannot be maintained, however, that the authorities were not legally justified in executing them, for both had been leaders, had held up the mails, and had indirectly caused the death of citizens. The execution of Lount, however, was particularly unfortunate and intensified the bitter feeling against the government. Egerton Ryerson considered that 'Sir Francis deserves impeachment just as much as Samuel Lount deserves execution. Morally speaking, I cannot but regard him as the more guilty culprit of the two'. See appendix K for supplementary material on the executions and the monuments, biographies by Mackenzie, and a letter to him from Mrs. Lount.

[4]Theller was a British subject according to English law at the time. The legal status of the American raiders was not clearly understood in Upper Canada, and the authorities were at first in doubt as to how they should treat them. See note 7, page 195, for a discussion of the subject.

From W. L. Mackenzie, *Caroline Almanack*

Execution of Lount and Matthews, April 12, 1838

ous Patriots who had languished in jail for many months. Theller and twenty-four others, chained in pairs, were shortly removed by wagon through crowded streets to the wharf, where they boarded the steamship *Commodore Barrie*. A plan to take possession of the boat was prevented, says Theller, by the cowardice of General Thomas Sutherland, and they arrived at Kingston without incident. Most of the Americans, however, after a night in Fort Henry, continued *via* the Rideau Canal to Montreal. There they remained overnight at the 'new jail', proceeding next morning by *calèche* and steamship to Quebec. A few hours later they passed through Prescott Gate between two lines of hostile citizens and entered the citadel.

The Fourth of July was not forgotten by these expatriated Americans. Colonel Dodge read the Declaration of Independence, Theller provided a lengthy oration in his usual flamboyant style, and 'the juice of the generous grape' was drunk with pleasure in 'the last stronghold of despotism that Britain held on this continent'.[5]

No sooner was this celebration over than five of the prisoners were planning an escape. Theller, having a lively imagination, goes into great detail about their various schemes, and one cannot but doubt the authenticity of many of the conversations which he records. But the escape was undoubtedly effected under great difficulties, and Theller describes vividly the intrigues and betrayals,

[5] A detailed account of the celebration, which included thirteen 'regular' and fourteen 'volunteer' toasts, is given by Sutherland in his *Loose Leaves*, 131-9. He thought it strange that it was permitted 'and the British Government paid the expense'. The fellow-prisoners of Dodge, Sutherland, and Theller were Pew, Partridge, Hull, Culver, Parker, Smith, and Thayer.

the treating of some guards and the drugging of others, and all the secret toil that was necessary to bring the plans to a successful consummation.

The circumstances, as well as Theller's statements, indicate direct aid from outside the walls and carelessness and gross neglect within. The prisoners were able to hold communication with sympathisers in the city, and a friend to whom they slipped a note brought not only the required tools, 'wrapped up in one of your *Gazettes*' (as Theller wrote William Lyon Mackenzie), but the promise of co-operation after the break. They prepared the aperture for their escape while the sentry stood near by. Talking, dancing, and singing smothered much of the noise of the saw, while the fifer of the schooner *Anne* did his share to increase the hullabaloo. But when all was in readiness they had to wait nearly six weeks for a stormy night suitable for the break.

Theller's account of the actual escape loses nothing in the telling. Somewhat corpulent, he squeezed through only by 'compressing my chest and scarifying my back and breast', and with the help of Partridge, who used his shoulder as a battering-ram. Lowering themselves by a sheet rope, they skirted the walls, keeping in the shade of the lamps which shed but a faint light near the doorways. The rain had stopped, but the wind, and the water dripping from the roof, smothered the sound of their footsteps. But an unfortunate accident almost led to their recapture at the outset:

'One by one we slowly moved along and got behind a small cook-house that was near, and which was to be the first rendezvous. While the last man was coming round he stumbled over a large tin pail that had been placed to catch the water under the spout, which made noise enough to create an alarm; and the attention of the sentinel on the wall above our room was directed to it. We watched his motions with anxiety. We could perceive him peering over the wall above, looking down where we were. We remained an instant motionless, afraid that we had been detected, when the sentinel beyond us challenged, "Who goes there?" Not a breath was uttered by us; and as he challenged again he was answered by the guard just emerging from beneath the gate, where the guard-house was: "Relief." . . . "Advance, relief, and give the countersign".'

Fortunately the noise made by Parker was laid to the approaching sentinels, who passed within a few feet of the fugitives—so close that their features could be seen by the light of the drummer's lantern. A moment later those relieved came over the same path, and then all was quiet. Passing onward on hands and knees, their escape was again jeopardized by Parker's clumsiness, but the sentinel nearest apparently attributed the clatter to prowling dogs.

Several sentinels had still to be passed, but they were at a greater distance, and the worst seemed to be over. They avoided another challenge and were soon on top of the wall. But not only was the promised aid from outside lacking, but one of the fugitives had tripped over a pile of lumber and once more aroused the guard:

'From where we stood we could plainly discern the whole commotion: the picket guard turning out; the officers, who had not arisen even at that time of night from their mess-table, also turning out to ascertain the cause of alarm; some buckling on their swords and other trappings, while others had run forward to the wood-pile. An artillery-man with his dog detected Parker,[6] and as soon as he was discovered by the light of a lantern the cry arose, "The American prisoners! The American prisoners escaping!" This shout added still more to the hubbub; many of them ran towards our late prison-room, while others dragged Parker away to the guard-room, and others began the search around to discover the rest of us.'

Dodge, meanwhile, was busy cutting the rope from a flag-pole, but the noise of the pulleys was too great, and it was hastily decided to take a chance on the forty-foot jump at the King's Bastion. Theller leapt first, landing on his feet on the solid rock of the ditch. The second descent was negotiated by the help of a cedar post and a rope, the last man being caught by his fellows below. Dodge, Culver, and Theller moved along painfully, assisted by Hull, who had escaped injury. Climbing the precipitous ascent to the glacis, they sat down for a moment's rest and observed torches flashing in every nook and cranny of the ramparts, with only the fifty-foot ditch between them and the garrison. Continuing downhill by a precipitous road which had been enclosed for a promenade, the fugitives passed through a turnstile and entered the streets of the Upper Town.

It was now immediately essential to locate the friends whose co-operation was to get them out of the city. Theller's knowledge of French was put to good use, nor was his usual swashbuckling attitude a detriment under the circumstances. 'We passed the sentry at Sir John Colborne's door, who challenged us,' he boasts. 'We advanced boldly, and he, mistaking us from our caps and cloaks to be some of his own officers, carried arms to us as we passed.' Proceeding through Hope Gate to the Lower Town they sought information from passers-by. A magistrate whom they inadvertently addressed promised not to inform upon them; while more definite directions from a workman led them to the home of friends. It was just in the nick of time, for the alarm having been given, all gates were shut and no one could get in or out until daylight. Soldiers and constables were scouring the streets in all

[6]This was R. G. Parker, brother of John G. who was recaptured after the break from Fort Henry. He was released the following spring and deported to the United States.

directions, 'rushing through the lanes like madmen, . . taking up everyone that was either tall or short—or who wore glasses, or who were blind—opening the coffins of the dead—examining all the old women they met with'. But Theller and Dodge were safely, if precariously, secreted.[7]

Few events in Quebec's history have aroused the same pitch of excitement. The drugged soldier, who slept for hours after the event, paid bitterly for his neglect of duty, as did the provost sergeant, Norman, who was held to have made the escape easy through his relaxed surveillance. Even when the prisoners were outside the walls it was considered impossible that they could evade the dozens of special constables who were ordered to hunt them down, and it was expected that they would be taken before they could leave the city. Private houses, public buildings, even convents were carefully searched, but the birds had always flown. The escape was the more remarkable because the crack Coldstream Guards were in charge of the prisoners; and so acutely was the disgrace felt that the corps offered a thousand dollars additional to the two thousand reward already posted by the government for the apprehension of the fugitives. That such a sum was not sufficiently attractive to tempt the dozens of French-Canadians who must have been in the secret is a pleasing commentary on their loyalty to the cause which Theller and Dodge represented.

Fifty pages are hardly sufficient to enable Theller to describe his experiences in Quebec and its environs as he and Dodge fled. From other sources, however, we obtain a clearer idea of the course of events between midnight on October 16, when the break took place, and the third of November, when they finally left the city. The principal agents in the escape were Messrs. Drolet, Hunter, and Grace, and owing to the suspicion directed against them they all became fugitives. Theller gives a description of a night of concealment under Grace's stable floor, first alone, and then with Dodge:

'About midnight intelligence was brought to our friends of a new search by the police,—in the very quarter I was in. . . In the rear of the house was a stable built of square timber. We entered there, took off the litter and raised the planks of the floor. A hole like a grave was dug by Mr. Grace and another friend; which, as soon as completed—and they hurried fast, for the voices of the police could be heard and their lanterns seen— a buffalo robe was placed in it and I laid down. They then put on the

[7]After the break Culver and Hull were left in hiding near the summerhouse in the governor's garden while Theller and Dodge sought a better place of concealment. They remained in the bushes until morning, when, thoroughly chilled and believing their companions had been captured, they entered a tavern and were shortly in custody. With the other American prisoners taken from the *Anne*, they were kept in the citadel until May 4, 1839, when they were deported at St. Regis.

boards and I was left till near daylight to enjoy the solitude of my living grave...

'At daylight we went into the stable again and descended into the grave, now enlarged for the accommodation of two... We remained there in far from a pleasant state—myself famishing with thirst, and not knowing anything of what was transpiring out of doors—or rather in the world above us. The horse, however, kept us busy. He had been foundered, and they had given him some diuretic medicine which, operating frequently, very soon drenched us completely.'

While separated from Theller, Dodge had had very similar experiences. Hidden for a time at Hunter's, he was then removed to a house in St. John's suburbs; and soon after he was hurriedly taken to St. Roch's suburbs, immediately under the Côteau St. Geneviève. There he remained in a cellar for several hours, crouched knee-deep in water, and was then removed to a house in St. Paul's Street.

The time was finally ripe for an attempt to cross the frontier. On Saturday, November 3, they crossed the St. Lawrence and rode to Saint Denis de Lauzon, four horses having been carried singly by the ferry-boat to Point Levis under the direction of J. B. Carrier, who had been over the route of escape frequently as a tea smuggler, and who had, consequently, been secured by Charles Drolet as the key man to lead the refugees out of the country. The fourth in the party was one Heath, or Bacond, and they spent the night and Sunday at Carrier's home, seven miles south of Point Levis.

Furnished with arms and money by sympathizers, the refugees resumed their journey on Monday, making their way by unfrequented by-roads to Saint François de Beauce; and thence in the same manner to the Kennebec Road, along which Carrier led them with courage and good judgment through three separate pickets.[8] Theller describes the final stage of the flight in characteristic fashion:

'We rode on, laughed at their guarded bridges, passes, and barricadoed posts, and on Tuesday morning, a little after daybreak, our hearts were gladdened at the appearance of the Frontier House, one-half of which was built on either side the lines. About the centre of this building stood a large post on which was hung a sign; on the one side was painted the royal arms—the lion and unicorn; beneath was in large letters "Lower Canada". On the other side the glorious eagle and the stars of our country; underneath, "State of Maine". As we looked in that wild spot upon the emblem of our country our hearts bounded with joy, and we gave three loud cheers that re-echoed in the woods, startling the inmates of the house from their slumbers. We rode on to the first house, a distance of six miles, and although we were scarce able to sit in our saddles, before

[8] So Theller says in his book, but in his earlier narrative he indicates that they followed circuitous routes and avoided all guards: 'We had intended to pass for a small squad of volunteer cavalry sent out at Quebec to pursue deserters or ourselves'. (*Niles' National Register*, 1838, 204.)

we arrived at the haven of our hopes joy had invigorated us so that we cantered our weary horses until we arrived at it.'

An incident occurred in this Maine tavern which illustrates Theller's unbounded vanity and indiscretion. The innkeeper had heard of the escape, and asked particularly if these travellers did not include Dodge and Theller. Carrier shrugged his shoulders and, as he and Bacond had to return to Lower Canada over the same route, gave him to understand that they were not of the party. But such a prosaic termination of his flight could not satisfy the egotistical Theller, who said: 'Why deny who we are? We are in safety. Yes, sir, I am Theller, and I have the honour to present my friend, Mr. Dodge.' Carrier could hardly believe his ears. 'A thunderbolt falling at my feet could not have produced a greater effect. I reproached Theller sharply for his indefensible conduct, pointing out that if Dodge and he were in a safe position, as he said, Bacond and I had still great perils to face.'[9]

Carrier was constantly in danger of arrest, and was finally apprehended. Through the interest of T. T. Taschereau he was admitted to bail, and eventually was included in the general amnesty. Charles Drolet, however, who had formerly been a Member of Parliament, was immediately suspected of complicity and arrested at St. Gervais. He was forwarded to Quebec under guard, but upon being allowed to visit his mother for a few minutes *en route,* he seized the opportunity to escape. He was not retaken, though the *Quebec Gazette* of November 14, in announcing the arrest and escape, said that hope was held out that he would shortly be in custody.

A recapitulation of the escape, as reported in the contemporary press, provides much of interest. The news, of course, reached the public piecemeal, and only the bare facts came to light at the time. The *Quebec Mercury* of October 16 first announced the break, indicating that the block of houses surrounding the Ursuline Convent was suspected of harbouring the fugitives; and it is also stated that Parker remained inside the walls because he had not the courage to make the jump which the other four did. The *Quebec Gazette* of the following day, in observing that 'the *soi-disants* General Theller and Colonel Dodge', together with Parker, Culver, and Partridge (an error for Hull), had escaped, expressed the opinion that excessive indulgence was the cause of the break. On the nineteenth, reference is made in an apologetic tone to the

---

[9]'La foudre tombée à mes pieds n'eut pas produit plus d'effet', wrote Carrier. 'Je reprochai vivement à Theller son inqualifiable conduite, lui faisant observer que si Dodge et lui étaient en lieu sûr, comme il le disait, M. Bacond et moi avions encore de grands périls à affronter, que grâce à cette declaration intempestive ces dangers allaient se trouver décuplés.'

useless and unnecessary searches which were antagonizing many citizens against both civil and military authorities. On October 22 the *Gazette* mentions the rewards offered by the government and the Coldstream Guards, and quotes the *Mercury* as denying rudeness on the part of posses which searched the Ursuline Nunnery, the only annoyance to the women, it is said, being 'the presence of a number of men within their walls'; the *Gazette*, however, believed that 'everybody admits there was irregularity'. On the twenty-sixth the *Burlington Sentinel* is quoted as stating that Theller and Dodge had reached the United States; and it is observed that the *Sentinel* should know, being 'one of the *sympathizing papers*'. The arrest and subsequent escape of Drolet is chronicled on November 14, together with the information that the four horses supposed to have been used by the fugitives were seized on Mr. Pozer's seigniory but later were given up to their respective owners. On the nineteenth the comment on the incident is closed with the quotation of the New York *Daily Express* that Theller and Dodge had reached that city *via* Boston and had reported that the pursuit was hot, particularly in Quebec, where the fugitives changed their place of concealment as often as five times in one night.

The reaction of the Canadian people to these events depended upon political views. The *Quebec Gazette* commented that 'the escapes from the citadels of Kingston and Quebec do not tend to give any very high idea of their security'—a sentiment which was echoed by the Toronto *Patriot* of October 23 with the remark that 'if our fortresses are no better for keeping people out than for keeping them in we are in a poor case'. This newspaper, however, included even British Whigs among the hated Reformers, and suggested that 'treachery' in London, and 'very close to Her Majesty', was responsible for the jail deliveries from Fort Henry and Quebec:

'This unfortunate country is regularly humbugged. Last night, following the example of Quebec and Montreal, the populace here hung and burned Lords Brougham, Melbourne and Glenelg in effigy, but we do not expect any particular relief from this piece of chivalry; we would have better hopes from a general calling out and arming a sufficient number of militia. However, it is well enough that Her Majesty's Ministers should know the opinion entertained of them in this country.'

One can readily imagine the pleasure that the talkative Theller would take in recounting his experiences. He addressed an audience at Vauxhall, New York, on November 13, in which he described not only his escape but his impressions of the languishing state of liberty in the Canadas. His five changes of hiding-place had by that time increased in true Falstaffian fashion to eight, and he had many other exciting incidents to relate to an audience variously estimated at from 200 to 1,000. After he and Dodge had reached the streets of Quebec, he recalled, 'a poor labourer—a caulker', ignoring the chance to obtain $3,000 by betraying them, led them instead to a friend's house. The audience clamoured for this man's name, but were content to rise and give three cheers for him. He said they escaped from Quebec 'in disguise as British officers, with a band of gold lace about their caps', and passed the sentinels just prior to the closing of the gates which were expected to keep them in. Theller said, also, that he had posed as 'a poor labouring Frenchman who didn't understand English', and later both he and Dodge 'joined the Queen's forces and went in pursuit of the escaped prisoners, . . Theller after Theller, and Dodge after Dodge—disguised all the time'.[10] But at least he had still a sprained foot to prove that he actually jumped from the wall!

Though Theller had it on the best authority that the reward for his apprehension would be paid 'even for my head or my scalp', it is quite probable that the British Government was quite as glad to see the last of him as he was to escape. But he was never noted for discretion, and his violent language led to his arrest. He was allowed bail, however, and does not again appear in the limelight as an agitator.

William Kingsford, Canadian historian, ran across Theller in Panama in 1857 and found that he was landlord of the Cocoagrove Hotel, 'one of the most beautiful spots I ever recollect to have seen'. He describes him as 'kindly and good natured, and certainly not wanting in courage'. He adds that Theller had the reputation thereabouts of being 'not unwilling to engage in a quarrel wherever it might lead him'. He favoured his guest on this occasion with the recollection of his many adventures, and his story was communicated in the same garrulous and gasconading spirit that ever characterized Brigadier-General Edward Alexander Theller. Shortly afterwards he removed to California, where he entered journalism and became a superintendent of schools. He died at Hornitos in 1859.

[10]'The Canada Meeting in New York,' Philadelphia *Inquirer*, November 16, 1838. A day or so later Theller and Mackenzie addressed 2,000 in Philadelphia. Similar meetings were held in Baltimore and Washington, difficulty being experienced in the capital in getting a chairman.

BIBLIOGRAPHY

Theller, as above. Egerton Ryerson's comment on the execution of Lount and Matthews is in Sissons, I 439-41. Charles Durand's description appeared in the *Caroline Almanack*, while the event was widely publicized by the press. An official reconsideration of the condemned men's cases is in State Book K, Public Archives of Canada. See appendix K for other documents. The escape of Theller and Dodge is based on three narratives: (1) Theller's original account, written in New York

David Gibson
One of the leaders at Montgomery's Tavern who succeeded in escaping to the United States

Chief Justice Robinson presided at many of the trials

From Dent, *Upper Canadian Rebellion*   William Bengough

Mrs. Lount Petitioning Sir George Arthur for Her Husband's Life

> The Canadian Tragedy:
> A Faithful Narrative
> of the Lives and Sufferings
> of Colonel Samuel Lount,
> and Captain Peter Matthews,
> Leaders in the Insurrection near
> Toronto, December, 1837;
> their Trials for High
> Treason, before
> the Chief Justice of Upper Canada,
> and Barbarous
> Execution, April 13, 1838.
> together with
> Brief Notices of the Relentless Persecution.
> By William L. Mackenzie.
> cut of the Gallows.
>
> Motto.
>
> Imprint
> 1845.
>
> crown, pica
> common
> brevier
> Dble column
> roy. 8vo

From the Lindsey Papers

MS. Title Page of a Work that Never Appeared

on November 18 for *Mackenzie's Gazette*, from which it was reprinted in the *New York Express*, the *Cobourg Star*, *Niles' National Register*, and in other periodicals in England and America; (2) Theller's long description in his *Canada in 1837-8*, II 102-235, which is full of imaginary conversation and confusing details; and (3) L. N. Carrier's, *Les Evénements de 1837-38. Esquisse Historique de l'Insurrection du Bas-Canada*, the original account of the escape being written by Dr. Charles De Guise and appearing in the *Journal de Québec*, 1852. Sidelights on Theller and the escape have been obtained from Sutherland, *Loose Leaves*, 131-9, Kingsford, *History of Canada*, X 467-8, and the contemporary press as noted in the text. The meetings subsequently addressed by Theller and Mackenzie in the United States are described in the Philadelphia *Inquirer*, while letters in the Lindsey Papers illuminate little-known aspects of these incidents.

CHAPTER XIV

The Battle of the Windmill

WHILE the attention of the authorities was being directed towards these notable jail deliveries, new schemes of invasion were hatching. During the summer of 1838 there had been several disturbances on the upper St. Lawrence, notably the destruction of the steamship *Sir Robert Peel* by Bill Johnston's gang, but these depredations were not closely connected with the new manifestation of Patriot agitation—the Hunters. The origin of this aspect of the movement is somewhat uncertain, but it is thought that the first lodge was organized in Vermont by Dr. James Hunter, a refugee from Whitby, Upper Canada. Two invasions of the province were carried out by Hunters' Lodges, but there was little attempt at co-ordination, with the result that neither had the slightest chance of success.

The main aim of this elaborate secret organization was to obtain a republican form of government for Canadians, and they were persuaded that on their arrival the populace would rise to their support. In the oath which was taken by each Hunter the promotion and defence of republican institutions and ideas throughout the world was included, and 'especially never to rest till all the tyrants of Britain cease to have any dominion or footing whatever in North America'.

A convention of the lodges of Ohio and Michigan was held at Cleveland during September, 1838, and there a 'Republican Government of Upper Canada' was formed, with numerous officials and a long list of officers from Commander-in-Chief L. V. Bierce downward. There were at least four degrees taken by the Hunters, each including a lengthy oath. They were known to the members as the Snowshoe, the Beaver, the Master Hunter, and the Patriot Hunter; of these, privates used the first, commissioned officers two, field officers three, and commanders-in-chief four or more, but all members took the four degrees whether they used them or not. The lodges are said to have numbered 1,174, with 80,000 members and $300,000 at their disposal.

William Lyon Mackenzie was not a member of the organization, but as editor of his *Gazette* he was kept informed of events. He took no direct part in the Hunters' activities, though among other political addresses which he delivered in the United States was

THE BATTLE OF THE WINDMILL 133

one on February 12, 1838, to the citizens of Ogdensburg, later a centre for the raid of Hunters upon Prescott. Canadian refugees, in fact, held but minor positions in the organization, but a promise of 160 acres of land, a cash bounty of twenty dollars, and ten dollars a month while on service induced many young and adventurous Americans to embark upon military expeditions for which they were destined to pay a heavy penalty.

The original leader of the ill-fated Prescott expedition was General John W. Birge, who was, from all accounts, a coward, and who apparently assumed the command without the knowledge of Bierce. Canadian spies[1] kept the authorities posted on the development of the Hunters' organization, and it was known that members were secretly concentrating at Syracuse, Salina, Oswego, Sackett's Harbor, and Watertown. Particulars of the Salina[2] contingent indicate the character of the movement and the general course of events. Onondaga County was particularly prominent in the agitation, and the excitement was intense during the early days of November. Some men sold their property or mortgaged their homes to raise money for the support of the organization. A considerable proportion of those engaged in the Prescott expedition were American militiamen, a few being officers. Eighteen gathered at Salina on the evening previous to election day, among them four leaders, including the eventual commander, Von Schoultz, who were subsequently executed for their part in the expedition, and six who were transported to Van Diemen's Land.

Captain Christopher Buckley was a salt manufacturer of Salina, and a number of the workers in his plant accompanied him, the party leaving Salt Point by the last regular Oswego packet boat. At Watertown they were drilled in the Amsterdam Hotel by Colonel Woodruff; and afterwards General Birge delivered a fiery oration in which he said that from 20,000 to 40,000 men would assemble on the State election day, and that nine-tenths of the Canadians and three-fourths of the troops would rise to their support. Sampson Wiley and Phares Miller, the drummers of the company, then 'beat the long roll in the centre of the hall while Birge flourished his sword and called for volunteers for the liberation of Canada'. A considerable number had withdrawn from the expedition by morning, but the rest proceeded to French Creek (Clayton), informing the inquisitive that

[1] Among Patriot spies was Captain E. Wingate Davis, who spent a week in Toronto, Port Hope, Cobourg, and Kingston to learn the views of the inhabitants. Davis was from Salina, but died in Wisconsin in the late eighteen-nineties.

[2] Salina, much older than Syracuse, was long noted for salt-boiling, while Syracuse, built on a swamp, first became important when the Erie Canal was constructed. When Syracuse became a city in 1847, Salina was included within its boundaries.

they were merely going hunting—for many of them were armed with the best of rifles, including several three-barrelled pieces.

On the morning of Sunday, November 11, about 400 Hunters embarked at Sackett's Harbor in the *United States,* which then proceeded eastward. The force was considerably augmented at Cape Vincent, French Creek, and Millen's Bay, and at the last-named point two schooners, the *Charlotte of Toronto* and the *Charlotte of Oswego,* were taken in tow by the steamer, whose captain is said to have been paid a hundred dollars by Daniel George, paymaster of the Patriots. Most of the men were transferred to the schooners, which were also loaded with provisions, arms, and ammunition. As soon as the voyage was again under way the men took from the boxes their swords and pistols, many of which were of most beautiful workmanship, and a few miles above Prescott the schooners were cut loose; but the cowardice of Birge led to the desertion of about 200 men, who went on to Ogdensburg in the steamer.

On the way down the river it was discovered that the leaders were not unanimous upon the procedure to be followed. One of them, Colonel Nils Szoltevcky Von Schoultz, was a native of Poland, where he had held the rank of major. He wished to surprise Prescott, being unaware that the inhabitants had been aroused several days previously. He wanted to go at once to McPherson's Wharf, for he expected that if a stop were first made at Ogdensburg more of the men would desert than would be made up by additional recruits. He planned to lead the main body through the centre of Prescott, while Colonel Martin Woodruff would lead the left wing around the north side, and Colonel Dorrephus Abbey the right wing on the south or river side. The forces were to come together between Fort Wellington and the town and advance on the fort. Had this been attempted the situation might have been even more serious than that which resulted at the windmill, but Birge and others opposed Von Schoultz's plans.

Birge, who had proceeded to Ogdensburg, promised to obtain reinforcements and cross over to the aid of the others on the schooners; but he fell sick with a suddenness that was imputed by his followers to cowardice.[3] The leadership thus fell upon Von Schoultz, who took charge of about 170 men on board the *Charlotte of Toronto* and crossed to the Canadian side. The other schooner was in control of the notorious Bill Johnston, who managed his ship so poorly that it ran aground on a delta of mud

[3]Truax describes how Birge, 'pale as a ghost', shut himself in a cabin of the *United States;* while Daniel Heustis refers to him as a 'coward, sick with a complaint vulgarly called the belly-ache'.

deposited in the St. Lawrence by the Oswegatchie River. The *United States* went from Ogdensburg to the assistance of the *Charlotte of Oswego,* but did not succeed in getting her off; later she returned to the task with a larger hawser but was still unsuccessful.

Meanwhile Von Schoultz's schooner had reached Prescott, and he succeeded in tying up to the wharf; but indecision prevented the Patriots from seizing the opportunity to invade the town, and the rope broke before an agreement was reached. The schooner floated on down the river, and those on board landed a mile and a half below Prescott, where they dragged their three guns up the steep bank and took up a position behind stone fences and houses near a large six-storey windmill.

The small British steamer *Experiment,* in command of Lieutenant Fowell, R.N., opposed the landing with two cannon, and poured shot into the *Charlotte of Oswego* as well as into the steamer *Paul Pry,* which was attempting to haul her off the sandbar. The *United States* was also prevented by the *Experiment* from approaching Prescott, and soon both steamers retired disabled into American waters. On the last trip of the *United States* a cannon-ball from the *Experiment* entered her wheelhouse 'and instantly beheaded a young man by the name of Solomon Foster, who stood as a pilot at the wheel'. Most of those on board the grounded schooner reached the windmill, and two guns were sent over on a scow. During Monday there was considerable activity on the river, and a number of men effected a crossing back and forth in small boats;[4] but on Tuesday the American naval forces seized both schooners.

When news of the invasion reached Captain Sandom, commander of the Royal Navy at Kingston, he rushed to the spot with armed steamers, the *Queen Victoria* and the *Cobourg*. These ships arrived at Windmill Point late Monday night with seventy marines and regulars on board. During the same night Captain George Macdonell arrived at Prescott in command of a detachment of the Glengarry militia, and the men lay on the ground during a heavy rain, expecting an attack at any moment; 140 men of the 9th Provincial Battalion under Lieutenant-Colonel Gowan also reached Prescott shortly afterwards. On Tuesday morning 300 men of the Dundas militia under Colonel John Crysler and a part of the 1st Grenville militia arrived at the scene of action,

[4]Truax reports that Bill Johnston not only deserted the force in the night but took some thirty men and considerable munitions with him; while Captain Malcolm, who had been forced aboard the *United States*, subsequently gave evidence that Johnston said he would 'have nothing to do with the expedition, but that he would volunteer to run down that damned little boat, meaning the British steamboat *Experiment*'.

and the combined companies were organized to drive the invaders from Canadian soil.

The British force advanced and drove in the invaders' pickets, forcing them, after an hour's engagement, to retreat from their outer defences into the circular stone mill, one hundred feet in circumference and eighty feet in height. The walls of this structure were three and one-half feet thick, and such gunfire as the ships could bring against it made very little impression. In fact, as the stones were set in the shape of a wedge the artillery merely drove them more firmly into place. The British force then decided to await the arrival of heavy artillery from Kingston before attempting to dislodge the invaders from their stronghold.

The Hunters held an excellent position, and from the small windows of the upper storeys of the mill their sharp-shooters kept up a heavy fire upon the British forces, which were situated in an exposed position on rising ground. At 3 p.m. a barn which had been used for shelter by the British was burned by the invaders, and the first phase of the battle ended in at least partial success of the Patriots. An American account of the battle says that British officers on horseback 'were seen distinctly to fall here and there on the field, and the ranks of the soldiers to waste away under the unequal contest'.

The invaders had meanwhile built a six-foot stone wall on the exposed side of the mill, and had three cannon in place to defend their position. They had lost a number of men who were captured by a flanking movement during Tuesday's engagement, but the rest of the force was in the mill or the neighbouring houses. Sandom's naval detachment, with the co-operation of Americans from Sackett's Harbor under Colonel Worth, prevented additional Hunters from attempting to cross over from Ogdensburg by capturing all the boats that had been used and patrolling the river. The dead and wounded lay on the field of battle until Wednesday morning, when an hour's truce was arranged to remove them. Both sides engaged in this work for a short time, though the lack of shovels handicapped the Patriots. During the rest of Wednesday and all day Thursday the opposing forces remained in comparative inaction.

The Patriots attempted to obtain medicine and surgical supplies from Ogdensburg, and Charles Smith, William Gates, Daniel George, and Aaron Dresser volunteered for the dangerous exploit.

'The only means we could secure for crossing', wrote Gates, 'was an old dilapidated yawl that lay half filled with sand and water on the beach one hundred rods below the mill. Forty rods below this were stationed several regulars. . . We crept along unseen to the yawl, but in the attempt to free it we were discovered by the regulars, who started at full speed to secure us. With a strong and hasty effort we upset it and pushed into the stream.'

But with armed steamers patrolling the river the odds were all against them, and it was not long before they were forced to exchange their sinking yawl for the quarter-deck of the *Cobourg*, where they lay handcuffed 'for three bitter hours'. Next morning they were in Fort Henry.

The invaders had meanwhile realized the hopelessness of their position, and efforts to arrange a retreat were made both by the men in the windmill and their sympathizers in Ogdensburg, who were practically in control of that town for nearly a week. The Patriots sent a man across on a plank to try to make terms; and Colonel Worth of the American force had an interview on board ship with Colonel Young of the British. It was suggested by Colonel Worth that the invaders be allowed to escape if they would retire from their position. This was refused, but it was learned, either from inadvertence or design, that the machinery of the *Experiment* needed repairs that would prevent her being used until two o'clock the next morning, and the *Cobourg* and *Victoria* having gone up the river the night before, it was very naturally inferred that 'no means of annoyance would be in the possession of the British during the early part of the night'. Therefore, the *Paul Pry* was sent over under command of postmaster King of Ogdensburg; but a man who accompanied Mr. King disembarked first and advised the Hunters to hold their position, as reinforcements and supplies would soon come. The emissary then went ashore himself, but did not succeed in getting the men to withdraw.

On Thursday night 117 men made up the force in the mill, and three of these escaped across the river by canoe. Stephen Wright describes the sleepless nights when the invaders realized how hopeless was their position. They made the best of it, however, and, although their ammunition for the three small field guns was soon exhausted, they loaded them 'with pieces of broken iron, butts, and screws that we tore from the doors and fixtures of the mill'.

At noon on Friday, the sixteenth, Colonel Dundas and four companies of the 83rd Regiment, with two eighteen-pounders and a howitzer, arrived on the steamboat *William IV*. The British were then ready to put an end to the invasion. One eighteen-pounder was placed back of the mill under Major McBane; a gunboat was posted below the mill, and a heavily-armed steamer above it, so that the shots from these three points had the mill in their focus. They were beyond the range of rifle fire, and sufficient to accomplish the demolition of the tower. While the guns bombarded the mill furiously a company of regulars supported by militia was drawn up on either flank to prevent the escape of the occupants. Von Schoultz states in a letter written a few days previous to his execution that his force at that time numbered only 108. His own actions were worthy of a better cause: 'As I could get no one to take the defence of the men,' he writes, 'I kept my position, though the roof crumbled to pieces over our heads.'

Those in the mill now hoisted a white flag; but the exasperated British kept up the cannonade, and every building near the mill was soon on fire, the raging flames outlining the whole field of battle with a lurid light. Under cover of night Von Schoultz and ten men withdrew from the stone house into the brushwood on the bank of the river, where they were easily captured. Those still in the mill, 'without ammunition, betrayed, deserted, and disheartened', again sent a flag of truce to the British, but the four men with the flag were fired on, so they returned and the Hunters 'made ready for a desperate resistance'. The British force advanced to within thirty rods and then halted; whereupon, much to their surprise, the Patriots were called upon to surrender unconditionally. They immediately 'disarmed and marched out, defiling between the soldiers of the 83rd who formed on each side of us'.

In the mill the British found several hundred kegs of powder, 200 stand of arms, and many swords, pistols, and cartridges; some of the weapons were silver-mounted, with their handles elaborately carved. A flag, said to have cost one hundred dollars and to have been presented to Von Schoultz 'by the patriotic ladies of Onondaga County', was also captured. On it was worked a full-spread eagle surmounted by a star, and beneath the design was wrought in silk: 'Liberated by the Onondaga Hunters'. In a bakery oven near the mill the bodies of two of the invaders were found. They had hidden there and been burned to death.

Patriot writers greatly exaggerate the British force which attacked the insurgents and compelled their surrender, one of them stating it to be

'5,000 regulars and militiamen; two large gun boats; seven steam boats, each of them armed with heavy cannon, mortars, rockets, carcasses, and every kind of warlike projectiles. To oppose this mighty host the lionhearted Patriots had only 152 men able to bear arms; they had some artillery, but no ammunition to serve them.'

The same writer states that the British lost 450 killed, but their

THE BATTLE OF THE WINDMILL

casualties were officially announced as two officers and fourteen men killed and about sixty wounded. Enthusiasm for the cause led McLeod to publish also an imaginative account of Von Schoultz's capture:

'At midnight all but their heroic commander were taken. He took possession of the stone house alone, and fired so incessantly that the enemy thought it was full of Patriots. At length they rushed in, and he jumped in their midst. They instantly pounced upon him like a pack of bloodhounds, tore the clothes from his back, robbed him of his hat, watch, and vest. This terminated the most extraordinary engagement that ever took place on the continent of North America.'[5]

Among the very few who escaped across the river—either before or after the battle—was N. Williams. He had been in a small group who had stationed themselves in a stone house at some distance from the windmill. As they expected to be attacked they made ready to defend their position to the last. The British force, however, gave undivided attention to the main body in the mill, and they decided to escape to a pine grove near the shore. Williams was soon on the road to Prescott, the others having fallen behind; and he resolved to attempt to pass as a traveller. Challenged by a sentry, he ran off through the fields and in the darkness fell into a deep mud-hole. This proved his salvation, for the militiamen, sent in search of him and his companions after the surrender, passed by at top speed, and he was soon on his way in another direction. Several miles from the river he took refuge in a barn; but the cold forced him out, and he went back towards the river in the hope that he might have a chance to cross. All approaches were well guarded, however, and he sought refuge at a farm-house. Although the occupants were very poor he was made as comfortable as possible, and, after being concealed there throughout the following day, he was given the watchword that would be required by the guard and made his way to the shore. No boats were available, so he constructed a raft out of rails, and with a stake for a paddle reached the American shore 'after a pleasant voyage of about two hours'.[6]

The prisoners were marched to Prescott in a long line, single file and tied to a rope. After being exhibited to the populace of the town, where a celebration of the victory was in progress, the men were 'crammed into the forecastle of a small steamboat' (the *Brockville*) and taken to Kingston. The march to Fort Henry, where they were imprisoned while awaiting trial, is described by one of the prisoners:

[5]M'Leod *A Brief Review*, 257. Besides those taken with Von Schoultz near the shore and four taken earlier in the yawl, two prisoners were captured at a tavern about twenty miles north of Prescott, having deserted the expedition the day after landing.

[6]Williams's narrative is given in full in appendix N(2).

'It was about midnight when we arrived at Kingston. We were tied together in couples, Von Schoultz at the head, a rope passing between us... In this condition, with a line of soldiers on each side, we were marched to Fort Henry, about one mile distant from the landing, the band playing *Yankee Doodle.*'

The evidence given at the court-martial brought out the information that steamboats and schooners of wealthy merchants had been made available to the invaders, who were encouraged by American officials and, in some cases, supplied with government arms. A judge, a member of Congress, and other men of influence were said to be members of the lodges, but did not take part in the expedition. The stories of most of the men were similar to that of Jeremiah Winnegar, a resident of Brownsville, Jefferson County, fifty-nine years old, who was sentenced to be executed, but was eventually pardoned. He stated that he

'had not expected to fight when he left home, but came for the sole purpose of giving liberty to the people of Canada. He thought when he was coming that he was doing God service, for he had heard Ministers of the Gospel encouraging the people to support the Patriot Hunters.' He said in an address to the court-martial: 'I presume many of the Court have families—I have a family as near and dear to me as them—I have left a wife—seven sons and four daughters... Though a poor man I have the same feelings as others, and my family are dear to me, and though old I am their main support—I have now only to throw myself on the mercy of the Court.'

At his trial Von Schoultz[7] emphasized that he had been deceived but admitted his leadership, and the court-martial found him guilty. He was executed on December 8, ten others being hanged later.[8] His last letter—to Warren Green, Salina, whose sister may have been the 'Emeline' to whom he was betrothed—indicates his character:

'When you get this letter I am no more. I have been informed that my execution will take place to-morrow. May God forgive them who brought me to this untimely death. I have made up my mind, and I forgive them... I wrote to you in my former letter about my body. If the British government permit it, I wish it may be delivered to you to be buried on your farm. I have no time to write long to you, because I have great need of communicating with my Creator and preparing for his presence. My last wish to the Americans is that they may not think of avenging my death. Let no further blood be shed; and believe me, from what I have seen, that all the stories that were told about the sufferings of the Canadian people were untrue. Give my love to your sister and tell her I think on her as on my mother.'

Most of the remaining prisoners were young men who little

---

[7] Von Schoultz, who was thirty-one years old at the time of the raid, lived near Salina and entered the Patriot movement through the influence of Stone, a merchant of the town. In October Von Schoultz signed commissions in cipher in New York City as Commander of the Patriotic Army, and he paid the expenses of several German and Polish recruits who joined him there. His statement and address to the court are given in appendix N (4), and a biography by Warren Green in N (5).

[8] They were Abbey, George, Martin Woodruff, Peeler, Sweet, Buckley, Phelps, Anderson, Leach, and Sylvester Lawton. For a list of participants in the raid and the disposition of the prisoners see appendix N (1).

THE BATTLE OF THE WINDMILL

realized the gravity of their offence, some fifty of them being between sixteen and twenty-one years of age. The Reverend Anson Green, a Methodist minister who preached to them at the request of Captain Beach, a member of the court-martial, wrote in his diary: 'I never preached to a more attentive and solemn assembly; still there were two God-forsaken looking men who lay upon the floor regardless of what I was saying! These were afterwards condemned and executed.' Like many other citizens, he 'was pleased to learn from Mr. Draper, the Judge Advocate, that but few others would expiate their guilt on the gallows'.[9] The younger prisoners were eventually pardoned and sent back to the United States; but sixty men were transported to Van Diemen's Land.

Von Schoultz appears to have been much the superior of those with whom he was associated. One of the members of the expedition describes him as 'an elegant scholar—a good military engineer—and spoke several languages with great fluency. . . His whole bearing and conduct were noble. . . Even regardless of his own sufferings he generously tried to render his companions in arms every service in his power'. In a letter to a friend Von Schoultz acknowledged the kind treatment experienced at the hands of the officers and men of the 83rd Regiment and the sheriff at Kingston; and in his will he left £400 to the dependents of the militia who had been killed.

From all accounts it would appear that the Regulars had to protect the prisoners from the militia of Glengarry, Dundas, and Grenville, who were greatly incensed at the invasion; and some of those captured suffered brutal treatment before it could be prevented. This was to be expected when such items were found on prisoners as a list of the citizens of Prescott who were to have been hanged upon the capture of the town. A Select Committee of the House of Assembly of Upper Canada reported that 'not only were the brave defenders of the province shot down and deliberately murdered by their fiendish assailants, but their dead bodies were mangled and mutilated and hung up as objects of scorn and derision by these inhuman monsters. The body of an intrepid and promising young officer, Lieutenant Johnson of the 83rd Regiment, was thus treated at Prescott'.[10] The Patriot

[9] On December 3 Sir George Arthur issued a proclamation appointing the fourteenth as a day of 'public fasting and thanksgiving, . . . earnestly imploring Him to guard us alike from the machinations of domestic traitors and foreign foes'. See the *Church* (Cobourg), December 8, 1838.

[10] *Report of Select Committee*, 20. It was brought out in Von Schoultz's trial that the mutilation could not have been done by hogs; and, of course, Dr. Hume's body was similarly treated at Windsor, as was Lieutenant Weir's in Lower Canada. Truax stated that a Polish fellow-exile of Von Schoultz 'stripped the uniform from the body and escaped that night, thus disguised, through the British lines'.

writers deny all such charges, claiming that the mutilation was the work of hogs.

At times during the four days' battle of Windmill Point thousands of Americans lined the opposite shore and witnessed the unequal fight. Some of them cheered at every slight advantage gained by the insurgents, but they took care to remain on their own side of the river. 'It embittered our hearts to know,' says Stephen Wright,[11] 'that they whose tongues could beguile so successfully had not the moral courage to aid us in the hours of trial'. For many years the mill, which had been erected in 1822 by a West Indian merchant, remained a battered and blackened ruin, a reminder of the ill-fated expedition. In 1873 it was repaired, whitewashed, and transformed into a lighthouse, the light being first shown on the anniversary of Waterloo, June 15. The old building still stands, a landmark which calls forth memories of exciting times along the border.

[11] The charge against Wright is given in appendix N(3).

BIBLIOGRAPHY

The most detailed description of the Hunters' Lodges is given in Preston, *Three Years' Residence in Canada from 1837 to 1839*, I 159 *et seq*. The sources relative to the activities of the Patriots from Onondaga County are (1) 'Survivors of a Bloody Opera Bouffe War Tell Their Story', Syracuse *Sunday Herald*, November 26, 1899. This is based upon the reminiscences of Nelson H. Truax of Watertown, and George H. Kemble of Pamelia, 'two old and tottering men' who met in 1899 to celebrate the 61st anniversary of the battle. With Price Senter, native of Ohio, but in youth and old age a resident of Auburn, they were in 1899 the sole survivors of the engagement. Cuts of Truax and Senter and representations of the expedition and battle accompany the article. (2) 'Invading Canada', by 'A Veteran Syracusan', Syracuse *Sunday Herald*, November 16, 1884. (3) 'Syracusans in Battle of Windmill Point', *Syracuse Post-Standard*, March 14, 1937. The invasion is described in some detail in Heustis, *Narrative of the Adventures and Sufferings of Captain Daniel D. Heustis*, in Wright's narrative printed in Lyon, *Narrative and Recollections of Van Dieman's Land*, and in Gates, *Recollections of Life in Van Dieman's Land*. Of these accounts the best is that of Heustis, who possessed many of the qualifications of the historian. An excellent official record was compiled by the Honourable W. H. Draper and enclosed in the despatch of Sir George Arthur to Lord Glenelg, February 5, 1839; while a good account largely from the Patriot point of view was printed in 1853 in Hough, *A History of St. Lawrence and Franklin Counties, New York*. Uninformed and propagandist writers like Donald McLeod (*A Brief Review*) add to the misinformation. The official records of the trials, in the Public Archives of Canada, contain valuable evidence on the course of the invasion. Von Schoultz's statements are given herewith in appendix N (4), while several letters of his are given by Heustis and Lyon, and some minor information about his burial in Lizars, 209. The depositions of the prisoners are in *Imperial Blue Books*, XIII; while some of the evidence at the trials, with comment, is found in *Report of the Select Committee of the House of Assembly, 1838*. Anson Green's *Life and Times*, 224, describes the executions, which are also referred to in the *Quebec Gazette* and other contemporary newspapers. The activities of the spy, Davis, are outlined in the Syracuse *Sunday Herald*, November 26, 1899, and Bill Johnston's part in the raid is indicated in evidence summarized in 'Escape of Johnson and Birge', *Albany Daily Advertiser*, December 4, 1838. Williams's narrative of his escape was reprinted in the Toronto *Mirror* of February 8, 1839, from the *Fort Ontario Aurora*, and is given in full in appendix N (2). Lieutenant-Colonel Bog's 'Reminiscences', Archives of Ontario, adds to our knowledge of the militia engaged in the battle, and gives seven verses composed by a volunteer and sung to *The Girl I Left Behind Me*. Two narratives of the expedition quoted in Lindsey, II 206, but of which the author has been unable to locate a copy in the United States or Canada, are Sebastian John Meyer, *A Narrative of the Expedition to Prescott*, and *Account of the Prescott Expedition*, which Lindsey ascribes to both Bierce and Bierge. The latter is probably by J. W. Birge, and it is likely that both were newspaper articles rather than pamphlets or books. Another newspaper account appears to have been written for the *Fort Ontario Aurora* by N. Williams, who escaped. See appendix N for related documents and a collation of data on participants in the raid.

CHAPTER XV

THE BATTLE OF WINDSOR

THE final Patriot invasion of Upper Canada, and the second engineered by the Hunters' Lodges, was a movement against Windsor early in December, 1838. General Henry Handy had been replaced by L. V. Bierce, lawyer of Akron, and under his orders Hunters from Ohio, Pennsylvania, Michigan, Buffalo, and Rochester assembled along the frontier. A central rendezvous for the easterly bands was at Swan River, near the mouth of the Detroit; while those from western points encamped at Bloody Run, north of Detroit. The former party, numbering 362, remained ten days at Swan River and then marched to a predetermined junction point four miles below Detroit, where they were equipped for a winter campaign through the money raised by the Patriot banking scheme.

There was in this movement the element of failure at the outset, for a steamboat that was to carry them across the river failed to appear. They made a night march to Detroit, where a vessel was engaged—but Major-General Bierce, who was to command, was not ready. The following night when they returned from their camp, Bierce claimed that he was ready but the steamer was not. At Bloody Run, similarly, cowardice and indecision prevented an embarkation, and Bierce restricted himself to bombastic addresses and proclamations. Angered by such tactics, two companies of Patriots left the camp, and at the same time the lack of secrecy enabled the Upper Canadian authorities to make preparations to meet the advertised raid.

Shamed by the offer of a junior officer to lead the expedition at once, Bierce finally got up courage enough to make a start, and on the evening of December 3 the men marched through the streets of Detroit without interference, taking possession of the steamer *Champlain* as she lay anchored in the harbour. Locking the crew in their quarters they manned the vessel and quietly passed the word to all other Patriots at hotels and boarding-houses. At 2 a.m. the *Champlain* crossed the river amid floating ice and landed 135 men at the Pelitte farm, about three miles above Windsor. Ordering the crew of the vessel to move her out into river, General Bierce said to his followers: 'We have no back doors now, boys; we must conquer or die!' At the same time he ordered his men to shoot any who refused to leave the boat.

The expedition then marched off towards Windsor, which at that time contained a population of but a few hundred.

A considerable number of the invaders were poorly armed, and others not at all. John Sullivan, an eye-witness, saw several men in the ranks with no firearms whatever: 'I saw some with long poles with a spur or lance on the end, and I think there were two poles with eagles on the ends. I could not see what use they were going to make of them.'

On the site later occupied by the Town Hall was a small frame barracks in which were twenty-eight men. These opened fire upon the invaders, killing an officer and wounding several men, whereupon Bierce ordered the building to be set on fire. Some of the garrison were shot down in attempting to escape, while others were burned to death. Thomas Robinson, one of the garrison, gives details of the attack:

> 'I went outside to see how many there were, and finding there was a large body of men I returned into the Barracks and recommended to the Sergeant, Frederick Walsh, to retreat to Sandwich. He replied "No—we will have a slap at them". As the rebels approached nearer to the Building the Sentry, Austerbury, fired, and loaded and fired a second time, when he was wounded by three balls. All of us below stairs fired at the rebels about the time the sentry fired a second time. As soon as our ammunition was spent the Sergeant said—"Now let us run!" He and another man went out at the Front door and made their escape—as two others followed they were killed. I and another followed, and when we saw the two persons before us fall we turned back into the Barrack, and I tried to make my escape through the back part of the Premises and was prevented owing to its being on fire. It was set fire to by the Brigands, I supposed, as I heard some of them say "Burn them up!" I tried to get over a pile of wood which was on fire when a bayonet was put to my breast by one of the Brigands and I was taken Prisoner immediately.'

After the burning of the barracks the Patriots moved to the centre of the village, where Bierce addressed them and issued a proclamation to the citizens of Canada. 'The spirits of Lount, Matthews, and Moreau are yet unavenged,' he shouted. 'The murdered heroes of Prescott lie in an unhallowed grave in the land of tyranny... Arouse then, soldiers of Canada! Let us march to victory or death!' The proclamation was dated November 30 and was signed by William Lount, Military Secretary, a son of Samuel Lount; and it emphasized that they were not 'pirates, robbers, banditti, and brigands', but had come 'to restore to our beloved country that liberty so long enjoyed and so tyrannically wrested from us.'

These oratorical efforts concluded, the force seems to have divided into three detachments, one of which burned the steamer *Thames,* which lay at the dock near the barracks. Two neigh-

THE BATTLE OF WINDSOR 145

bouring houses were also burned, and a negro named Mills, who refused to join the invaders and, instead, gave three cheers for the Queen, was immediately shot. As clouds of smoke rose from the burning structures, loud cheers from 5,000 sympathizers on the American shore greeted the first evidences of success. But the jubilation was short-lived.

The greater number of the Patriots had meanwhile come into contact with a force of militia under Colonel Prince and Captain Sparke. The site of this engagement was an orchard in the western part of Francis Bâby's farm, now bounded by Sandwich, River, and Chatham Streets, and Dougall Avenue. The invaders faced north and the militia south, at a point immediately north of the intersection of Church and Pitt Streets. As the Canadians advanced upon the enemy's position they were met by an irregular fire, but aimed too high to do any damage. A volley from the militia was all that was necessary to scatter the invaders. Their standard-bearer, Colonel Harvell of Kentucky, was killed defending the flag of the Provisional Government, while another leader, General Putnam,[1] fell during the retreat. An attempted rally failed, and several additional Patriots were killed as they made a short stand. The rest made for the woods.

While the battle was at its height the town of Detroit was in a state of great excitement. An eye-witness observed that 'amid the cheers and huzzas of the People on this side of the River (for the docks and Roofs were covered with spectators), they fought for about 3 minutes very well, and men fell on both sides, when to our surprise *both* parties *retreated,* and neither one claimed the victory'. He saw enough, however, to convince him that 'war is not the thing it has been cracked up to be'.

Four of the militia were killed and four wounded during the raid. Forty-four of the invading force were captured, and the official report of Colonel Prince stated that 'of the brigands and pirates, twenty-one were killed, besides four who were brought in at the close and immediately after the engagement, all of whom I ordered shot upon the spot, and it was done accordingly'. An eye-witness describes the Colonel's method of applying the ancient Indian sport of running the gauntlet:

'I saw Colonel Prince in his hunting-suit—grey coat, short coat and pants, a red-fox skin fur cap, long fur gloves, and black sword belt. . . He gave the captured Rebels a running chance for their lives: they were all to start from a line, and any that got over the fence and clear into the country were to go free. I believe there was not one who got clear over the fence.'

[1]Mackenzie states that Putnam was American-born but left a widow and eight children in Canada.

The killing and mutilation of Dr. John Hume, assistant surgeon, was among the worst acts of the invaders. Upon refusing to surrender to Bierce's detachment he was followed, and, defending himself to the last, was shot in the breast and finally killed with an axe; his body is said to have been partially devoured by hogs before burial. This mutilation and the charred remains of several men who had been burned when the barracks was fired, provided Colonel Prince with an excuse for the barbarous treatment he meted out to several prisoners. One Patriot named Miller, badly wounded in both knees, was among the five ordered shot by Prince, and he was killed in cold blood.

'There were,' John Sullivan says, 'a lot of starved hogs running around owned by a colored man named Gambeli; and smelling the fresh blood they gathered around in great numbers. I went over to where the body lay and drove off the hogs several times... After dark I left. Next afternoon a man came with a spade and dug a hole about three feet deep and as long as his legs, and shut poor Miller up like a jack knife, head and feet together, rolled him in, and covered the body with the soil.'[2]

Such are some of the most unsavoury details of the Battle of Windsor—an engagement which reflects but little credit on those engaged in it.

A detachment of the 34th Regiment under Captain Broderick, with a field piece, arrived from Fort Malden after the battle was over, and were in time only to pick up one or two prisoners. Colonel Prince ordered the pursuit discontinued almost immediately after the battle, and the Patriots were off to a day's start before it was resumed. Hearing the order given, one of the 'dead' got up and made for the woods, but he was killed by the militia, one of whom, a negro, took his boots, was subsequently taken prisoner by straggling Patriots, and finally rescued by militiamen. Charles Bâby, realizing that there had been negligence in the pursuit, describes his success in rounding up Perley and others at Shaver's Tavern, thirteen miles from Sandwich:

'I stopped at the House of a person by the name of Shaver. I went upstairs for the purpose of writing a letter, and in the room where I went I found the Prisoner Purley in bed between 11 & 12 o'clock in the daytime... I made enquiry of the Master of the house how long the Prisoner had been there and was informed by him that the Prisoner had arrived with the party which was then below stairs on that morning. I then made up my mind he was one of the party which crossed—he had his clothes on in bed. I made him get up and put on his boots and desired him to follow me downstairs, and with the other Prisoners who had been taken by other persons I took him to Sandwich—the other Prisoner Gooderich was among them.'

[2]Stephen Miller, aged thirty-five, left a widow and one son in Florence, Huron County, Ohio. Dennison, also wounded in the battle, and Bennett, 'late a resident of the London District', were two of the others summarily executed. The details, with affidavits, are given in Lyon's *Narrative*, 59-62. The epitaph which Prince is said to have written for Hume's tombstone is given in appendix O(5).

Courtesy Ontario Historical Society

A Patriot Commission

E. J. Roberts was also 'Brigadier-General of the First Brigade'

From Willis, *Canadian Scenery*, 1842   W. H. Bartlett

The Citadel of Quebec

Scene of the celebrated escape of Theller and Dodge

SEVEN YEARS OF MY LIFE,

OR

NARRATIVE OF A PATRIOT EXILE.

WHO TOGETHER WITH

EIGHTY-TWO AMERICAN CITIZENS

WERE ILLEGALLY TRIED FOR REBELLION IN UPPER CANADA IN 1838,
AND TRANSPORTED TO VAN DIEMAN'S LAND.

COMPRISING A TRUE ACCOUNT

OF OUR OUTRAGEOUS TREATMENT DURING ITS MONTHS IMPRISONMENT
IN UPPER CANADA, AND FOUR MONTHS OF BUFFELING
FEELING IN A TRANSPORT SHIP ON THE OCEAN.

WITH A

TRUE BUT APPALLING HISTORY

OF OUR CRUEL AND UNMERCIFUL TREATMENT DURING FIVE YEARS OF EMIGRATED
SUFFERING ON THAT DETESTABLE PENAL ISLAND, SHOWING ALSO THE
CRUELTY AND BARBARITY OF THE BRITISH GOVERNMENT TO
ITS PRISONERS OF WAR ALL IN THAT PENAL COLONY.

WITH A

Concise account of the Island its Inhabitants, Productions, &c. &c.

BY ROBERT MARSH.

Freedom before Aristocracy; if Liberty be your motto, support and defend it under
all circumstances, otherwise you aid and assist the French of Monarchy

BUFFALO:
FAXON & STEVENS.
1848.

A

NARRATIVE

OF THE

ADVENTURES AND SUFFERINGS

OF

CAPTAIN DANIEL D. HEUSTIS

AND HIS COMPANIONS,

IN

CANADA AND VAN DIEMAN'S LAND,

DURING A LONG CAPTIVITY;

WITH

TRAVELS IN CALIFORNIA,

AND

VOYAGES AT SEA.

BOSTON:

PUBLISHED FOR REDDING & CO,
BY SILAS W. WILDER & CO.
1847.

Title Pages of Two of the Rarest and Most Informative Patriot Narratives

THE BATTLE OF WINDSOR

Constant Ganthier gave evidence that he saw two men making efforts to arrange a passage over Lake St. Clair, and though at first not suspecting who they were, he next day got help and arrested the men, who proved to be Goodrich and Cunningham. Doan was taken in a similar manner. Antoine Demande, who lived about eleven miles from Windsor, gave evidence at the court-martial that he saw

'three men near my house trying to get a canoe out of the ice and I supposed they wanted it to go hunting in. After a while they succeeded in getting it out and they appeared so anxious to cross I suspected they were some of the Party of rebels who had been beaten at Windsor. I armed myself, took two men with me, and pursued and arrested them.'

The experiences of many others prior to capture were no doubt similar to those recorded by Samuel Snow and Robert Marsh. Snow and a few companions, finding themselves isolated after the battle in the orchard, dressed the wounds of two of their fellows, and after sending them to a neighbouring farm-house wandered further into the thicket:

'At night, cold, weary, and hungry, we built a fire and lay down to rest. Some time in the night, when all was silent and the fire nearly extinguished, a flash of light was seen, followed by a loud report which brought every man of us from our horizontal posture with the dexterity of minute men. We at first supposed we had been fired upon by Indians, . . . but one of our party who had a large quantity of powder in his pocket had taken quarters too near the fire. . . In the morning myself and two others took to the ice on the St. Clair River, and after travelling all day found supper and lodging at the house of a man whose name I have since forgotten.

'In the morning we continued up the St. Clair; passed a Camp of Indians who offered us no molestation; and towards night came to Baubee's ferry. The ferrymen had received instructions to take no one across the river who had not a pass from the captain of the guard. We went boldly to the captain and requested of him to cross over, but were told that in consequence of the late disturbance at Sandwich he should be under the necessity of detaining us and sending us back; and if we were not recognized as belonging to the Patriot service we could then cross the river.'

So Snow soon found himself before a magistrate in Chatham, but as no witnesses appeared against him he spent the night in the guard-house across the river. On the following day the Patriot prisoners were confronted by three of their number who had turned Queen's evidence to save themselves, and conviction was then certain. 'This,' says Snow, 'did not look to me like administering equal and exact justice to all, but I could take no exception to the proceedings.'[3]

Robert Marsh's experiences were more exciting. At a short

[3]Snow, *The Exile's Return*. Snow lived in Strongsville, Cuyahoga County, Ohio. He was aroused in the Patriot interest when he heard Dr. Charles Duncombe speak in the Cleveland Court House.

council of war in the woods it was decided that every man should do the best he could for himself:

'We accordingly separated and I found myself pursued by a man hollowing at the top of his voice, "Stop, there! stop! you damned rebel, or I'll shoot you!".. I discharged my rifle but cannot say whether it hit the mark or not, for I did not look but immediately rose and walked off. At any rate I heard no more of "Stop there, you damned rebel!"'

But Marsh did not long remain at liberty. He hid in a hayloft and was almost punctured by a pitchfork, but after a sleep escaped during the night, though he narrowly avoided capture by Indians. He was finally forced by hunger to knock at the home of a French settler, hoping that the inhabitants might be friendly to the revolutionary cause. The small daughter of the house asked him if he was a Patriot, which he had no sooner admitted than the father and three other men came from another room and took him prisoner, saying they would take him to Sandwich. He had hopes of escaping on the way, but they tied him securely to the back of an old nag.

He asked to be taken at once before Colonel Prince, who, he was assured, would lose no time despatching him; but Marsh had decided 'to draw my pistols and rid the country of one of Britons favourites', though his purpose was defeated when it was learned that the colonel was at dinner. He was shortly lodged in jail, where he naïvely protested that as he owed the Queen no allegiance he was consequently not a rebel; but he was fated to spend periods of unvarying misery in the jails of Sandwich, London, and Toronto, as well as some months in Fort Malden, Fort Henry, and Quebec, before he was finally transported on the *Buffalo* to Van Diemen's Land.[4]

A considerable number of the Patriot raiders, however, made good their escape. Some were hidden in the lofts and garrets of friendly farmers until the border waterways were sufficiently frozen to enable them to cross to Michigan. Nathan Toles was one of these, a farmer's wife having sheltered him and obtained clothes from Detroit, by means of which he contrived to cross without suspicion; while another fugitive was brought into Windsor in a load of hay, and reached the American shore by canoe. One Irish peasant woman hid four refugees for six weeks, finally delivering them safe and sound to Detroit.

One Patriot narrative, Jedediah Hunt's *An Adventure on a Frozen Lake,* records a remarkable escape across Lake St. Clair. He gives some details of the battle in the orchard, indicating

[4] Marsh, *Seven Years of My Life*. He had been on Navy Island, and while on his way to Detroit participated in the raids upon Bois Blanc and Fighting islands, which he confuses with the Pelee raid. The subsequent experiences of Snow and Marsh are described in chapters XIX, XX, and XXI.

THE BATTLE OF WINDSOR 149

that his fellows were panic-stricken at the approach of the Canadian force, and adding, 'I knew too well that we had no business with British Regulars'. Escape was soon the uppermost thought in every mind, and he set off at top speed with the rest after seeing Harvell and others killed. As he ran along, his cartouche box was blown away, but he observed that the British, fearing an ambush by a larger force in the woods north of Windsor, did not follow far. Some twenty Patriots gathered there for a moment, and then broke up in small groups to facilitate escape. Hunt went with one Thompson, whom he described as one of the greatest dare-devils the world ever knew, and the deeds credited to him certainly bear out the reputation.

Passing onward they came up with a man who had had part of his face blown away. He accompanied them some distance, but, being unable to keep up, was shortly taken prisoner. Hiding behind a tree, Thompson wounded a militiaman who still followed, and finished him off at close range with a pistol. At a point about twelve miles from Windsor and six from Lake St. Clair they joined a camp of sixteen refugees. Five of this party were wounded, and two appeared to be dying. Colonel Cunningham, suffering greatly from a bad wound and begging to be put out of his misery, was among the number. During that night one man was blown up when his powder-horn caught fire, and in the morning two others reached the camp with the news that seven of their fellows had perished from cold.[5]

Hunt and Thompson pushed on some miles and approached a hut. A knock brought two or three women to the door, and their hostility led to a fight, after which the two men made off with a goose and a large store of other food. An Indian who followed them was killed by more of Thompson's bullets, but they outdistanced other pursuers and reached a log house where they were temporarily hidden. But it was an Irish sympathizer who did most to make escape possible, for they were some fifteen days in a loft in his house. Paying for their accommodation, they kept within while their protector crossed to the American side and returned with a letter from their friends, suggesting an escape across the ice on Christmas Eve, when there would be a moon.

This meant a twenty-one-mile tramp over Lake St. Clair, but the two men made what preparations they could and set out. Some miles from shore a body of open water was encountered, but they finally got around it. They suffered greatly from the cold, and held their general direction only by keeping the wind on the same

[5] Sir Richard Bonnycastle states that the bodies of nineteen Patriots were found frozen in the woods; while a militiaman saw five dead on cakes of ice in the Thames.

side of them and hoping it did not change. But Thompson soon became hopelessly cramped with the cold, and Hunt had to leave him in a dying condition after fruitless efforts to move him onward over ice 'piled up in long winnows eight or ten feet high, which rendered my progress very difficult'.

Hunt kept on doggedly and several hours later reached land, though he was uncertain whether he was in Michigan or back in Canada. The first house he came to was occupied by French settlers, and after learning the joyful news that he was in the United States he proceeded to Detroit, where he was welcomed by fellow-Patriots.

The main body of those who escaped, however, did not participate in the battle of the orchard. These were about thirty under General Bierce, who contrived to keep well in the rear throughout the raid. John H. Harmon describes how they effected their return to the United States:

'When we came to our landing place of the morning the *Champlain* had disappeared. We began a search for canoes and soon had half a dozen but no paddles... We used the stocks of our guns to get the canoes over to Hog Island.[6] When on the Island the canoes were abandoned and we walked across to the opposite side. A single canoe was found there, with which the party, a few at a time, were ferried over... The steamboat *Erie*, having the Brady Guards on board, was close at hand for the purpose of capturing all persons violating the neutrality laws of the United States. We dropped our guns overboard and waited for the *Erie* to come up.'

The trial of the forty-four prisoners took place in London during December, 1838, only one, Abraham Tiffany of Albany, being acquitted. Five of them—David McDougall, Daniel Sweetman, George Putnam, Sidney Barber, and William Bartlett—turned Queen's evidence, and no time was lost in disposing of the cases. Marsh says that the prisoners were not sentenced, but merely taken away, ignorant of their fate until told a few hours before their execution to prepare for death. All forty-three were sentenced to be hanged, but the informers were recommended to mercy. Six were executed,[7] eighteen of the more prominent selected for transportation to Van Diemen's Land, while the rest were largely 'young men to whom it is proposed to grant a free pardon at no very distant date'. One of these escaped, two of the informers were shortly set free, and the remaining sixteen were deported to Lewiston in April, 1839.

The conduct of Colonel Prince with respect to the prisoners aroused great excitement not only in the Canadas but in the United

[6]Hog Island is now Belle Isle.
[7]Those hanged were Doan, Perley, Lynn, Bedford, Clarke, and Cunningham. Details of the executions, a full list of the prisoners and their disposition, Doan's last letter to his wife, and the address prepared by Perley to deliver from the scaffold are given in appendix O. Tiffany, the only prisoner acquitted, was thought insane.

THE BATTLE OF WINDSOR   151

States and Great Britain. An investigation by court-martial was ordered and evidence taken at Sandwich; but the result was tantamount to an acquittal, if not quite a vindication. In Detroit, however, placards were posted offering one thousand dollars for Prince's capture or eight hundred dollars for his dead body, and an American was shortly afterwards arrested in Sandwich on suspicion of having come over to murder him for the reward.[8] For several years his life was in jeopardy, and his farm was placarded with notices that spring-guns and man-traps endangered the lives of trespassers; but he continued to carry on his public duties regardless of all personal danger.

Opinions upon the colonel's conduct were extreme. To many he was 'a great rascal', while others found him the impersonation of everything admirable. A considerable number of persons signed a protest condemning his actions, but the only result was that the redoubtable colonel challenged them all to mortal combat, and one Wood, with whom he exchanged shots, was wounded. Newspapers with Reform sympathies, like the Toronto *Examiner* and the *Christian Guardian*, similarly criticized his actions, while the *Mirror* castigated 'the murderous conduct of this coward and bully'. There was, however, no lack of support for Colonel Prince, particularly in such ultra-Tory newspapers as the *Quebec Mercury, Cobourg Star*, and Toronto *Patriot*; for there was widespread disappointment and criticism that numerous prisoners should have been able to escape from the strongest Canadian fortifications, and that leaders like Sutherland and Parker were released by British courts on technicalities or writs of *habeas corpus*. The *Patriot* considered it a severe public grievance that all the Pelee Island prisoners were not forthwith executed; and letters of Colonel Prince in the same publication show that his conduct at Windsor was not the result of sudden impulse in the heat of action, but a predetermined policy, which had the support of a Sandwich public meeting and the backing of a large body of Canadian citizens who were exasperated at the repeated incursions of 'bandits' and their unsatisfactory disposal after capture.[9]

In the spring of 1839 Colonel Prince was tendered a triumphal dinner by the inhabitants of Toronto in token of their appreciation of his conduct, and those present were regaled

[8] Howland Hastings was the man, and Samuel Wilcox was held by him in Detroit because he was 'a damned Tory'. On the latter's evidence Hastings was sentenced to six months in jail, but he was ordered liberated by the provincial authorities. Colonel Prince withheld the warrant and received a sharp reprimand, another order being sent direct to the sheriff. See Enclosure 5 in Arthur to Glenelg, February 18, 1839. See p. 235 for another example of his impetuosity.

[9] At least one officer, Colonel W. Elliot, was dismissed from the service for denouncing Prince's conduct. See *Imperial Blue Books*, XII, No. 106, and Lyon, 60.

with a fighting speech from the guest of honour. As he rose to address his friends he was greeted by the singing of *The Fine Old English Gentleman*. Frequent applause punctuated his speech as he outlined his version of the course of the Battle of Windsor, emphasizing that 'John Prince has done his duty'. He proudly took credit for the despatch of five men; and observed with characteristic vigour that 'the rest, I presume, will be kept to fatten in our Jails, or will be sent at an enormous expense to some distant colony, instead of being (as they ought to be) swept off the face of God's Creation, for where are sinners equal to them?' In succeeding months he was made an honorary member of numerous St. George's societies, and cheered whenever he appeared from Amherstburg to Halifax.

The controversy over his actions extended to England, where there were debates in both Commons and Lords, and the Battle of Windsor was refought by Brougham, Wellington, Melbourne, and Normandy. It is significant, however, that the disastrous defeats at Prescott and Windsor were the last Patriot invasions; and, apart altogether from the justice or injustice of his actions, Colonel Prince's summary treatment of his prisoners may well be credited with a salutary and deterrent effect.[10]

[10] In private life Prince was a lawyer, and in 1841 he was elected to the Legislative Assembly. He was appointed judge of the District of Algoma in 1859 and lived in Sault Ste. Marie until his death on November 30, 1870, at the age of seventy-four. Latterly, he was an ardent advocate of Canadian independence. One of his sons, Captain William Prince, established the first effective police force in Toronto, 1858-74.

BIBLIOGRAPHY

For despatches of Sir George Arthur to Lord Glenelg, with enclosures relating to various aspects of the border excitement, see *Imperial Blue Books*, XII and XIII. Evidence at the trial by court-martial of Doan, Perley, and Goodrich is from the official records in the Public Archives of Canada. Colonel Prince's report is reprinted in the Toronto *Patriot*, December 14, 1838, from the Sandwich *Herald*; while his Orderly Book, November 2, 1836, to January 26, 1839, is in the Burton Historical Collection, Detroit Public Library. The narrative of Marsh, *Seven Years of My Life*, that of Snow, *The Exile's Return*, and that of Hunt, *An Adventure on a Frozen Lake*, give accounts of the invasion. Hunt's narrative was printed in Cincinnati in 1853, and the only copy the author has seen in the United States or Canada is in the Burton Historical Collection, Detroit, where also are Levi Bishop's MS. 'Recollections of the Patriot War of 1837-1838', and a MS. letter of Charles Ford, December 7, 1838, describing the battle. The Patriot proclamations are given in Lindsey, II 228-9. Incidents during the invasion, and the capture or escape of participants are described in considerable detail and largely from reminiscences of those concerned, in Ross, 'The Patriot War', 555 *et seq.*, and Detroit *Free Press*, December 7, 1884, Lizars, 262-3, Essex Historical Society, II 5-33, and Bonnycastle, *Canada As It Is*, II 179. Details of value are also found in Mackenzie's *Caroline Almanack*, 99, and in the contemporary press. The capture of Doan is described in detail in the *London Gazette*, January 14, 1839, and in the *St. Catharines Journal* of the twenty-fourth. A recent study of the disposition of the prisoners, including related documents, is Fred Landon's 'Trial and Punishment of the Patriots Captured at Windsor in December, 1838', *Michigan History Magazine*, XVIII. For the controversy over the summary execution of prisoners see, among others, the *Mirror*, July 26, 1839, the *Patriot*, August 21, 1838, and the *Cobourg Star*, April 17, 1839, in the last of which is described the dinner held in Toronto in honour of Colonel Prince. See appendix O for related documents and a collation of data on the participants in the invasion.

CHAPTER XVI

BILL JOHNSTON AND THE BURNING OF THE SIR ROBERT PEEL

NOTHING exemplifies the degeneration of the Patriot movement so well as the activities of William Johnston and Benjamin Lett; for whatever justification there may have been for the various military invasions over the border, there was none for the predatory raids upon steamships, churches, and other public or private property by gangs under their leadership. The similarity in their depredations did not extend to their methods, however, for while Lett usually carried out his plans secretly and under careful disguise, Johnston was arrogant enough to admit his attacks publicly and to advertise their continuance. He was different from Lett also in that he played a lone hand most of the time, taking little or no part in activities in which others were leaders and organizers. Although he was in command of a schooner at the commencement of the Hunters' raid upon Prescott, he appears to have been more relieved than grieved when his vessel grounded on the American shore, for he made no further effort to come to the aid of Von Schoultz's force at Windmill Point. He was by nature a buccaneer, and had no intention of allowing himself to be surrounded by enemies with all hope of escape cut off.

Johnston was born at Three Rivers on February 1, 1782, and so was considerably older than most of the Patriots. In 1784 his family moved to Upper Canada. In early life he was a farmer and merchant near Bath, but when part of his property was confiscated for smuggling[1] he removed to Sackett's Harbor, vowing vengeance against the British. During the War of 1812 he was a spy in the American service, and, being 'of a powerful frame and of great fearlessness and energy of character', he performed many bold and hazardous exploits. Darting here and there among the Thousand Islands in his six-oared barge, Johnston's gang intercepted despatches, attacked small craft, and harassed Canadian settlements. On one occasion he robbed the mails between Gananoque and Kingston, took off the clothes of the coach's occupants, beat whoever refused him, and tied the coachman to a tree. Upon capturing a dragoon carrying official papers he shot

[1] Sir James Alexander says that Johnston's claim against the government amounted to £1,500, for which he would have fought on the British side as he did on the American. F. B. Hough states, however, that Johnston was in the Canadian militia in 1812, but was jailed for insubordination and escaped to the United States.

his horse and sent the man on foot to report to his commanding officer the loss of his despatch-bag. Once a gale drove him ashore, but while all his crew were captured he eluded his pursuers, and two weeks later escaped to Sackett's Harbor, thirty-six miles across Lake Ontario, in a canoe. When the war was over he took up residence at French Creek, becoming both trader and smuggler.

Johnston first appeared in the Patriot War at Navy Island, where he was apparently appointed by Van Rensselaer to be 'Commodore of the Navy in the East'. Among the recommendations which Silas Fletcher bestowed upon 'Admiral' Johnston were that he was 'a gentleman of intelligence, equal to fifty ordinary men', could raise 'two hundred bold volunteers as ever drew a trigger', and—still more important—was certain to 'greatly annoy the Kingstonians'. Early in the spring of 1838 Johnston and a party of Canadian refugees prepared a rendezvous on an island at the head of Wells Island, within British territory; this he named Fort Wallace, and boasted that with twelve men he could defend his position against 200. Another hide-out was located on Abel's Island, opposite Alexandria Bay. Johnston stated he had 150 men under him, went about with six pistols, a dirk, and a bowie knife in his belt, and announced to his enemies that they might expect him to sell his life 'at the dearest rate'.

The whole district was ideal for banditry. Not only did the rough granite islands form a perfect defence in themselves, but the larger of them were inhabited by 'a lawless race of half banditti' who preferred the freebooter's life to all others. Augmented in 1838 by hundreds of embittered Canadian refugees,[2] the island population controlled a hundred boats of one type or another; and Johnston sometimes used a very swift forty-foot vessel which was so light that it could readily be portaged a long distance. Neither the American nor the Canadian militia in the vicinity were in any sense adequate to cope with such a situation; and it was pointed out to the American Government that only a force 'sufficient to explore the islands and expel the marauders' would be of any value, and then only if other military and naval detachments and an armed steamship were active at various frontier points. But meanwhile the depredations were well under way.

True to Fletcher's prophecy, Johnston was not long in causing the Kingstonians a great deal of anxiety. In the latter part of February numerous rumours of Patriot movements among the islands began to alarm the inhabitants of the Canadian shore of the upper St. Lawrence. A large number of men from Jefferson

[2] The *Albany Argus* estimated there were 1,000 refugees on the islands and several thousand more between Ogdensburg and Niagara. The influence of many less would have been sufficient to induce raids over the border.

JOHNSTON AND THE BURNING OF THE PEEL 155

and neighbouring counties had assembled in sleighs and on foot, and it was learned that a force of 'the pirates' had left Grindstone Island for one or another of the towns along the river. Johnston was quoted by 'a gentleman who was at French Creek' as stating that Gananoque was the object of the raid.³ Hickory Island, 'uninhabited, save by one poor widow,' shortly became the rendezvous, and several hundred Patriots and three pieces of artillery were assembled for whatever purpose the leaders might decide upon; but General Van Rensselaer was there, and not sober, and after frittering away a day of two of bitter cold weather, the force melted away. On February 28 someone called for volunteers to invade Canada, but as only thirty-five answered the call this motley band dispersed, the officers with the utmost difficulty retaining a sufficient number to remove the arms they had taken over.⁴ On the island was afterwards found a large quantity of scrap-iron sewed up in bags, intended to be used by their artillery in place of grape or canister.

Meanwhile Kingston was in a state of siege, having heard among other rumours that all but Van Rensselaer were in favour of an immediate march on that town; and that the Patriots had a friend in the fort who had engaged to spike the guns on the night when the attack was to be made. Several streets were barricaded, and many other elaborate preparations made to meet the invasion which never occurred. 'I shall not easily forget the dismay which prevailed amongst the Kingstonians', wrote T. R. Preston, who found that people had taken all their plate, money, and jewels to Fort Henry, and most of the able-bodied had joined the town guard.⁵ The inhabitants of French Creek were also excited, fearing a British invasion; and the occupants of one or two houses, known to be Tories, burnt blue lights in their windows that the British might spare them in case of an attack. But Johnston, who had found himself trammelled in this project by the inefficient Van Rensselaer,⁶ was soon to act more successfully on his own.

³Elizabeth Barnett, Gananoque schoolmistress, crossed on the ice on November 20 and warned the inhabitants of the intended raid. Even if 'never thanked or rewarded', she met Warren Fairman, one of the militiamen, and shortly became his wife. See 'An Unsung Heroine', Montreal *Gazette*, February 26, 1934.

⁴They fled, recalled Nelson Truax, 'at the approach of two Canadian farmers with a load of hay'. Mackenzie records that five American farmers—John Pockard, George Holseburgh, John Martin, Ebenezer B. Stores, and John Herman—were captured and taken to Fort Henry, from which they were released on August 16 'after very cruel usage'.

⁵Details of the plans and precautions in Kingston are given by Sir Richard Bonnycastle, who commanded a corps of engineers and was knighted for distinguished service. Companies of militia were established also at Bath, Gananoque, Brockville, Prescott, Cornwall, and intermediate villages.

⁶With the Hickory Island fiasco General Van Rensselaer passes out of the picture. He was shortly sentenced to a year in prison and a fine of $250 for breaking American neutrality laws. On January 1, 1850, he committed suicide in Albany.

The burning of the steamship *Sir Robert Peel* was probably the most outrageous of all Patriot activities along the frontier. The vessel, carrying from twenty-five to thirty cabin passengers and forty in the steerage, stopped about midnight of May 29 to take on wood at Wells Island, the largest of the Thousand Island group. One Ripley of Abel's Island, who was in charge of the the wood on the wharf, told the captain that he had seen a longboat filled with men running past the island at two or three different times that night, and that upon the first appearance of the steamer he had heard someone in the boat say 'She is coming!' Because of the presence of these suspects, Ripley suggested to the captain that the vessel should not stay long, but he laughingly observed that 'if there were not more than 100 or 150 men he did not fear them', and the crew thereupon left the vessel to carry wood.

At 2 a.m., when they were about finished, some twenty-one men[7] came out of the bush, dressed and painted as Indians or negroes, and shouting 'Revenge for the *Caroline!*', ordered the captain and all passengers ashore. They were variously armed with guns and bayonets, pistols and swords, and 'with implements resembling lance or spear on a red painted pole, about eight feet long'. They placed a guard on the gangway to prevent the crew from coming aboard, and six of them took possession of the engine-room. A passenger, awakened by the tumult, thought it was occasioned by a quarrel among the crew, but he was quickly disillusioned when five armed men broke into his stateroom and were about to run him through, believing him to be a British officer. He persuaded them that they were mistaken, but not before they had seized him. A man who took some pains to learn 'facts, and not rumours', describes the scene:

'At this time great alarm was created among the ladies, in consequence of the ruffians dashing their bayonets and lances through the cabin windows and breaking open the various doors. At first those gentlemen who attempted to get out of the cabin on deck were pushed back, either by a slight push of the bayonet or by a strong one with the butt end of the guns. The next order was for all passengers and hands to be put on shore; they at the same time shouted if they would go on shore quietly no one would be hurt. As all the passengers were in bed at the time many of them rushed on deck nearly naked, and were not allowed to return for either their clothes or trunks, but rudely pushed on shore if they did not walk off at

[7]This is the number in Governor Marcy's list. The captain said they numbered from fifty to seventy, while one of the passengers, Colonel Frazer, thought there were 150, of whom 100 were in reserve. Donald McLeod, who was among the number, says that twenty-eight intended to seize the ship and invade Upper Canada, but many lost their way and only thirteen took part in the attack. Bill Johnston told F. B. Hough, historian, that they numbered thirteen, though the Cleveland Committee that planned the attack had promised him 150 men. It is probable that the estimates made by those attacked are the least reliable.

JOHNSTON AND THE BURNING OF THE PEEL

once. There were only two cases in which they allowed those who came on deck to return for their clothes, but those who brought their clothes or trunks on deck were allowed to take them away. Several of the ladies were driven on shore in their night dresses, and the Ladies' Maid told me they were not even allowed to take their jewellery.'

After all the passengers had been driven ashore the raiders put off in the vessel, allowed her to drift down stream about fifty rods, and dropped anchor. They remained aboard about half an hour, 'probably pillaging all that was valuable and portable'; then they set her afire in five places and left for Abel's Island in three small boats. Unknown to them, the mate and pilot, Roderick M'Swain, was still on board and did not wake until the flames burst into his room. Badly burned, he yet was able to swim ashore. The passengers had taken refuge in a shanty, where 'a ruffian' who told them 'it served them right' was knocked down by Captain Bullock, formerly of the *St. George,* who quickly dragged him outside by the scruff of the neck. The captain obtained a skiff and rowed to Gananoque, and thence by express to Kingston, with the result that all Canadian steamboats were ordered to remain in port. A few hours after the attack the *Oneida* took the *Peel's* passengers aboard and carried them back to Kingston before proceeding on her voyage.

A survey of the damage revealed heavy losses. The ship itself was valued at about $11,000, while it was reported that she was carrying £20,000 in specie to pay off the troops in Upper Canada. Mr. Holditch lost some £1,520 in bank notes, while Colonel R. D. Frazer of Brockville was robbed of £300. Altogether the passengers lost much baggage and jewellery and about £15,000 in specie. Some three or four passengers were reported missing, and they were accounted for by the belief that they belonged to the raiders and joined their fellows after the attack. A traveller on the *Oneida* saw the doomed vessel a few hours after she was fired and described her appearance as she settled in shallow water:

'I had a full view of the remains of the *Sir Robert* as we passed down; she must have upset when the fire reached near the water, as the engine had fallen outward, partly into the water, and partly on one side of the hull, the other side and keel raised out of the water, the shaft almost perpendicular, and the skeleton of one wheel out of the water, nearly in a horizontal position. The fire was then smouldering near the keel.'

There was intense indignation in both the United States and the British provinces when news of the destruction of the *Peel* was received. On the day following the attack Sir George Arthur issued a proclamation requesting the inhabitants to forbear from any outrage or insult in retaliation. On June 2 Lord Durham offered $1,000 reward for information procuring the conviction of any participants. Similarly Governor Marcy of New York posted rewards of $500 for the apprehension of Johnston, $250 for Donald McLeod, Samuel C. Frey, and Robert Smith, and $100 each for any others. He also went immediately to the scene of the outrage and spent ten days gathering information as to the sentiments of the inhabitants, the peculiarities of the region in which Johnston operated, and the nature of his rocky retreats among the islands. He found that there was sympathy for the Patriots even among the American militia. As a result of his investigations Federal troops were sent by the President to Sackett's Harbor and Plattsburg and armed men placed on a Lake Ontario steamer under orders to patrol the region and prevent further piratical attacks.

Not to be outdone in the matter of proclamations, Bill Johnston issued 'to all whom it may concern' his declaration of war against the British Crown as 'Commander-in-Chief of the Naval Forces and Flotilla'. Admitting the destruction of the *Sir Robert Peel,* he said his confederates were largely English-born but included some American volunteers. He announced that he had studied the latest treaties and maps concerning the boundary line among the Thousand Islands, and knew very well what he was about. 'The object of my movement,' he declared, 'is the independence of the Canadas'. From that time Johnston invariably carried with him the colours of the *Sir Robert Peel,* and proudly exhibited his trophy at every opportunity.

Every effort was made in the United States to apprehend the perpetrators, though conditions in the neighbourhood of the attack apparently prevented much in the nature of punishment. Three men were arrested almost immediately. Nathan Lee had considerable booty when captured—'a lady's silk cape, a book of gold leaf, a considerable quantity of coppers, some silver spoons, and a cap'. The other two were Seth D. and Chester Warner. Passengers and crew believed they could identify Bill Johnston, Frey, Phillips, and Wells, 'the latter three Upper Canada refugees, the former a notorious bad character, and chief of the gang from French Creek'; and some of them observed that 'those in command were above the common, and had delicate, slender fingers more used to picking and stealing than to honest labour'. Within two or three days nine men had been arrested and were committed for trial on the evidence of Dr. Thomas Scott.[8] The Brockville *Statesman*

[8] Scott was a passenger on the *Peel.* The raiders asked him to tend a wounded man, who proved to be Hugh Scanlon. He then accompanied them to Abel's Island. Next day he promised that he would not inform and they took him to French Creek, where he identified all the prisoners.

ascertained the names of the raiders, and published them.[9] Twelve men were imprisoned in Watertown jail for six months, but only Anderson was tried and he was found not guilty, presumably by a sympathetic jury.

Bill Johnston, meanwhile, continued to appear here and there among the islands. On June 7 one of his gangs descended upon Amherst Island, near Bath. Sir Richard Bonnycastle received information that

'three isolated farm-houses were plundered, and many valuables and some money obtained; whilst one farmer, in the defence of his property, was inhumanly shot at and lost three fingers and a part of his hand. The pirates were dressed as sailors and well armed, and it is said had one sixteen-oared boat, mounting two three-pounders.'

On June 13 Johnston was reported to be on the Ducks Islands, at the foot of the lake. Shortly afterwards he again struck terror into the inhabitants of the Canadian shore by appearing in the vicinity of Brockville, though he committed no crime on this occasion. The following report of the incident appeared in the Brockville *Statesman*:

'On last Monday this notorious Brigand made his appearance with four armed men in one of his *gigs*, in the River about 10 or 12 miles above this place. The Commander and Mate (we are informed) of the steamer *Oswego* lowered their small boat and went out in the river, where they remained for some time in close *confab* with the Pirate. Some sensation was created in town on Thursday night by a report which was brought in of his being at Oak Point (7 miles from this) with a strong party of armed men.'

Among later depredations was an attack upon a farmer named Preston on the Island of Tanti. The possessions of the family were completely plundered, a son died of wounds, and Preston himself had part of his hand shot off. But in spite of these piratical attacks it was reported that 'the Yankees have actually had the audacity to dub the notorious Bill Johnston "Sir William!"' This, it was stated, they considered proper enough, since the British had knighted MacNab after the destruction of the *Caroline*!

'Sir William' continued to maintain a sort of feudal sovereignty

[9]The following combines the names and information in the *Statesman's* list and Governor Marcy's: Hugh Scanlon, 'an absconding debtor from Kingston'; William Nickles, a deserter from the militia; Robert and William Smith; Marshall W. Forward and William Anderson, Bath; Seth D. and Chester Warner, Bastard Township; Henry Hunter and Samuel C. Frey, Brockville; Donald McLeod, Prescott; and — Thayer, James Potts, Nathan Lee, William Johnston, William Coopernoll (Coppernell), William Leister (Leston), — Robinson (Robertson), James Hunter, William Robbins, and John Tarr. The *Statesman's* list indicates eleven Americans and nine Canadians, while Marcy's shows five Americans and sixteen Canadians. Reports implicating William B. Wells, James Phillips, William H. Leavitt, Ebenezer Wilson, and Patrick Walsh had not been substantiated. Even the ardent Patriot, Hill, referred to the burning of the *Peel* as an 'outrage' by 'an armed band of British refugees and robbers', though he hoped that such activities would lead to war: 'It must come. And if it does the British must bid farewell to Canada—Good times may yet be in store for the Patriots'.

at Fort Wallace for some months, though effective measures were restricting his movements. He declared his island the only independent part of the British domain, and received friends who came to pay their respects. 'His lovely little daughter, about sixteen years old,[10] visits him daily', we are told, while at her home at French Creek she had to put up with the bad language of American soldiers who were constantly haunting his premises. On the Fourth of July a celebration was held at Fort Wallace in honour of that independence which Johnston held in such high regard. A combined British and American force of eighty men tried to surround one of his hide-outs, but owing to the density of the brush on the island the two parties did not reach it simultaneously, and most of the occupants escaped. Two men, Riley Toucy and Jonathan Turnacliff, were found asleep, but Johnston, John Farrow, Robert Smith, William Robbins, John Van Clute, and Allen Early made off into the woods. The two prisoners and Johnston's famous twelve-oared boat[11] were taken on the steamship *Telegraph* to Sackett's Harbor.

Johnston's four stalwart sons, John, Decater, James, and Napoleon, had much of their father's fearlessness. In November, 1838, shortly after the ill-fated raid upon Prescott at the inception of which Johnston was prominent, Federal troops attempted to clean up the district in which his gang operated, and they first captured one of his sons, who had a boat and was awaiting his father. 'Old Bill' was then tracked through the woods, and rushed down to the river shouting, 'My boat! My boat!'; but the boat was gone, and there was nothing left but surrender or death. He made a last effort to escape, but before he reached the woods two troopers were upon him. Even then he made his own terms of surrender, stipulating that his son should be allowed to take his arms. He handed him 'a Cochran rifle (twelve discharges), and two large rifle pistols', and then started with C. T. Burwell and A. B. James for Ogdensburg. He still retained four small pistols and a bowie knife, but in the course of a few minutes he gave these to his son. His arrest and delivery to a file of soldiers was effected three miles from Ogdensburg, and he was removed to the American Hotel, Auburn, where, with John W. Birge, he was placed under guard while indictments were being

---

[10]Kate, 'Bill's very handsome daughter, . . . the Queen of the Thousand Isles', as Sir James Alexander wrote after meeting her, was nineteen at the time. Two novels woven around the activities of Bill and Kate Johnston are: Charley Clewline, *The Empress of the Isles, or the Lake Bravo, a Romance of the Canadian Struggle in 1837* (185?); and P. Hamilton Myers, *The Prisoner of the Border: a Tale of 1838* (1857). Copies of both are in the Toronto Public Library, and the former is in the New York Public Library.

[11]The boat, which had one set of sweeps and another of short oars, was 'clinker built' and painted inside and out in red and yellow, with a black bottom. One Botell, six miles below Cape Vincent, built boats most to Bill's liking.

JOHNSTON AND THE BURNING OF THE PEEL 161

made out. After preliminary evidence was taken as to his part in the Prescott raid Johnston was apparently acquitted, but N. Garrow, United States Marshall, decided he should be held pending other investigations. In some manner, however, he and Birge escaped from custody during the night.

A reward of $200 was offered for his recapture, and he was arrested ten miles from Rome. Trial at Albany resulted in a sentence of a year in jail and a fine of $250, and his daughter Kate[12] sought and obtained permission to share his imprisonment. Six months later he escaped early one evening, walking forty miles before dawn. Remaining in hiding until things had quieted down, Johnston then proceeded to Washington with a well-signed petition for his pardon. This was refused by Van Buren's administration, but soon afterwards granted by the incoming President Harrison.

His Patriot activities at an end, Johnston returned to French Creek, where he was shortly appointed keeper of the Rock Island lighthouse, located on the spot where the *Peel* was burned. He later became a tavern-keeper, and had the reputation of engaging in smuggling when the opportunity offered. In 1843 Sir James Alexander crossed the St. Lawrence in search of deserters from the Kingston garrison and had some intention of employing Johnston in the work. In appearance he found him 'hale, straight, and ruddy; his nose was sharp, as were his features generally, and his eyes were keen and piercing; his lips compressed and receding; his height about five feet ten inches; he wore a broad-brimmed black hat, black stock and vest, frock and trowsers of dark duffle. He was very charitable and a good father', and other characteristics of the man became apparent during the visit. Sir James learned that he owned Ball, Shot, Powder, and other islands, no doubt appropriately named by himself, and he was shown his favourite galley, which he offered to sell for sixty dollars. The old bravado asserted itself when he offered to row or sail against any boatman on the St. Lawrence. As a parting question Sir James asked him what had been gained by the Rebellion. 'Do you call the expenditure of four millions of British cash nothing? That is what our side has gained', he answered. A colourful life came to a close on February 17, 1870, when William Johnston died in the Hotel Walton,[13] Clayton (French Creek), at the age of eighty-eight years.

[12] Kate Johnston married Charles H. Haws, Clayton, and died in March, 1878, aged fifty-nine.
[13] Kept by his son Decater. Bill's brother John was at one time a member of the New York Assembly and President of the First National Bank of Clayton. Captain Henry Johnston, Clayton, whose family came from the same part of England, recalls Bill as an old man and is well acquainted with the locale of his activities.

BIBLIOGRAPHY

For the Hickory Island occupation see 'Contemplated Attack on Kingston', and 'Further Particulars of the Threatened Attack upon Kingston', *Cobourg Star*, February 28, 1838, quoting the Kingston *Upper Canada Herald*; 'An Unsung Heroine', Montreal *Gazette*, February 26, 1934; Hough, *Jefferson County*, 520; Syracuse *Sunday Herald*, November 26, 1899; *The Growth of a Century*, 344-9; *Caroline Almanack*, 28; Heustis, *Narrative*, 32; Preston, *Three Years' Residence*, I 138 *et seq.*; and Bonnycastle, *Canada As It Is*, II 79 *et seq*. The main sources of biographical information on Johnston are (1) 'Bill Johnson, the Lake Buccanier. Scenes on the Frontier', reprinted from the *Albany Argus* in the Toronto *Patriot*, July 17, 1838; (2) Alexander, *L'Acadie*, I 309-12; and (3) 'Frontier Events of 1837-39. William Johnston, the so-called Pirate of the Thousand Islands', by Henry S. Johnston, in the Clayton *On the St. Lawrence*, January 9, 1936. For copies of his historical articles the author is indebted to Captain Johnston and to Mrs. Arthur L. Williams, Public Librarian of Clayton, N.Y. The main accounts of the burning of the *Sir Robert Peel* are: (1) 'Outrage! Steamboat Sir Robert Peel Burned!', the narrative of Mr. Holditch, Port Robinson, quoted from the Oswego *Commercial Herald* in the Toronto *Patriot*, June 1, 1838; (2) Narrative of 'A gentleman on the Oneida', purporting to contain 'facts and not rumours', *Cobourg Star*, June 6, 1838; (3) 'Another Outrage', Philadelphia *Inquirer and Public Courier*, June 4, 1838; (4) 'The Frontier Outrage', containing Captain John B. Armstrong's deposition, *Inquirer*, June 6; (5) MS. letter of A. B. Hill, Ogdensburg, to William Lyon Mackenzie, June 3, 1838, Lindsey Papers; and (6) Account given by Donald McLeod, one of the raiders, in his *A Brief Review*, 242-3. Johnston's proclamation is dated June 10, 1838. It was printed in the *Albany Argus*, from which it was reprinted in the New York *Albion* of June 16. Among local histories which contain a reprint of it are Leavitt's *Leeds and Grenville*, 45, and Haddock's *The Thousand Islands*, 156-63. Lord Durham's proclamation appeared first in an extra of the *Quebec Gazette*, from which it was reprinted in the Toronto *Patriot* of June 8 and in numerous other periodicals. For Governor Marcy's proclamation and his list of participants see Bonnycastle, II 186-7. Johnston's subsequent activities, as well as sidelights on his character, are described in Bonnycastle, II 136; Lindsey, II 135; Alexander, *L'Acadie*, I 309-12; Preston, I 138 *et seq.*; 'More Canadian Difficulties', Philadelphia *Inquirer*, June 13, 1838; 'Bill Johnston Again', *Cobourg Star*, June 27; *Patriot*, July 17; 'Canada and the Frontier', *Inquirer*, July 17; Letter *ibid.*, July 19, quoted from *Mackenzie's Gazette*; 'Bill Johnston', *Cobourg Star*, December 12, 1838, quoting the *Oswego Palladium* and the *Albany Argus*; and 'Escape of Johnson and Birge', *Albany Daily Advertiser*, December 4, 1838. Two novels based upon the activities of Bill and Kate Johnston are Charley Clewline, *The Empress of the Isles, or the Lake Bravo, a Romance of the Canadian Struggle in 1837* (1851); and P. Hamilton Myers, *The Prisoner of the Border: a Tale of 1838* (1857). Copies of both are in the Toronto Public Library, and the former is in the New York Public Library. The trial of Anderson in Watertown for participation in the attack on the *Peel* is outlined in the Toronto *Patriot*, July 6, 1838.

From Daniel Heustis, *Narrative*, 1847
The Battle of the Windmill, November, 1838
The most serious engagement of the Patriot War took place below Prescott

From Smyth, *Sketches in the Canadas*, 1842   Coke Smyth
Defeat of the Rebels at Dickinson Landing, 1838
Coke Smyth was drawing master to Lord Durham's children

in palliation are of opinion that the prisoner Nils Szoltevcky Von Schoultz is guilty of the charge preferred against him in violation of the provisions of the statute passed in the first year of Her Majesty's reign entitled "An act to protect the inhabitants of this province against lawless aggressions from subjects of foreign Countries at peace with Her Majesty" and they do therefore adjudge him the said Nils Szoltevcky Von Schoultz to be hanged by the neck till he be dead at such time and at such place as Her Excellency the Lieutenant Governor shall be pleased to direct and appoint

[signature]
Col & President

[signature]
Col & Judge Advocate

The Lieutenant Governor in Council approves of the finding & sentence of the Court Martial upon Nils Szoltevcky Von Schoultz as set forth & contained in the foregoing proceedings —

Done in Council at Government House the 3.d day of December 1838.

Geo Arthur
Lieut Gov

Courtesy Public Archives of Canada
Final Page of the Von Schoultz Trial Record

CHAPTER XVII

BEN LETT AND THE COBOURG CONSPIRACY

BENJAMIN LETT's activities in the Patriot War were as outrageous as those of William Johnston. Lett was of Dutch and Irish extraction, his ancestors having removed to Ireland in the reign of William III. During the Rebellion of 1798 his mother was twice imprisoned at Wexford for loyalty to the British Crown, and her brother, Benjamin Warren, was murdered by the rebels. In 1819 Robert Lett, his wife, two daughters, and four sons, including Benjamin, aged five, emigrated to Canada and settled on the Ottawa River near Montreal. There the father died, and his widow and her children removed in 1833 to Darlington Township, Upper Canada. The family, who were Protestants and Orangemen, were owners of a farm on lot 27, concession 7, and they were known as respectable and cultured people; while Ben's sister was a poetess of something more than local reputation and merit. A local historian recalled that Lett was

'a dangerous, queer man to have a difference with. He was a man of studious habits, and when he brought his grist to the mill east of Harmony he would borrow a book, disappear all day in the forest, return at night, and set off silently with his flour. He was arrested as a rebel in 1837 although he took not the slightest interest in politics. He was sentenced to prison as a conspirator by Colonel Reid of Bowmanville, and while being conveyed to the jail at Kingston by three guards he overpowered them by sheer strength and cunning and escaped.'

Our knowledge of Lett's participation in the Rebellion of 1837 and Patriot activities thereafter is beclouded by a mist of rumour and legend, as a result of which it may be that he has been blamed for certain nefarious actions of others—as well as credited with numerous escapades and feats of daring which have no existence in fact. A relative states that Ben became identified with the Patriot cause because he was 'furious at the injustice' of a group of Orangemen who fired at him near his home for refusing to join in an expedition to hunt down Mackenzie sympathizers. Apparently he did not join the Patriots at Montgomery's Tavern in December, 1837, but it is said that after the battle a refugee came east through Darlington, looking and acting 'like a gentleman, one who had occupied a good position in life, but presenting the appearance of a hunted deer, without boots and only partly clothed. Ben took him under his protection. They went east and caught the Kingston stage, and finally landed in the United States'. Another source of information in the vicinity of Lett's home suggested Lount as his companion, stating that they came to the Powers home in Clarke Township and begged shelter, were allowed to spend the night there, and continued eastward through the woods early the next morning; while there is also the story of John Frank, who claimed he had found Lett, armed to the teeth, sound asleep in his corn field, but 'with the true nobility of an Englishman' he gave him something to eat and allowed him to go his way.

Whatever may have been the circumstances of his crossing the frontier, there is no doubt that Lett participated in a number of Patriot activities originating in the United States in 1838. He was among Mackenzie's force on Navy Island, and his conduct there was commended by his leader. General Donald McLeod states that he was in the force which invaded Fighting Island on February 24 and 25, and helped carry off a wounded man; while a relative credits him with the same gallantry a few days later at the Pelee Island raid. Reports, however, that he was at Windmill Point and participated in the burning of the *Sir Robert Peel* are almost certainly wrong; and other generally believed stories of his depredations are open to very considerable doubt. But enough is known to warrant his having the reputation of being fearless and unscrupulous.

Among the depredations in which he is believed to have participated was the murder of Captain Edgeworth Ussher on November 16, 1838. Unknown persons knocked upon the door of Ussher's home in Chippewa after he had gone to bed, and upon going down to ascertain the purpose of their visit, he was shot through a side window.[1] In January, 1839, there was a plan to fire 'the whole British fleet, lying in Kingston harbour', and Lett is said to have come 'very near' achieving his design. A few months later he was engaged in a raid which ranks among the most outrageous of the Patriot War. An outline of the setting in which these conspirators played their parts will fit the event into its proper place.

When the contents of Lord Durham's *Report on the Affairs of British North America* became generally known, the Reformers, who had had perforce to restrain somewhat their public utterances, eagerly welcomed their new champion and seized the opportunity to hold 'Durham meetings' to further the interests of

---

[1]The Toronto *Palladium* of November 28 describes the inquest and funeral of Ussher. It is recorded on his tombstone in Chippewa that he was 'cruelly assassinated at the early age of thirty-four years'. T. R. Preston says Lett admitted receiving money for the deed.

reform. The Tory press, on the other hand, were as quick to label all such gatherings as treasonable, and their members as rebels, Yankees, and republicans.[2] Two of these meetings were in the background of the notable but little-known[3] Patriot conspiracy which developed in the vicinity of Cobourg in the last days of July, 1839, and in which Ben Lett is believed to have taken a prominent part.

On July 1 a Durham meeting was held in the Township of Haldimand. Some 300 Reformers were present, and the meeting was orderly, with no interference on the part of either Tories or magistrates, two of the latter being on hand to see that the law was respected. Those who participated in this meeting were as public-spirited men as might have been found in any assemblage of the opposite political persuasion, but the *Cobourg Star* labelled them 'Canadian Chartists, . . chiefly liberated traitors'.

A week later a similar meeting was held in Cobourg, 'the Durhamites', says the *Star,* having 'determined on insulting the Conservative town of Cobourg'. A considerable part of the assemblage came in from Haldimand by wagon, flying two flags, one of which was inscribed 'Lord Durham and Reform!' A rough hustings having been constructed in front of the Town Hall, 'a crew of the most ill-favoured, Yankee-visaged democrats' mounted the platform and commenced the meeting. But a group of Old Countrymen, principally Irish, found this 'audacious display of insolence and rebellion' too much for them, and armed with shillelaghs, demanded the surrender of the Durham flag. One of the 'Jack Cades' on the platform drew a pistol, but the flag was given up after a tussle and 'torn into a thousand shreds and trampled on with contempt'. A volley of stones quickly put the 'Durhamites' to flight, one being carried off wounded. After this typical old-time battle, the town was quiet for a while, though among minor demonstrations of loyalty, one man was given a ride on a rail and forced to give three cheers for the Queen. One of the Reformers' wagons was closely pursued until the driver fired a pistol into the mob, whereupon his 'good-humoured & sober' assailants, somewhat taken aback, permitted him to escape, though not without wishing most audibly that they could have killed him. The *Cobourg Star* trusted that the warning implied in the day's proceedings would be heeded, and that no more

[2]The *Cobourg Star* ranked with the Toronto *Patriot* in Tory partisanship. The Toronto *Mirror* of July 26 called it 'a vile Tory journal'.

[3]T. R. Preston, who refers to the raid in his *Three Years' Residence*, states that Sir George Arthur was aimed at with a rifle as he passed near Cobourg in October, 1838, and was saved only when it missed fire. The Lieutenant-Governor had also paid a visit to the town during that summer, and 'a humble mechanic was very much maltreated because he refused to take off his hat in respect' to the ex-Governor of the Van Diemen's Land convict colony. See the Cobourg *Plain Speaker,* August 23, 1838.

people would be 'inoculated by the pernicious virus of his Lordship's Report, for rebellion must not be allowed to show itself unresisted for a single moment'.[4]

Among the results of this affair, which was described by the Toronto *Examiner* as a peaceful meeting disturbed by a band of Orange ruffians,[5] at the instigation of the Family Compact, was the cancellation of the regular Orange Parade in Cobourg. This was stated to be as a mark of appreciation of the Roman Catholics who joined in breaking up the Durham meeting, though it was probably suggested by a fear of retaliation on the part of the Reformers. But a plot was being hatched which, rightly or wrongly, was at once associated with Durham meetings in general and the Cobourg riot in particular.

Samuel P. Hart, the son of an old soldier in the British Army and a resident of Cobourg and Belleville, was the leader in the conspiracy. In the early eighteen-thirties he published in Cobourg an ephemeral sheet, the *Weevil,* and he became more and more radical. In 1836 he commenced The *Plain Speaker* in Belleville. His opinions aroused resentment, and a mob of militiamen attacked his press and dragged him through the mud and slush when his paper came out one morning with the British coat-of-arms upside down.[6] He fled to the United States, where he became prominent in the Patriot organization as editor of the *Lewiston Telegraph.*

John Montgomery's boarding-house in Rochester had become a Patriot rendezvous almost as well known as his former hotel

[4]Numerous accounts of such meetings are found in the contemporary press. On October 15 the 'Responsible Government party' met at Davis's Temperance Hotel, Yonge Street, but 'Mr. Sheriff Jarvis armed his murderous faction', and 'aided by Mr. Mayor Powell with *his* Aldermen and Police' and all 'the low, drunken carters, &c., each armed with pistols and bludgeons', drove the Reformers from the spot. They tried to continue their meeting a hundred yards away but were followed, and every man 'who had not a purple ribbond in his bosom' was 'beat, stabbed, and maltreated'. (*Mirror,* October 18, 1839). Mackenzie refers to the riot as the 'Toronto Massacre', and states that two Reformers were 'murdered' on the spot and two others died later.

[5]William R. Lount, son of Samuel, wrote Mackenzie describing a visit to his old home, which he found 'plundered', and 'my mother and all our family driven out by a band of those blood-thirsty wretches, the Irish Orangemen, our beloved country's curse'. On the other hand, 'old Tory Mayerhoffer', earlier a Roman Catholic priest but during the Rebellion a Church of England clergyman to the German settlers in Markham and Vaughan townships, found 'the Orange Boys' his chief defenders. They alone were 'faithful and courageous', and proceeding to the church 'drove away the rebel guard' and broke open the doors, telling him to send word of any further trouble to Brown's Corners and they would oblige by hanging the offenders 'on the first tree'.

[6]Incidental information about 'Sammy' Hart, as he was called in Cobourg, may be found in McAllister, *Historical Reminiscences,* 72. The Reverend James Gardiner, who was a journeyman printer in Hart's office at the time of the attack, said that the coat-of-arms inversion was accidental. While Hastings County was not among the most disaffected, Mackenzie received a list of 482 pledged Patriots from C. H. McCollom, merchant, one of the leaders. McCollom was in jail three days but on December 20, 1837, was set free, and fled to Montgomery County, N.Y. Sir Richard Bonnycastle refers to the 'many specimens of furious revolutionists' in Belleville and the Township of Sydney, and describes 'many plots and counterplots', among others the presence in Belleville of 'an American gunsmith' to provide munitions for the rebels.

near Toronto, and there about the middle of July Hart had a talk with Henry J. Moon, another Patriot. Upon being asked if he wished to go into a money-making business, Moon replied in the affirmative and was let in on the scheme, which was to get a schooner, put two pieces of cannon on it, and 'go skulking'. Hart then went to Oswego to arrange for a boat, while Moon went to Cobourg, presumably to further the plan there. Hart promised to write to him in care of Montgomery, but a message came to Moon while he was still in Cobourg, asking him to meet Hart in Rochester or Oswego.

Meanwhile Hart was completing the arrangements for the enterprise. On Friday, July 26, he had a long talk with Captain Terry of the schooner *Guernsey*, of Genesee, and on that day nine men went aboard, including Ben Lett. Most of them were American Patriots or Hunters, among them being Peter Wilkins and William Baker, 'a scoundrel who upon his own statement was concerned in the robbery of Mr. Taylor on the Niagara frontier'. There were also Edward Kennedy and Henry Wilson, described generally with the others as 'strong, powerful-looking men'.

In the early hours of Saturday the *Guernsey* set sail from Oswego with another schooner on which was a party 'under command of one Anderson, who is gone on a similar expedition to the Niagara frontier'. The crew thought the head of the lake was the destination of the *Guernsey*, but her direction was shortly changed towards Cobourg, where the captain said passengers were to be landed. There was but little wind at the start of the voyage, and by daylight she was only four or five miles from port; but a good breeze rose during Saturday, and the lake was crossed. Among the baggage was a trunkful of weapons, and the conspirators spent time in practice with pistols and bowie knives, fitting on their military belts with evident satisfaction. The sailors also observed bundles of matches and bottles of turpentine, and by overhearing chance bits of conversation were able to gather that Cobourg was to be burned after the bank had been robbed and two or three individuals plundered or murdered. Sheppard McCormick, who, the conspirators thought, was still custom-house official in the town, was to be murdered[7] for his part in cutting out the *Caroline,* supply boat of the Navy Island Patriots. Hart was apparently the leader of the party, and one mariner heard him say that he had lost his house and property and had been driven from home, and that he was determined to have satisfaction.

[7] In a letter to Mackenzie 'Jonah' states that the general belief in Cobourg was that the real object of the expedition was to take McCormick across the border 'and deliver him to justice at Lockport', presumably in connection with the firing of the *Caroline.*

It was after midnight when the *Guernsey* lay to off the north shore of the lake and landed six men from a small boat. They were Hart, Lett, Kennedy, Wilkins, Wilson, and Baker, and the party was put ashore near the Evans farm, some five miles east of Cobourg. The other four men were probably not concerned in the enterprise, for they disembarked at Whitby the following night. The Cobourg conspirators wore belts loaded with arms when they landed, and a sailor observed them hiding other weapons on the shore. They then went to their rendezvous, which was the farm of Joseph Ash, about two miles east of the town. During Sunday Henry Moon rode to 'the blue house' on Ash's invitation and was taken by him to a neighbouring dwelling occupied by Ash's son, Joseph, jr., to which they were admitted by the secret Patriot rap on the door. Wilkins, Baker, and Hart were there, and from them Moon learned that they planned to rob Maurice Jaynes, a wealthy farmer, after which they intended to plunder the private bank operated by 'Squire' Henry in his residence, which still stands at the south-east corner of Church and King Streets, Cobourg.

Later Ben Lett appeared and by way of introducing himself told Moon that he had already 'cost the Province about £6,000'; and he introduced Wilkins by describing him as a captain at the Battle of Prescott, and for whose head the government would give a great deal.[8] As Lett strutted about in his belt, which contained four pistols and a bowie-knife, they discussed the possible means of escape after their proposed exploit had been achieved. Moon's suggestion that they take to the woods brought nothing but angry responses, for they wished to return to the United States without delay. One Downer had a schooner in Cobourg harbour at the time, and it was decided to seize his boat. After much argument about the most effective method of using the schooner, the majority agreed that the crew should not be put ashore at once but sent in by small boat after the raiders were well out in the lake.

There were many suggestions as to the best means of robbing Jaynes. Hart said that he 'kept his money in a pail, in a churn, in the inner room, and that it could be easily got at'. Lett volunteered to go with one other and effect the robbery, but his departure was delayed by a lengthy discussion as to the suitability of a bag for the money, and as to whether the family should be forced to lie face down or be called out one by one. When Lett approved the latter plan, Baker rejoined that such

---

[8]This is mere braggadocio unless he fought under an alias and was one of very few who escaped, for no such name is found in Heustis's list of participants.

was the method attempted at Taylor's, but that Mrs. Taylor 'had concealed the money in her bosom, and so they had got far less than they expected'. It was then decided to commit the robbery in the evening so that an escape could be effected during the night. After leaving the Jaynes farm it was intended to rid Cobourg in particular and Upper Canada in general of two prominent members of the Boulton family, strong supporters of the Family Compact. The Honourable George S. and D'Arcy Boulton were not only objectionable as political enemies of the Patriots, but Moon, at least, had some personal antipathies arising out of property. The dogs of the Boultons, it appeared later, had been poisoned to facilitate entry to their homes. It was anticipated that Robert Henry's bank could hardly be plundered without breaking open the door and, if need be, taking his life, for he always kept the keys about his person. Lett and Hart were busy in the kitchen 'running bullets by the stove', while Moon rode to Cobourg wearing Lett's coat and hat as a partial disguise. Walter Woolcott was counted upon to provide a wagon for some part of the enterprise, and his inability to do so until Monday night led to a postponement. Foster Sprague, a sailor, was at the Ash home when Moon returned, and he apparently intended to join the conspiracy.

But Moon had already made up his mind to inform the authorities. As he walked to Cobourg with Sprague (he had lent his horse to Kennedy) they talked the matter over, and apparently his intention was clearly enough expressed, for he observed that he was a Patriot but would not be 'a midnight assassin'. He admitted he was afraid of the consequences, and particularly he 'did not like to be near Lett, who had fire in his eye and would as soon murder me as anyone else'. His wife urged him to go through with it, saying that he would doubtless be murdered if he informed. When they separated Sunday night, Sprague was uncertain what he would do.

Early Monday morning Moon sought an interview with D'Arcy Boulton, who, when he learned his business, called Benjamin Clark, a magistrate, into his office, and had Moon give a full account of the conspiracy, describing the men and taking an affidavit as to the truth of his deposition. It was decided to surround the houses of the two Ashes that evening, while Moon kept up appearances with his former confederates. He had tea at Sprague's, Kennedy also being present; but it was apparent that he was suspected. Privately he advised Sprague to stay away from the conspirators. After the meal he tried to hasten the attack on the houses, and even as he was doing so he saw Kennedy running through 'the fields by the Seminary',[9] presumably to escape from the district.

Early that evening 'a body of trusty men' met at Captain J. C. Boswell's home, mounted their horses, and proceeded eastward along the Kingston Road. They included Messrs. Manners, Tremaine, Boswell, Charles Clark, Charles Ruttan, D'Arcy Boulton, Kenneth Mackenzie, and John Brady. A few others, including R. D. Chatterton and Benjamin Clark, magistrates, arrived in time to take down the prisoners' depositions. Dividing into two groups the posse quickly surrounded the houses of the Messrs. Ash.[10] Captain Boswell, demanding entrance in the Queen's name into the home of Joseph Ash, sr., arrested Wilkins, Wilson, and Baker; while Captain Clark, after offering to blow the brains out of anyone who resisted entry, led the search of the house of Joseph Ash, jr., capturing Hart as he was attempting to climb out of a window. The elder Ash was found hiding in his pig-pen, and both father and son, after at first denying that any men were in their homes, later made excuses for their presence. Miles Luke, formerly a Cobourg tanner, was visiting one of the homes at the time, but had no connection with the conspiracy and was not detained.

In addition to powder-flasks and bullet-moulds, a formidable array of pistols and bowie-knives was found hidden under beds and elsewhere in the houses. Bullets were found in Baker's pockets, but Hart was unarmed when taken. The depositions of the prisoners were taken down, Baker explaining his presence in the district by an exceedingly improbable story, while Hart refused to sign his after it was written. The six prisoners were then tied up and conveyed to Cobourg jail.

The conspirators were brought to trial on September 13, during the regular Newcastle District Assizes, though there were apparently some who hoped for a court-martial. Mr. Justice Jones presided, and he was assisted in his duties by the Honourable Messrs. Burnham and Boswell. The Judge's charge consisted of a lengthy disquisition on the crime of treason, leading up to the case in point. It was stressed that British subjects only could be charged with treason, while Americans might be indicted for felony.[11] The law on conspiracy was similarly explained, after which the prisoners were charged with 'conspiracy to murder Robert Henry, Esq.; to enter the dwelling-house of the said

[9] Upper Canada Academy, later Victoria College. The original building still stands, and the fields to the east of it remain as in 1839.

[10] The family still occupy the same farm, near the 'Kingston Crossing'. Records in the Cobourg Registry Office show that the first patent for land in Hamilton Township was taken out by Joseph Ash in 1798.

[11] This was the view at the time, though incorrect. See note 7, p. 195.

Robert Henry, and to induce one Henry J. Moon to aid and assist them to rob and murder'. The indictment contained seven counts, and the prisoners pleaded not guilty.

It was apparently felt from the start that the Messrs. Ash were not as deeply involved in the conspiracy as the other four prisoners; perhaps the use of their houses as a rendezvous was the extent of their complicity. In any case they were allowed to sit in front of the prisoners' box occupied by the others. The *Cobourg Star* set them down as 'two reformers of the Durham school who figured at the late meeting in Cobourg'. Hart, 'long a resident of this village, . . seemed unconscious of the situation in which he was placed, and behaved throughout with a great deal of levity'; while Wilkins had 'every appearance of a desperado, and the loss of the right eye gives his face a peculiarly sinister appearance'.

The result of the trial was pretty much a foregone conclusion, for the circumstances under which the prisoners were taken admitted of but little defence; nor were the times such that any sympathy was wasted on American Patriots—much less upon conspirators whose depredations could advance no cause but their own. The Attorney-General opened the case by an impassioned address on the heinous nature of the crime, which, he said, was 'the most atrocious, the most cold-blooded'. Referring to Hart particularly, he said it was 'horrible to think that he, the son of an old soldier, should conspire to imbrue his hands in the blood of innocent and inoffensive men and endeavour to subvert the government of this country'. In fact he blamed the whole scheme upon the political controversy, 'the demon of change and innovation which had upset the province from end to end'. Referring next to Henry Moon, the Honourable W. H. Draper gave him credit for exposing the conspiracy when he saw that murder was intended, and suggested that for this public service he should be honoured. After further references to the law regarding conspiracy, the first witness was called.

The Crown's case was, of course, largely built around the evidence of the informer Moon, but it was strengthened and corroborated by the story of the trip across the lake in the *Guernsey*, as told by George Hart, the mate, and James Stewart, a sailor, who received a hundred dollars for appearing in court. Sheriff Ruttan made a determined effort to bring back Sprague, who had apparently gone to the United States when the conspiracy was uncovered; but although he was offered immunity from prosecution and part of Moon's reward, and appears to have accompanied the sheriff from Rochester to Oswego in the steamer *Express*, he refused to return to Cobourg, and it was suggested in court that his fellow-Patriots prevented him from doing so.

Two letters attributed to Hart were produced to show that this particular conspiracy was not the first in which he had been engaged behind the Patriot cloak. Much contained in the letters was obscure, but they indicated that 'the villains' (Tories) had destroyed his Belleville printing office, and he was seeking compensation of £50 from the brother of the owner of the steamer *Traveller*; for Hart claimed that he had persuaded Bill Johnston to give up his plan to seize and burn this steamship as she lay at anchor at the mouth of the Genesee. He indicated in the letter that if refused he would try to get the money from the Buffalo executive of the Patriot Hunters. It was also stated that 'some M. P. P.'s are to be assassinated in order to create disorder in Toronto at the opening of Parliament', the object being to cause a concentration of troops there while the Patriots effected a landing elsewhere. The second letter indicated a scheme to destroy all Canadian steamboats on Lake Ontario, and said that 'if the Canadian government wish my services they must forward me three hundred pounds before I leave here' (Lewiston). In these communications Hart appears as both a blackmailer and a traitor to the Patriot organization.[12]

The evidence submitted in defence of the prisoners consisted almost entirely of an attempt to break down Moon's story. Their case was in charge of D'Arcy E. Boulton, who made a somewhat unnecessary apology for acting as defence counsel. His cross-examination of Moon did not alter his evidence in any essential, but he elaborated somewhat his membership in the Patriot Hunters. An attempt was made to draw from Moon the names of Hunters on the Canadian side of the frontier, but it was defeated when the Judge decided that such a question could not be put. This has the appearance of an effort to inject local politics into the trial, but it was considered at the time to be an attempt to discredit Moon's testimony by proving false his information in this respect. Robert H. Williams, a brother-in-law of Moon's, gave evidence of Moon's complicity in the plot, suggesting that he had told him he was the captain. The purpose of the conspiracy, he had learned, was to get all the money possible and stir up an invasion of the province. On being questioned as to Moon's character he injected a little humour into the case by replying: 'You may judge what it is; he was first a Methodist, then a Baptist, next

[12]Mackenzie referred to Hart as 'a spy for the Hamiltons', and said that he had 'offered for £300 to go fully into the Judas trade for Arthur'. The references are, respectively, to the owners of the steamer *Traveller*, and the Lieutenant-Governor.

an Infidel, and now a Traitor'. He elaborated upon his remark by observing that Moon had said 'he commanded a company of 80 near this place. . . He has led men into difficulty and deserted them, and disclosed the cause of the men whom he had joined'. Williams indicated that he also was a sworn Hunter. Several other witnesses were brought forward by the defence in an effort to discredit Moon's testimony, four of them—Samuel Stevens, Jacob W. Myers, J. C. Bush, and Nelson G. Reynolds—stating they would not believe him on oath. D'Arcy Boulton, defence counsel, spoke at length in the same vein and made an eloquent plea to the jury to disregard Moon's evidence as entirely unreliable. The *Cobourg Star* admitted that many of the townspeople were similarly inclined to impugn his veracity, called him traitor, and 'pointed and hooted' at him as he passed through the streets; some of the bolder, indeed, had declared vengeance against him, and his position was obviously not an enviable one.

The depositions of the prisoners, however, largely bore out the general truth of Moon's story. The elder Ash's statement corroborated his evidence in many particulars, as did also the depositions of Hart and Wilkins, though Baker explained his presence in the country by a story that was palpably absurd. The younger Ash stated he had intended to inform the authorities of the condition of affairs at his home, but, as the Judge remarked in summing up the case, he made no effort to do so; for he had 'gone to meeting' in Cobourg on Sunday evening, which would have furnished a good opportunity. Mr. Justice Jones considered there was no doubt that father and son were willing participants in the conspiracy, being both members of the Hunters' Lodge; while their depositions were characterized by contradictions which rendered them by no means satisfactory. As for Moon's story, the Judge told the jury that in his opinion it bore the air of truth.

A trial of seventeen hours' duration was concluded when the jury brought in a verdict of guilty. The following morning the Judge addressed the prisoners and passed sentence upon them as follows: Hart, seven years in the penitentiary; Joseph Ash, sr., six months in jail and a fine of £100; Joseph Ash, jr., twelve months in jail and a fine of £50. It can hardly be said that the punishment was not fairly apportioned according to the guilt of the parties; nor, considering the times, are the sentences as heavy as might well have been expected.

So ended 'another atrocious attempt of the American pirates to murder and pillage the inhabitants of this unfortunate country under cloak of assisting us to obtain in a more summary manner the blessings of "Responsible Government" recommended by Lord Durham'.[13] It was a far-fetched deduction, however, that such a criminal conspiracy must be closely related to Durham meetings and the Reform party in general, and the Reform press denounced the *Star* for its 'wicked and infamous attempt' to identify them.[14] The escape of Lett and Kennedy through a thickly-settled territory was deprecated by the *Star* as indicating that they had plenty of sympathizers and protectors. 'One man openly declared', wrote 'Erinensis' to Sir George Arthur, 'that if he knew where Lett was asleep he would not assist in his capture, or even give information'. It would have been no more than justice, wrote the same correspondent, had 'every one of the villains been shot down', and the house which sheltered them burned to the ground. Immediately after the flight of the two conspirators the following description of them was printed:

'DESCRIPTION OF THE PIRATES LETT AND KENNEDY.

'LETT is a man about 25 years old, 5 ft. 11 inches high, rather slim, sandy hair and whiskers, very red face and freckled, light skinned, very large muscular hands, with round, long, and very white fingers. Eyes light blue and *remarkably penetrating*. Had on a black fur hat, rather high in the crown and broad brim; blue coat with black velvet collar; mixed pantaloons and *laced boots*; dark coloured vest with light spots on it and figured metal buttons; common cotton shirt.

'KENNEDY is about 23 to 25 years old, 5 ft. 9 or 10 inches high, slender figure, full face, dark hair, clear complexion, dark eyes, and altogether a handsome looking man. Wears generally a dark frock coat, dark pantaloons and vest, white full-bosomed shirt, and black stock.'

There is a possibility that the man who called himself Walker may not have been Lett, as generally supposed; for Rochester newspapers had but recently suggested that he was on his way to Texas. Kennedy is a somewhat nebulous figure, for his real name is said to have been Owen Molson. The direction he was taking when last seen does not suggest that he went to Ash's to warn Lett before escaping; nor does it appear likely that Hart and the others would have remained there if they had learned that Moon had informed the authorities. It is probable, therefore, that Kennedy met Lett elsewhere, or that Lett became suspicious and departed Sunday night or early Monday; for there is no indication

[13] On May 15, 1839, a Grand Jury of the Newcastle District declared Lord Durham's Report a 'seditious, false, and dangerous libel'. Mackenzie gives the names of the jurors and some incisive comment in his *Caroline Almanack*, 51.

[14] The *Examiner, Mirror, Palladium*, and 'other kindred prints' are so quoted in the *Star* of August 14, which also observes that 'the *New York Commercial Advertiser* sneers at the account in the *Star* of the late intended murder, and insinuates we have designedly mis-named the pirates AMERICANS. We respectfully inform our contemporary that with the exception of Hart and, we believe, one other (the younger Ash), all concerned in the affair *were* Americans'. The informer, Henry J. Moon, was a resident of Ameliasburgh Township until 1836, when he removed to Cobourg.

BEN LETT AND THE COBOURG CONSPIRACY 175

whatever that either of them escaped when the houses were surrounded Monday night.

There remain to be considered but a few results of the conspiracy. The schooner *Guernsey*, after a short stop at Whitby, continued to the River Credit, obtained a cargo of lumber, and returned to Oswego. But the American authorities had heard of the affair and immediately seized the vessel. In Cobourg, meanwhile, there was the greatest apprehension that the conspiracy was but the forerunner of open and secret violence, and renewal of American 'sympathy' on a large scale. On August 1, three days after the arrest of the six men, the magistrates of the town addressed a letter to Sir George Arthur expressing their fears and requesting immediate and effective protection. On the fifth, as their request had not been met with, they wrote again in stronger language. Finally, on August 11, nearly a fortnight after the discovery of the plot, a company of militia, 'consisting of eighty men, rank and file', reached Cobourg on the steamship *Commodore Barrie*.[15] They apparently remained until the trial was over, and their presence prevented the rescue of the prisoners—if any such attempt was contemplated.

Benjamin Lett evaded arrest, but was occasionally observed along the frontier. The *Quebec Gazette* of September 30, 1839, noted that 'the notorious Lett was seen in Manchester a day or two since'. A year later the attention of Sir Richard Bonnycastle was drawn to Lett, a loafer on Buffalo wharf. 'He boasted of having blown up Brock's monument and of shooting Captain Ussher', wrote Sir Richard. Perhaps on that account he has generally been assumed responsible for the destruction of the Queenston Heights monument on Good Friday, April 17, 1840, but the following item from the *Christian Guardian*, though implicating Lett in another raid, states that others were known to be guilty of that outrage:

'It is beyond doubt that John H. De Witt, whose trial appears in to-day's impression, was a leading instrument in the execution, if not the actual planner, of most of the outrages which took place on this frontier a few years ago. From information the accuracy of which is not questioned it appears that in addition to the offence for which he has been sentenced to incarceration for life, he and a man named Wheeler were the parties by whom Brock's Monument was blown up; by the same men was Dr. Mewburn's barn burnt down; De Witt and a man named Caswell were the destroyers of Chippewa Church, and De Witt and Benjamin Lett were the persons who set fire to Mr. Henry Miller's Barn.'

[15] The *Mirror* of August 9 announced that Lett had not been arrested, 'although a company of the 1st incorporated Battallion, under Sir Allan McNab', was in hot pursuit. MacNab was not present, the company being commanded by Captain Ussher, brother of the man assassinated by Lett.

On June 25, 1840, Lett engaged in an unsuccessful attempt to burn the steamship *Great Britain* at Oswego, and was arrested when his confederate, David Dafoe, turned state's evidence. A trunkful of high explosives had been conveyed aboard, and Lett was convicted of attempted arson and sentenced to seven years in Auburn prison. The *Kingston Chronicle* commented that 'the verdict and sentence are honorable to both Court and Jury', at the same time expressing the hope that the American Government would 'act in the same spirit' and let him serve the whole term. But a few days later Lett escaped in a sensational manner about four miles from Auburn, as he was being conveyed to prison by rail. The sheriff published a description and offered one hundred dollars for his capture.[16] Carelessness or connivance of guards was only too apparent in Lett's scape. The *New York Commercial Advertiser* commented:

'All this makes up a story that does not sound well in the telling. After so many "escapes" as one and another of these "patriot" scoundrels have effected, one might have looked for something like precaution in the management of Mr. Lett; but he has escaped also. . . If "well secured by shackles", how did he contrive to jump out? If the car was going at the rate of 20 miles an hour, how did he escape being dashed to pieces? Mr. Sheriff, we have no disposition to think hardly of you, but your account of this matter—if it is your account—does not hang well together.'

Governor William H. Seward of New York offered a reward of $250 for Lett's apprehension, observing that 'the felony of which the said Benjamin Lett was convicted was of an aggravated character; and the cause of public justice and the peace and welfare of the State are deeply concerned in his exemplary punishment'. Lett left the state, but the blasting of a lock of the Welland Canal in September, 1841, suggested that he was again active, and he was arrested in Buffalo the same month. The press commented that the Governor's reward overcame the fidelity of Lett's friends.

After spending four years in prison Lett settled on a farm at Northville, Illinois, where he is reported to have become a good citizen. He was for a time in De Kalb County, and later in Milwaukee, Wisconsin. His end was characterized by tragic circumstances in keeping with his earlier life. On October 15, 1858, he left home to engage in a trading expedition on Lake Michigan, but on December 1 he was suddenly taken ill, was carried by steamer to Milwaukee, and died there on the ninth. An autopsy showed that he had been poisoned by strychnine, but it

---

[16]E. J. Pierce wrote that after jumping down a twenty-foot embankment Lett 'slipped off the handcuffs and cut the shackles off his legs'. A comparison of the *Auburn Journal's* description of Lett with that earlier printed in the *Cobourg Star* leaves little room for doubt that he participated in the Cobourg raid.

BEN LETT AND THE COBOURG CONSPIRACY 177

was never learned who was responsible. He was buried in La Salle County, one of the two tombstones on the plot carrying the following peculiar inscription: 'The records of American partnership in the case of Benjamin Lett. They are like a Christian hell without a Jesus Christ. No escape'.

BIBLIOGRAPHY

The sources of information upon the Cobourg conspiracy are the depositions, evidence, and judicial comment at the subsequent trial of the conspirators, as reported in the *Cobourg Star*, September 18 and 25, 1839, together with press comments on these and other dates. Mackenzie printed an account, compiled from the *Star*, in his *Gazette* of September 28 under the caption 'Trial of the Editor of the Lewiston Telegraph and Others at Cobourg, U.C.'; and a letter of comment from Cobourg, written by 'Jonah' and addressing 'Dear Mac', appears in the same issue. A search in Osgoode Hall and elsewhere has revealed no trace of the trial record, MS. or printed. More extensive treatment of the political background of the district may be found in the author's 'The Cobourg Conspiracy', *Canadian Historical Review*, March, 1937. The raid has never previously been referred to in an historical work, but is mentioned in Preston, *Three Years' Residence in Canada from 1837 to 1839*, I 177-8. The main sources of facts or rumours on Lett's early life are Fairbairn, *Bowmanville*, 5; Farewell, 'Early Day Tales in Ontario County', *Toronto Daily Star*, July 5, 1913; Squair, *Darlington and Clarke*, 163-6; and a letter in Ross, 'The Patriot War', 607-8, of E. J. Pierce, whose aunt, a cousin of Lett's, lived near Lewiston and was frequently visited by him. A letter of Nelson Gorham's, quoted in Dent, II 224 fn., states that Lett was one of five who spent some days in hospital on Navy Island; and M'Cleod, *A Brief Review*, 216, refers to his bravery on Fighting Island. Preston, *Three Years' Residence*, I 176-7, and Marsh, *Recollections, 1837-1910*, 8-9, give incidental information, while Sir Richard Bonnycastle, *Canada and the Canadians*, I 229 and 243, is among several contemporary writers who refer to Lett as the one who blew up Brock's monument. Newspaper sources upon his activities after the Cobourg raid are particularly 'A Scoundrel', *Niagara Chronicle*, April 10, 1844, reprinted in the *Christian Guardian* of April 24; the *Kingston Chronicle*, quoted in the *Guardian* of July 1, 1840; 'A Rogue Abroad', *Guardian*, July 8, 1840, quoting the *Auburn Journal*; and the *Niagara Chronicle*, quoted in the *Guardian*, September 15, 1841. Material on the assassination of Ussher is found in Bonnycastle, *op. cit.*, I 301 fn.; Preston, I 176-7; in the account of the inquest and the funeral, Toronto *Palladium*, November 28, 1838; and on his tombstone in Chippewa cemetery. Hart's printing activities in Cobourg prior to the Rebellion are referred to in McAllister, *Historical Reminiscences*, 72; while the Reverend James Gardiner, who was employed in Hart's office at the time, outlines the Belleville riot in 'When the *Plain Speaker's* Type Was Pied', Ontario Historical Society, XX, and an issue of Hart's newspaper is described in Riddell, 'An Old Provincial Newspaper', *ibid.*, XIX. See also the *Historical Atlas of Hastings and Prince Edward*, III, and for references to Belleville and Hastings County during the Rebellion, Bonnycastle, *Canada As It Is*, II 79, and *The Canadas in 1841*, II 63-5, and McCollom's letter in the Lindsey Papers. In addition to the *Cobourg Star*, the following sources have provided information and comment on Durham meetings, the activities of Orangemen, and kindred subjects: 'Lynch Law at Cobourg', *Mirror*, July 26, 1839, and October 18, 1839; Mackenzie's *Caroline Almanack*, 86-7; William Lount's letter, Lindsey Papers; and *Twelve Years a Roman Catholic Priest, or the Autobiography of the Rev. V. P. Mayerhoffer, M.A.*, 96-7.

CHAPTER XVIII

The United States and the Patriot War.

It was the complex nature of the American Patriot movement which caused its failure, for it was characterized throughout by divided leadership and petty jealousy. The motives which led men into the campaign for Canadian independence were correspondingly varied. Hatred of all things British was still felt in the United States, and there were yet living many who had vivid memories of the War of Independence.[1] Closely connected was sympathy for the under-dog, and the belief that it was the duty of Americans to propagate republican institutions. Nor was hope of conquest and the desire for personal advancement by any means a minor incentive, for the financial panic of 1837 had left many unemployed, and they were ready to embark upon any undertaking which might improve their circumstances.

If any race dominated the movement it was the Irish, who had an historic antipathy to Great Britain; for it is evident that the leaders of the agitation desired to bring about war between Great Britain and the United States. The New York *Gazette* reported in November, 1838, that

'M'Kenzie, about the paltriest of the *patriots*, but prominent at the same time as an advocate of Van Burenism in this city, advertises that he will deliver lectures and prove the propriety of a war between the United States and Great Britain for the purpose of "liberating" the Canadians from the state which a very great majority are perfectly contented with. He is organizing societies . . . and administering secret oaths to the initiated.'[2]

Among considerations which accelerated the Patriot movement were the north-east boundary dispute and the interplay of state and federal politics; while a larger number were aroused by the severity of the repression in the Canadas, or by some incident—notably the burning of the *Caroline*—in subsequent frontier events. Whatever the motive, there is no doubt of the enthusiasm which characterized the movement. All sorts of secret societies were formed to further Canadian freedom. There were 'Hunters

---

[1]'I hope there are yet remaining in the Republic a majority of men professing the same noble spirit which actuated the Patriots of the revolution; who would rather see the last resources of our mighty empire exhausted, than to behold her the patient endurer of British injury and insult.' (Hill's letter, Lindsey Papers).

[2]'Meeting of American Sympathizers and Canadian Rebels at New York,' *Quebec Gazette*, November 19, 1838. Dr. Wolfred Nelson and Fanny Wright, the 'Venus of equal Rights', also spoke. In his *Gazette*, December 22, 1838, Mackenzie denied that he desired war.

Courtesy *Watertown Daily Times*

'The Pirate of the Thousand Islands'

Colonel John Prince

Prominent loyalist, whose summary execution of prisoners aroused intense excitement on two continents

From Smyth, *Sketches in the Canadas*, 1842   Coke Smyth

Engagement in the Thousand Islands, 1838

Courtesy Buffalo Historical Society

Figurehead of the *Caroline*
A relic of a *cause célèbre*

Courtesy Niagara Historical Society

Brock's Monument
Blown up by Patriots in 1840

Courtesy Public Archives of Canada   Lieutenant P. Bainbrigge

Cobourg in 1840
Scene of a projected Patriot raid under Benjamin Lett and Samuel Hart
and the trial of the conspirators

and Chasers in the Eastern Frontier', 'Lodges of Patriotic Masons', and various other associations planning 'deer hunts' and 'exploring expeditions' to hunt 'red foxes' or 'kill the tories'. People mortgaged their homes to provide funds for the movement, and at one time three-fourths of the citizens of Rochester and seven-eighths of those of Buffalo were claimed to be supporters. A barber manufactured balls with which to shoot the Tories when not engaged at his trade, and a woman was seen casting bullets in her own home from a mould that ran sixty at a time. At the height of the Hunters' Lodge movement the membership was variously estimated at from 15,000 to 200,000, and many neglected their occupations to engage in Patriot activities.

Such a complex organization required capable and unified control, but it was entirely lacking. When a member of the expedition to Prescott commented that the attack was deranged because of ineffective leadership he was explaining the failure of the entire movement. While there were plenty of efficient agitators, there is but little indication that any of the self-styled generals and commanders possessed the skill and ability to carry a military campaign to a successful conclusion. At the same time jealousy and treachery were so rampant among them that friend and foe were at times not distinguishable. Some of the commanders had received training in the American militia, in a few instances as officers, but the greater number had no other claim to prominence than enthusiasm in the cause.

The rank and file of the American agitation were largely recruited from the so-called working classes. Sir Richard Bonnycastle, whose duties brought him close to the movement, considered that three-fourths of them

'had been brought up without any fixed religious notions, and they all really imagined that they were serving their country as well as themselves in attempting the conquest of Canada. They were in fact chiefly those restless frequenters of tavern bars who begin smoking cigars and drinking spirits before nature has developed their perceptions of right and wrong'.

Such men were particularly susceptible to the type of oratory that was served out; for they were not among the more prosperous portions of the community, nor did they take the trouble to inquire into the truth of propaganda. The tangible inducements offered were variations of Mackenzie's 300 acres of land and $100 in silver. Some of those who participated in the Prescott raid were promised that their families would be cared for in their absence, $10 a month while on service, a bounty of $20, and 160 acres of land on the establishment of a new government.

The depositions of the prisoners indicate other means by which recruits were obtained. A large number attempted to excuse their participation by claiming they were forced to cross the border, or were innocent passengers intending to proceed elsewhere to accept work as lumbermen. Several said they were made drunk and taken across the frontier; while the importance of an officer's position gratified the vanity of others. There is good reason to believe, in fact, that adventure and excitement proved the main incentive to many.

In spite, however, of the presence of mercenary and other ignoble considerations, there was a strong feeling that they were helping the Canadians by crossing the border, and this belief was encouraged by gross misrepresentation. Joshua Doan, who forfeited his life in the movement, stated that he was told 'there were six hundred men ready to join the moment I landed; and also that they had risen near London and taken one half of the 32nd regiment'. Only three Upper Canadian inhabitants joined the Prescott raiders; while Samuel Snow wrote with some bitterness that 'not a Canadian met us on our arrival save a few who joined us in Michigan, and some of these turned traitors soon after'. There were undoubtedly thousands of Upper Canadian Reformers who bitterly hated the Tory administration, but most of them were not prepared to go the length of armed revolt—much less to risk their necks to aid ill-advised invasions.

The Patriot activities of Daniel D. Heustis may be taken as typical of the more intelligent members of the organization. He was born in Vermont in 1806, the son of a farmer. During the course of his early life he followed a number of occupations, becoming in 1835 a commercial traveller for a firm of morocco dressers. It was while travelling in Upper Canada that he listened to 'the bitter complaints of the Canadian people' and was filled with a strong feeling of sympathy for them. In 1837 he observed that the rumblings of discontent were more pronounced; while the events of the Lower Canadian Rebellion made a deep and abiding impression on his mind. The defeat of Mackenzie in Upper Canada, the escape to the United States of many refugees, and the burning of the *Caroline* intensified the excitement along the border, and on January 10, Heustis, who was then in Watertown, decided to devote himself to 'the cause of Canadian liberty'.

Armed with four rifles and four muskets he set out for Rochester by stage. There he met McLeod, Fletcher, and Rolph, all refugees, who entrusted to him three cannon to be used by the insurgents on Navy Island. Proceeding by stage and railway to Buffalo he put up at the Eagle Tavern, Patriot headquarters,

THE UNITED STATES AND THE PATRIOT WAR   181

where he learned that the island had been evacuated the day before. He was cordially received by Mackenzie and his wife, and spent a few moments in talking over plans for future operations. On the following night it was decided by the Patriot leaders to discontinue for the time being all operations in the neighbourhood of Buffalo, but to attempt the capture of Fort Henry about February 22.

Accompanied by David Gibson and the Mackenzies, Heustis proceeded to Watertown, where a circular was issued and distributed through Jefferson County soliciting aid for the next enterprise. The abortive occupation of Hickory Island caused great excitement, and several Americans, Heustis among them, were arrested for breach of the neutrality laws. During the stage trip to Auburn to stand examination he playfully assumed the name 'General Mackenzie', and large numbers gathered to shake his hand, while 'the sparkling glances of youthful maidens and the eager gaze of aged matrons' abashed him not a little! At Auburn he was discharged from custody.

A few weeks later Heustis was among some 1,900 who joined the Watertown branch of the Hunters' Lodge; but he did not participate in the burning of the steamer *Sir Robert Peel*. He was one of fifty who soon afterwards congregated at Youngstown for the purpose of delivering from Niagara jail the Patriots who had been captured at the Short Hills in June, seventeen of whom were under sentence of death. A day or two before the appointed time, however, the sentence was commuted to transportation and the prisoners removed to Fort Henry, so the raiders dispersed. Heustis's next Patriot activity proved his last, for he was captured after the raid upon Prescott and sent to Van Diemen's Land.

Linus W. Miller's activities represent another angle of the movement, for he entered Upper Canada as an emissary of the Canadian Refugee Relief Association. He was nineteen years old, somewhat psychopathic, and had begun the study of law. His narrative is among the most bitter, and is composed in a bombastic style which emphasizes his 'smartness' and conveys the impression that he considered himself a martyr. But he was possessed of spirit and initiative and the good opinion of his fellow-Patriots. Benjamin Wait calls him 'the gallant young American', and Mrs. Wait considered that his 'noble bearing was ever admirable'.

On April 12, 1838, Samuel Lount and Peter Matthews were executed in Toronto jail, and nine of the London District prisoners were sentenced to die in Hamilton on the twentieth of the month.[3] Miller says he was consequently selected at a secret meeting in Lockport of the Refugee Association to proceed to Upper Canada and contrive in some manner to deliver these nine men from jail. The plan formulated by Miller and Dr. John Wilson was bold enough:

'I purposed to cross into Canada that evening, raise 200 efficient men, proceed in secret to Hamilton, and on Thursday evening at the hour of twelve the Doctor with a piquet was to attack Dundern Castle as a ruse; another small party were to take possession of a steamboat which always lay at the wharf during the evening, and by the aid of an engineer of our own to prepare her for the reception of the main body, with whom I was to surprise the jail, force the doors, etc., and press the prisoners on board; there to be joined by the Doctor and all hands, to whistle *Yankee Doodle* until we landed our valuable freight on Yankee ground.'

But these and subsequent schemes fared badly, and Miller was soon to have plenty of time to whistle *Yankee Doodle* in several remote parts of the world. Jacob Beemer was let in on the plan, and his treachery is blamed for the failure.[4] However that may be, the two men set forth upon their mission, and friendly settlers along the route to Hamilton provided horses and shelter. 'I got neither sleep or rest for four days and nights,' wrote Miller. 'For forty-eight hours it rained or snowed incessantly, in consequence of which my overclothes were frequently covered with ice an inch thick.' But everyone who was approached wanted to participate in the raid. 'Thousands, instead of hundreds, were ready to risk their lives to save the doomed men... Old men seemed to forget their age, and young men their sweet-hearts.'

Miller altered his dress and wig and entered Hamilton to find the town full of soldiery, who 'greatly feared the vengeance of the whole country'. But he had been betrayed, and all the objects of attack were closely guarded. As the prisoners had been granted a respite and were in no danger of execution, the Patriots who had congregated in the vicinity were ordered to return to their homes, while the authorities, 'after much investigation came to the conclusion that there had been no rising'. But the fearless Miller argued with British officers about the rebels and the comparative bravery of the Yankees and British, and had the satisfaction of

---

[3]They were William Webb, John Hammil, Horatio Hills, Stephen Smith, Charles Walrath, Ephraim Cook, John Tufford, Nathan Town, and Peter Malcolm. Hills died in jail, Walrath shortly escaped, Cook was banished, and the rest eventually pardoned. The Canadian Refugee Association was particularly active at this time. The President, Dr. A. K. Mackenzie, formerly of Hamilton, stated they were hostile only 'to a Canadian aristocracy which lived in open violation' of the policy of the British Government. He wrote requesting Sir George Arthur to meet a delegation of refugees to effect a reconciliation, but was refused. The situation consequently became worse, and Mrs. Samuel Lount was sent along the frontier to arouse sympathy and support. See also appendix K(6) and L(4).

[4]Mackenzie refers to him as a 'Judas' and a 'wretch'. He escaped from the London District, where his father's tavern in Scotland had been Dr. Duncombe's headquarters. See also pages 106-10, 205 fn., 207, 213 fn., and 229.

THE UNITED STATES AND THE PATRIOT WAR 183

hearing himself described as a 'tall, ferocious-looking Yankee'. He then went to Mills's store, whither he was shortly followed and examined by Sir Allan MacNab, Colonel Lang, Judge Jones, and a large number of other gentlemen. He says they recognized him as the leader, but were satisfied to leave two policemen at the door while he and Mills[5] concluded their business in a back room. 'In five minutes I had altered my disguise—passed through a trap door into the cellar, and from thence into a back street. . . I hastened out of town and in half an hour joined my good friend Dr. Wilson.' To assure themselves of Beemer's duplicity they hid near the Patriot rendezvous and saw several companies of infantry and cavalry march into the field at twelve midnight.

Two months later Miller was again sent to Upper Canada by the refugee organization, this time in connection with the Short Hills raid. But he was captured and transported to Van Diemen's Land, where the severity of his punishment was intensified by the eccentricities of his temperament.

The departure of Sir Francis Bond Head for England provided the opportunity for an incident of a humorous nature, and quite characteristic of the times. Sir Francis was somewhat lacking in personal fortitude and planned a secret exit from the scene of his triumphs. His original intention was to make a quick trip to Halifax, and thence by warship to New York, for he feared that some group of American Patriots might kidnap him for Mackenzie's Navy Island reward of £500. Believing, however, that a conspiracy was on foot to murder him *en route,* he made a last-minute change. On March 24, 1838, he left Toronto by steamer and was assumed to be bound for Montreal; but at Kingston he left the vessel and with Judge Jones went in a small boat through floating ice to Cape Vincent, and thence to Watertown by special stage. Watertown was then a headquarters for Canadian refugees, and Mackenzie, Van Rensselaer, and other prominent Patriots were at the Mansion House. Into this nest of hornets was landed the citizen of Kingston and the erstwhile Lieutenant-Governor, disguised as a gentleman's gentleman. The situation had distinct possibilities, and Sir Francis thought discretion the better part of valour:

'It was just after the breakfast hour, and the lobby was filled with the Patriot community. . . Hugh Scanlon, an Irish-Canadian, a bright and shrewd fellow, noticed that the valet was missing and his suspicions were aroused. . . He at last found the lost valet cosily sitting in a wheelbarrow near the stables. Introducing himself, Scanlon invited him to breakfast and to meet his late subjects, assuring him that he would be

[5]Michael Marcellus Mills, merchant, Gore District, was among the sixty-one leaders against whom indictments were found for high treason but who had left the province.

welcome and receive every courtesy due his rank. The governor accepted the invitation and came forward. He was met by all in a courteous and friendly way, and was assisted in his arrangements for departure. He left town in a coach and four, with cheers, and without a single uncomplimentary remark.'[6]

The attitude of the United States Government during the first stages of the Patriot agitation was complicated by inadequate neutrality laws, but there was a determined effort to prevent unfriendly acts. The Secretary of State announced in December, 1837:

> 'Some of our citizens may, from their connection with the settlers, and from their love of enterprise and desire of change, be induced to forget their duty to their own Government and its obligation to foreign Powers. It is the fixed determination of the President ... that we shall abstain, under every temptation, from intermeddling with the domestic disputes of other nations.'[7]

It was apparent during the Navy Island occupation, however, that there was open recruiting and the movement of arms and ammunition, some of it even from state arsenals. In his Message to Congress, January 5, President Jackson pointed out that events on the northern frontier showed defects in the existing laws and the insufficiency of their penalties. News of the *Caroline* incident reached the White House on the evening of the fourth. As a result a law providing for 'Punishments of Military Expeditions against the conterminous Territory of Foreign Governments at peace with the United States' was passed. But while it was then possible to seize the leaders and the arms and equipment of persons engaged in invasions or acting with apparent hostile intent, there was no provision for preventing enlistment in projected expeditions. Conflict between federal and state rights intensified the difficulties at times, and there were notable variations in the attitude of the governors of the border states.

The incoming administration of President Martin Van Buren was more hostile to the Patriot movement, and, in the face of considerable public demand for hostilities, succeeded in preventing war with Great Britain. By stricter supervision along the border many incipient raids were rendered abortive, and the possibility of the success of others greatly lessened. After the failure of the Pelee Island invasion in March, 1838, the situation was quiet until the burning of the *Sir Robert Peel,* which aroused a storm

[6]Haddock, *The Thousand Islands,* 163. The story is also told in *The Growth of a Century,* 346-9, but the Lieutenant-Governor is called Sir Allan McNab! Bond Head was generously paid for his two years' misgovernment of Upper Canada, his salary and allowances totalling £9,079. The two books he subsequently produced, *A Narrative of the Canadian Rebellion* and *The Emigrant,* are of some historical value in spite of his prejudices. For many years he received a pension of £100 a year 'for his services in the cause of literature'. He died on July 20, 1875.

[7]Forsyth to the attorneys of border states, December 7, 1837.

THE UNITED STATES AND THE PATRIOT WAR 185

of protest on both sides of the border. Commenting upon the attack, the Albany *Evening Journal* observed that 'there is not a Government in the world so corruptly and wretchedly administered as ours', though it is difficult to see how any precautions could have prevented the destruction of the vessel. A Special Message to Congress on June 20 stated that the attack afforded 'the most painful anxiety to this government. . . Every effort has been and will be made to prevent the success of the designs apparently formed,—to involve the nation in a war with a neighboring friendly Power'. Troops were sent to Sackett's Harbor and Plattsburg, and an armed steamer was despatched to prevent a repetition of the piratical attack.

A few days after the *Peel* raid there occurred a lesser attack on the part of the British, but which the Americans were glad to set off against the greater outrage. As the American steamship *Telegraph* was passing Brockville she was 'hailed by soldiers upon Maynard's & Morris's wharf & ordered to halt'. She stopped and the captain awaited the approach of a small boat; but twelve shots were suddenly fired at her, two piercing the ladies' cabin, one the engine room, and one the cook's room. The ship thereupon steamed away. Two soldiers later swore that they 'fired *four* shots, and without orders, which, however, was desired by their officers'. Referring at considerable length to this incident and the earlier burning of the *Caroline,* an ardent Patriot, A. B. Hill, wrote Mackenzie that 'war must be the inevitable result'.

There was frequently much more behind Patriot activities than appeared on the surface. Political considerations were particularly prominent during the summer and autumn of 1838, and one of the obligations of the Hunters was to vote for members of the order in the state and congressional campaigns which were then in progress; and the Ogdensburg *Republican* stated that the raid upon Prescott was part of the Whig campaign to carry the New York State election.[8] Mackenzie, however, remained a warm supporter and admirer of President Van Buren, in spite of the evident hostility of his administration to the Patriot cause.

The raid upon Prescott in November caused a notable expansion of the United States Government's policy of strict neutrality. Cordial co-operation with Great Britain and the Canadas in ending vexatious border troubles was promised in the proclamation of November 21, and it was stated in no uncertain terms that those who 'without the shadow of justification or excuse' had 'nefariously invaded' a friendly power's dominions had

[8] In the Lindsey Papers are many letters to Mackenzie making comments or suggestions as to his attitude to American politics.

forfeited their claims to the protection of their country and need not expect the interference of the Government in any form on their behalf.

The invasion of Windsor three weeks later found the American forces active. They 'flew to the spot and exerted themselves to the utmost', arresting some of the principal offenders who had escaped from Upper Canada. General Scott passed along the entire frontier, addressing immense gatherings, principally of sympathizers ready to embark on some hostile expedition. He appealed to their patriotism, and to the necessity of strict obedience to the laws of the land; and showed them that a war to be successful must be differently commanded and conducted.

A change in public opinion was noticeable after the defeat at Prescott. There was quite general opposition to a continuance of the Patriot agitation, and the law-abiding element now controlled the situation. During December and January there were protest meetings in Jefferson County, and resolutions against secret societies were adopted. A Grand Jury made similar comments, and a large gathering at Watertown resolved that the frontier population should do everything in its power to prevent invasions, and permit Canadians to enjoy the government of their choice; and in advocating the disbanding of all Hunters' Lodges the meeting hoped to see justice tempered with mercy in the punishment of the Prescott raiders.[9] Though eleven of the leaders were shortly hanged, there was some desire in official circles to be lenient to the rest, but coupled with it was the irritating feeling that the chief agitators were continuing to stir up trouble in the United States almost without molestation. The Executive Council went on record that 'were it positively understood that such men as Johnston, Birge-Birce, and Mackenzie would be seized and delivered up as having violated the refuge afforded them, there would be no objection to the release of hundreds of obscure criminals'.[10] But it was obviously impossible to suggest such an exchange, so it was decided to pardon the numerous minors and those who had turned Queen's evidence or were for some other reason recommended to mercy, while all others were transported to Van Diemen's Land.

[9] On the other hand, elements in the American press considered that too much leniency had already been shown to the Patriots. After the Short Hills raid the New York *Gazette* carried the following comment: 'We say again, as we have repeatedly said before, that the highest mercy that the Canadian authorities can exercise towards the people on both frontiers is to hang every villain that crosses from our territory to commit murder and rapine in the provinces; and that if Sutherland and his associates had been promptly executed when they were taken, it is not very likely that the sixteen new victims would ever have been in the situation they are.'

[10] Enclosure 6, Arthur to Glenelg, February 6, 1839. 'Birge-Birce' indicates that Birge and Bierce were considered the same man.

THE UNITED STATES AND THE PATRIOT WAR 187

Though the importance of the movement had passed with 1838, the agitation died hard. In the spring of 1839 General Donald McLeod claimed to have 3,250 'efficient men ready for service when called for', and reported numerous alliances with western Indian tribes. The ramifications of the agitation are apparent from his report, which showed that 1,500 Indians and 500 volunteers were available at Coldwater, Missouri, under General J. B. Stewart, formerly of the United States Army; 560 Roman Catholic Irish at Chicago under A. Smith; 250 men, probably Indians, on the Desplain River under Colonel W. R. Miller; 140 French Canadians at Kankakee under Francis Brodieau; 300 Canadians, Dutch, and Irish on the line of the Illinois and Fox rivers under Major Luddington; and donations of lead, etc., in various quarters. But lack of funds and decreasing enthusiasm was shortly to cause the collapse of the entire movement. The correspondence of McLeod indicates his poverty, and shows that continual begging for money to pay tavern bills and similar debts had replaced any dependence upon voluntary contributions. The conviction and imprisonment of Mackenzie and Van Rensselaer further decreased the waning enthusiasm, and the movement rapidly degenerated into predatory raids under the Patriot cloak. There was still some hope, however, that war would be produced by the cumulative effect of innumerable irritating attacks of a minor nature; for it was expected that bank robberies, mail hold-ups, the burning of public buildings, the destruction of crops and barns, and an occasional murder would provoke retaliation which would embroil the governments in hostilities. Meanwhile they took what comfort they could from small indications of success. It was 'glorious news for the Patriots' when the Chancellor of the Exchequer announced in the British House of Commons that the Rebellion and border troubles had cost the government over £2,000,000; and they had been equally elated when Sir John Colborne was recalled because of his severity in Lower Canada, and Sir George Arthur censured for the execution of Lount and Matthews in the upper province.

Late in 1839 the publication of Lord Durham's *Report* had both a quieting and an exciting effect; for it appeared to the Reformers that their agitation was at last bearing fruit, while it greatly incensed the Tories, who saw their monopoly of public administration slipping from their grasp as the 'treasonable' utterances of 'republicans' assumed respectability and importance. A report found on a Patriot spy highly commended 'Durham meetings' as forerunners of reform and in enabling Patriots to assemble; but indicated that 'burning the barns of the Tories' might be continued with advantage.[11] In the United States, however, the agitation was rapidly becoming a boisterous offshoot of the celebration of Independence Day:

'On July 4, 1839, a patriot celebration was held in Ben Woodworth's Steamboat Hotel, at the northwest corner of Randolph and Bates streets, Detroit, at which the officers were: President, John Biddle; vice-presidents, Andrew Mack, De Garmo Jones, D. C. McKinstry, James Summers, E. D. Ellis, Reynolds Gillet and A. T. McReynolds. After the usual patriotic toasts were given, the whole of the speaking was devoted to the wrongs of Canada. The toasts of Mackenzie and Theller were responded to eloquently by the latter, and the memories of Van Schoultz, Lount, Matthews, Putnam, and Harvell were drunk in solemn silence. Dr. Theller gave "The patriot mayor and aldermen of the city", which was drunk with enthusiasm. Ald. McReynolds responded in the absence of Mayor De Garmo Jones, who had retired. . .

'He was followed by Luther B. Willard, afterward Poor Director of Detroit for many years, who gave the following remarkable toast which is said to have been founded on an occurrence after the battle of Windsor: "True French hospitality, exemplified by the Canadian, after the affair at Windsor, who, when the bloodhounds were in pursuit, put the hunted patriot in bed with his wife to save him." This toast produced long and uproarious applause, and the celebration broke up at 1 a.m.'

During the year there were several minor but aggravating incidents which tended to keep the frontier in a disturbed condition. On April 14 British troops at Prescott fired upon the steamer *United States* on her first trip of the season; while on the twenty-second certain depredations were committed by Canadian militiamen against the schooner *Gerard* at Port Colborne as she was passing through the Welland Canal. On April 25 the steamer *Traveller* was subjected to a 'most insulting ransack' while in the harbour of Charlotte, the port of Rochester. Someone had taken an affidavit that two Patriot prisoners bound for Van Diemen's Land were on board, and the sheriff, with Mackenzie and a party of armed followers, 'posted down to the vessel to search it, in the hope, doubtless, that Captain Sutherland would be rash enough to resist them, and so give them a pretext for burning it'. The incident caused a temporary interruption in communication with Rochester, and the *Traveller* was sold to the government.

Succeeding events indicate still further the deterioration of Patriot motives and plans. On April 28 some of Bill Johnston's gang robbed the Canadian mails near Kingston, and similar attacks were reported in June. On June 25 a fracas occurred in Ogdensburg when a party from Prescott tried to abduct a deserter.

---

[11] Report of a spy, enclosed in Arthur to Normandy, October 15, 1839. It also said that 'the English church at Toronto' (St. James') was to be burned when completed. Typical of numerous items in the contemporary press is one in the *Quebec Gazette* of September 30, 1839, describing the burning of the barn of Ogden Creighton, near Drummondville, and the arrest of one Brown for setting fire to a St. Catharines tannery 'on the night of the Thorold Durham meeting'.

THE UNITED STATES AND THE PATRIOT WAR 189

A crowd surrounded them, applied plenty of tar, and marched them back to their boat under an armed guard. In July a number of cases of incendiarism against Tory property occurred, while a conspiracy to rob and murder in the vicinity of Cobourg was uncovered and promptly blamed upon Durham's *Report* and the 'Durham Meetings'. In September there were daring robberies along the St. Clair and the St. Lawrence; while the Episcopal Church at Chippewa was burned by incendiaries on the thirteenth of the month. There were plans for another invasion of Upper Canada at Windsor, with risings at various interior points to prevent the despatch of troops to the frontier, but the schemes came to nought. In his Message to Congress on December 2, 1839, the President was consequently able to declare the danger past. He observed that the misguided sympathy of certain American citizens had subsided, and that they were now strongly opposed to all intermeddling with the internal affairs of neighbours.

Among the expiring efforts of the movement was the senseless and infamous destruction of Brock's Monument in April, 1840, and the attempt to blow up the Welland Canal locks in September, 1841.[12] On September 5 President Tyler issued a proclamation calling for the suppression of secret clubs, but the flagging Patriot enthusiasm was temporarily revived by the trial of Alexander McLeod, which threatened serious international complications. McLeod was reported to have boasted in a tavern in November, 1840, that he had killed Amos Durfee, but in his trial, which took place between October 4 and 12, 1841, he proved an alibi and was acquitted.[13] Patriot agitators attempted to trump up another McLeod trial,[14] but the coming of Lord Ashburton in April, 1842, and the deliberations resulting in the Treaty of Washington put an end to the agitation. The Oregon dispute aroused a brief excitement a few years later, and the Hunters had some hopes of further employment; but not until the mid-sixties did their legitimate successors—the Fenian raiders—come into prominence to disturb the peace along the border.

12See chapter XVII for a more extended reference to these depredations. The attacks provoked a private circular from General McLeod:
'Officers and non-commissioned officers and men engaged in Patriot service, detected crossing the lines to plunder, destroy monuments, public works, or private property, shall be tried by a Court Martial, and punished accordingly.'
Dent quotes another of McLeod's papers implicating Mackenzie in these activities; but considering the number and general type of the recriminations that were bandied about among the leaders of the agitation, the author prefers to accept none without corroboration.
13McLeod sued the State of New York for false imprisonment but was unsuccessful. The British Government eventually awarded him a pension of £200 a year, at the same time despatching a belated apology to the United States Government. He died in 1871.
14John Sheridan Hogan and Dr. A. K. Mackenzie were parties to a scheme by which the former would be 'the goat'. He was twice arrested in Rochester in the spring of 1842 but not tried. On December 1, 1859, Hogan was murdered in Toronto. An account of the tragedy may be found in the author's *Toronto: From Trading-Post to Great City*, 224-5.

THE LIVES AND TIMES OF THE PATRIOTS

BIBLIOGRAPHY

The Messages to Congress, proclamations, and other official American papers quoted are in the public collections in Washington. Despatches in the *Imperial Blue Books*, and others in the Public Archives of Canada, are indicated more particularly in the notes; while Q413, I 37-40, describes the change in American feeling after the Prescott raid, and is corroborated by Hough, *Jefferson County*, 525-7. The depositions of the Prescott and Windsor prisoners are given in detail in Enclosure 4, Arthur to Glenelg, February 5, 1839, *Imperial Blue Books*, XIII. In the Lindsey Papers are many letters to Mackenzie making comments or suggestions regarding his attitude to American politics in relation to the Patriot agitation. Several comprehensive studies have been made of the relations between the United States and Canada during the Rebellion years. The most complete is Tiffany, 'The Relations of the United States to the Canadian Rebellion of 1837-1838', Buffalo Historical Society, VIII. See also Shortridge, 'The Canadian-American Frontier during the Rebellion of 1837-1838', *Canadian Historical Review*, March, 1926; and Callahan, *The Neutrality of the American Lakes* (1898), and *American Foreign Policy* (1937). There are several contemporary printed accounts of the McLeod trial, while among the best studies of the repercussions arising from it are in Tiffany, 37-40 and 107-12, and Watt, 'The Case of Alexander McLeod', *Canadian Historical Review*, June, 1931. Bond Head's experiences on his homeward journey through the United States are detailed in his books, in Haddock, *The Thousand Islands*, 163, and in *The Growth of a Century*, 346-9. The narratives of Heustis, Snow, Wait, and Miller, Donald McLeod's correspondence appended to Tiffany and in Dent, II 271-2, and A. B. Hill's letter to Mackenzie, June 3, 1838, Lindsey Papers, indicate the Patriot attitude. These are supplemented by Ross, 'The Patriot War' and Mackenzie's *Caroline Almanack*, while much of value from the loyalist point of view is found in Bonnycastle, *Canada As It Is*. Various contemporary issues of the following newspapers give supplementary information: New York *American*, New York *Gazette, Albany Daily Advertiser, Albany Argus*, Philadelphia *Inquirer*, Quebec *Gazette*, Toronto *Patriot*, Toronto *Mirror*, *Cobourg Star*, and *Mackenzie's Gazette*. For purposes of comparison, see appendix G for a discussion of the social status of the Upper Canadian rank and file in the Patriot agitation.

CHAPTER XIX

JAILS AND CONVICT-SHIPS

THOSE who were arrested during Patriot insurrections and invasions or as alleged sympathizers were imprisoned either in the district jail or in one or another of the British fortifications then maintained in Upper Canada. In general, the conditions in local jails were worse, though the forts were equally overcrowded by the unusual number of prisoners; but the severity of treatment was greatest where the rancour of politics or the ultra-loyalty of militiamen replaced the matter-of-fact attitude of British regulars.

While only a small number of the Reform party were directly implicated in the revolt, almost the entire membership suffered in the repression. Bitter feelings and personal animosities rendered rebel-hunting an agreeable occupation to many, and their high-handed assumption of legal and judicial powers is among the most remarkable phases of the Rebellion. The proceedings of a half-armed body of militia from the vicinity of Bradford as they gathered in Reformers and marched towards Toronto, hooting and jeering at the unfortunate prisoners, typifies the method. An eye-witness states that not one-third of the militia had arms of any kind, while the rest

'had nothing better than pitchforks, rusty swords, dilapidated guns, and newly manufactured pikes, with an occasional bayonet on the end of a pole. These persons, without the least authority of law, set about a disarming process; depriving every one who refused to join them, or whom they chose to suspect of disloyalty, of his arms. Powder was taken from stores wherever found, without the least ceremony, and without payment. On Thursday a final march from Bradford for Toronto was commenced, the number of men being nearly five hundred, including one hundred and fifty Indians with painted faces and savage looks... Each prisoner as he was taken was tied to a rope; and when Toronto was reached a string of fifty prisoners all fastened together were marched in'.[1]

John Doel saw them as they entered Toronto in mid-winter 'like so many slaves driven to market;... some of them were old grey-headed men—some without overcoats;... some never saw their homes again but perished thro' privation and neglect'.

The families of those arrested were frequently subjected to

[1] While in the vicinity of Toronto, Hamilton, and London arrests were made wholesale, in other districts comparatively few were apprehended. Similarly, in some regions the Crown did not press for conviction. Sir Richard Bonnycastle refers, for example, to the acquittal of Reynolds, Le Sage, Myers, Lewis, Orr, La Fontaine, Marsh, and Day from Kingston and vicinity, many of whom were admittedly guilty but were freed through 'the privilege of an almost unlimited challenge of the jurors'.

persecution. John Doel and his son were arrested several times, and while they were in jail 'a drunken soldiery' terrorized their family, billeted half a dozen men upon them, and periodically ransacked the house and threatened to burn it. The Orangemen, who were blamed for the outrage, were described as 'no better than Organized Gangs of Drunken Ruffians'. In Toronto jail, meanwhile, Doel was cooped up with '28 or 29 in two small rooms'. They were not fettered, though the clanking of chains could be heard through the partitions, where other Patriot prisoners were more closely confined. The windows were boarded up and no newspapers were allowed in the jail, but friends sent in a plentiful supply of books, and those who did not care to read spent the time in carving and similar activities. 'We had family Devotions every day', Doel recalled, 'and religious Services on the Sabbath. We had a good deal of singing and profitable conversation, especially in the evening'.[2] Charles Durand describes secret means of communication devised by the prisoners. The Reverend William Ryerson was greatly affected by the unrelieved misery in the poorer cells:

'I visit the goal daily, generally preaching twice each visit to the prisnors in the different rooms, where a few of the more respectable & wealthy are confined, & the cells where the much greater number are kept. Many of those in the latter are in a truly pitiful situation. There are two departments or rather cluster or halls of cells, in each of which from 45 to 50 are confined with very very little room or air or any other comfort. Sickly & dirty, some crazy (at least one of them), some gloomy & despairing. My dr. br. I can hardly write about them; you may then well think what my feelings are when among them & seeing & hearing their misery & groans, many of whom are not yet tryed nor can they tell when they will be. Some have been frightened by the execution of Lount etc. to confess & petition the Governour, whom I do not believe are any more guilty of *treason* than I believe you are, merely having attended some political meetings last summer & fall, etc. etc. The A. G. has informed them that this is all treason. . . I feel, I assure you, like leaving Canada too, & I am not alone in these feelings.'

As weeks of incarceration passed, the treatment became harsher,[3] and many suffered from the debilitating effect of cold and damp cells. William Alves refers to the excessive cold, wet, and frost which he experienced in Toronto jail; while Van Egmond's death was hastened by pneumonia contracted in an underground cell. William Wilson, a farmer near Toronto, was 'treated with great cruelty all winter in the dungeons of Toronto',

[2] The Reverend John Doel escaped conviction when he proved that he was selling a cask of ale to one of the commissioners at the time of the skirmish at Montgomery's.
[3] Reports were current in the United States that prisoners in Hamilton jail were treated 'with severity, cruelty, and neglect'; but a Grand Jury of the Gore District reported that their treatment was 'humane, attentive, and indulgent', and that they fared 'as well as if they had been at home'. (Toronto *Patriot*, April 13, 1838).

JAILS AND CONVICT-SHIPS 193

and died in hospital[4] on April 12, 1838. Charles Durand contracted jail fever, and at the hospital was placed 'amongst over fifty patients, half of whom had the smallpox'. Those acquitted or discharged from custody were generally set free only upon providing excessive bail. On May 10, fifty-five prisoners were called before the court which had just sentenced Charles Durand to death. Chief Justice Robinson stated that they would be discharged upon 'entering into recognizance themselves in £200, and two sureties of £100 each, to keep the peace and be of good behaviour to Her Majesty and all Her liege subjects for three years'. The forfeiture of their property—the usual penalty of rebellion—was not remitted, but it was suggested that they might hope for its eventual return if their behaviour was satisfactory. A comment of the Toronto *Patriot* gives a sidelight on their suffering:

'The scene was one of most intense interest; the space in front of the dock was crowded with prisoners, whose bleached and sunken countenances show the inward misery of their bosoms. During the Address, which was delivered with that fine, clear, solemn, and forgiven tone which together with its subject seemed to partake more of Heaven than of Earth, many a tear stood trembling in the corner of an eye which would have darted scorn upon a gibbet.'[5]

A few days later the press published two curious documents. The 'Address of the Prisoners who have been lately liberated from Jail' was phrased in terms of the most abject contrition:

'Transgressors as we were, we do not now attempt to offer any apology for our offence; but we are led sincerely to believe that your Excellency has with clearness observed how easily the ignorant though honest inhabitants of the country were led astray by the artifice and chicanery of designing men. . . Restored again to our wives and little ones through the feeling humanity of a magnanimous Government, with the hope held out to us that the forfeiture we subjected ourselves to will not be exacted, we fondly cherish the belief that we will be permitted to remain in the country of our birth and adoption. . . GOD SAVE THE QUEEN!'

Very similar in tone and phraseology was the 'Address of the Wives and near Female Relatives of the Prisoners lately liberated from Jail':

[4] See Mackenzie's *Caroline Almanack*, 100-2 and 42. While the element of propaganda was prominent in much of Mackenzie's post-Rebellion writing, the suggestion that none is to be relied upon is based upon ignorance. A glance at the 'Register of Prisoners Committed to the Home District Gaol' fully corroborates his statements in this respect, for numerous prisoners are marked 'Sent to Hospital'. According to official records at least two other Home District prisoners died in hospital—Peter Grant on January 30, 1838, and Thomas Hill on February 27.

[5] An honest effort was made to classify the prisoners according to guilt and to apportion punishment. Of the 824 arrested in Upper Canada prior to the Prescott and Windsor invasions, including American raiders on the schooner *Anne*, at Pelee, the St. Clair, and the Short Hills, three were executed, fourteen escaped, twenty-seven were sentenced to transportation (thirteen of whom were subsequently released), twenty were banished, twelve sentenced to the penitentiary, 140 pardoned, and 608 acquitted or dismissed from custody. Apart altogether from the merits of their cause, the 216 convicted were, of course, rebels, and had to be dealt with as such.

'We, the undersigned, are desirous to approach Your Excellency thus to tender our expressions and acknowledgment of gratitude with which our minds are affected for the extension of your clemency towards our husbands, our children, and our friends... From which act of theirs we have been deep partizans in their sufferings, having been often debarred from even looking at them through their windows from the street.'[6]

Their experiences in Canadian jails and British prison-ships formed no small portion of the punishment of the captive American Patriots, and their narratives, the general truth of which there is no reason to doubt, provide detailed accounts of hardship and ill-usage, relieved at times by more humane treatment. Robert Marsh's *Seven Years of My Life* is one of the most illuminating of Patriot narratives. He was a lieutenant in the raid on Windsor, and his first experience of Canadian jails was at Sandwich. Here he was placed in a cell which had but one small window, closely covered with bars of iron, so that there was barely light enough to see that 'the cracks were literally alive with large body lice'. Marsh relieves himself of a little venom by accepting the opportunity to compare them with 'their brother Tories', whose persecution was just as intensive. The prisoners were closely packed in, and only the crudest of accommodations and food were supplied. Though the weather was cold, there was neither fire nor bedding; and the cells were so crowded that the prisoners could not lie down. Late at night a little coarse bread and thin soup was brought in, but their fitful snatches of sleep were continually disturbed by shouts that all would shortly be shot or hanged. After five days at Sandwich they were removed to Fort Malden. Marsh notes that stops were made at each tavern while the militia officers drank, and the prisoners froze in their tracks:

'About five miles farther and we halted before another grog shop, and about the same manoeuvering here as at the former place; after sitting another hour, shivering and freezing, bound tight together with irons, and receiving repeated insults, orders were again to march. After traveling seven or eight miles further we were ordered to turn out; some three or four on reaching the ground could not stand; being so long in one position, chilled, their feet frozen, the irons being so tight as to prevent circulation of blood, were obliged to be carried or led into Fort Malden.'

After they had been left twenty-four hours without food, 'a large bucket of Beefs head boiled, and in the water', was finally thrust among them, but they had no means to cut or serve it:

'We were strongly ironed, two together hand and foot, and but one hand at liberty. Two approached the bucket and with one hand managed to extract a little from the head, both obliged to kneel to sup a little of the broth, which was warm and revived us a little; this couple then stepped

[6]They were addressed to Sir George Arthur, and his replies are also given in the *Patriot*, May 18, 1838. The tone of abject contrition is similar to that in the London District petitions, and they were probably composed by a Tory lawyer.

Courtesy Liverpool Public Library   W. Herdman

The 'Old French Prison', Liverpool, England

'A great number of ladies and gentlemen called to see us the day after we landed. They were warm in their expressions of sympathy and good wishes. . . The prison surgeon, Doctor Archer, and the chaplain, the reverend Doctor Buck, spent some hours with us; and we were soon made to feel that we had come less to a land of strangers than of friends.'—*Linus Miller*

From an old print

View of the Inside of Newgate, London, England

Upper Canadian Patriots transported without trial spent several months in these prisons while a motion on the return of a writ of *habeas corpus* was being argued before the Queen's Bench and Exchequer courts. Their detention was declared illegal and they were released.

From the London *Sun*, 1839

Upper Canadian State Prisoners in England

From left to right: Paul Bedford, Linus Miller, William Reynolds, Finlay Malcolm, John G. Parker, Randal Wixon, Leonard Watson, Ira Anderson, William Alves, James Brown, Robert Walker, James Grant

JAILS AND CONVICT-SHIPS 195

back and another approached and performed in like manner. Though each one took but little, three or four that were last had nothing... Messrs. Woodman, Sweet, Higgins, myself, and two or three others suffered extremely by frozen feet. They were so swolen in a few days after our arrival there that we were obliged to cut our boots from our chains down, as the chains prevented us from getting them off;.. for weeks they felt as though they were in hot embers...

'I solemnly declare to you that our sufferings here were almost beyond endurance:.. not more than half enough to eat, and that filthy;.. some obliged to sit while others were trying to sleep;.. and perhaps one would want to get up to go to the *tub* which was sitting in one corner of the *same room*, but could not go without his mate, who was perhaps asleep, and in getting to it obliged to pass over others that were sleeping, causing them to cry out, "Get off! Oh God! you are killing me!".. But to the tub you must go, which frequently was not emptied until the contents were all over the floor and running under us while sleeping... Then the lice,.. when our clothes were not off our backs nor a change of linen for ten weeks.'

The 'Black Hole' of Malden was succeeded by a similar experience at London, to which the Patriots were taken by sleigh in two groups, four days apart, and where their trials[7] and six executions were carried out. The food was 'not fit for hogs', and a brutal turnkey often stole it. Continual efforts were made to get the men to incriminate one another before trial, and there were frequent changes from one cell to another to prevent plans of escape. Marsh remained in London about three months,

'and my treatment had been so severe that the second week after my arrival at that place, being chilled through and suffering from frozen feet, starvation, galling chains, vermin, and filth, that I had a fever and pain in my breast, so that for six weeks I was not expected to live'.

The jail surgeon, Dr. Moore, did everything he could to ease their suffering, which suggested that he was 'a reformer at heart'; while David O. Marsh[8] and his wife, who lived near London, when they heard that a man of the same name was in the jail, brought him a blanket, three pounds of tobacco, and other luxuries from day to day.

[7]The disposition of the American prisoners caused much concern. It was thought necessary to pass a special Act, January 12, 1838, 'to protect the inhabitants of this province against lawless aggression from subjects of foreign countries at peace with her Majesty'. The Act provided that either courts-martial or the regular courts might be used. There was a disposition in England to disallow the Act, for it was considered that Americans crossing the border owed a temporary allegiance and upon its violation might be tried for high treason. There was, however, no interference with the Upper Canadian legislation. Of the 220 prisoners apprehended after November 1, 1838, most of whom were Americans, seventeen were executed, seventy-eight transported, six acquitted, twenty-one discharged, and ninety pardoned, while two died in hospital and six remained in jail in the province for some months after the disposition of the rest.

[8]Both David Marsh and Woodman were in jail in London the previous summer as suspects. Woodman recorded in his diary that the prisoners took turns at a small window to avoid suffocation. Neither name appears in the official list of those arrested—one of many indications that it is by no means complete. Prior to his arrest Woodman had been warned to flee the country as he might be assassinated; but he wrote in his diary on April 15, 1838, that he replied that he had done nothing except 'assist the prisoners in their trials, and that was no crime'.

On April 3, 1839, the prisoners started for Toronto in wagons, crowds of people turning out to see the cavalcade. Elijah Woodman[9] wrote in his diary:

'Very early this morning we were unlocked, and bread served to each man with a small piece of meat, with orders to be ready immediately to take our departure. Soon the jailer appeared and commenced calling to receive us... We started and passed along Dundas Street, getting a nod of the head from a few true friends who took an interest in our fate...

'I thought, why should I be cast down, for I am only in the hands of men and am able to stand all the trials that are put upon me, so with William Stevens I struck up *Pretty Susan* and continued singing for some time'.

The journey lasted nearly a week, but the inconsiderate treatment of the militiamen was offset by kindness from sympathetic innkeepers. The prisoners had high expectations, as they drew near Toronto, of having superior quarters, but Marsh found them, 'if possible, worse than the place we had left':

'We were put into a hall that was occupied during the day by thirty or forty, and at night all locked in different cells—from five to eight in a cell. The jail was crowded full; some crazy, some for murder, some for stealing, some for desertion, and various other crimes.[10] This old jail, as well as all others, was alive with vermin. It is out of my power to describe this place, and our feelings at our entrance and during seven weeks confinement in this horrible place. Our rations were hardly sufficient to keep us alive; what there was more filthy, if possible, than any before. Bullock's heads, boiled with a very few peas that the rats had been among,— and I declare it was impossible to tell, many times, of what our scanty meal consisted,—it appeared to be their intention to poison us here. The bullock's heads were boiled with brains, teeth, and often the hair was so thick in the broth, together with the effects of rats and mice, that we could not stomach it; we came to the conclusion that our days would be ended here...

'I must here mention that after we had been two weeks in this place a gentleman by the name of Richardson, a Methodist[11] Minister residing in the city, visited us; he said he had heard of our condition, fearing we could not long survive under such treatment, had brought with him what we most needed, excepting liberty, which was a large basket of provisions; he said he had tried to see us before but was not allowed till then, and expected that would be the last. He stopped a few moments and comforted us in our affliction by telling us he could not say for certain but he believed it was their intention to liberate us in a short time. This kind

[9] Woodman was captured on the road to Chatham on December 5. He stated in his deposition that he was a citizen of the United States but had lived in London six years. Like many others, he said he was forced off the boat at Windsor. Robert Marsh describes Woodman's wife as 'a regular down easter, a yankee', stating that she came to the jail and told him 'not to inform on others on any account'.

[10] The 'Register of Prisoners' shows numerous entries of deserters and lunatics. Until the erection of the Lunatic Asylum in Toronto in 1846 there was no place else to send the insane.

[11] This is but one of numerous examples of visits to the Patriot prisoners by Methodists. A contributory factor in their interest was sympathy with many of the aims of the movement, but the denomination was always prominent in social service work. Charles Durand says that the Reverend John Strachan, Church of England, and the Reverend John Roaf, Congregational clergyman, also visited the prisoners in Toronto jail. A group of other clergy co-operated with the Reverend John Ryerson, Methodist, in presenting a petition to the Lieutenant-Governor praying for clemency to Lount and Matthews.

JAILS AND CONVICT-SHIPS

act was received with grateful hearts, was often spoken of, and I believe will not be easily forgotten by any of us.'

A plot to escape was well under way, but there were always traitors in the Patriot camp and the authorities received word of the plan. On May 25, just as the plot was scheduled to hatch, they were removed to the deck of a steamship where 'amongst cattle and hogs' they were taken to Kingston. Their quarters and treatment were now very much better. 'We were permitted', says Samuel Snow, 'to get out and play ball once a day for exercise, but strictly watched all the while by British regulars'. Stephen Wright records a visit from Sir Allan MacNab and an inspection by Sir George Arthur, 'the bloody Robespierre of the Canadian Revolution'.[12] The Fourth of July was not forgotten. Wright says:

'We thought of the thousand crowded churches in the land of the free, where millions of happy hearts were bringing meet offerings to that liberty whose claims we advocated at the sword's point, and for which we received a dungeon in this British Bastile as our reward; we sang *Hail Columbia, Happy Land,* and our hearts fluttered as in spirit we visited our thrice dear kindred and our native shores.'

'The ever glorious Fourth of July we celebrated as well as circumstances would permit', says Daniel Heustis. 'Out of several pocket handkerchiefs a flag was manufactured, as nearly resembling the "star-spangled banner" as we could conveniently make it. We procured some lemons and sugar, which enabled us to pass round a refreshing bowl of lemonade. We then let off our toasts, in which the heroes of '76 were duly remembered. . . We had faced the enemy as did the heroes of Bunker Hill, and we saw no cause for self-reproach.'

As the months passed there was less likelihood of further executions. William Gates's mother crossed the frontier to present a petition for his release, and he claims that he and twenty-four others were at one time slated for pardon but that mercy was withheld because a British officer was mistreated in Jefferson County, N.Y. There was a scheme on foot, with the help of guards, to effect an escape, but the weather remained too warm to form ice on which they could cross the river. The whole group[13] were finally marched out of Fort Henry on September 22, 'attached by pairs to a long chain'. They showed their joy—and something of their spirit—by breaking into song, and *Hail Columbia, The Star-Spangled Banner, The Hunters of Kentucky,* and *Yankee Doodle* enlivened their embarkation upon a Durham

[12]The only Patriot who has anything good to say of Sir George Arthur is Linus Miller, who experienced, through the representations of friends, a comparatively kindly reception. Miller observed during his interview with Arthur that 'if he had feelings they were hidden by his exterior; . . but there was a compression about his lips which strikingly evinced his great perseverance, determination, promptitude, and decision of character'. See also appendix L(2) re conditions at Fort Henry.

[13]Six Windsor men and eleven captured at Prescott had been hanged, and seventy-eight were in the group transported.

boat which was to carry them to Quebec *via* the Rideau Canal. There were eighty-three[14] in the group, and 'loaded with chains' and surrounded by detachments of the 83rd Regiment, the Patriots were soon disconsolate enough as they were slowly towed along the canal. 'We suffered considerable on our passage', says Marsh, 'there being so large a number in so small a space, and all being in irons'. At Montreal they were transferred to the steamer *King William,* which carried them eastward to Quebec.

On September 27 they were placed aboard the armed prison-ship *Buffalo,* bound for Van Diemen's Land, though some thought they were *en route* to England. On board were also fifty-eight prisoners from Lower Canada, destined for New South Wales, and at 5 a.m. on the twenty-eighth the *Buffalo* set sail. Some of the Patriots wrote to their relatives while the ship proceeded through the Gulf, and on October 3 the pilot was dropped and carried the letters back to Quebec.

Long descriptions of the ship and life at sea are given in the narratives. Double bunks with a little bedding, and 'tubs for the reception of filth' constituted 'the sum total of our conveniences', wrote Gates, whose account of the effects of a storm leaves little to the imagination:

'Ordinary sea sickness furnishes no comparison to that we experienced in the hold of the *Buffalo.* If one should wish to observe its effect in all its horror—the loathing that takes hold of the soul—the energies of the mind deadened—ambition quenched and hope put out—let him become the unwilling inmate of a convict ship and he will receive his gratification in full.'

For food they were daily served 'one-half pound of bread, one-half pound of meat—pork and beef alternately—a pint of skilly in the morning, a pint of cocoa or tea at night, a pint of water, and a small quantity of duff'. These rations, however, were generous in comparison with those of emigrant ships, nor were the other conditions of travel severe for sailing-ship days. A mutiny was planned with the intention of sailing the ship to New York and freedom, but the captain became suspicious and the captives were prevented from carrying out their plans. Heustis claims that two of the civil prisoners informed the captain of the plot, while Wright states that one of the Patriots was responsible for the failure. In any case it was fortunate that Captain Wood

[14]In addition to the seventy-eight Windsor and Prescott prisoners, there was another, Horace Cooley, arrested June 28, 1838, in the Western District, and convicted of participation in the St. Clair raids. Four others, civil prisoners, were also included. Edwin Merrit, John McMunegall (McMuligan), and John Dean had been convicted of murder, while William Highland was a deserter. Robert Marsh believed them to be spies, stating that 'two accompanied us from Toronto, and we found two at Fort Henry'. The list is given in its entirety in the *Quebec Gazette,* October 9, 1839, while the Patriots are named in Heustis and, with two omissions, in Marsh.

was 'a kind, humane man', for otherwise the punishment would have been much more severe. On October 19 Asa Priest, who had been sick from the commencement of the voyage, died.[15]

The miseries of the passage increased as the tropics were reached, and particularly since numerous privileges had been withdrawn when the projected mutiny was uncovered. Many of the prisoners were ill and lost several teeth through the predominance of salt provisions and a restricted issue of water. On November 12 the equator was crossed, and after a stormy passage of two months the *Buffalo* put in to Rio de Janeiro, where a little fruit was obtained to allay the ravages of scurvy. An English admiral and a post-captain visited the *Buffalo*, and as their attitude was 'respectful', Wright was convinced 'that it was but the *scum* of England who ruled in Canada'. Once again a Methodist missionary visited the prisoners, inquiring about their treatment and giving them Bibles. A celebration was in progress at the port, and the Patriots were impressed with the beauty of the scene.

On New Year's Day, 1840, the *Buffalo* doubled the Cape of Good Hope, a stop at Cape Town being prevented by storms. Home was in every man's mind as he contrasted his position with happier times. For several days the *Buffalo* flew before the gale under a close-reefed main topsail and a reefed foresail. During the crossing of the South Pacific and Indian oceans the wind continued high but generally favourable. The ship leaked a good deal, however, and the prisoners had to take their turn at the pumps. On February 8 the *Buffalo* was in sight of Van Diemen's Land, and four days later dropped anchor off Hobart after 134 days at sea. On the fifteenth the Upper Canadian prisoners were conveyed ashore after a minute examination, but the Lower Canadians continued to Sydney, New South Wales.

Somewhat earlier in reaching Van Diemen's Land were thirteen men who had been captured during the Short Hills raid. The experiences of these men were more varied even than those from Windsor and Prescott. Their leader, James Morreau, had been hanged, and several others might have suffered the same fate if it had not been for the efforts of Mrs. Benjamin Wait. Her husband lost no time in initiating a series of petitions, sending the first while in Niagara jail. He claimed that he was confined 'in the main hall, attended by night only by one or two of his companions who volunteered for that purpose, the wind and rain beating into the hall, which was open to its full force, having no sash or glass in the large rear window'. At other times he was locked in 'a small damp cell so closely

15Marsh describes Priest as 'a very quiet, social man', who left a widow and three children. He was a native of Massachusetts, aged forty, was captured at Prescott, and stated in his deposition that he had been forced ashore. Gates says he died of 'a broken heart'.

that even the diamond door through the main door was fastened, thereby cutting off all communication with the outside, and the whole time not allowed a light even for the purpose of making his bed. . . That the keeper is in the habit of making use of language towards the prisoners too horrible and vulgar to repeat, much to the discomfiture of the quiet and devotionally disposed.'

Deputy-Sheriff Alexander McLeod described the petition as 'lies from beginning to end', and it would appear to be merely part of the Wait propaganda for release. 'He is one of the most consummate villains I have ever met,' wrote McLeod, who added that Wait's wife was 'elegantly dressed, and generally has her pockets well stuffed with Martin Overholt's hard dollars'. Beemer, Wait, and Chandler were described as 'three of the most notorious vagabonds unhung; the two latter I have known these several years and I don't know one redeeming quality they possess'. The sheriff agreed that Wait's petition was 'a tissue of gross misrepresentations as well as inconsistency and absurdity. . . One of the most bare-faced pieces of impudence that can well be conceived'.[16]

But Maria Wait's petitions to Lord Durham procured a last-minute stay of execution, and further respites were succeeded by a commutation to transportation, though Wait says that his acceptance was conditional, for he 'would prefer death to being banished to Van Dieman's Land'. In any case he and the others were transferred to Toronto on October 6. From 'an immense multitude crowding the wharf and lining the street' came 'mingled shouts of imprecations and pity—derision and sympathy'. But Wait considered that it was 'by the squalid alone that imprecations were uttered, while compassion was visible in the countenances of all who appeared worthy respect'.

After an unpleasant night in Toronto jail the prisoners were again moved, proceeding to Kingston by the steamer *St. George*. During the journey Captain Moodie asked them 'if they were not sorry for their conduct'. Wait and Beemer replied that they were not, and that 'they would join the patriots again to-morrow if they were at liberty. They shook their chains and called to the passengers to see what they were suffering for liberty'.

From Kingston they were taken across the Rideau to Fort Henry by wagon, accompanied by numerous officials and a company of regulars. Other prominent Patriots from the Home and London districts who had petitioned were already there, and the new-comers joined them in two large rooms. Wait, Wixon,

[16] Wait and his wife were born propagandists. Their book, *Letters from Van Dieman's Land*, maintains the same tendency, giving the impression of studied composition rather than extempore correspondence. English officials considered Wait to be 'a cunning, designing fellow, and his associate convicts are his dupes'. See appendix L(5). Chandler's daughter accompanied Mrs. Wait to Quebec.

JAILS AND CONVICT-SHIPS

Watson, Tidey, Parker, and McLeod formed an association for 'literary improvement and amusement', and in other ways the prisoners contrived to pass the time. Their rations were 'one pound of bread, three-fourths pound fresh meat, and a small quantity of vegetables served us twice per week—tea and sugar we supplied ourselves. . . The bread seldom lasted the time it was designed, and I have known eighteen extra loaves brought in our ward in one week'. The rooms were inspected daily, presumably to avoid a repetition of the jail delivery of the previous August. Mrs. Wait visited her husband, resolving to follow him to Quebec, to England—even to Van Diemen's Land if necessary.

On November 9 twenty-three of the prisoners were chained and removed to the steamer *Cobourg*, where they passed a disagreeable night:

'Our quarters were most uncomfortable, crowded on the bow deck and penned in on all sides by the military guard, with three horses among us, and the deck covered with their litter upon which we must either lie or stand, while the weather was very cold and we had nothing but our own clothes to protect us from it.'

The next morning they reached Prescott, where they were transferred to the armed steamer *Dolphin*. Although still standing unprotected on the deck the prisoners suffered less, for the weather was fine until afternoon. The *Dolphin* reached Cornwall at 2 p.m. in pouring rain, and the prisoners were marched to jail. Wait states that

'the road was uncommonly bad, and it was with exertions painful in the extreme that we drew our chained limbs along. . . We finally reached the jail, a large brick building three quarters of a mile from the landing, with an imposing appearance upon the outside. But inside, like the Jewish sepulchres, "filled with dead men's bones", alias filth, vermin, and a number of the drunken orange soldiery, thrown in the cells for a few hours to give time for their superabundant spirits to evaporate.'

But the 'large dirty hall' provided at least a place to throw themselves, though their clothes, saturated with rain and steaming in the heat, made them exceedingly uncomfortable. The iron clevies upon their wrists had caused them to swell 'in such a manner that on some the iron was buried in the flesh'. The morning following, however, a 'very good breakfast of beef steak and tea was furnished by the good natured Dutch jailer'.

Rumours of Patriot raids along the St. Lawrence made officials very nervous, but after two days at Cornwall the prisoners proceeded eastward on the steamer *Neptune* and landed at Côteau du Lac early in the evening. French tumbrils, with four men in each cart, carried them to the old fort, where they took turns lying on the floor in a small guard-room. No food was given out that night, but on the following day their guards, Glengarry militia, shared 'fruits, vegetables, and other comforts' brought by their wives and friends.

The following night they were provided with more space, and the cuffs were removed from their wrists. On the morning of November 15 an effort to proceed eastward by Durham boat was rendered futile by a heavy wind, so wagons were pressed into service. Rain and sleet covered them with ice as they moved slowly along, and at the village of Cedars, where a short stop was made, they saw the 71st Regiment and thousands of volunteers— 'the scum of society'—fresh from 'scenes of conflagration, carnage, and ruin', and 'loaded with the booty and plunder of Beauharnois'. The night was spent in a room at the Cascades, where a supper of boiled potatoes was provided.

The steamer *Dragon* carried them to Lachine next day, and from her deck they could see smoking embers and smouldering ruins of the homes of French-Canadian Patriots. Bateaux hauled by horses carried them along the Lachine Canal, and they reached Montreal at nine in the evening. It was midnight, however, before they had any shelter from the cold, and then they were forced to make the best of a 'small hole', the inner room of a lawyer's office, where it was 'impossible to sit down, and scarce practicable to stand'; but later an additional room relieved the congestion, though no food was supplied until the next afternoon— just as they were ordered to embark on the *British North America*. This vessel had a cabin heated by a large stove, and some bunks where they were allowed to sleep without their manacles; but ice delayed their passage and it was 1 p.m. when they reached Quebec. Amid jeers they passed through crowded streets and were placed in a large room in the old City Jail, where tea and bread were supplied for supper, and 'a large pot of oatmeal gruel, with a quart of molasses and a half pound of bread', for breakfast. The nine prisoners[17] who had petitioned to escape trial protested against their transportation, but without success; while those from the Short Hills[18] were wise enough to delay further moves for freedom until they should reach England. On November 22 a blacksmith rivetted chains and handcuffs upon them, and they were shortly driven on sleds to the dock, embarking with eleven felons in a yawl which carried them to the bark *Captain Ross*. A winter

[17]They were Paul Bedford, Finlay Malcolm, John G. Parker, Randal Wixon, Leonard Watson, Ira Anderson, William Alves, James Brown, and Robert Walker.
[18]This group consisted of Linus Miller, Benjamin Wait, William Reynolds, John Grant, Jacob Beemer, Samuel Chandler, Norman Mallory, James Waggoner, John J. McNulty, Garret Van Camp, John Vernon, James Gemmell, George Cooley, and Alexander McLeod. See appendix L(4) for the warrant transporting them.

voyage across the Atlantic was never pleasant in sailing-ship days, and Wait describes the passage as full of horror:

'When the whole number, including twenty-three state prisoners and eleven felons, had been searched and sent below together, and the trap or hatch of iron grates locked down upon us, a scene of confusion and tumult commenced which beggars description. . . The shouts and curses of the felons fighting for pre-eminence, mingled with the clanking of chains, aided by the frigid chilliness of the atmosphere and the damp fetid smell arising from the bilge water, created peculiar sensations of gloom and dread and forebodings. . . For my own part I felt that the last trials of life had arrived. . . *Then* I would have given worlds to have terminated my life upon the gallows.'

During the first fifteen days the prisoners were not allowed on deck, and the straw mattresses and blankets were constantly wet by frequent deluges of sea water and drippings from the lumber and ice above deck. An attempted mutiny led to still stricter discipline, and Wait and John G. Parker were fastened together with a fifty-pound chain; but in the last stages of the voyage the treatment was less severe, and twenty-five days after leaving Quebec they sailed into the Mersey.

Jail in Liverpool proved a welcome change. Coaches conveyed the prisoners to the borough jail, more commonly called 'the old French prison' because it had sheltered French prisoners during the Napoleonic wars. Kindness from visitors, their lawyers, the prison doctor, and the chaplain rendered imprisonment here comparatively pleasant, though the regulations were strictly enforced. Mattresses were provided, and the prisoners were either in separate cells or in groups of three; while satisfactory meals at regular times replaced the 'mouldy biscuit and salt pork' of the ocean passage. On Sunday all attended chapel. 'The female prisoners were hidden from our view by a screen', observed Miller; 'but their voices, when they chanted the service, satisfied me that they were a set of termagants, and cured me of any desire to take a peep behind the curtain'. The service was 'well conducted', and the sermon by the Reverend Dr. Buck 'appropriate to the condition of the prisoners'. The Patriots established contact with prominent Whigs whose influence might be useful. Lord Brougham and Messrs. Hume and Roebuck[19] were addressed by Wait and others; a petition to Lord John Russell would, it was hoped, reach the Queen; while another was sent to Lord Durham. But in the end

[19]Roebuck and Hume, writer of the famous 'baneful domination' letter of 1834, took out affidavits that twelve of the prisoners had been transported without trial, though three of these were to be test cases as to the status of the Short Hills prisoners. On November 24, 1840, Hume replied to a letter of January 27 from Joseph Beemer, Townsend, U. C., enclosing petitions in behalf of his son Jacob. He attempted to secure the pardon of all state prisoners at the proclamation of the Act of Union, and failing in that, was active in securing amelioration of their punishment. See appendix L(5) for a letter to Hume *re* Wait's complaints.

only twelve[20] of the prisoners, of whom Wait was not one, had their cases reviewed by British courts.

On January 4 eleven of the Short Hills prisoners were separated from the rest. J. G. Parker describes in his diary the parting of the two groups:

'At daylight the rattling of chains announced to us that the eleven prisoners were being prepared to embark for Portsmouth. Their chains were riveted on them, as well as on the eleven convicts from Quebec. After dinner they went on board—Dr. Buck having previously prayed with us—and the separation was affecting, as their leaving was under apprehension that they should not see us again. Dr. Buck saw them on board the *Meteor*, which is but a small vessel, and the Governor spoke to the Captain of the steamer of the good conduct of the prisoners while in his custody.'

A bed each and wooden trencher, bowl, and spoons were provided for the eleven men in the bow cabin of the *Meteor*, and at six in the evening she put out to sea. A violent storm almost wrecked her during the next three days, for she dare not even enter the harbours of Cork or Holyhead without a pilot. The engine stopped, the sails and equipment were swept away, but with great skill the captain sailed her back to Liverpool under almost bare poles, and she came to anchor in safety on the seventh. After effecting repairs the *Meteor* set out again and reached Portsmouth on the sixteenth, the prisoners being conveyed at once to the *Leviathan* hulk, and an hour or so later rowed by convicts to the *York*, a similar prison-ship. These antiquated vessels sometimes accommodated prisoners for years, but those sentenced to the longer terms were usually shipped off to Australia and Van Diemen's Land in 'Bay-ships'.

Wait's account of life on the *York*, together with that of Miller concerning his experiences some months later, shows that no time was lost in making the prisoners appreciate their situation. Convict apparel—a gray jacket, waistcoat, knee-breeches, long stockings, striped shirt, checked handkerchief, thick shoes, and sheepskin cap—replaced their own, and the heads of all were shaved. The rations were oatmeal and four ounces of ship biscuit for breakfast and supper, and for dinner a pint of soup, a half pound of salt beef, and a pound of 'a coarse black substance which the officers called bread and the prisoners "brown tommy" '. Every third day a little cheese and sour ale were substituted for the meat and soup. Cold, damp quarters without a fire, the prevalence of

[20]These were the nine *ex post facto* prisoners (see note 17, above), and Linus Miller, William Reynolds, and John Grant. Miller was a Rochester law student, Reynolds a Philadelphia saddler, and Grant a Canadian wheelwright. There is no indication how they were selected as test cases.

JAILS AND CONVICT-SHIPS

vice and crime of the worst types, and 'suffering, privation, insult, reproach, and shame' made life on the hulks sheer misery. On March 12 nine of the men[21] were removed to a vessel bound for Van Diemen's Land. Preparations for the voyage consisted of a physical examination, shaving the head, and depriving them of almost all personal possessions. Loud protests were of no avail, the officers telling Wait with considerable reason 'that they knew what they were doing and would hear nothing from me'. After receiving an issue of bedding the prisoners proceeded to their berths, four men being allotted to each. For meals they were divided into messes of six, 'with only a "kid" to bring the food down in, one tin cup, one wooden spoon, and one knife and fork as table furniture and eating apparatus'. The 600-ton *Marquis of Hastings*, carrying 240 prisoners into exile, set sail on Sunday, March 17. All but the nine men from Canada were criminals sentenced by British courts to transportation—'a mass of corruption and crime', says Wait.[22] The horrors of the 16,000-mile passage are outlined in one of his letters:

'On the embarkation the weather was cold, but as we approached the equator it gradually became more and more warm until the intense heat rendered our situation not only inconvenient but shockingly uncomfortable. The hospital incumbents were daily increasing, until the salt waves closed over thirty unhappy victims of cruelty and starvation. Vermin, the most loathed of all objects to an American, generated too in such abundance that our beds and clothing became literally alive with them. My dreams were always about them, and I would often awake in the act of killing them. . . You cannot conceive the slightest approach to the torment we endured. . . The erysipelas or scurvy broke out among us and continued to carry off the poor fellows long after we had landed; so that one year from the date of our arrival, out of 240 persons the *Marquis of Hastings* was freighted with only 103 were alive.'

The passage exemplifies the uncertainty of sailing-ships. A fair wind carried the vessel to the Bay of Biscay, but a storm drove her back to the coast of Ireland. On regaining her course and reaching the Azores she was suddenly struck by high winds which carried her to the coast of South America. Attempts to round Cape Horn were fruitless, and the ship bore off towards the Cape of Good Hope, near which she lost some of her rigging in stormy weather. After this the *Marquis* was more fortunate, proceeding eastward without incident; in fact the last 1,500 miles were made in fifteen days, and about the middle of July she reached Hobart Town.

[21] Two were temporarily omitted. Gemmell was in hospital, while Beemer was believed by his companions to be busy informing upon them in connection with the abortive mutiny on the *Captain Ross*, and that in the hope of pardon he had made himself sick to delay his departure. See appendix L(5) re life on the *York* hulk.

[22] Evidence was given before a Parliamentary Committee in 1861 that 'the horrors of convict ships are really past description'.

When Mrs. Wait learned that her husband had been sent to Van Diemen's Land, she made plans to go to England in his behalf. Cash contributions from sympathizers, certificates of character, and introductions to prominent persons were first collected, and Bidwell, Mackenzie, William Merritt, and Jesse Ketchum were among those who aided her. After a short 21-day Atlantic passage she reached England, and, armed with her letters of introduction and assisted by the lawyers who had been in charge of the appeals of the state prisoners, she went immediately to work. There were petitions to Lord Durham, Lord John Russell, Lord Normandy, and indirectly to the Queen; introductions to Elizabeth Fry, the great prison reformer, who wrote to the Governor of Van Diemen's Land in behalf of Wait; and to Lady Barham, Lady-in-Waiting to the Queen; and even 'female prayer meetings', where 'the most earnest and affectionate appeals were made to the throne of Heaven'. As a result of the exertions of his energetic and resourceful wife,[23] Wait, as well as his friend Chandler, received preferential treatment and an early parole. Her efforts resulted in improved conditions for the other Patriots as well, and they were quick to thank her, Daniel Heustis observing that 'her devoted and heroic services, embalmed in all our hearts, shall be handed down to other generations as a bright example of conjugal fidelity and active philanthropy, worthy of an immortality of honor'.

Meanwhile, on January 9, the nine *ex post facto* prisoners and three of the Short Hills men, Miller, Grant, and Reynolds, had left Liverpool by rail for London, where their cases were to be tested under a writ of *habeas corpus*. They were taken to Newgate prison, 'a living tomb—the receptacle of the poor, the lost, the ruined, the doomed of earth'. The accommodation, however, was 'decidedly better' than that of Liverpool, for they had two large airy rooms, 'good rations and comfortable bedding', and they were permitted to walk in the yard once or twice a day. 'The officers of the prison,' wrote Miller, who was by no means easily pleased, 'were exceedingly kind and obliging, and we were made to feel ourselves quite at home'. Here they were kept entirely separate from the other prisoners, though Miller was obviously disappointed that he had not been sent as a state prisoner to the Tower of London! On January 14 they attended the Court of Queen's Bench at the opening of the discussion of their cases, and were duly impressed by their sur-

---

[23] A letter written by Wait on the *Marquis of Hastings* on March 15 reached her at Lockport in May, and she immediately made plans to proceed to England. While there she supported herself by teaching in an infants' school and acting as lady's companion. See appendix L(3) for one of her unpublished letters.

JAILS AND CONVICT-SHIPS

roundings. But after six months of deliberation by two courts the sentences of Miller, Grant, and Reynolds were confirmed, though the nine who had been ordered transported without trial were released,[24] Lord Denham giving judgment on January 21, 1839, that their pardon had been authorized by the Upper Canadian Legislature if they petitioned before arraignment. Reynolds also was shortly set free on the ground that he was the youngest[25] of the Short Hills prisoners. Miller and Grant were ordered on July 14 to prepare for removal to Portsmouth. 'Strange as it may appear', says Miller, 'a confinement of six months in Newgate had actually produced an attachment to its old, gloomy walls'.

In chains and handcuffs they proceeded through Old Bailey court-room into a dark passage underneath, where some 200 executed felons were buried, and into a covered van with twenty-six English prisoners. The whole group were chained to a bar of iron which ran through its centre. Upon arrival at the *York* hulk in Portsmouth harbour they found James Gemmell and Jacob Beemer, who had been left in hospital when the others were sent to Van Diemen's Land.

Miller and Grant spent two weeks carrying coal and skinning logs in Portsmouth dockyard, for which they were paid twopence a day. As a result of their protests against manual labour they were placed in the invalid gang, and while engaged in light work at Chelsea beach they planned an escape; but they had apparently informed Gemmell, who inadvertently told Beemer, and their plans failed.

The four prisoners were transferred in September to the 'Bayship' *Canton*, 'with about as much ceremony as would have been shown to so many swine'. But they were unquestionably much better off than they would have been on the average emigrant ship of the day. The height of the between-decks was six feet eight inches as compared with a legal minimum of five feet six inches on passenger vessels; while the berths were better and the issue of food much more varied, including a little wine or lime juice to keep down the ravages of scurvy. The doctor in charge received £1 for each man landed alive at Hobart, so it was to his advantage to keep them in good health; though such an inducement was un-

[24] Of the nine men released, all except Alves sailed from Liverpool for America on the *Wellington* on July 27. Alves apparently went to the United States about the same time, and was still residing there in the eighteen-fifties.

[25] Reynolds was pardoned through the influence of American Ambassador Stevenson, who stressed that he was but eighteen years of age. Miller claims that he was really three years older than himself. Reynolds was apparently active with Bill Johnston's gang before the Short Hills raid, for he observed as they were proceeding through the Thousand Islands on the steamer *Cobourg*: 'Many are the happy hours I have spent here under *Old Bill*; would to heaven he was here now to serve the *Cobourg* as we did the *Sir Robert Peel*'. Miller says his real name was David Deal, but that he altered it to avoid recognition as one of Johnston's men.

208   THE LIVES AND TIMES OF THE PATRIOTS

necessary in the case of Dr. John Irvine, for he was 'an Irish gentleman of mild deportment and christian principles'.

Owing to the good offices of interested parties in England the four Patriots were accorded privileges on the voyage which made it less arduous than that experienced by the nine who had sailed earlier in the year. The irons were removed from all prisoners, and there was a school for their improvement; but fighting was more popular, and the Patriots did not enjoy their crude surroundings.

In order to double the Cape of Good Hope effectively they sailed far westward to Trinidado, 'a barren lofty rock'. On November 10 a stop was made for provisions at Tristan d'Acunha, a small island 1,500 miles off Africa, with a population of fifty-nine, largely shipwrecked sailors. The one American among them told Miller that they lived in peace and amity under a communistic form of government, and that 'nothing could tempt him to abandon the island'.

Between September 22 and January 12 the *Canton* sailed the 16,000 miles between England and Van Diemen's Land—a fast passage over the route. Only two prisoners were buried at sea during the sixteen weeks, and it was in many other respects a satisfactory voyage. But it was with mixed feelings that the Patriots viewed Hobart Town; and their first experiences ashore plainly indicated that any special consideration they had been shown aboard ship was at an end.

BIBLIOGRAPHY

The printed Patriot narratives upon which this chapter is based are as follows: Marsh, *Seven Years of My Life*; Snow, *The Exile's Return*; Wright, in Lyon, *Narrative and Recollections of Van Dieman's Land*; Heustis, *Narrative of the Adventures and Sufferings of Captain Daniel D. Heustis*; Gates, *Recollections of Life in Van Dieman's Land*; Wait, *Letters from Van Dieman's Land*; and Miller, *Notes of an Exile*. All of these are now rare, and the author has not found a complete set in any city in the United States or Canada except Toronto, where six are in the Public Library, and the seventh, Marsh, is in that of the University of Toronto. The unprinted diary and other papers of Woodman are in the Library of the University of Western Ontario, London. The quotations in this and the next two chapters are from Landon, "The Exiles of 1838 from Canada to Van Diemen's Land", London and Middlesex Historical Society, XII, and the writer is indebted to Mr. Landon for supplementary information. Charles Durand's account of his stay in Toronto jail is among the valuable parts of his very rambling and incoherent *Reminiscences* (1897). Other primary sources are Doel's 'Recollections', Archives of Ontario; Parker's diary, in Wait, 191; William Ryerson's letter, in Sissons, I 459-61; the Alexander Hamilton Papers, Public Archives of Canada; and verse on the *Caroline*, 'the Tories', etc., 'By a prisoner in Toronto jail for a charge of high treason' (Lindsey Papers). Family history and traditions relative to John Montgomery are given in York Pioneer and Historical Society, 1927. Much valuable material is found in Bonnycastle, *Canada As It Is*, and in Mackenzie's *Caroline Almanack*. The *habeas corpus* proceedings in England are detailed in Miller and Wait, and in Fry, *Report of the Case of the Canadian Prisoners; with an Introduction on the Writ of Habeas Corpus* (London, 1839). The disposition of Rebellion prisoners is best covered in Watt, "The Political Prisoners in Upper Canada, 1837-8', *English Historical Review*, XLI, 1926; while comment on legislation relative to the American prisoners is given in Robinson, *Life of Sir John Beverley Robinson*. The names of the prisoners on the *Buffalo*, with related material, are given in the *Quebec Gazette*, September 27 and October 9, 1839, and in the Montreal *L'Ami du Peuple*, September 28 and October 23. Conditions on convict-ships are described in the Patriot narratives; in Griffiths, *Memorials of Millbank*, and *Chapters in Prison History*, II; and in Browning, *The Convict Ship and England's Exiles*.

CHAPTER XX

Van Diemen's Land

It is not easy to appreciate the full force of a sentence of transportation to Van Diemen's Land, for the other side of the world is not now the remote region that it was a century ago. The Patriot prisoners were exiled to a Devil's Island from which a return could not be made without the greatest difficulty, and then only by shipping on a whaler or merchant vessel which chanced to pass that way.

The nine state prisoners who disembarked from the *Marquis of Hastings* in July, 1839, were the first to reach Van Diemen's Land and were better treated than those who followed. This was partly due to uncertainty as to their status, and partly to a subsequent change in administration in the prison colony. Three of the nine, however, did not long survive the passage. John McNulty, who had become consumptive during the Atlantic crossing in the *Captain Ross,* died four hours after landing. Alexander McLeod showed evidences of galloping consumption at the close of the voyage, and died two days later, his body being dissected and then buried in a nameless grave among thousands of 'felon mounds'. Garret Van Camp was injured while drawing wood, and his death occurred three weeks after arrival at the island.[1] Chandler and Wait were also in hospital, the latter with erysipelas complicated by treatment with a 'foul lancet' on the *Marquis of Hastings.* There were compensations in Wait's case, however, for he avoided the labour gang and was placed on 'full diet, with extra wine, tea, and sugar'.

The other men, Waggoner, Vernon, Mallory, and Cooley, after being addressed at debarkation by Sir John Franklin in front of the prison barracks, spent several weeks macadamizing the streets of Hobart, though Wait says the superintendent informed them that labour was optional in their cases. The 'tormenting annoyances' of convict overseers worried them, but they were shortly relieved by being assigned or 'sent on loan' to settlers. Chandler was made 'ward's-man' in the barracks, and Wait proceeded thither when he had fully recovered. The accommodations were

[1] McLeod and McNulty had participated at Montgomery's Tavern prior to their capture at the Short Hills; Van Camp was an American. Miller refers to McNulty and Van Camp as 'upright, well disposed men, and esteemed by their comrades'; while McLeod was 'comparatively faultless in person, mind, and heart—never have I known a more noble specimen of the human race'.

but little better than those on the *York* hulk. The beds were 'almost black with fleas and alive with lice', so Wait took narcotics to enable him to sleep, observing that the 'worst conceptions of misery' would be *'far short of the real state in which I spent two weeks'*. But he was not put to work, and was occasionally allowed to walk to town to interview the redoubtable William Gunn, superintendent of convicts.

On October 11 Chandler was assigned as carpenter to Commissary-General Roberts, and Wait as clerk, store-keeper, overseer, and teacher of his five children. Both remained there until they were granted a ticket-of-leave on August 3, 1841. Their good fortune was due to the exertions of Mrs. Wait, and later Patriot prisoners were similarly benefitted in being paroled after two years' labour in place of the usual eight, though they suffered much more severely when probation replaced assignment to settlers.[2]

The sight as the convict-ship *Buffalo* landed seventy-eight Upper Canadian state prisoners in Van Diemen's Land must have been a strange one; for the 'Yankees' were objects of curiosity by reason of the remoteness of America and the cause of their exile, as well as from their unsteady gait after the long voyage. Their reception was ominous, for a row of gallows welcomed them here, and two hundred members of a chain gang a little farther on. Gates says:

'We had hardly our feet on the soil when almost the first objects that greeted our vision were gibbets, and men toiling in the most abject misery, looking more degraded even than so many dumb beasts. Such sights, and the supposition that such might be our fate, served to sink the iron still deeper in our souls.'

The Lieutenant-Governor of Van Diemen's Land was the famous Arctic explorer, Sir John Franklin. The Patriot narratives do not speak well of him, alleging that he was incapable of a proper appreciation of his duties or application to his office; but at least he had not the reputation of a heartless tyrant, as had his predecessor, Sir George Arthur.[3] Some of the Patriots approached Franklin immediately after their arrival, hoping that the nature of their crime would excuse them from the labour gangs; but they were told that he had no orders to give them preferential treatment.

The convict's suit was shortly issued to each. Gray trousers

[2]The assignment of convict labour to settlers ended and probation was substituted on May 20, 1840. The penal colonies in New South Wales and Van Diemen's Land were considered a satisfactory type of colonization as well as a place to send undesirables. In fifty years nearly 100,000 convicts were sent out and £7,000,000 expended upon administration. Transportation was abandoned in 1853.

[3]Sir George Arthur was Lieutenant-Governor of Van Diemen's Land from 1824 to 1836. He was noted for harshness and an autocratic manner, while at the same time he amassed a fortune by investments in land. The best account of his administration is Forsyth, *Governor Arthur's Convict System, Van Diemen's Land*. See also Jesse Morrell's letter to Benjamin Wait, in Wait, 343-4.

Courtesy *Canadian Magazine*
Sir John Franklin
Lieutenant-Governor of Van Diemen's Land, 1836-43

Courtesy Louis Blake Duff, Esq., Welland
Benjamin Wait
Prominent Patriot who was exiled to Van Diemen's Land

William Carey
The *York* Hulk in Portsmouth Harbour
A temporary prison for convicts awaiting transportation

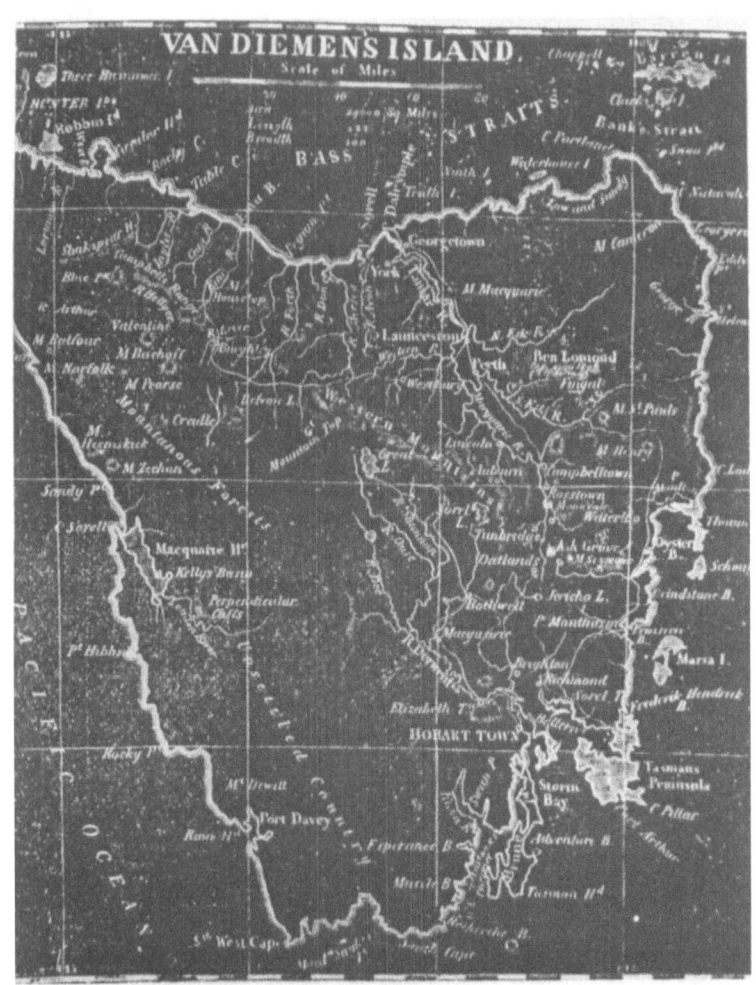

From Benjamin Wait, *Letters from Van Dieman's Land*, 1843

Van Diemen's Land in the Times of the Patriot Exiles

and jacket, 'coarser and rougher even than common carpeting', two striped cotton shirts, a skull-cap of stiff sole leather, and 'a pair of thick clumsy shoes without socks' constituted the entire wardrobe, and each article was marked with a large R. 'When we were thus accoutred,' says Gates, 'we looked so grotesquely that we could not help bursting into a roar of laughter'. But the laughter was short-lived, for shovel, pick-axe, wheel-barrow, and cart were quickly to become accustomed implements of toil, and blistered and bleeding hands and strained muscles the daily portion of each man. Daniel Heustis, in recording bitterly the details of the continued 'slavery', was yet not without a sense of humour:

'On the 28th of May eight of our men were taken to Jerusalem, in the interior. On their journey they passed through Jericho and crossed the River Jordan, and at Jerusalem they "fell among thieves". There were no Samaritans in that region, and the Levites, as of old, "passed by on the other side".'

Flogging was a common punishment in the convict colony, and Heustis saw as many as one hundred lashes laid on—'enough to shock every feeling of humanity'; but he definitely states that 'none of the Americans were flogged',[4] the whipping-post and triangle being reserved for the hardened characters from English jails and brothels. But the heaviest labour, solitary confinement, and short rations were not avoided by the Patriots, and at times there were other miseries. William Gates particularly detested the Sunday church parade:

'We were mustered out, formed into double rank, and marched with the most soldier-like precision to the convict's church at Hobart town, to hear the detested ritual of the Church of England. . . We were considered the lawful butt of every vagabond loafer or high-bred gentleman that chanced to meet us. Our American blood boiled in our veins. . . But there we were, helpless and forced to submit to it all, and compelled to endure the purgatory of two and three long doleful hours—rising, kneeling, and sitting according to the most precise formula, all the while holding our faces as grave as an owl. This done, we were marched back to the station, and back again to endure an afternoon purgatory of increased misery. Thus had we to submit to those above us and sit under the ministrations of Parson Bedford, . . who made no other impressions on our minds than those of hatred and disgust.'

For two years the prisoners worked on the roads, dragging heavy carts of stone. 'We were bowed down with suffering,' says Gates. 'We exhibited symptoms of disaffection—we gave vent frequently to our curses.' The visit of the captain of an American whaler aroused the suspicion of the overseers, and the convicts

[4]Letters from American sailors, suggesting that the state prisoners had heavy chains attached to their legs and were often flogged, appeared in the *Canada Times* in 1841, but they were in error in both respects. See 'Les exilés canadiens à la Nouvelle-Galles', *Le Bulletin des Recherches Historiques*, juillet et août, 1936.

were suddenly removed from Sandy Bay to Lovely Banks station. An effort to effect a wholesale escape was unsuccessful, and again the group was removed. Their sufferings were so great that 'the only wonder is that we were not all tumbled into the dead hole or carried away to the dissecting room'.

Samuel Snow, among the most philosophical of the prisoners, relieved his suffering by a keen sense of humour: 'At Sandy Bay we were divested of our threadbare garments and enrobed in nice suits of domestic manufacture got up after the latest improved convict fashion.' A 'rigid course of *dietetics*' suggested that they had been sent there 'for the cure of dyspepsia', for 'our food was uniformly of the lightest kind—not in the least hard of digestion'. He assumed that Sir John Franklin, 'in the plentitude of his benevolence, wished us to expend all our energies in McAdamizing *our ways*, not in digesting English luxuries', and he gives daily menus to bring home his point. Sugar, tea, coffee, and tobacco were 'unknown to us while we were prisoners', and there were occasions when they were glad to appease their hunger with boiled potato skins and cabbage leaves gleaned from refuse dumps. Two ounces of soap was issued daily, 'with the injunction for every man to wash his own shirt Saturday afternoon'.

At times discipline was most severe, but occasions are recorded when friendly overseers allowed their men to work for wages every Saturday afternoon and to procure luxuries with the proceeds. Certain magistrates similarly evinced a desire to soften the rigour of their punishment, though the type of overseer was common who 'would subdue that damned independent Yankee spirit of ours', and who well merited the description—'inhuman, overbearing, unprincipled, incarnate devils'.

Primitive living conditions and insufficient clothing caused great suffering. Wright notes that the clothes issued did not last long, and the prisoners were soon

'bare-footed and had but a small blanket tied about us to hide our nakedness. Exposed to biting winds and storms of sleet and snow, the huts in which we slept were built of slabs set up endways, very poorly thatched, and the top covering thin and leaky. . . Our floor was the ground, and after a rain pools of water stood for hours in the hut. No fire was allowed us either to warm or dry our clothing. . . Many a time have we, barefooted and in the snow four inches deep, gone to work shivering with cold, half naked, with our bodies wrapped in tattered blankets, and so hoarse with colds that our groans alone were audible.'

Solitary confinement was the punishment for minor breaches of regulations. At Brown's River station Stephen Wright was given twenty-one days' solitary imprisonment for not telling who gave him a piece of tobacco. The usual cell had an uneven floor flagged with stone, and was not high enough for standing erect; it was two feet wide and six in length, ventilated with irregular crevices in the wall, which were also the only means of securing light. 'The filth of these dens of infamy surpasses all description'. On another occasion Wright was given the same punishment 'for refusing to carry, in an overworked and debilitated state, a bar of iron weighing one hundred pounds to the station, the distance being four miles'.

Several of the Patriot prisoners were seriously ill with inflammation of the eyes, and one died after going blind.[5] But the miserable existence did not break the spirit of Elijah Woodman, and Linus Miller describes how he courageously aided in maintaining the morale of his companions-in-exile:

'The party in general bore their misfortunes with manly fortitude. There were several aged men among us, who mostly set the younger an example worthy to be followed in the school of adversity. Elijah C. Woodman of London, Upper Canada, and Chauncey Sheldon of Michigan were the eldest. I shall never forget a little circumstance which occurred, connected with the former. We had worked hard all day in the cold rain, and as usual were locked into our cheerless huts after the day's toil, to sleep in our wet clothing until the morrow should again call us to the performance of our cruel tasks. Some sat upon the forms, some in their berths, while others had covered themselves with their thin blanket and rug to court the warmth, sleep, and rest which they so much needed. All were silent... Suddenly Mr. Woodman sprang from his berth to the floor, and in a tone of voice that might have been heard a mile struck up *The Hunters of Kentucky*. The effect was instantaneous. As if electrified, every man sprang to the floor; sick, blind, and halt joined in the chorus; some danced, others shouted, and all shook off the gloomy horrors of Van Dieman's Land.'

There are frequent references in the Patriot narratives to fellow-prisoners' treachery. Wright, for example, alleges that two of the Prescott men were made overseers for their zeal in informing upon their friends, one of them being earlier blamed for the failure of the projected mutiny aboard the *Buffalo;* while after their promotion they attempted to encourage a revolt among the prisoners, intending to inform upon them in the hope of receiving a pardon.[6]

Groups of prisoners were continually making a break for

[5]This was James P. Williams of Cleveland. His real name, however, is variously given by his companions as John Stuart or Steward, Nelson Recker, and James Rykard. Marsh says his body was dissected after death. The following also died in Van Diemen's Land: Andrew Leeper, Foster Martin, John Simmons, Thomas Stockton, Alson Owen, Lysander Curtis, and William Nottage. Nottage was blown up while engaged in blasting, while Curtis and most of the others died 'in consequence of bad treatment'.

[6]In addition to the informers at the trials, who were freed, and to Beemer, who was universally suspected, there are references in Wright's narrative to the alleged treachery of Orrin Smith, John Tyrrell, and James Aitcheson. But it is not improbable that some of the comments were based on personal dislike or jealousy.

liberty, but the chances of success were strongly against them. Robert Marsh fled but was soon retaken, and thereafter he was dressed in magpie—half black and half yellow. Four others, Michael Morin, Horace Cooley, Jacob Paddock, and William Reynolds, attempted a break from Sandy Bay station, but three weeks later they were captured on a desolate island in Bass Strait, where the small boat in which they had hoped to reach New Holland had been wrecked. They were almost starved, having subsisted largely on shell-fish; and a trial resulted in a sentence of two years' hard labour at Port Arthur. This prison was as secure a place as could well be imagined, but to add to the natural difficulties, the narrow approach was protected 'by chaining large savage dogs so close to each other that a man cannot pass between them without being seized and torn in pieces. These dogs are provoked daily to aggravate their ferocious dispositions'.[7]

Linus Miller, with Grant and Gemmell, had been sent to Brown's River Road station, where they felled trees and carried spars. Miller was shortly made a watchman, but he could not forget his situation—'I am an American citizen—I am a British slave'. Upon learning of the arrival of the main body of seventy-eight Upper Canadian prisoners in the *Buffalo,* Miller, who never knew when he was well off, obtained permission to join them at Sandy Bay station. There he worked harder, the party being engaged in breaking and hauling stone. Scant rations were supplemented by cockles, muscles, and other shell-fish from the beach, but these excursions were discovered and prohibited. Miller was kept at heavy work in spite of all efforts to obtain preferential treatment. On August 29, 1840, he and Joseph Stewart left the camp without leave to make arrangements for a wholesale escape in an American whaler which they learned had arrived at Hobart:

'We traveled until early dawn, and then made our bed for the day under cover of a thick cluster of the wattle tree. The reappearance of darkness was the signal for renewing our journey. Carefully avoiding the habitations of men, we made the bush our highway and the warm lairs of the kangaroo (as they sprang up and bounded away, measuring from twenty to thirty feet each leap), our resting place. Climbing high hills and descending dark and dangerous precipices, clinging to rocks and bushes to prevent a plunge into the abyss below, our progress was neither swift nor uniform. Occasionally we found the under brush and high grass so thick in the valleys as almost to defy our efforts to advance, and often spent an hour of great exertion in gaining one fourth of a mile.'

When they reached Bridgewater they were in the open, but

[7]There is no exaggeration here. Only two prisoners are said to have escaped from Tasman's Peninsula, one being recaptured and the other dying in the woods. Norfolk Island was an even more severe place of punishment. A priest stated that those who were condemned to death for mutiny after a period there 'appeared to be rejoiced'. See *Speech of Sir William Molesworth, Bart., on Transportation* (1840), 16.

they made their bed in a rocky region. A district constable stepped into their retreat, but Miller persuaded him to let them go their way. An effort to engage the help of an innkeeper drew half a dozen constables in pursuit, but the fugitives quickly outdistanced them. After a couple of days under a stone bridge the two men decided to return to Lovely Banks and surrender, and a few days later they were in jail. Trial at Green Ponds brought the usual sentence of two years' hard labour at Port Arthur, but they were first given a taste of the treadmill:

'There were about one hundred persons in this establishment, mostly convicts, but freemen were sent there by the police magistrate of the town for drunkenness, etc. An immense wheel about thirty feet in diameter and sixty feet in length was kept in constant motion fourteen hours of the twenty-four by thirty prisoners. Every four minutes one the men descended from the wheel at one end while another mounted it at the other, each man upon the wheel thus periodically shifting two feet towards the place of descent, which was reached in two hours... Stewart and I, owing to the hardships and privations we had lately experienced, were very weak, but being poverty stricken were of course obliged "to tread out the corn", as it was significantly termed.'

At night 'vermin of every description' made sleep almost impossible; and to the misery from this source was added the 'most revolting and diabolical' activities among the prisoners. Four weeks later the brig *Isabella* arrived to take them to Port Arthur, and sufferings 'ten-fold greater than we had before experienced' were the lot of Miller and Stewart during the thirty-six-hour passage:

'The space between decks was not four feet in depth, and could not have exceeded six feet by ten; yet into this narrow hole forty-six prisoners were crowded, all of whom were doubly ironed and hand-cuffed in pairs. Only about one-fourth of the number could enjoy the luxury of sitting upon the floor at once, and the remainder could not stand upright, but yet were obliged to support themselves upon their feet and lean forward, at the same time clinging with their manacled hands to their companions.

'When the vessel pitched and careened from side to side we were thrown into heaps upon the floor, the wrenching of the irons upon our limbs producing the most excruciating pains and torture, and the weight of the uppermost crushing those beneath half to death. The most horrid oaths and imprecations mingled with the cries and groans of the poor wretches. Nearly all were sea-sick, and the deck was literally a pool of nauseous matter produced by vomiting. Every man was wet to the skin with it, and the stench was intolerable... "Water! water! for God's sake, some water!" was constantly vociferated by a dozen voices at a time; but the monsters who had charge of us would only hand down a tin pannakin full (less than a pint) at stated intervals. Many fainted, but it was with the greatest difficulty that they were dragged to the hatchway in order that a little fresh air might save their lives. At the end of thirty-six hours we reached Port Arthur in a state of misery which language cannot describe.'

Brutal overseers enforced the heaviest labour which men can stand, and the lash was laid on those who would not 'endure the horrors of the carrying gang'.[8] Being the tallest, Miller was 'literally crushed to the earth' by the large sticks of timber. 'We were allowed to rest only once on the way, and when we reached the settlement I was nearer dead than alive.'

The next work was easier. Three miles off was Mount Tongatabou, and from its summit bundles of shingles weighing 70 to 100 pounds had to be carried to the settlement. 'We were obliged to go seven turns a day', says Miller, 'making a distance of forty-two miles, with this load half that distance on our backs; yet it was the lightest work which we had performed since our arrival and we esteemed it quite a *treat*'.

Shortly after Sir John Franklin's visit to Port Arthur, Miller was removed to the invalid gang and became gardener and then washerman in the camp. The five workers in the wash-house were given 1,300 shirts each Monday morning, and their work was to return them clean and dry to their owners. Seven weeks later Miller was given the chance to be church clerk and schoolteacher for the convict settlement. He called upon Sir Eardley Wilmot, who had succeeded Franklin, and a ticket-of-leave enabled him to become tutor in the family of General Lemprière, commissariat officer.[9]

Stephen Wright obtained his parole on February 16, 1842, and at once attempted to find employment; but this was not easy, as there were large numbers of others similarly situated. It was bluntly brought to his notice that ticket-of-leave men were still subject to regulations, for at Campbelltown, where he had joined a group of mechanics, he was given seven days' 'solitary' and had his head shaved for being on the street after 8 p.m. But the paroled prisoner was able to move about, and the strange feeling of comparative freedom as these ragged and exhausted men proceeded slowly to the interior, alternately cast down by their hardships and cheered by an occasional word of kindness, is described by Robert Marsh:

'Now, kind reader, just imagine yourself in a foreign land, destitute of friends, no money, no clothes, discouraged, sick, and worn out by hard labor, a substitute for horses and oxen, starved and insulted in various forms

[8] Sir George Arthur considered the punishment of chain gangs 'as severe as can be inflicted upon men'; while Sir William Molesworth, in stating that 'the convict code of the penal colonies has not its equal in severity in the civilized world', gave numerous examples of excessive crime and punishment. There is no indication, however, that Miller worked in chains, though 'the most desperate characters were chained to a heavy log'.

[9] Miller states that his companion, Stewart, was also made a gardener, then after a year obtained 'a comfortable situation in the family of an officer', was subsequently signal man, and finally pardoned by Sir Eardley Wilmot. Miller named one of his children after his benefactor Lemprière.

that cannot be described, for nearly three and a half years, and meeting a stranger, in all appearance a man of knowledge, addressing you, though in a policeman's garb, with words of sympathy and kindness; do you think you could manifest any other than feelings of gratitude, and rejoice to see such a man, though sorry to see him obliged to serve the government which he despised? . . We met four constables during that afternoon, each one demanding who we were. To each one we had to produce what was called "next thing to freedom".[10]. .

'Night comes and finds us about nine miles from Hobart town; we find lodging in a shepherd's hut; although it was on the ground, there was a temporary covering to the hut. We got a frying-pan of the shepherd, but when we had our mutton ready for frying found not a particle of fat. So we were obliged to boil it in the pan. We had to go nearly a mile for some water, and then partook of our humble fare. Being tired we spread out our old blankets and soon fell asleep. Morning came, and two of the party upon being told we were ready to start exclaimed, "Why the bell has not yet rung!" Upon being told it had, and the gang had all gone to work, they sprang up, apparently in a complete state of bewilderment. This was the first night for two years that we had been allowed a good night's sleep without being obliged to turn out at the ring of the station bell.'

But employment was scarce, and many months were spent in vain efforts to obtain a living wage. Some of the men became outlaws; others petitioned to be allowed to change their parole district to another which might offer more work. Marsh and Snow were among a group of fourteen who worked an estate for a year and a half on shares, the owner subtracting the cost of food supplied to them. They finished with little to show for their labour except a poor living.

When Daniel Heustis received his parole he set out for the interior with a few companions. They encamped by the roadside at the end of the first day, but the landlord of a tavern invited them to sleep in his bar-room. On the following day 'Mother' Barnes gave them a supper and comfortable lodgings in Good Woman's Inn. As they journeyed onward, some diverged from the main road, obtaining employment as farm labourers or 'tree-grubbers'. Alson Owen died from epileptic fits and was buried in a coffin made by his fellow-exiles.

Heustis went to Campbelltown where he was engaged first in making winnowing machines and then in the manufacture of shingles. In January, 1843, he and Elon Fellows introduced the cradling of grain, sickles being in universal use at the time. They made the cradles, became expert in their use, and were so successful in introducing them that their employer gave them an extra pound in payment. But the regular reapers were jealous of

[10]The 'first step towards freedom' was the official name for probation, while a ticket-of-leave was the second stage. A large number of the Patriot prisoners were paroled in February, 1842, when their two years' labour was completed. Bad conduct and other reasons delayed the probation of the rest.

the innovation, and the cradles had to be guarded at night. At the end of February, Heustis was visited by his brother Charles, who had come to Hobart in a whaler; and though there was some thought of escape, he was too closely watched to make the attempt.

Standards of life were not high in Van Diemen's Land. Wright observed that the manners of the inhabitants were 'gross and sensual. . . There is an article which, if imported there, would command the highest price: it is *female virtue*; licentiousness, libertinism, drunkenness, and debauchery being the order and fashion of the day; and a really virtuous person is looked upon with as much disgust there as a vicious one is here'.[11] Some of the paroled prisoners were not long acquiring dissolute habits, and Wright and a few companions formed 'a little temperance society; and we doubt not that it has saved them many weeks from the wretchedness of those living graves'.[12]

Among the worst features of the colony was the bush-ranger, driven to the life of an outlaw to escape the cruelties of prisons and convict camps. Murders and robberies became so common and the fear of bush-rangers so general that to effect their capture a large number of posses of constables were formed from ticket-of-leave men, who were offered a pardon if successful. Over 1,500 men were so engaged in 1842. Wright and Aaron Dresser were among them, and obtained their quarry:

'After we had roamed over mountains and across rivers and valleys for twelve days[13] and had nearly despaired of any success, we heard of a shepherd's hut about three miles distant; and as it had rained incessantly for the last two days we wished to get to it and dry our clothes, cook some meat, and bivouac for the night. We all had separated so that it might be impossible for it to escape our observation; and when we reached it we all came from different directions. When within about twenty rods of the hut we saw two men armed to the teeth coming out of the door, and from the description we knew them to be the brigands. When near them our constable cried "Halt!"; but they seemed to have just discovered us, and giving a wild look around them they ran to the woods. We were ordered to follow them and to fire if they did not halt. They found that we gained ground, and each taking a tree took steady aim at us from behind it; but not one of their pieces would go off, as they had been out the last two days in steady rain. One was armed with a double-barrelled gun and four pistols; the other with a rifle and the same number of small arms. After finding that resistance was useless they surrendered in a very gentlemanly style . . . I visited their cave upon the side of a mountain, and if they had had plenty of provisions they would have been secure for years.'

[11]Upon the average there were some 30,000 convicts in Van Diemen's Land, and only 37,000 inhabitants 'free and without stain'.

[12]As Gates left Van Diemen's Land in 1847 he commented that several of his companions were of dissipated habits and seemed to care little whether they ever returned to America.

[13]Heustis and Gates also acted as bush-rangers, the former stating that on one occasion he was out seventy-three days, 'during which time I never had my clothes or boots off'. See appendix P(4) for Wright's pardon.

VAN DIEMEN'S LAND 219

The third stage of life in Van Diemen's Land began when the prisoner was officially pardoned. Then only was it legally possible for him to leave the country. From two to three years commonly elapsed before a paroled man received his freedom, and the interval would have been longer if it had not been for the American Ambassador to London and others who interested themselves in the fate of the Patriot exiles. In 1844 it was announced in the American press that 'official correspondence between our Minister and the British Government, for the release of David Allen, of New York State, transported to Van Diemen's Land for taking part in the Canadian Revolt, has been published. Allen is to be released provided his conduct in the penal colony has been good'. Lord Aberdeen stated that if clemency was extended to Canadian prisoners it would also be applied to citizens of the United States.[14]

But the Patriot prisoners were impatient at the delay, and some twenty of them planned to escape by whaler. Long-continued activity of a large group of widely separated men was required. James Fero went secretly to Hobart and arranged the details of the rendezvous at Wabs' Boat Harbor, a remote and unfrequented point on the east coast some 200 miles distant. Two of the men, Garret Hicks and Riley Whitney, rented a farm to mature the plans. By bribery and other expedients the party made their way thither from diverse quarters. Huts and caves provided shelter, and firewood was hauled to the spot. More than two tons of potatoes were carried five miles in kangaroo skins for food aboard ship. The nerves of every man were continually at breaking point when at any moment an unguarded action might result in their capture by constables and the consequent failure of the whole plan. The whaler appeared as arranged and sent a small boat ashore to establish contact with the fugitives, but she had come in the morning instead of the afternoon and the group had not assembled; and in the afternoon an armed patrol schooner hove in sight and remained. Hope of freedom turned to desperation as the whaler was forced to set sail without them; but they tried to keep out of sight in the hope that she might return. Suspicion had been directed towards the locality, however, and the men were apprehended and sent back to their respective districts. The bitter disappointment of last-minute failure was succeeded by a punishing journey of one hundred miles over a difficult terrain, and a lengthened interval before pardon.

[14]'Canadian Prisoners', New York *Presbyterian*, quoted in the Toronto *Christian Guardian*, April 24, 1844. See appendix P(2) for Ambassador Edward Everett's letter to Daniel Heustis, describing his activities in behalf of the American exiles; and P(3) for his list of fifty-six men pardoned as a result.

Not all the Patriot exiles returned to America, but the more fortunate were eventually able to echo fervidly the words of Samuel Snow,

'Farewell, Van Dieman,[15] ruin's gate,
With joy we leave thy shore;
And fondly hope our wretched fate
Will drive us there no more.'

[15] All the Patriot narratives and letters so spell the name, though there is no basis for it. When he discovered the island in 1642, Tasman named it Van Diemen's Land after his patron, the Governor of the Dutch East Indies. The name was changed to Tasmania in 1853, when the transportation of convicts came to an end and representative institutions were inaugurated.

BIBLIOGRAPHY

Narratives of Marsh, Snow, Wright, Heustis, Gates, Wait, and Miller, and the Woodman diary, as above. Gates says that the prisoners were not allowed to keep a diary and that parts of Woodman's were seized. For corroboration of the narratives see Griffiths, as above, and *Speech of Sir William Molesworth, Bart., on Transportation* (1840). See also note 4, above, with reference to the reported use of chains and flogging; and appendix P(2) and (8) relative to efforts to secure the release of American citizens.

CHAPTER XXI

The Exiles' Return

THE hard conditions in the Van Diemen's Land prison colony made survival difficult. Of ninety-two[1] Patriots who were transported, thirteen are known to have died,[2] while there is no record of the return to America of three times as many more. The rest reached some part of the continent, though often remote from their old homes.

The first to leave the island were three of the Short Hills prisoners—Benjamin Wait, Samuel Chandler, and James Gemmell. Wait and Chandler, having received their parole in August, 1841, were not closely confined and entered into plans of escape. When Chandler saw press notices of the arrival of several American ships, he obtained a ten-day pass and went to Hobart. A little later certain circumstances enabled both men to be absent without creating suspicion, so they spent Christmas in seclusion in Hobart, and early in January made a bold break, assisted at various stages by fellow-Masons approached by Chandler. Wait says:

'Hiring a small whale boat under the guise of a party for fishing, no one taking us for prisoners, we put to sea for the purpose of evading the consequences of the strict harbour laws, with the spot designated where we could be found; yet it was not until we had tossed about for several days in danger, destitution, and extreme anxiety that the *proper ship picked us up in "distress"*, and offered us comfortable berths in the cabin.

They reached America seven months later, but only after surviving shipwreck in a hurricane off Brazil and spending a month in Rio de Janeiro. In July, 1842, they were welcomed by many hundreds at the railway station in Niagara Falls, N.Y., where Wait's wife[3] was teaching school. As Wait had not been pardoned he could not openly return to Canada, but he sometimes crossed the Niagara at night to visit his sister, Mrs. Michael Gonder, in Willoughby Township.[4] His wife died shortly after his return, and he married again, moving to Michigan. For the last twenty years of his life he resided in Grand Rapids, where he engaged in lumbering and was one of the founders of the *Northwestern*

---

[1] See appendix P for a collation of data relative to those transported.
[2] In addition to the twelve named in chapter XIX, note 15, and chapter XX, notes 1 and 5, Elijah Woodman died *en route* to America in 1847.
[3] Maria Smith Wait died on May 21, 1843, after giving birth to twins. No stone marks her grave in Buffalo, in spite of her exertions in behalf of her husband, and the exiled Patriots in general. Their *Letters from Van Dieman's Land* was published in Buffalo in 1843.
[4] In his reminiscences to R. B. Ross when in his 77th year Wait described trips back to the Grand River region to drill a new generation of Patriots, but this is obviously an old man's tale.

Lumberman. Judge Woods, staunch loyalist militiaman during the Rebellion, was introduced to 'Colonel Waite' in Duluth in 1881 and writes that he found him a 'fine, genial person'. The two veterans talked over their experiences in the Patriot War, Wait stating that he was in charge of the guns which fired at Woods and his companions as they returned from cutting out the *Caroline*. Wait's second wife predeceased him by one year, and he was supported in his last days by old business friends. When he died at the Union Benevolent Home on November 9, 1895, he was among the last survivors of those prominent in the Patriot War.

Samuel Chandler went almost immediately to Iowa, where he took up residence near Maquoketa and was a prominent citizen for twenty-five years. In 1852 he visited Canada, selling his property near the village of St. Johns. He died suddenly on March 25, 1866, while on business in Colesburg, Iowa. Chandler was seventy-six years old and left a family and 'a large circle of friends to cherish his memory'. He was buried with Masonic honours, having been a member of the lodge for fifty-five years.

Gemmell similarly escaped on an American whaler, leaving Van Diemen's Land a month after Wait and Chandler but reaching America a month earlier. In a public announcement he ascribed his good fortune to the freedom he had under parole, the early receipt of which he attributed to Mrs. Wait.

Stephen Wright and Aaron Dresser were the next to leave the convict colony. Among numerous other Patriots they had been assigned to the dangerous duty of hunting bush-rangers, with the promise of one-sixth of the £200 reward, a pardon, and a passage home; and they alone left the prison colony by this means. The director of convicts asked Wright if he would again interfere with British rule in Canada. 'Not until the Canadians are worthier of liberty than they are at present', he replied. On July 22, 1843, they embarked upon the brig *Areta*, bound for London.

Five months later they reached England. Wright was no royalist, as his comments on 'Victoria Cobourg' show. Edward Everett, American Ambassador to London, aided in procuring them a passage to New York on the *Quebec*. Before setting out for Denmark, Lewis County, N.Y., Wright spent a day or two in New York City.[5] 'I would here thank the generous-hearted William Lyon Mackenzie,' he says, 'whose gentlemanly sympathy and hospitality was extended to us while in the city.' When he

[5] On February 17, 1844, Wright and Dresser wrote to the New York *Tribune*, drawing attention to the plight of their comrades in Van Diemen's Land. Wright's narrative is printed with this letter and many other documents in Caleb Lyon, *Narrative and Recollections of Van Dieman's Land* (New York, 1844). The letter is given in appendix P(1).

reached home his aged father received him as the prodigal son, and crowds of people welcomed him. Dresser was similarly greeted at his home in Alexandria, Jefferson County. The greater number of the Patriot prisoners were pardoned in 1844, and many succeeded in leaving Van Diemen's Land within a few months. David Allen,[6] John B. Tyrrell,[7] and John Morrisette were among the first to set out for America, but they were followed in January, 1845, by twenty-six others[8] who were accepted by Captain Selah Young as substitutes for an unsatisfactory crew on the whaler *Steiglitz*, which had put in to Hobart for repairs and was bound for New Zealand and northwest America. Three of the writers of narratives—Heustis, Marsh, and Snow—were in this group. With the help of John Thomas and Nelson Griggs, Heustis had succeeded within three days in assembling the men from various parts of the island. They bonded themselves to the extent of thirty dollars per man, the sum to be raised upon arrival in America.[9] Heustis felt 'as rich as Croesus! British tyranny had fastened no stain upon my reputation, and already visions of home and brighter days were flitting before me and I was buoyant with hope!' 'None of us had formed attachments that would cause pain in dissolving,' says Snow. Robert Marsh, who had become consumptive from the severity of the life, reflected bitterly upon their experiences:

'One of my comrades remarked, "It has just occurred to me that we must be in hell." It must be, for we have found devils here in all shapes, big and little; the big one told us as soon as we had landed in his dominions that we need never expect mercy but perpetual punishment, at the same time intimating that good conduct should be rewarded; but I suppose it was

[6] See also chapter XX, note 14. Pressure was exerted to secure the release of Allen, who was a Massachusetts labourer. American Ambassador Edward Everett (1794-1865) was influential in securing also the pardon of fifty-five other American prisoners. A letter summarizing his activities in the Patriot interest is given in appendix P(2) and (3). American Consul Hathaway at Hobart co-operated in securing a passage on the whaler *Steiglitz* for many of the men.

[7] At his trial Tyrrell said he was an unwilling participant in the raid on Windsor. He returned to Elgin County about 1845, where he became a cheese-maker and a 'prosperous and respected citizen'. He died on May 22, 1874, in his sixtieth year, and was buried in Claus Burying-ground, near Vienna.

[8] Slightly varying lists are given by Marsh, Snow, and Miller. The Buffalo *Commercial Advertiser*, September 1, 1845, gives the names of the twenty-six men, who are reported as having reached Honolulu: Nelson Griggs, Jerry Griggs, Luther Darby, Daniel Heustis, Orrin Smith, John Thomas, Gideon Goodrich, Nathan Whiting, Bemis Woodbury, John Cronkhite, John G. Swanberg, Ira Polly, Leonard Delano, Edward Wilson, Elon Fellows, John Gilman, Joseph Thompson, David House, Chauncey Sheldon, Henry Barnum, Samuel Snow, Alvin Sweet, James Fero, Robert Marsh, Elizur Stevens, and John Grant. The first eighteen were captured at Prescott, the next seven at Windsor, and Grant at the Short Hills.

[9] Marsh and Heustis state that the men signed two joint notes, one for the twenty east of Buffalo, another for the six west of that point. Measures were taken to raise the money upon arrival in America, but Heustis's request in 1847 for contributions suggests that the notes were probably not met in full. By September, 1846, only about half of those who sailed on the *Steiglitz* had reached the United States.

for the purpose of enhancing our misery, for certain I am that if men, women, and children are sent here for the purpose of reforming and making them better they must experience different treatment, or the reverse is and will be invariably the case; for as they are now situated, there is no prospect of reform or of their becoming in any degree better.'

On March 20 the *Steiglitz* stopped off the Society Islands, and the crew bartered for yams, bananas, and other supplies. Heustis and Captain Young dined at Oheterva with the king, 'the young princesses waving cocoa leaves over our heads'. On April 27 the *Steiglitz* cast anchor in the harbour of Honolulu, where the Patriots disembarked and 'were received by the American residents as brothers'.

The group broke up here. Seven shipped with Captain Young's whaling expedition to the northwest coast of America; three took service on the New Bedford whaler *Samuel Robertson*; two went to the Columbia River, and two to California. Eleven others, including Snow, remained for the time being at Honolulu, for at Tahiti Captain Young had arranged with the master of the whaler *Canton* to pick them up after his voyage. Before she arrived, however, six more had shipped on the *Samuel Robertson* when she returned to Honolulu three months later, and Chauncey Sheldon[10] had taken passage on the American sloop-of-war *Levant*, bound for the west coast of Mexico; so only Elizur Stevens, Gideon Goodrich, and Samuel Snow were left to sail with Captain Dyke on November 12. The *Canton* reached New Bedford on May 2, 1846, the only stop having been made at Bahia, Brazil, for water.

Seven years and five months had passed since he had joined the raid on Windsor, and Snow approached his old home in Strongsville, Ohio, with unspeakable delight. He had not heard from his wife since he left Fort Henry in 1839, but found his family in good health. And this likable Patriot takes his leave in pleasing manner by tendering his 'heart-felt gratitude to all who have relieved my wants, and have contributed to the comfort of my family while I was separated from them'.[11]

Robert Marsh and John Grant were among the six who shipped aboard the *Samuel Robertson* at the second opportunity, and nine ex-Patriots were working their passage to New Bedford when she

[10]Sheldon was fifty-seven years old when taken at Windsor and was by far the oldest transported. He is described as 'a free and easy blade' who came to Detroit from Utica with a load of wheat, became the worse for liquor, and joined the expedition. Upon his return he found that his wife had died. He became a lighthouse keeper, then a bartender, and died about 1855. During the War of 1812 he had fought against the British at Lundy's Lane.

[11]Samuel Snow's narrative, *The Exile's Return*, was published in Cleveland in 1846. A local history of Strongsville states that 'Dr. Leonard wrote a book describing Mr. Snow's adventures', though his name does not appear in title page or preface. The Western Reserve Historical Society, Cleveland, Ohio, states that the Cuyahoga County cemetery records indicate that Mary Snow, wife of Samuel, died in Strongsville on February 17, 1863, when he was apparently still living.

set sail on October 1. She stopped at Pernambuco for fresh provisions, and reached New Bedford on March 13, where the men were well received and aided financially by former Patriots.

Delano, House, Orrin Smith,[12] Darby, Grant, Whiting, and Thompson took the stage for Jefferson County, while Fero and Marsh went by 'the cars' to Canandaigua. There they separated, Fero continuing westward to Michigan, and Marsh locating a brother in Canandaigua and accompanying him to Buffalo, where he found his parents in good health. Shortly afterwards he journeyed to Toronto and was pleased to find plenty of Reformers as he proceeded north on Yonge Street. One of them, 'Mr. N. M. H. of the New Market District school', had particularly liberal views. 'May God send many such teachers,' observed Marsh, as he pondered upon the 77,000 miles he had travelled and the sufferings he had undergone for his activities in aid of republican institutions.[13]

Daniel Heustis and John Thomas had contracted in Honolulu to spend a year in California as overseers of a large cattle ranch, and on May 7 they set sail in the *Fama*. Upon reaching Monterey they found their services were not required, but they were given one hundred dollars compensation for breach of contract. In the latter part of June, after waiting in vain for a passage home *via* Cape Horn, they set out by land for St. Louis with a trapper. During extensive preparations for the journey the American consul gave a fandango in their honour. 'We had a fine dance, an excellent supper, and a gay and happy company,' says Heustis. 'Everything was conducted with propriety and in good taste. The Spanish ladies made an elegant appearance in form, dress, and manners.'

Crossing the Coast Range and following the course of the San Joaquin and Casna rivers, they travelled eastward, having to keep close watch upon their equipage because of Indians. A number of considerations, however, shortly led them to abandon the trip over the Rockies, and by calling upon Captain Sutter at Neuva Helvetia, on the Sacramento, they learned that a whaler bound for the United States was then at Yerba Buena. A schooner took them there in six days, but the ship had just left. Heustis then took work as a cattle-driver and spent several weeks in

[12]Gates describes Orrin Smith as 'a single man of considerable property', and says that he suffered greatly from the heavy labour. J. Donald Garnsey, Clayton, states that Smith was born in Charlotte, Vermont, on May 13, 1810, and worked with a lumbering firm on the Grand River, Upper Canada, for several years prior to the Rebellion. After his pardon he returned to French Creek (Clayton), and shortly removed to Peru, N.Y., where he married a sister of Mr. Garnsey's maternal grandmother. Returning to Clayton, he was postmaster from 1867 to 1885. He died on January 6, 1892. His pardon is given in appendix P(5) and facing page 243.

[13]Marsh's *Seven Years of My Life* was published in Buffalo in 1848. On the outside cover is imprinted 'New Book of Martyrs'.

Yount's Valley, going from there to the coast. A letter from Thomas informed him that a vessel at Sousaleta would take them to Chile. He set out at once and took passage on the bark *Fame*, Captain Mitchell refusing payment for the three months' voyage to Valparaiso.

On April 5, 1846, Heustis secured a berth on the 800-ton *Edward Everett*, out of Valparaiso for Boston, arriving there on June 25. When he reached Watertown, Heustis was accorded a rousing reception by his family and friends, who 'fired a cannon and called out a band of music'. Shortly afterwards he visited 'the battlefield at Prescott', and although time had worked some changes in its appearance, 'the recollections of the past were still fresh in my mind, and I will leave the reader to imagine the feelings with which I trod again that field of deadly strife'.[14]

Other Patriots had meanwhile left Van Diemen's Land in smaller parties. Linus Miller spent a year in a lawyer's office after receiving his pardon, leaving for England on September 25, 1845, on the *Sons of Commerce*. But he had no desire to visit any part of the British Empire, and at Pernambuco transferred to the American barque *Globe*, bound for Philadelphia, certain passengers contributing towards the cost of his passage. He disembarked at Newcastle, Delaware, and hastened to Stockton, N.Y., where he found his relatives in good health. In spite of his eight years' servitude he closes his *Notes of an Exile* with the characteristic boast that he was 'still blessed with a strong arm and a willing heart to wield a sword in the sacred cause of LIBERTY, either in the defence of my own country or the rights of an oppressed people'. He married in 1850 and settled on the old homestead, half a mile from the village of Delanti. William Henry Seward, to whom his narrative was dedicated, offered to take him into his law office, but to please his aged parents he remained on the farm, a decision which proved 'a life time regret'. He died in April, 1880, aged sixty-one years.[15]

Others left Van Diemen's Land from time to time. George Brown took passage on an American whaler in January, 1845, arriving home in the spring of 1846. Michael Murray shipped the following June on the whaler *Fame*, bound for the United

[14]Heustis's *Narrative of the Adventures and Sufferings of Captain Daniel D. Heustis* was published in Boston in 1847 and is the most scholarly of the Patriot narratives.

[15]Miller's *Notes of an Exile* was published in Fredonia in 1846. A copy inscribed 'Presented to A. Tyler by the author, March 10, 1852' is in the Legislative Library of Ontario. For a letter written by Miller to the New York *Express* upon his return to America see appendix P(6). Mrs. Harriet J. Thompson, Jamestown, N.Y., only survivor of Miller's five children and now in her 81st year, states that he wrote two other books, *Design of Creation* and *Meal Feeding—Animal Digestion*.

Embarking for Van Diemen's Land

Convict Labour on the Roads

Prisoners Carrying Timber

Scenes in the Life of the Patriot Exiles

Courtesy New York Public Library

Hobart Town from the Barracks

Many Lower Canadian *Patriotes* were transported to Bermuda and New South Wales, but a large number of prisoners from Upper Canada, mostly American citizens, were sent to remote Tasmania

Courtesy New York Public Library

Hobart Town, Van Diemen's Land, from the Harbour

After years of hard labour the prisoners were 'sent on loan' to settlers or placed on parole, and a pardon eventually rewarded those whose conduct was good; but of ninety-two Patriot prisoners transported from Upper Canada, thirteen shortly died and less than half are known to have returned to America

States. Emmanuel Garrison, Garret Hicks,[16] and Daniel Liscombe left for Sydney the same month in the American merchantman *Eliza Ann*, the first two intending to work their passage home in that vessel; and in August Hiram Sharp set out in the *Belle* on a whaling voyage to the South Seas. Others went first to Australia, hoping to earn sufficient there to carry them homeward. In September, Jehiel Martin and James Pearce reached Sydney in a colonial vessel, and William Gates, Riley Whitney, and Chauncey Bugbee left in a lumber schooner for Melbourne the same month.

Gates, who had been overseer of a farm while awaiting his pardon, was hired by a settler 150 miles inland. 'It was sweet to be free,' he commented as he took a last look at Van Diemen's Land. 'Yonder lay the island whose first welcome to us was the sight of men in gibbets, and whereon we had been forced to drag out some five and a half years of most degraded servitude, and whose last greeting was the more disgusting sight of women in those same gibbets'. After two years' work as farm labourer, shepherd, and sheep-shearer Gates had saved ninety pounds. A vessel carried him and Whitney from Melbourne to Sydney, where the captain of the whaler *Kingston* agreed to convey them to America for two hundred dollars.

On May 31, 1848, Gates and Whitney landed at New Bedford, proceeding to Utica, where Gates took the stage for Watertown. As he approached his old home in Cape Vincent with half a dollar in his pocket he learned after many enquiries that his relatives had removed to various parts of the United States and Canada. A Kingston gentleman offered him his home and 'a life of ease' for his sufferings in behalf of liberty, but Gates would not live on British soil. A sister in Niagara County informed him that his parents were living in Aylmer,[17] Canada West, to which he proceeded. Fate decreed that he should travel on the *Experiment*, one of the steamers which had cut off the retreat of the Patriots from the Windmill ten years before. After three months he induced his parents to return to the United States, for he 'could not bear the idea of staying in Canada, to become a citizen of her most gracious majesty's government—a government that I had come to loathe with an abhorrence as sincere as it was deep'. The family went to Wilson, Niagara County, N.Y., their former home.

16Heustis describes 'Old Hicks' as 'a coarse, careless, independent sort of fellow'. His home was in Alexandria, Jefferson County.
17One of Gates's sisters had married one Touzer, who lived near Aylmer, and two other sisters resided in the vicinity. Gates's *Recollections of Life in Van Dieman's Land* was published in Lockport in 1850. In his preface he expressed the hope that 'it may meet with encouragement sufficient to give him help to assist in maintaining his aged parents'.

Many of the Patriot prisoners were still in Van Diemen's Land. Some, says Gates, were 'rather dissolute in their habits and could not get means to leave'. Perhaps the most tragic case was that of a Canadian, Elijah Woodman, who was ill and unable to raise funds for a passage to America. He approached the Masonic lodge in Hobart, outlining his connection with the fraternity in Canada and the United States and stating that he had been 'confined indoors for two years with sore eyes, and almost blind, and am now in a very destitute situation'. Some aid came from this quarter, but Woodman was left in Van Diemen's Land while others worked their passage home. Sometimes he slept in the open air and had no food for forty-eight hours, and his clothes were in such a tattered state that he was often ashamed to be seen. He was in this condition for over a year and a half after he had received his pardon.

Finally, on February 8, 1847, he recorded in his diary that 'Captain Lathrop of the whaler *Young Eagle* has agreed to take me to America with him. He is very generous'. He wrote a note of appreciation to the Masons 'for that kind feeling you have manifested towards me during my sickness, distress, and privations'. The American consul in Hobart gave him an overcoat, and others made small gifts to aid him on his long voyage. His last letter home—he had at times been as long as two years without word from his family—was dated February 15, 1847:

> Dear wife, children, and friends,
> I am, through the all wise providence of God, yet alive. He has surrounded me with his tender care and protection and I am recovering and gaining strength from my affliction which has confined me to this hospital for eight months.
> I shall leave, if God willing, this island for home one day this month on board the *Young Eagle*, Captain Lathrop, from Cape Cod, Massachusetts, and shall mail this the day the vessel leaves.
> You will probably receive this letter three months before my arrival, as the *Eagle* will fish some to complete her load of oil. Now do not put too much dependence in seeing me, for the All Wise Disposer of events may remove me from the shores of time before I reach my native country. I should have been home some time ago but for sore eyes and my other afflictions. The cuts—the result of five operations—are about healed up, and I have been able to walk about for the last three weeks. Since I wrote you with my own hand, August, 1845, I have been quite blind; indeed I did not know if I would ever see again, but thank God I have recovered so that I can see quite as well as ever, and I find my eyes as sound. . . It will be nine years next August since we were all together, but I have faith I will see you all once more, so keep up good courage and think as little as possible of me.

A small boat carried this courageous Patriot to the *Young Eagle,* and he found his berth so comfortable that he slept as he had not slept for months. The vessel sailed on March 2, and on the fourth Woodman noted that they 'got clear out to sea and of that cursed land of Van Dieman'. As later entries record his increasing weakness we are not surprised that Woodman was finally unable to write, and Benjamin Chase, the mate, began to make short entries for him in his diary. On June 15 he cryptically states that 'at seven thirty this morning Mr. Woodman died without a struggle. . . Henry Shaw[18] is employed in making a coffin'. And so Elijah Woodman, who deserved a much better fate, was buried at sea off the Juan Fernandez Islands. The mate of the *Young Eagle* took charge of his papers, which he was finally able to forward to the family in London, in spite of the wreck of the ship a few days after Woodman's burial. His letter to the widow completes the tragic recital:

'Your husband having taken passage for home in the *Young Eagle,* in which I was second officer, and having formed a very strong attachment to him, and his most intimate and confidential friend while on board, it was my pleasure to attend him during his last illness. His last request was that I should write to you on my arrival and convey to you his last words, which I took down at the time (June 6th) and most cheerfully now communicate. Perhaps you are aware that our ship was cast away and lost all on board a few days after his burial. Fortunately the scrap of paper on which I noted down his remarks at the time was by mere accident saved.'

In his last letter home Woodman gave the names of thirteen Patriots still 'in bondage': 'Asa Richardson, William Reynolds, Calvin Matthews, Chauncey Matthews, John Goodridge, John Bradley, Patrick White, Hugh Calhoun, James English, Harris Cooly, George Cooly, James Waggoner, Jacob Beemer.' It is possible that there were many others—one, John Berry, was certainly still there, and as Moses Dutcher had married in Van Diemen's Land it is likely that he permanently settled there or in Australia; but however incomplete it may be, Woodman's list forms the last detailed information concerning the transported Patriots.

John Berry, a Canadian,[19] was unfortunate, for he remained in Van Diemen's Land some thirteen years after he had been pardoned through the efforts of Mr. Everett. Not until 1857

[18] He is everywhere else referred to as Henry Shew. He was from Philadelphia, Jefferson County, N.Y., and upon his return found his wife married to another.

[19] John Berry owned 200 acres in the 6th Concession of Elizabethtown, Upper Canada. An 'ardent Patriot', he was imprisoned in Brockville jail at the outbreak of the Rebellion. Upon his release he became a refugee in Columbia County, N.Y., and was active in the Hunters' Lodge movement which resulted in the attack on Prescott. In his deposition upon capture Berry said he had been 'engaged by Captain Benedick at 16 dollars a month to assist in fortifying an island between Ogdensburg and Morristown as winter quarters for the Patriots preparatory to their attacking Canada'.

did he learn that he was 'discharged from further servitude'. After three years at road work he had received his ticket-of-leave and hired out as a shepherd, in which occupation he apparently remained some fifteen years. Upon learning that he had been pardoned he immediately determined to return to Canada. He worked his passage on a South Seas whaler, and the ship finally reached New York, where Berry disembarked early in June, 1860. From Cape Vincent he crossed to Kingston and took a steamboat to Brockville. Judge William H. Draper, who as Solicitor-General had been Crown prosecutor at his trial, was on board, and recollecting John Berry, 'shook hands with him and generously helped him onward'. 'Last Monday,' observed the *Brockville Monitor*, 'Berry landed in Brockville after an absence of twenty-two years since he had left for Oswego'.[20]

Of several hundred men who were directly implicated in Upper Canadian Patriot activities but escaped execution or transportation, those concern us here who were banished[21] or whose known complicity—or merely their neighbours' persecution—led them to flee the country. A large part of this group apparently returned to Upper Canada when it became legally possible, but no information is available as to the time or circumstances of the repatriation of the greater number. This is easily explained, for the attitude long persisted in some quarters that such men were criminal conspirators, and as such their return was not usually announced publicly; while many local histories, where such information might readily have been recorded, deliberately omit all reference to the Rebellion as too sore a topic. Many did not return until the lapse of years had almost consigned them to oblivion, and others settled in some remote region where their past was entirely unknown.

Those who fled to the United States of their own volition were divided by official proclamation into two classes, according to their prominence in the revolt. The first amnesty, 1 Victoria

[20] Of the ninety-two who were transported, there is no record of the departure from the prison colony of eighteen men, in addition to those in Woodman's list. Assuming that he was substantially correct, the following had left the island between September, 1845, when Miller compiled a list of those remaining, and February, 1847: Moses Dutcher, Robert Collins, Orlin Blodget, Thomas Baker, Michael Fraer, Joseph Lefore, Hiram Loop, Andrew Moore, Jacob Paddock, Solomon Reynolds, Joseph Stewart, and Samuel Washburn, all captured at Prescott; John Sprague, James Aitcheson, Riley Stewart, and John C. Williams, taken at Windsor; and John Vernon and Norman Mallory from the Short Hills. It is probable that a number of these removed to Australia. Towards the close of 1847 William Gates heard from the captain of a whaler that only three of the prisoners were still in Van Diemen's Land. Only one of the group, John Guttridge, appears in the list of those pardoned in 1844 on application of Edward Everett, American Ambassador to London.

[21] The following were sentenced to banishment for life: John Browne, Asa Wixon, Charles Durand, Home District; Ephraim Cook, Gore District; Caleb Kipp, Lewis Norton, Uriah Emmons, Amos Bradshaw, London District. The following were sentenced to three years in Kingston penitentiary and then banishment for life: George Lamb, Colin Scott, George Barclay, Francis Robbins, Luther Elton, Joseph Watson, John Rummerfeldt, C. C. Scott, John Haling, John Robinson, John D. Staples, all of Home District; and Edward Carmon, London District.

c. 10, was passed on March 6, 1838, and enabled a conditional pardon to minor participants. Fifty-nine leaders were, however, excepted from its effects.[22] The men to whom it applied were assured in the Queen's name that they might 'return to their homes, and that no prosecution for or on account of any offence by them done or committed, and in any way related to or connected with the said revolt, shall be instituted or continued'.

The scope of the Act of 1838 was gradually extended. During 1843 five leaders—Charles Duncombe, John Rolph, David Gibson,[23] Nelson Gorham, and John Montgomery—were pardoned under its terms, and all except Duncombe returned to Upper Canada. Various comments greeted this act of clemency. The Toronto *Patriot* exemplifies the Tory attitude. In announcing that Sir Charles Metcalfe had issued a pardon to Rolph and Duncombe, this publication recalled the hanging of Lount and Matthews with the observation that thousands then wished that they might have been replaced by 'a Rolph, a Duncombe, or a Mackenzie. Every one knew *who* was the dupe and *who* the seducer'. It was Mackenzie's opinion that they were 'not hung for treason, but because Rolph and I were not then forthcoming'.

Dr. Rolph had settled in Rochester after his flight from Toronto, and in the spring of 1838 he appears to have given up Patriot activities. When he returned to Toronto in 1843 he restricted himself for some years to the practice of medicine, but gradually re-entered political life, becoming one of the founders of the Clear Grit party. In 1851 he was elected to represent Norfolk in the Legislative Assembly, and in the same year was appointed Commissioner of Crown Lands. In 1853 he became President of the Council, but four years later retired from political life. His death occurred in Mitchell, Ontario, on October 19, 1870.

Dent includes Dr. Morrison in the group pardoned in 1843, but as he had been acquitted upon trial and was not among those attainted of high treason by proclamation, there was no reason to pardon him. He appears, however, to have come back from Rochester about the same time as Rolph. He was not politically prominent upon his return to Canada West, but resumed the practice of his profession in Toronto, and died there on March 19, 1856. David Gibson lived for a time in Rochester, and then obtained, through the help of Marshall Bidwell, employment in connection with the enlargement of the Erie Canal, whereupon he removed to Lockport. He returned to Canada West in 1848 and

[22] See appendix G. Two others, Joshua Doan and Alexander McLeod, were included but were subsequently captured, the former at Windsor, the latter at the Short Hills. Doan was executed, while McLeod died in Van Diemen's Land.

[23] Gibson's pardon has been preserved and is given in appendix Q.

was immediately employed by the government as a surveyor. In 1853 he was appointed Superintendent of Colonization Roads, a position which he held until his death in Quebec on January 25, 1864, in his sixtieth year. Charles Durand returned from Chicago in 1844 and commenced the practice of law in Toronto, where he died on August 16, 1905, in his ninety-fifth year. John Montgomery again kept tavern in Toronto.[24] Nelson Gorham returned to his home in Newmarket. In May, 1885, he was in Yarmouth, Massachusetts, and Durand refers to him as still living in 1897, sole survivor of those who had been prominent at Montgomery's Tavern. Other refugees were gradually brought under the operation of the Act, but many are known to have become well established in the United States and to have had no desire to pay more than a visit to their former homes.[25]

The experiences in exile of William Lyon Mackenzie, 'the last of the rebels', were almost uniformly unfortunate. The early months of 1838 were largely spent in organizing Patriot activities along the border, though Mackenzie abstained from active participation in any of the raids which succeeded the Navy Island occupation. On May 12 the first issue of *Mackenzie's Gazette* appeared in New York, and it continued to be published there until January 26, 1839, and then in Rochester until the close of 1840. On March 19, 1838, a meeting of refugees was held in Lockport and the Canadian Refugee Relief Association organized. Mackenzie had apparently no part in its activities, nor in those of the Hunters' Lodges. The attack upon Prescott in November, 1838, however, led to a proclamation by Sir George Arthur renewing the offer of a reward of £1,000 for the apprehension of Mackenzie, and for a time he feared that an attempt might be made to kidnap him and take him back to Canada.

During the last weeks of 1838, meetings in favour of Canadian independence were held in New York, Washington, Philadelphia, and Baltimore, and Mackenzie was prominent both as organizer and speaker. Shortly afterwards he removed to Rochester, where he continued his newspaper and organized the Association of Canadian Refugees, of which John Montgomery was President. The object was to aid Canadian movements for reform rather than to organize raids from the United States, but the project had no important results.

On June 12, 1838, Mackenzie was indicted at Albany for a

---

[24] In 1849 he was proprietor of a tavern near the corner of Yonge and Albert Streets, and subsequently at Church and Colborne Streets. See also chapter XII.

[25] John Anderson, for example, was in old age a resident of Florida, and Alves, Morden, and Fletcher remained for a considerable period in the United States. Several letters in the Lindsey Papers are from Canadian refugees in remote parts of America. Many settled in Iowa. See pp. 33 and 111, *supra*.

breach of the neutrality laws in invading Upper Canada at Navy Island, but the trial was several times postponed. The case was finally brought up in Canandaigua on June 20, 1839, and Mackenzie was found guilty and sentenced to eighteen months in Monroe County jail and a fine of ten dollars. The sufferings of his dependents were very great during his imprisonment, and his own accommodations and surroundings were primitive and debilitating. Sickness and death were added to the extreme poverty in which his family lived. Almost every article of furniture went to buy food—even the highly-prized gold medal presented to him in 1832 had to be melted down. John Montgomery devised a scheme to enable a last visit to his dying mother, but Mackenzie watched her funeral from the prison. Nor was the hardship greatly relieved when he was set free on May 10, 1840. 'My daughter Janet's birthday, aged thirteen', he wrote in his diary. 'When I came home in the evening we had no bread; took a cup of tea without it, and Helen, to comfort me, said it was no better on the evening of my own birthday.'[26]

Mackenzie made every effort to earn a living for his family. He published the *Caroline Almanack*, attempted to enter the legal profession, and again issued a newspaper, the *Volunteer;* but finding his circumstances becoming steadily worse he removed on June 10, 1842, to New York. There he secured work as actuary of the Mechanics' Institute, but as he was paid largely through fees the position did not prove satisfactory. In 1844 he again entered newspaper work, but gave it up soon after to take a minor office in the New York Custom House. His circumstances improved as books and essays were published, and he became a correspondent of the *Tribune*; but he was never free from financial worries.

His experiences in republican United States not having equalled his expectations, Mackenzie was willing enough to admit the error of the movement he had led in 1837-39. He wrote to Earl Grey on February 3, 1849, two days after he had been pardoned:

'A course of careful observation during the last eleven years has fully satisfied me that had the violent movements in which I and many others were engaged on both sides of the Niagara proved successful, that success would have deeply injured the people of Canada, whom I then believed that I was serving at great risks; that it would have deprived millions, perhaps, of our own countrymen in Europe of a home upon this continent, except upon conditions which, though many hundreds of thousands of immigrants have been constrained to accept them, are of an exceedingly

[26] Of Mackenzie's thirteen children five died in infancy and one at the age of fourteen. A list of his descendants, of whom the most noted is his grandson, the Right Honourable William Lyon Mackenzie King, Prime Minister of Canada, is given in Johnson, 'After One Hundred Years', *Toronto Star Weekly*, November 27, 1937.

onerous and degrading character. I have long been sensible of the errors committed during that period to which the intended amnesty applies. No punishment that power could inflict or nature sustain would have equalled the regrets I have felt on account of much that I did, said, wrote, and published; but the past cannot be recalled. . .

'There is not a living man on this Continent who more sincerely desires that British Government in Canada may long continue and give a home and a welcome to the Old Countrymen than myself. Did I say so or ask an amnesty, seven or eight years ago, till under the convictions of more recent experience? No; I studied earnestly the workings of the institutions before me, and the manners of the people, and looked at what had been done, until few men, even natives, had been better schooled. The result is—not a desire to attain power and influence here—but to help if I can, and all I can, the country of my birth.'[27]

There could hardly have been a more complete abnegation of his earlier course of action, but the document must be interpreted with due consideration to the state of mind which prompted it. He had suffered greatly in the United States and wished to return to Canada, and his attitude was not that of the fiery Reform leader of 1837 but of a disappointed and broken man. As he recovered something of his old spirit he referred merely to his 'honest, even if mistaken effort', and stated that 'my worst error, call it crime if you will, arose out of an excess of zeal for your welfare'.[28]

His final judgment upon his life work combined a sense of achievement with an admission that there might be opposing opinions upon the necessity of armed revolt in 1837:

'I think that however much we may have disagreed as to the move by which Canada would be benefitted, you are not insensible to the fact that from 1st to last of my political career I have striven to promote the general welfare, and that even in those parts of my proceedings most liable to objections, good has arisen by means of a superior class of governors and a better system of Gov.t'[29]

When the petition for his pardon was being circulated in 1847 the *Cobourg Star* reflected the high-Tory attitude in commenting

[27]This was no sudden decision. In the last number of his *Gazette*, December 23, 1840, Mackenzie said: 'Over three years' residence in the United States and a closer observation of the condition of society here have lessened my regrets at the results of the opposition raised to England in Canada in 1837-8.' Private letters similarly indicate a progressive change in attitude.

[28]Mackenzie's address 'To the Resident Land-owners of the County of York', dated at New York, November 6, 1849, Toronto *Examiner*, November 21, 1849. A reply by 'Justice' noted that the Queen had pardoned 'his *one false step*', and that the 'debt of gratitude' owing to the old Reform leaders should be paid 'by placing them once more in the Legislature'. The election of Mackenzie and Rolph in 1851 indicates that this view was fairly general.

[29]MS. letter of Mackenzie to Robert Fairbairn, Darlington (Bowmanville), December 24, 1852. All but the ultra-Tory press had been for some time ready to agree with these sentiments. On February 23, 1848, the *Cobourg Star*, which had mellowed with age and a change of editors, referred to the time when the province was 'misgoverned' by the Maitlands, Colbornes, and Heads: 'We have seen a Military Governor—like all of his class—ignorant, indolent, and with a profound contempt for Civil Government'; and Sir Francis Bond Head, 'taken by midnight from the Fens of Lincolnshire. . . The people knew that as subjects of Great Britain they were entitled to the blessings of a limited monarchy, and they were determined to have them. *And they have got them*'.

that the document was 'going the rounds of the horse thieves and others of that ilk, in favour of the recall of the murderer and outlaw, W. L. Mackenzie'. That this 'cruel censure' had by no means abated by 1849 was apparent as he returned to Canada on the receipt of news that his pardon had been granted.

Mackenzie went first to Montreal, where Parliament was in session under a Reform administration. Nothing of a vexatious character occurred until he visited the Legislative Library on March 1: While consulting the catalogue he was approached by Colonel John Prince of 'shot accordingly' notoriety, who immediately demanded that he show the member's ticket by which he was introduced. 'I will kick you downstairs if you don't leave this moment', was the ultimatum served upon him by Prince, and Mackenzie left without putting it to the test; but he was followed to the lobby and the threat repeated, and the 'distinguished ruffianism' of the colonel was imitated by one of the House messengers.

Another version of the incident indicates that Mackenzie had two separate encounters with Colonel Prince. The Montreal correspondent of the Toronto *Patriot* relates that 'W.L.M.' called at Prince's residence but he was very definitely 'not at home', and Mackenzie left his card. When Colonel Prince returned and saw the card he 'swore he would horsewhip him for his impudence in calling upon him'. The correspondent was an eye-witness of 'the last and best and *richest,* aye, and "gloriousest" of all', which he details in great glee. His version is that 'the little man' returned after the first encounter in the library and was regularly introduced by a member, at the same time casting 'a little leering glance of triumph upon his quondam adversary'. The colonel

'without a word stepped up to him and laid his iron paw upon his throat and dragged him out of the Library, through the door, down the stairs, across the lobby, down another stair, across the hall, through the outer door, and pitched him into the slush in the open street, with one kind word of warning to his unresisting victim, to keep out of his way in future lest he should break his neck. I wouldn't have missed witnessing this scene— no, not for a king's ransom. The Colonel will of course be prosecuted for assault and battery, but the costs and fine I have reason to know will not come out of *his* pocket if he should be.'

There was no court case, however; nor did Colonel Prince ever apologize for his boorish attack upon Mackenzie, though he regretted his impulsive action.

A few days later Mackenzie proceeded by stage towards Toronto. At Kingston he saw himself burned in effigy. On March 18 he reached his old home, though his presence was not generally known for some days. But on Thursday, the twenty-second, there occurred one of those riotous demonstrations which, like 'bloody battles' at elections, were apparently to be expected from time to time. The mob was dignified by the *Patriot* into 'a band of loyal citizens, determined to save Toronto from shame'; while the *Examiner* found them merely 'an assembly of unshaven, dirty-looking, half-intoxicated men, and ragged boys'.

The pre-arranged signal for the assembling of the mob at the old 'rebel corner', Queen and Yonge Streets, was a false fire alarm. The ringing of the bells brought many from their homes, though the more peaceable returned when they learned there was no fire. The rest were roused to action by the shout, 'Drive Mackenzie out of town!', and the riot commenced. Effigies of Baldwin and Blake had been prepared in tar barrels and the mob marched down Yonge to Front Street and burned them in front of their residences. Continuing thence to the Market and the Police Office, the rioters learned that Mackenzie was at the home of John Mackintosh,[30] M.P.P., his brother-in-law, at Albert and Yonge Streets. Bearing the third effigy and several tar barrels, and accompanying their actions with 'horrid threats, hideous grimaces, and drunken imprecations', some 1,500 men marched to the house, burned Mackenzie's effigy, and bombarded the building with rocks.

The Toronto police force consisted of half a dozen men, and some of them were present; but when they arrested one man he was immediately rescued. It would appear, indeed, that effective action was out of the question, though the *Examiner* suggests their apathy was due to their 'Tory masters'. The windows of Mackintosh's house were all smashed, and an effort made to set it on fire. The 'glare of ferocity' on their faces suggested that the rioters were in earnest as they shouted 'Remember Colonel Moodie!' and howled for Mackenzie's life. All night the mob roamed the streets, venting their hatred on prominent Reformers. John Montgomery's Tavern, almost opposite the Mackintosh house, was bombarded by a large number of stones, and Hervey Price[31] was wounded and narrowly escaped with his life. At 4 a.m. the rioters attacked the residence of George Brown on Church Street, and then 'staggered to their homes, the supply of liquor being exhausted'. Mackenzie had meanwhile escaped out the back door of the Mackintosh house, and, accompanied by his daughter Janet[32] and a young political friend, unbarred the gate

---

[30]Mackintosh, although a party to the plans for revolt, was not suspected at the time and escaped arrest and persecution.

[31]Price did not participate actively in the Rebellion. He shortly removed to England, where he died on July 13, 1882.

[32]A year earlier Janet Mackenzie carried the petition to Lord Elgin which resulted in her father's recall from exile. She married Charles Lindsey, biographer of Mackenzie.

THE EXILES' RETURN 237

leading to the street and walked boldly through the mob to the home of an acquaintance. The riot continued sporadically during Friday and Saturday nights, but the presence of two hundred special constables and sixty men from the Garrison with orders to shoot to kill dampened their enthusiasm.

The proceedings were thoroughly canvassed during the next few days, and the Reform press learned that printed circulars had been sent into the rear townships as far as Bond Head, urging the inhabitants to participate in the riot, and that 'numbers of low Orangemen' had joined their brethren in Toronto; it was also maintained that their course of action followed very closely the incendiary editorials of the Tory organ, the *Patriot*. The next meeting of the City Council was given over entirely to a debate upon the riot. Alderman Duggan blamed the affair upon the fact that 'that wretch Mackenzie had come to town, and his presence insulted the inhabitants'; and Alderman Carr contributed the enlightened comment that 'it was bad policy to prevent a mob of people'. Aldermen Dempsey and Dennison had been seen in the front rank of the rioters, and the latter, in admitting that he was there to see 'the fun', said that 'if it were not for the law I would not hesitate a minute to take his life'. He objected to special constables, claiming that thirty-six dollars expense had already been incurred, and asking, 'Are we to tax ourselves to protect a little rebel?' He admitted that he loved 'to see a spree', and 'the most violent portions' of his harangue brought cheers from 'the loafers in the gallery'. Dennison further stated that if the Mayor called on him to fight the riot he would refuse; whereupon Alderman Workman interjected the apt comment that he ought in that case to be shot immediately, and it would be 'done accordingly' *à la* Colonel Prince!

Mackenzie shortly left town, and Toronto was soon back to normal. Many among the 'respectable' class considered that the good name of the city had been stained, but others were 'proud that they had saved the reputation of loyal Toronto'. There was no attempt, however, to repeat the riot upon Mackenzie's return after his 'Winter Journey through the Canadas'. On May 1, 1850, he removed his family from New York to Toronto, and in April, 1851, re-entered political life and was elected to the Legislative Assembly as member for Haldimand, his chief opponent being George Brown. The return of Rolph and Mackenzie at this election indicates that their past was approved—or at least pardoned.

It was perhaps to be expected that the career of the Rebellion leader after his return from exile would be to a considerable extent an anti-climax, for the system of government had been greatly changed during his absence. Lord Durham's investigation of the abuses which had precipitated the revolt resulted in the decreased importance of the lieutenant-governor,[33] and a corresponding increase in the scope and powers of the Legislative Assembly. In 1849 the full implications of responsible government were recognized when Lord Elgin signed the Rebellion Losses Bill. There was, consequently, no longer the necessity of exposing administrative abuses—a field in which Mackenzie had been pre-eminent.

Though hardly at home in his new environment, the great agitator took a prominent though independent part in the debates on the questions of the day. His occasional reference to the Rebellion in semi-jocular fashion in Parliament was considered in bad taste by many, for it had proved no joke to hundreds still living; though his attitude was probably intended to indicate that he did not retain the bitter feelings of earlier times. In other matters his course of action was entirely consistent. To the end he remained the untiring opponent of administrative extravagance, of monopoly and privilege in any form. In advocating prohibition of intoxicants and the extension of educational facilities he was the friend of the poor man. He was not impressed with the results arising from the achievement of responsible government, considering it rather a new distribution of patronage than a positive gain.

In 1858 he resigned his seat and retired to the 'Mackenzie Homestead',[34] which his friends had provided after several years' exertions. Until 1860 he continued to publish *Mackenzie's Message*, which he had commenced in February, 1853. Financial difficulties and a depressing malady rendered miserable the last months of his life, and his death on August 28, 1861, was a welcome relief to a man 'heart-broken with disappointment'.[35] He was buried in the Necropolis, whither he had helped remove the

---

[33] The prospects were disheartening to the Tories. The following epigram by 'Philo Quoz' appeared in the *Cobourg Star* of March 14, 1849:

> 'The Governor a *cypher?* No!
> Let's hope, at least, it is not so;
> I grant his ministers' vile tricks
> Have plac'd him in an awkward *fix*;
> That they no *value* can confer
> Who cannot boast one *integer*,
> Though they're a villainous *whole number!*
> My Lord! awaken from your *slumber!*
> To shew you loathe their wicked actions,
> Reduce them all to *vulgar fractions!*'

[34] This historical landmark at 82 Bond Street, threatened with demolition, was purchased in 1936 by a group of Toronto citizens led by T. Wilbur Best, and will be preserved as a library and museum of Rebellion relics.

[35] Mackenzie's last days are described in Charles Lindsey, *Life and Times of Wm. Lyon Mackenzie*, I 13.

bodies of Lount and Matthews but three years earlier, and his grave is surmounted by a granite column crowned by a Celtic cross.

All parties and creeds united to follow his funeral *cortège*, for his services in the cause of human liberty were widely recognized. 'It was a funeral which demonstrated that in the long run honesty is cherished—that blunders and even crimes are forgiven by the people if their author has but acted under the pressure of disinterested impulses', said the *Ottawa Citizen*. Friend and foe alike found much to commend in his life and work. A political opponent considered him remarkable for 'his indomitable perseverence and unhesitating self-reliance'; while J. C. Dent described him as 'a man of great ability, true patriotism, and sterling integrity of purpose', and the holder of opinions 'which were honestly entertained, which were just in themselves, and most of which have since been approved by the general voice of the Canadian people'.

Moreover, it is not necessary to minimize Mackenzie's defects to justify his life work. While eminent as the organizer of an agitation, he was unsuited by temperament to the exacting demands upon leaders in a revolution. His fiery nature incited enthusiasm, but he lacked the poise and personal magnetism to reconcile divergent opinions and iron out potential difficulties; and yet, though he made not the slightest claim to skill in military tactics, there would have been at least initial success in the capture of the capital if he had had his way at Montgomery's. He was continually actuated by a desire to right the wrongs he saw everywhere around him, and his unbounded energy, unselfishness, courage, and sincerity of purpose outweigh his impetuosity, which was incited and exaggerated by the deliberate and continual aggravation under which his agitation was carried on. In retrospect, the passing of a century has obliterated not only all the actors in the drama but their violent feelings, and sentiments expressed in Mackenzie's lifetime by a friend may be the eventual verdict of history: 'For all your exertions and great sacrifices in the cause of human Liberty you will ultimately be rewarded—if not by success, by an honorable name in the annals of history and by the gratitude of the unborn *freemen* of Canada'.[36]

Unsuccessful revolt is always followed by recriminations, and Mackenzie took his full share in the charges and counter-charges

---

[36] Soon after his death there were suggestions that a memorial be raised to commemorate his part in the achievement of responsible government, but they did not materialize. A monument is now under construction near the Ontario Parliament Buildings, Toronto. A detailed description of the plans is given in Johnson, 'After One Hundred Years', *Toronto Star Weekly*, November 27, 1937.

that were bandied about; but while others sought to evade their share of the responsibility he ran a straight course to the end, even to the extent of apologizing most abjectly when he came to believe that many of his actions were unjustifiable. The same cannot be said for the other leaders who survived the revolt. Bidwell took but little part in the final break, but that little was not to his credit, for his timidity prevented a clear-cut stand one way or the other. Morrison was much more involved, but he too was unwilling to carry through to its logical conclusion the enterprise which he was prominent in launching; and after his return from the United States he sank with lesser leaders into merited obscurity.

Rolph's rise to greater prominence after the revolt places him in an unique position. He was generally considered at the time to be 'the secret Executive of the rebels', and it was undoubtedly intended that in the event of a successful rising he should be the leading figure in the new administration. After the failure and his flight the opinion was expressed that 'insidious and treacherous men are always cowardly, and we suspect that *Rolph's* heart failed him on *coming to the scratch'*. The *Christian Guardian,* in no sense a Tory publication, condemned the 'degrading duplicity' of 'that arch-traitor John Rolph',[37] and historians have repeated the accusation with embellishments.

Shortly after the failure of the revolt, and while he was still in exile, Rolph wrote a 'Review of Mackenzie's Publications on the Revolt before Toronto', with the purpose of exposing 'numerous malevolent falsehoods'. He makes no effort to justify his noncommittal attitude during the revolt, nor does he even give a straightforward statement to explain the simplest of actions; instead he equivocates by referring to himself as 'either unable or unwilling to join his insubordinate officer' (Mackenzie). It is this reticence to steer a clear course that makes it difficult to place a favourable construction upon his activities during the Rebellion. Without the corollary of a definite statement, a denial in general terms of wrong intent[38] is insufficient, for those who are more capable of judging the culpability of his actions are prevented from so doing, and are left no choice but to assume correct the statements of the others most directly concerned, and especially when they corroborate one another beyond all reasonable doubt.

[37] Quoted in the *Patriot,* January 2, 1838. The issues of the *Christian Guardian* for December have been torn from the 1837 file in the Victoria College Library, while the whole year is missing from the set in the United Church Publishing House, Toronto. Since a number of Egerton Ryerson's letters of the period are also missing, the question arises whether these records were accidently or designedly destroyed.

[38] See appendix E for a discussion of the evidence on the Flag of Truce incident.

The real cause of the revolt in which Mackenzie and his supporters had given their best was a rebellion against the constitution by the ruling clique, a course of action in its essence worse than the consequent revolt against the Crown. 'I confess I have no sympathy with the would-be loyalty of honourable gentlemen opposite, which, while it at all times affects peculiar zeal for the prerogative of the Crown, is ever ready to sacrifice the liberty of the subject', said Solicitor-General Blake in 1849. 'That is not British loyalty. It is the spurious loyalty which at all periods of the world's history has lashed humanity into rebellion'.[39] A strong protest was inevitable, and that it developed into armed revolt is more the responsibility of Sir Francis Head than of the rebels.

The Patriot agitation failed through inefficient leadership and defective oganization. Both in the Canadas and across the border there was always some great lack, some fatal blunder or gross neglect of duty. At no time was there any realization of the importance of promptitude, precision, and discipline in military operations. Where there should have been close co-operation between the Upper and Lower Canadian movements there was only sympathy; while among the American Patriots particularly, jealousy among the officers and treachery in the ranks were continually in evidence, and the whole tone of the movement was consequently lowered. There was no George Washington to co-ordinate and unite the Patriots of the Canadas and their sympathizers in the border states into one great irresistible force.

The movement was by no means a wasted effort, however, for it brought forcibly to the attention of the Imperial Government a condition of administrative irresponsibility which was entirely out of place in the nineteenth century. That the same results might eventually have been achieved by constitutional means in no respect lessens the value of the Reform movement in forcing an immediate decision on the issue. The coming of Lord Durham not only provided the cure for all major grievances in the Canadas, but prevented the continuance of the repression which had followed the revolt and was threatening to blight the development of the nation. Nor was this all. The antiquated Imperial colonial system shortly came to an end, and the spirit of reform had far-reaching effects upon the basic principles of educational, religious, and financial institutions in Canada. The Patriot agitation is a notable example of the type of movement which, despite innumerable defects, may yet, through its results, lay claim to an honourable place in the history of human freedom.

[39] On July 9, 1897, the National Liberal Club, London, England, tendered Sir Wilfrid Laurier a complimentary luncheon. When Sir Robert Head, grandson of Sir Francis, pointed out the famous Bidwell banner, Laurier observed that 'in 1837 Canadians were fighting for constitutional rights, not against the British Crown'.

BIBLIOGRAPHY

Narratives of Marsh, Snow, Wright, Heustis, Gates, Wait, and Miller, and the Woodman diary, as above. State Book L, Public Archives of Canada, contains the official lists of those whose death sentence was commuted to transportation to Van Diemen's Land. As far as their actual transportation is concerned the lists are erroneous, for there were some last-minute changes. These are pointed out and the lists collated with those of Heustis and Miller, neither of which is entirely accurate, in appendix P. The author is indebted to Mr. Louis Blake Duff, Welland, for information upon Wait's later life. A biographical notice appeared in the *Buffalo Courier* after his death in 1895, and was reprinted in the *Welland Tribune* of November 15. Supplementary material is found in the *Niagara Falls Evening Review*, November 18, 1930, and in Judge Woods's *Reminiscences*, 3. Chandler's obituary notice in the Toronto *Globe*, April 6, 1866, describes his later life. Tyrrell's later life is outlined by Landon in the *London Free Press*, July 15 and September 21, 1935; while Sheldon's is described in Ross, 'The Patriot War', 568, with some traditional misinformation in Lizars, 262, making him out to be an Enoch Arden. Mrs. Arthur Williams and Mr. Donald Garnsey, Clayton, N.Y., have provided information on the later life of Smith, whose pardon has been made available for reproduction by Mr. Garnsey. See also notes and appendix P for supplementary sources and data.

The sources on the exiles and refugees in the United States are equally fragmentary, except in the case of Mackenzie, who is well covered in the official biographies of Charles and G. G. S. Lindsey, and in various contemporary newspapers. A biography of Gibson is given in Ontario Land Surveyors' *Report*, 1916, 51-2. An inconsequential treatment is bestowed upon his own life by Durand's *Reminiscences*. Rolph's 'Review' was not published in his lifetime but is printed in Dent, II 331-51. Mackenzie's address 'To the Resident Land-owners of the County of York', dated at New York, November 6, 1849, was printed in the Toronto *Examiner* of November 21, and the reply of 'Justice' appeared on December 12. Harsh American and Canadian comments on the petition for his recall are given by Mackenzie in Head's *Flag of Truce*, 6-7, while his own attitude may also be seen in various issues of his *Gazette* and in other writings, both printed and manuscript. The encounter with Colonel Prince is detailed from opposing points of view in C. Lindsey, II 293-4, and the *Cobourg Star*, March 14, 1849. For the Toronto riot see contemporary issues of the *Patriot* and *Examiner*, and particularly 'A Tory Riot. Toronto Delivered up to Mob Law', and 'City Council—Discussion of the Late Riot', *Examiner*, March 28, 1849. Comments on the Montreal riot and the repercussions of the point at issue throughout Canada are exemplified in 'The Last Desperate Struggle of Toryism', and 'Tory Sedition in Toronto', *Examiner*, May 9, 1849, and in 'Proceedings of Anti-"Rebellion Reward" Meeting in Seymour Township', *Cobourg Star*, March 21, 1849. Mackenzie's 'Winter Journey through the Canadas' is one of his lesser-known works. The ten articles appeared in the New York *Tribune*, from which they were reprinted in the *Examiner*, April 25 to July 25, 1849, omitting the issue of June 13. Obituary notices and comments on his life are found in the official biographies, in Thompson, *Reminiscences*, 136, the *Hamilton Spectator*, August 28, 1861, and in Dent *Canadian Portrait Gallery*, II 45-53, and in his *Upper Canadian Rebellion*, where is reflected the great change in his attitude. Scovell's letter is in the Lindsey Papers, where also are MS. and printed announcements of the Vauxhall meeting and various other items of value in connection with this chapter. A carefully documented estimate of Mackenzie's policies is given by R. A. MacKay in 'The Political Ideas of William Lyon Mackenzie', *Canadian Journal of Economics and Political Science*, February, 1937; while the banking crises attendant upon the Rebellion, and the resulting financial disturbances and commercial depression, are treated fully by D. G. Creighton in 'The Economic Background of the Rebellions of Eighteen Thirty-seven', *ibid.*, August, 1937. A recent valuable study of the Rebellion as an incident in the sequence of world social revolutions is Stanley Ryerson's *1837—The Birth of Canadian Democracy*. A large number of letters relative particularly to the later life of participants in the agitation, many of them from descendants, as well as photographic or photostatic copies of several documents, have been presented by the author to the Toronto Public Library.

Edward Everett
American Ambassador to Great Britain, 1841-1845, who expedited the return of the exiles

Lord Durham
The Father of Responsible Government, who ended the repression in the Canadas

The New Bedford South Seas Whaler *Canton*
A prison-ship in 1839, she transported four Patriots to Van Diemen's Land; and in 1846 carried three exiles from Honolulu to the United States

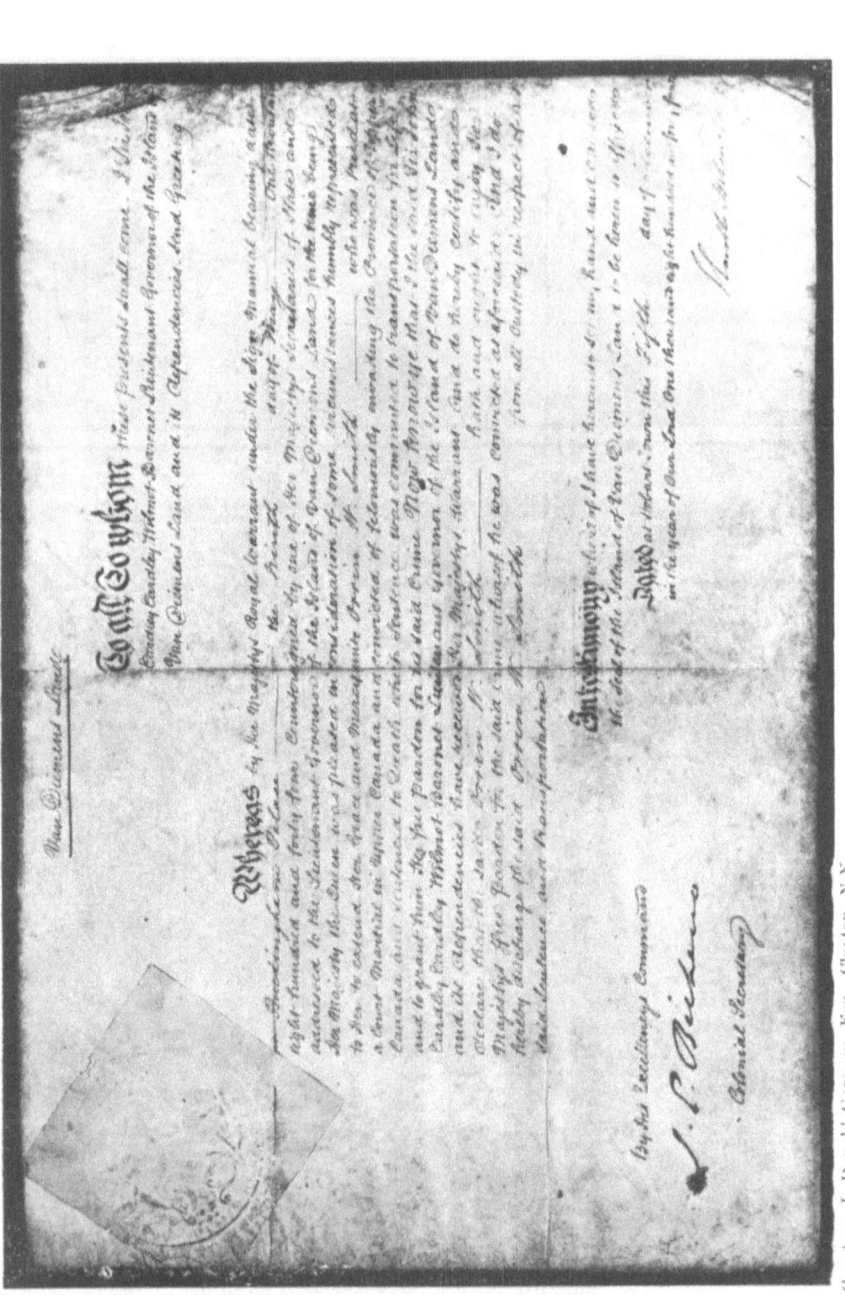

The Pardon of Orrin Smith

This parchment pardon is among the most notable relics of the Patriot War

APPENDIX OF SELECT DOCUMENTS

AND

COLLATION OF DATA RELATIVE TO THE PATRIOT MOVEMENT

APPENDIX A.

RESOLUTION DECLARING MACKENZIE UNWORTHY OF A SEAT IN THE LEGISLATIVE ASSEMBLY, DECEMBER 17, 1833.

(Proceedings of the Legislative Assembly, December 17, 1833.)

That this House, on the thirteenth day of December, 1831, in consequence of a false and scandalous libel published against a majority of its members by William Lyon Mackenzie, Esquire, one of the members then representing the County of York, of which he avowed himself the author and publisher, was induced to expel him, the said William Lyon Mackenzie, from this house: That notwithstanding the gross and scandalous nature of the said libel, this House, in the hope that the said William Lyon Mackenzie would abstain from a continuance of the offensive conduct for which he had been expelled, permitted him to take his seat on the third day of January following, as a member for the County of York, after being re-elected: That in this hope, so important to the deliberate transaction of public business, so essential to the respectability of the Legislature and peace of the country, a few days' experience convinced this House there was so little reason to rely, that on the seventh day of the same month of January, it was by a large majority again deemed necessary to expel the said William Lyon Mackenzie, for a repetition and aggravated reiteration of the aforesaid false and scandalous libel; and in doing so, this House, in order to support the dignity which ought to belong to a Legislative body, considered it just and proper to declare the said William Lyon Mackenzie unfit and unworthy to hold a seat in this House during the continuance of the present Parliament: That, as the said William Lyon Mackenzie has never made reparation to this House for the gross injuries which he has attempted to inflict on its character and proceedings, there is no reason to depart from the resolution of the said seventh day of January, 1832. And therefore he, the said William Lyon Mackenzie, again elected and returned to represent the County of York in this present Parliament, is hereby expelled.

APPENDIX B.

The 'Family Compact'.

[From W. L. Mackenzie, *Sketches of Canada and the United States* (1833), 405-9.]

When I left Upper Canada last year some of the offices, sinecures, and pensions of the Government were divided as follows:—No. 1. D'ARCY BOULTON, senior, a retired pensioner, £500 sterling. 2. HENRY, son to No. 1, Attorney-General and Bank Solicitor, £2400. 3. D'ARCY, son to No. 1, Auditor-General, Master in Chancery, Police Justice, etc. Income unknown. 4. WILLIAM, son to No. 1, Church Missionary, King's College Professor, etc., £650. 5. GEORGE, son to No. 1, Registrar of Northumberland, Member of Assembly for Durham, etc. Income unknown. 6. JOHN BEVERLEY ROBINSON, brother-in-law to No. 3, Chief Justice of Upper Canada, Member for life of the Legislative Council, Speaker of ditto, £2000. 7. PETER, brother to No. 6, Member of the Executive Council, Member for life of the Legislative Council, Crown Land Commissioner, Surveyor-General of Woods, Clergy Reserve Commissioner, etc. Income £1300. 8. WILLIAM, brother to Nos. 6 and 7, Postmaster of Newmarket, Member of Assembly for Simcoe, Government Contractor, Colonel of Militia, Justice of the Peace, etc. Income unknown. 9. JONAS JONES, brother-in-law to No. 2, Judge of the District Court in three districts containing eight counties, and filling a number of other offices. Income about £1000. 10. CHARLES, brother to No. 9, Member for life of Legislative Council, Justice of the Peace in twenty-seven counties, etc. 11. ALPHEUS, brother to Nos. 9 and 10, Collector of Customs, Prescott, Postmaster at ditto, Agent for Government Bank at ditto, etc. Income £900. 12. LEVIUS P. SHERWOOD, brother-in-law to Nos. 9, 10, 11, one of the Justices of the Court of King's Bench. Income £1000. 13. HENRY, son to No. 12, Clerk of Assize, etc. 14. JOHN ELMSLEY, son-in-law to No. 12, Member of the Legislative Council for life, Bank Director, Justice of the Peace, etc. 15. CHARLES HEWARD, nephew to No. 6, Clerk of the District Court, etc. Income £100. 16. JAMES B. MACAULAY, brother-in-law to Nos. 17 and 19, one of the Justices of the Court of King's Bench. Income £1000. 17. CHRISTOPHER ALEXANDER HAGERMAN, brother-in-law to No. 16, Solicitor-General. £800. 18. JOHN M'GILL, a relation of Nos. 16 and 17, Legislative Councillor for life. Pensioner, £500. 19 and 20. W. ALLAN and GEORGE CROOKSHANKS, connexions by marriage of 16 and 17, Legislative Councillors for life, the latter President of the Bank. £500. 21. HENRY JONES, cousin to Nos. 9, 10, etc., Postmaster at Brockville, Justice of the Peace, Member of the Assembly for Brockville. Income unknown. 22. WILLIAM DUMMER POWELL, father of No. 24, Legislative Councillor for life, Justice of the Peace, Pensioner. Pension £1000. 23. SAMUEL PETERS JARVIS, son-in-law to No. 22, Clerk of the Crown in Chancery, Deputy-Secretary of the Province, Bank Director, etc. Income unknown. 24. GRANT, son to No. 22, Clerk of the Legislative Council, Police Justice, Judge Home District Court, Official Principal of Probate Court, Commissioner of Customs, etc. Income £675. 25. WILLIAM M., brother to 23, High Sheriff Gore District. Income from £500 to £800. 26. WILLIAM B., cousin to Nos. 23 and 25, High Sheriff, Home District, Member of Assembly. Income £900. 27. ADIEL SHERWOOD, cousin to No. 12, High Sheriff of Johnstown, and Treasurer of that district. Income from £500 to £800. 28. GEORGE SHERWOOD, son to No. 12,

APPENDIX 245

Clerk of Assize. 29. JOHN STRACHAN, their family tutor and political schoolmaster, archdeacon and rector of York, Member of the Executive and Legislative Councils, President of the University, President of the Board of Education, and twenty other situations. Income, on an average of years, upwards of £1800. 30. THOMAS MERCER JONES, son-in-law to No. 29, associated with No. 19 as the Canada Company's Agents and Managers in Canada. This family connexion rules Upper Canada according to its own good pleasure, and has no efficient check from this country to guard the people against its acts of tyranny and oppression. It includes the whole of the judges of the supreme civil and criminal tribunal (Nos. 6, 12, and 16)—active Tory politicians. Judge Macaulay was a clerk in the office of No. 2, not long since. It includes half the Executive Council or provincial cabinet. It includes the Speaker and other eight Members of the Legislative Council. It includes the persons who have the control of the Canada Land Company's monopoly. It includes the President and Solicitor of the Bank, and about half the Bank Directors; together with shareholders holding, to the best of my recollection, about 1800 shares. And it included the crown lawyers until last March, when they carried their opposition to Viscount Goderich's measures of reform to such a height as personally to insult the government, and to declare their belief that he had not the royal authority for his despatches. They were then removed; but with this exception the chain remains unbroken. This family compact surround the Lieutenant-Governor, and mould him like wax to their will; they fill every office with their relatives, dependants, and partisans; by them justices of the peace and officers of the militia are made and unmade; they have increased the number of the Legislative Council by recommending, through the Governor, half a dozen of nobodies and a few placemen, pensioners, and individuals of well-known narrow and bigoted principles; the whole of the revenues of Upper Canada are in reality at their mercy;—they are Paymasters, Receivers, Auditors, King, Lords, and Commons!

APPENDIX C.

(1) THE FLAG OF TRUCE.

The controversial issues in the Flag of Truce episode revolve around Dr. John Rolph. His aim in accepting the office, his conduct during both journeys to the rebel camp, and his conversation with the leaders have all been the subject of bitter dispute. On October 28, 1852, he spoke upon the subject before the Legislative Assembly of Canada at Quebec, stating that on his first visit to the rebels as joint bearer of the flag of truce he neither said nor did anything which could be construed into impropriety on his part, and that Samuel Lount's deposition was false in that respect. Statements by all directly concerned, and by some who could hardly have known much about it but had plenty to say (or were told what it would be convenient to have said) may be found in Dent, II 69-91, in Lindsey, II 82-6, and in Mackenzie, *Head's Flag of Truce*; and this and many other controversial subjects are discussed at length in King, *The Other Side of the Story*. The attitude of W. W. and Robert Baldwin towards the insurrection in general and the flag of truce incident in particular is given in their letters to the *Palladium*, reprinted in the *Mirror* of January 6, 1838.

Two items of evidence not previously used in the controversy are among the most illuminating. The *Christian Guardian* and the *Patriot* (January 2, 1838) cite an affidavit by a Methodist who stated that he was 'made a prisoner by Rolph and detained *by him* until taken into custody by Mackenzie and a guard of armed men; and this too at the time when Rolph was returning to the City with his flag of truce!' Even more important is the evidence at Montgomery's trial of William Ketchum, a Reformer, for he gave it in such a straightforward and naïve manner that Chief Justice Robinson said he had practically convicted himself of high treason because he had not earlier told the authorities what he knew, and he forthwith fled to escape arrest. After visiting his farm above Montgomery's on Tuesday, and stopping to talk with John Montgomery on his way back, Ketchum had proceeded towards the city and shortly met Baldwin and Rolph on their first trip with the flag of truce. The original trial record states that 'Rolph then called Witness on one side and spoke to him—he told Witness that when he returned to the City, he must mind and say to every one that the party there was very strong. Witness was convinced from what he heard that they were not very strong'. (State Book K, Public Archives of Canada.) Without such direct corroboration Dr. Horne's statement relative to Rolph (see note 8, chapter II) might have been attributed to party rancour or desire for revenge, but the two taken together bear out the entire truth of each.

After a careful consideration of all factors in the dispute the author believes that the truth lies with Lount and Mackenzie. The very fact that the rebels proceeded a mile southward after the two hours' truce was declared indicates that Rolph told them privately to do so; for there is no possibility that Bond Head would authorize his delegates to permit them to march towards the city while the truce was in force and he was considering their demands.

Rolph's son Thomas, still living in Toronto, says he always understood that his father took a prominent part in the Rebellion, but that he never broached the subject to his family. This reticence was characteristic of the man, but it is unfortunate for his reputation that he chose never to make a positive statement of his course of action, for in the face of the evidence of others a mere denial in general terms is insufficient.

(2) DEPOSITION OF SAMUEL LOUNT UPON CAPTURE.

(Appendix to Journal of the House of Assembly of Upper Canada, 1837-8, 406.)

The Prisoner Samuel Lount, on being asked whether he wishes to make any statement, says that he did not know of any intention to rise in rebellion for more than two weeks previous to the Monday on which the Assembly took place at Montgomery's; that while he was with the rebels he disapproved of many of their acts, particularly the burning of the house, which he did not hear of till after it took place. I had no idea it was to be a rebellion; I was informed and led to believe that what we wanted could be obtained easily, without bloodshed. I opposed the burning of Mr. Jarvis's house, and exerted my influence to prevent the rebels from going there, as I understood that Mrs. Jarvis was unwell. When the flag of truce came up Dr. Rolph addressed himself to me; there were two other persons with it besides Dr. Rolph and Mr. Baldwin. He (Doctor Rolph) said he brought a message from His Excellency the Lieutenant-Governor, to prevent the effusion of blood, or to that effect, at the same time he gave me a wink to walk on one side, when he requested me not to hear the message but go on with our proceedings. What he meant was not to attend to the message.

Mackenzie observed to me that it was a verbal message, and that it had better be submitted to writing; I took the reply to the Lieutenant-Governor's message to be merely a put-off. I understood that the intention of the leaders was to take the City of Toronto, and change the present form of Government; I heard all that was said by Doctor Rolph to Mackenzie, which is as above related; this was the first time the flag come up—I was present also when the second flag come up; Dr. Rolph then observed that the truce was at an end. I do not know who shot Colonel Moodie; I do not know who was on guard.

(Signed) SAMUEL LOUNT.

Taken before the Commission,
18th January, 1838,
A true Copy,
A. B. HAWKE,
Secretary to the Commission.

APPENDIX D.

PROCLAMATIONS OF LIEUTENANT-GOVERNOR SIR FRANCIS BOND HEAD.

PROCLAMATION

By His Excellency Sir Francis Bond Head, Baronet, Lieutenant-governor of Upper Canada, &c., &c.

To the Queen's Faithful Subjects in Upper Canada.

In a time of profound peace, while every one was quietly following his occupations, feeling secure under the protection of our laws, a band of rebels, instigated by a few malignant and disloyal men, has had the wickedness and audacity to assemble with arms, and to attack and murder the Queen's subjects on the highway—to burn and destroy their property—to rob the public mails—to threaten to plunder the banks—and to fire the city of Toronto.

Brave and loyal people of Upper Canada, we have been long suffering from the acts and endeavours of concealed traitors, but this is the first time that rebellion has dared to show itself openly in the land, in the absence of invasion by any foreign enemy.

Let every man do his duty now, and it will be the last time that we or our children shall see our lives or properties endangered, or the authority of our gracious Queen insulted by such treacherous and ungrateful men. Militia-men of Upper Canada, no country has ever shown a finer example of loyalty and spirit than you have given upon this sudden call of duty. Young and old of all ranks are flocking to the standard of their country. What has taken place will enable our Queen to know her friends from her enemies—a public enemy is never so dangerous as a concealed traitor: and now my friends let us complete well what is begun—let us not return to our rest till treason and traitors are revealed to the light of day, and rendered harmless throughout the land.

Be vigilant, patient, and active—leave punishment to the laws—our first object is, to arrest and secure all those who have been guilty of rebellion, murder, and robbery; and to aid us in this, a reward is hereby offered of One Thousand Pounds, to any one who will apprehend, and deliver up to justice, William Lyon Mackenzie; and Five Hundred Pounds to any one who will apprehend, and deliver up to justice, David Gibson, or Samuel Lount, or Jesse Loyd, or Silas Fletcher; and the same reward and free pardon will be given to any of their accomplices who will render this public service, except he or they shall have committed, in his own person, the crime of murder or arson.

And all, but the leaders above-named, who have been seduced to join in this unnatural rebellion, are hereby called to return to their duty to their Sovereign—to obey the laws—and to live henceforward as good and faithful subjects—and they will find the Government of their Queen as indulgent as it is just.

GOD SAVE THE QUEEN

Thursday, Three o'clock, P.M., 7th December.

The party of rebels under their Chief-leaders are wholly dispersed, and flying before the Loyal Militia. The only thing that remains to be done is to find them, and arrest them.

Description of the above rebels.

One Thousand Pounds Reward for the apprehension of W. Lyon Mackenzie. He is a short man, wears a sandy-coloured wig, has small twinkling eyes that can look no man in the face—he is about five feet four or five inches in height.

Five Hundred Pounds Reward for David Gibson. He is about five feet nine or ten inches in height, red-faced, sandy hair and red whiskers, which curl rather closely—rather round-shouldered—speaks with a strong Scotch accent, age about thirty-five.

Five Hundred Pounds Reward for Samuel Lount, a tall man, say six feet or rather more, long face, sallow complexion—about six feet in height, and upright.

Five Hundred Pounds Reward for Jesse Loyd, he is rather an old man, say about fifty-five years of age, long straight hair rather thin and turning gray—stoops very much in his gait, has scarcely any teeth left—one remarkably prominent, which is much observed when he speaks, very round-shouldered, and speaks with a strong Yankee accent, height about five feet ten or eleven inches; generally dresses in a drab or brown homespun clothing.

Government-house, 8th Dec., 1837.

His Excellency the Lieutenant-governor warmly thanks, in the name of Her Majesty the Queen, the loyal and gallant Militia of Upper Canada, for their ready attention to the call of their country, when their services were required for putting down a cruel and unnatural rebellion.

His Excellency trusts that the service has now been effectually rendered, and it only remains for him to take whatever steps may be necessary for the peace and security of the several districts, and to announce with much satisfaction that there appears to be no further occasion for the resort of Militia to Toronto.

APPENDIX E.

THE COBOURG RIFLES, 1837.

(From 'The Adventures of the Cobourg Rifles during the Campaign of 1837', by 'One of Themselves', *Cobourg Star*, October 27, 1847.)

Captain Warren, late 66th Regt.
Lieuts. Chatterton, McDonald, late 59th, and H. Covert
Qr. Master Serg't H. E. Nichols

APPENDIX 249

Serg'ts G. M. Goodeve, H. H. Meredith
Corporals Saunders, R. Armour

Privates

Charles Perry	C. S. Finlaison
Rowe Buck	W. W. Hammond
J. McGarvey	R. D. Rogers
F. H. Burton	C. J. Owston
H. W. Jones	John Laurie
W. F. Harper	Henry Blackstone
Wm. Bancks	Angus Crawford
C. G. Buller	Geo. Pierce Marsh
Wm. Graveley	Jonathan E. Tremain
R. H. Throop	Henry Falkner
Wm. Butler	A. G. Allan
Charles Butler	F. P. Covert
Wm. Boswell	John Brady
James Mewburn, jr.	Henry J. Ruttan

APPENDIX F.

THE DEPOSITION OF PETER COON.

'Papers re Examination before Magistrates of Persons taken up for Treasonable and Seditious Practices.' (Public Archives of Canada.)

Gore District.
To wit.

Peter Coon of the Township of Burford, in the London District, Blacksmith, being duly sworn, deposeth and saith, that for about a fortnight past frequent meetings have taken place in the neighbourhood of his residence. Isaac Malcolm and Eliakim Malcolm, of the Township of Oakland, were particularly active and industrious in calling these meetings, and inducing people to attend them, that at some of these meetings, violent speeches were made by Eliakim Malcolm and Doctor Chas. Duncombe, and one McGuire a School Master, who advised the people to arm themselves and fight against the Government, and said they would lead and assist them.

Has seen Doctor Charles Duncombe armed with a sword, and the said McGuire armed with a gun. He also has frequently seen these three, so armed, drilling and training men, some armed and some without arms. He has also seen George Case, of the Town of Hamilton, armed, and he appeared to be acting in concert with the leaders before mentioned, has heard the Malcolms say, that Geo. Case was of their party, and that they considered him a very efficient person, who would do them good service. Has also understood, that a person of the name of Matthews, an auctioneer from Brantford, was in company with Case, aiding and assisting the rebels.

Deponent further swears, that on Sunday last, McGuire, the school master, and James Malcolm came to him and required him to manufacture a lot of Pikes, for the purpose of arming some of the rebels who had no other arms. He objected to doing so, and they returned on Monday last and insisted on his making pikes for them, and threatened if he did not do so, they would put their martial law in force against him. They required fifty, and he was compelled to proceed to work and made upwards of 20. On Tuesday evening following Doctor Duncombe came to his neighbourhood with about 180 men, Duncombe and the principal part of his men being armed, Duncombe sent a message to him, that he must make pikes or do any other work they required him to do, and charge the same to the party. George Case was in company with Duncombe and his party at that time he was told. James Malcolm gave orders, that everyone should throw his house open and give lodging to the men under arms. Some of them lodged in Deponent's house. Eliakim Malcolm and McGuire told deponent, that they would plunder everyone who would not turn out with them, in order to procure provisions, arms and other necessities, he knows, that they did take a quantity of arms from a person or persons at Waterford. He has heard Eliakim Malcolm and others of the party, say, that they had pills for the Lieut. Gov., Sir F. B. Head, and that they would shoot him if they could get a chance. Has heard Eliakim and James Malcolm and McGuire state, that if they could succeed they would establish an independant Government, without any connection with the Queen or the Mother Country, Great Britain. After it was known that a battle had taken place near Toronto, he had heard Eliakim Malcolm and McGuire say, that MacKenzie was doing well, and that they had acted and would act in concert with them, or words to that effect.

The Rebels heard on Tuesday that Col. McNabb was coming up with a body of armed men to oppose them. On Tuesday morning George Case and Matthews came in from Norwich, and when they heard that an army was coming against them, they went back to Norwich and returned again the same evening with Duncombe and his men. On Wednesday evening the Rebels forces in his neighborhood amounted in all to about 200 men. On Wednesday evening the Rebels, amounting in all to about 400, left deponent's neighborhood in a body and in tolerably good order. On Thursday morning Col. McNabb's men came to his neighborhood. He was called out to take care of Capt. Servo's horse, which had been shot. Shortly after that deponent was taken prisoner, as he was told for making the pikes already referred to.

his
PETER + COON.
mark.

Sworn before us at Hamilton this 17th day of Dec. 1837.

(Signed) Colin C. FERRIE, J. P.

(Signed) W. B. VANVERY, J. P.

APPENDIX G.

Upper Canadians Arrested and Imprisoned.

[The list which follows was prepared by J. W. Macaulay from returns furnished by the sheriffs, and included information as to the disposition of each case. A number of American raiders in the schooner *Anne,* at Pelee, and at the Short Hills are included. For the complete table see *Imperial Blue Books on Affairs Relating to Canada,* XI, 1839. The names only are given herewith, twenty-seven of the 885 being still in prison when the compilation was made. There are many evidences that the list is by no means inclusive of all who were arrested. A survey of their occupations is illuminating. A Cobourg militiaman, in describing those who answered Bond Head's call to the militia, unwittingly indicated the central truth that the Patriots were largely men of small property, while the loyalists were 'the Lawyers, the Clergy, the Gentry, the Farmers, and the Traders—in fact all who dreaded being plundered and had the most to lose'. ('The Adventures of the Cobourg Rifles during the Campaign of 1837', *Cobourg*

Star, October 27, 1847.) The rebels described here as having 'nothing to lose' included, however, many farmers and large landowners. In general the mercantile class found it to their interest to ally themselves with the government, but in the Patriot movement were large numbers of labourers and tradesmen, for it was essentially a workingman's agitation. The official list of 885 arrested or absconded contains some 375 yeomen (farmers), 345 labourers, 80 carpenters or other tradesmen, and a sprinkling of 85 'gentlemen', innkeepers, teachers, lawyers, doctors, merchants, artists, and preachers (one Baptist and one Methodist). The greater number would appear to be of American birth or descent; and while the leaders emphasized the constitutional issue, there were many among the rank and file who would have been quick to effect a social revolution. The official list contains many errors in spelling, and many more were introduced when it was reprinted in Lindsey, II, 373-400.]

NAMES OF PERSONS ARRESTED IN UPPER CANADA AND IMPRISONED ON A CHARGE OF INSURRECTION OR TREASON BETWEEN DECEMBER 5, 1837, AND NOVEMBER 1, 1838.

EASTERN, OTTAWA, AND BATHURST DISTRICTS—No prisoner confined.

JOHNSTOWN DISTRICT

Thos. Wilson	Charles Swift	James Malone
Wm. H. Sherman	George R. Brian	William Parrot
Wellesley Pike	John Thomas	

PRINCE EDWARD DISTRICT—No prisoner confined.

MIDLAND DISTRICT

George R. Huffman	John B. Wheeler	Ivy R. Roblin
Francis M. Weafer	Charles N. Phillips	Samuel Stephen
Augustus Thibodo	Thomas Mullins	Elijah Ockerman
John Burley	Samuel Parkeymore	Edward Hickey
William Cunningham	Christ. Lafontaine	Tobias Myers
Reuben White	Samuel Marsh	John C. Pennock
Joseph Canniff	Asa Lewis	John Pockard
Joseph Lockwood	Peter Orr	George Holsenburgh
Norr. H. Herns	Charles Marsh	John Martin
Joseph P. Cavalar	Wm. A. Forward	Ebenezer B. Stores
Gideon Turner	Hiram Mott	John Herman
Peter Davidson	Stephen Mott	Daniel Davidson
C. H. M'Collum	William Anderson	Nelson Long
Thomas Anderson	Abram Collard	Jacob Lott
Oliver Robinson	Samuel Babcock	William Leslie
Richard Tucker	Robert Bird	James L. Chatsey
Anson M. Day	Peter Robinson	Absalom Day
Anson Hayden	Joshua Smith	Christopher Greniser
Cornelius Parks	Robert Robertson	Harvey Stratton
John Jacobs	Amos Proctor	James Ketchipaw
James O. Harr	Blecker W. Myers	Vanranslaer Robins
James M'Cann	Peter Lott	Philo Smith
Hiram Banazar	John W. Stickles	Samuel Star
Nel. C. Reynolds	Nicholas O. Cave	Benjamin Proctor
John Belby	James Getty	Pierre Lasage

NEWCASTLE DISTRICT

William Purdy	John Davis	Charles Powers
William Richardson	Sylvanus V. Wicklin	John Gilchrist
Joseph Pearson	Francis Ferguson	Munro Merriman
Jacob Kellar	Peter Nix	Robert Waller

HOME DISTRICT

James Foster	John Anderson	Thomas Burrill
Jay Cody	James Smith	Thomas Rerdon
Daniel Winstow	Peter Deguire	John Kennedy
Louis Brine	Cornelius Duncan	John Kennedy (2)
James Raggat	Wm. Kendrick	Pat. McChrystal

Patrick Casey
H. Carlton
Arthur Laidlaw
J. M'Gilles
W. Young
John Dunn
William Pearson
Andrew Dragoon
Fred. Anderson
James Bergin
Henry Cowen
Christin Ninny
Wm. Alderney
Francis Lyons
Daniel Gamble
Wm. Robertson
Robert Stibbert
James Johnson
Gordon Burgess
John Burgess
John Pearson
James Hutchinson
Richard Taylor
Robert Baillie
Seymour H. W. Stogdill
Col. Van Egmond
James Hunter
William Watson
Leonard Watson
Eli Bateman
Joseph Sheppard
Jacob Sheppard
John Brown
George Hill
Joseph Gould
Abraham Haling
Joseph Newlove
George Wilson
William Asher
John Beilby
Joseph Wilson
Periphen Hawke
Gideon Vernon
Isaac Masterson
Weldon Hughes
Abraham Musselman
Peter Pence
Henry Johnson
James Johnson
Joseph Johnson
John Clarke
John Browne
Hugh D. Wilson
John D. Wilson
William Brougham
Peter Grant
Joseph Millburn
David Dean
Peter Munro
Samuel Munro
Abraham Wilson
Sampson Harris
Patrick Garry
John Marr
Thos. Wilson
Robert Berrie
Joseph Elthorp
John Graham
William Bently
Geo. S. Yeomens
William Graham
Nelson Flanagan
J. Matthews
Henry Weaver
George Barclay
Thomas Gray
Wilson Read
John Read
Wesley Duncan
John M'Lafferty
John Devins

George Ireland
Joseph Horne
Maurice Fitsgerald
George Carrol
Samuel Carpenter
James Latimer
William Alves
Edward Hilton
George Nelson
John Montgomery
Henry Brock
Edward Brock
Robert Brock
Michael Vincent
John Whiting
William Clay
James Egar
Robert Middleton
William Ballard
Samuel Read
John Russell
Wm. M. Plasted
Godlip Eickart
Gregory Innis
George Eickart
George Chewett
John Steeple
William Jackson
David Cash
Andrew Eickart
Robert Stiver
Daniel Hibner
Daniel Sheppard
John M'Kay
Peter Matthews
John Stewart
John Wilkie
Reuben Lundy
Emanuel Doner
Joseph Doner
John Sheppard
Jacob Troyer
David Blair
L. S. W. Richardson
George Robinson
Benjamin Winhup
Thomas Wilson
David Porter
W. G. Edmonstone
George Holborn
George Lamb
Townsend Wixon
Silas Bardwell
Colin Scott
John Gibson
Hasel H. Scott
Hiram Matthews
Russel Baker
John Prout
Charles Crocker
Randal Wixon
William Hill
Eli Irwin
Francis Robbins
Jesse Doan
Dougal Campbell
Donald Campbell
John Campbell
Adam Graham
Luther Elton
Joseph Watson
Andrew Rowand
Joseph Brammer
Francis M'Donald
W. J. Comfort
Jacob Lane
M. P. Empey
Gerard Irwin
William Doan
Thomas Thompson
Henry Styles

W. T. Kenedy
W. Milney
F. Wardrope
George Farley
Henry Hall
Frederick Eickart
William Pool
John Brett
Francis Way
Peter Storey
John M'Millan
Henry Earl
Edward Snider
Henry Shaver
Emanuel Tomlinson
William Rogers
Samuel Brock
Philip Busson
George Garbut
John Brammer
Philo Belfry
Alexander Read
William Nelson
John Cuyler
Joshua Stevens
W. R. Lount
Philip Wideman
Charles Burling
Richard Watson
Peter Rogers
William King
William Rogers
J. W. Kendrick
Gilbert F. Morden
James M'Queen
Michael Sheppard
Thomas Sheppard
Robert Walker
Joseph Clarkson
Arthur Squires
John M'Dougall
Peter Rush
William Wilson
Jacob Kirty
Adam Rupert
Adam Scott
William Stockdale
George Bolton
John Mitchell
James Harman
John G. Parker
Samuel Watford
Adam Baird
Asa Wixon
Charles Low
Solomon Sly
Joel Wixon
John Hill
Andrew Hill
William Wilson
James Long
William Curtis
Archibald Molloy
Arthur Kelly
James Keene
Joseph M'Grath
Thomas Sly
Thomas D. Morrison
Charles Durand
James Lesslie
—— Lesslie
John Doel
Robert Johnson
James Brown
Asher Wilson
Louis Terry
Robert Taylor
Thos. Hill
John Rummerfeldt
John P. Plank
William Kilburn

APPENDIX 253

Thomas Watts
William Read, jun.
Thomas Wilson
George Fletcher
William Carney
Nelson Carver
Joseph Noble
Charles Doan
Joshua Wixon
James Kane
James Barry
John Wilkie (2d)
Peter Grant (2d)
Burton Attwell
John P. Cherry
John Plank
R. S. Smith
Lazarus Ellis
Jonathan Doan
Lucius C. Thomas
Eber Thomas
Elias Crery
Royal Hopkins
Timothy Doyle
Alexander Cluny
D. Hutchinson
Michael Corrigan
John Haling
John Doyle
John M'Anany
James M'Guire
James Parker
Donald Cameron
Ewen Cameron
John Cameron
Chancey Hawley
John Robinson
Edward Keays
Simon Servos
Joseph Wixon
R. A. Parker
Joseph Earl
Francis Clarkson
Hugh Carmichael
Jesse Clever
William Delaney
Titus Root
Daniel Schell
John D. Staples
John Cane
Jas. Cane
Robt. Wilson
Jas. Squires
Timothy Munro
William Horon

Elisha Mitchell
Ebenezer Moore
Webster Stevens
John Gillingham
John M'Cormack
Ira Anderson
Jacob Lamoureaux
G. G. Parker
Duncan M'Nab
Charles Axtell
J. F. Farley
Gilbert Decker
Thomas Elliott
William Carroll
James M'Donald
Isaac Moins
John Houck
Matthew Hayes
Samuel Lount
James Murray
Martin Smith
Henry M'Garry
James Edmonstone
William Brewer
Terence Fergusson
Peter M'Conville
John Hawkes
John Kline
Michael Flood
William Irwin
James M'Isaac
Dennis Leahy
Dennis O'Connor
John Condon
John Keane
William Carney
Peter Milne
Edward Kennedy
Jno. Hill (2d)
Bartholomew Plank
William Wilson
James Yule
Ira White
Zachariah Dent
James Leland
John Randal
Michael M'Farlane
James Howie
Sylvanus Spencer
Thos. J. Sutherland
Edward Carmon
Horatio Fowler
Finlay Malcolm
Joseph Hart
James Bell

George Wright
C. C. Scott
Abraham Faulkner
Thos. Sherrard
Joshua Haskill
Joseph Martin
Charles Rayner
Abraham Anderson
Patrick Condon
John O'Brien
James Keane
Jeremiah C. Chapin
William Shaw
Ewen Cameron
Edward A. Theller
Stephen P. Brophy
Claude Campeau
Aug. D. Berdeneau
Francis St. Augustin
Henry Johnston
Abram W. Partridge
Theron Culver
Louis Lennoux
Francis Clutier
Benjamin F. Pew
Henry L. Hull
George Davis
Walter Chase
Squire Thayer
Nathaniel Smith
W. W. Dodge
Chancey Parker
William Ketchum
Aaron Freele
Thomas Tracy
John Arthur Tidy
John Kelly
Paul Bedford
Harvey Bryant
Enoch Moore
Philip Jackson
Diogenes M'Kenzie
Benjamin Warner
Philip Brady
Isaac Myers
William M'Carrick
Samuel Woods
James Mace
John M'Intyre
William Bell
John M'Leod
Ebenezer Wilcox
Robert Cook
Alvaro Ladd

NIAGARA DISTRICT

Ira Smith
Thomas Higgins
Fisher Hanagan
William Law
Samuel Chandler
Norman Mallory
James Waggoner
Benjamin Waite
Solomon Camp
John Grant
John J. M'Nulty
Edward Seymour
Garret Van Camp
James Gammell
Murdock M'Fadden

Robert Kelly
Freeman Brady
Loran Hedger
Street Chace
Abraham Clarke
Eber Rice
James Morrow
David Taylor
George Cooley
William Reynolds
George Buck
Linus Wilson Miller
Alexander M'Leod
Alexander Brady

Erastus Warner
Stephen Hart
James Doan
William Whitson
John W. Brown
John Vernon
William Yerks
Samuel D. Haslip
George Malcolm
Charles Malcolm
Neal Brown
Clarke Bowers
Duncan Willson
Jacob R. Beamer

GORE DISTRICT

Robert Armstrong
Philip Henry
Henry Winegarden
Robert Elliott

Oliver Edmonds
Joseph Beemer
Henry Goff
Jonathan Bishop

William Thompson
Charles Chapin
John Austin
Oiver Smith

254   THE LIVES AND TIMES OF THE PATRIOTS

William Stants
Abraham Vanduzen
John Tulford
Joseph Smith
Peter Coon
John Whalen
Alonzo Foster
John Heap
John L. Uline
Charles P. Walrath
Isaac Edmunds
Peter Ladon
John Lacklin
James Johnson
John Johnson
Albus Connor
Charles M'Intosh
Thomas Sirpell
George Roberts
Andrew Miller
Joshua Lind
Jacob Emery
Charles Hammond
Silvanus F. Wrigley
James Dace
Aaron Glover

James Benham
James Peters
James Butchart
Lyman Chapin
Dudley Newton
Malcolm Brown
Thomas Balls
Adam Winegarden
Horatio A. Hills
William Webb
Willard Sherman
John Sherman
Asahel Davis
Gilbert Davis
William Lyons
William Winegarden
Lord Wellington Winegarden
John Hammill
Duncan M'Phederain
Robert Laing
Collins Skelly
William Armstrong
Calvin Lyman
James Parkinson
Hiram Dowling
Nathaniel Deo

John Van Norman
John Malcolm
Isaac B. Malcolm
Finlay Malcolm
Norman Malcolm
Solomon Lossing
Ephraim Cook
Elias Snider
Garry V. Delong
Adam Yeigh
Nathan Town
Robert Alway
Michael Showers
George Rouse
Samuel Marlatt
David Ghent
John Tyler
Peter Malcolm
John Moore
William Sheppard
Horace Lossing
Calvin Austin
John Fish
Jesse Matthews
Edy Malcolm
Stephen Smith

TALBOT DISTRICT—No prisoners confined.

LONDON DISTRICT

Cyrus M'Cartney
James Canfield
Andrew Martin
James Woods
Alexander Sumner
Thomas Hewman
Judson Sweet
John O'Gorman
Joseph Alway
Robert Cavanaugh
Cornelius M'Carty
Levi Heaton
James Waterman
James Coleman
Benjamin Page
Luke Hogle
Moses Cook
William Norton
John Medcalf
Josiah Woodhull
Matthew Berry
William Cheeseman
John Legg
Moore Stephens
William Lymburner
Wm. Watterworth
Joseph J. Lancaster
David Curtis
Andrew M'Lean
Alfred Adkins
Lymon Davis
Solomon Sherrick
Nelson Leach
Sobeisca Brown
William Storey
Jonathan Steel
Losee Denton
Joseph Moore
Isaac Phillips
Andrew Connors
Lymanteus Chapel
Thomas Hall
John Kenny
Absolom Shaw
Wm. A. Everett
Albert Stephens
James G. Shaw
Uriah Shaw
Robert Taylor

George Lester
Charles Reeves
Jacob Esmond
James M'Clees
Simon B. Moses
John B. Nichols
Peter Phillip
James Defields
William Loop
Robert Larraway
Tracey Congdon
Thomas Pool
Isaac Moore
Caleb Kipp
George Ribble
Enoch D. Doxie
John Parker
Josiah Wood
S. Smith
Archibald Olds
George Phillips
James Nixon
Abel Cooper
David Willson
Duncan Willson
Elias Moore
Luther Hoskins
Nathan Doan
Alonzo Hall
William Hall
Gideon Tiffany
William Putnam
John Stephens
James Nash
Thomas Arker
Morey Whithey
Charles Travers
John Grieve
Descom Simons
Charles Lawrence
Anson Gould
Stephen Bronger
Joshua B. Moore
Jacob B. Allen
Abraham Graves
Jacob Deo
Sylvanus Shaw
John Day
Samuel Day

Robert Traney
Henry Emigh
Truman Sinclair
Robert Farr
Dennis Cavanaugh
John H. Carr
Sheldon Sweet
Mark Hogle
Charles Christie
James Oswould
Thomas Headman
Charles Coonrod
John James Jolly
John M'Carren
Egbert Hellaker
John Riley
William Watts
Lewis Norton
James Coville
Charles Latimer
David Hagerman
Daniel Bedford
Alexander Neilly
Samuel Sands
Uriah Emmons
Ezekiel Manns
William Childs
Abraham Sackrider
John D. Brown
Stephen H. Secord
Orlando Inglis
Patrick Malada
George Blake
Amos Bradshaw
George Hill
Joseph Bowes
Charles Tilden
Andrew M'Lure
Amos B. Thomas
Jacob Lester
Samuel Forbes
Amos Shaw
Alex. Leadbeater
William Hillaker
John Dennis
Benjamin Smith
Pety Sullivan
Benjamin West
Henry Spencer

James Tucker
Francis Jones
Abraham Kilburn
David Sherman
William Day
William Jackman

John G. Wells
Otis Inglis
Jacob Aubrey
William Gibson
Benjamin Hillaker

Isaac L. Smith
David Williams
John Long
James Lyons
Christ. Hendershot

WESTERN DISTRICT

Horace Cooley
Charles Bourman
Louis Burnham
Orlando Boyington

Henry B. Nugent
Reuben Markham
Lambert Beaubien
Malcolm Burnham

James Coll
Isaac Phillips
William Herrington

RETURN OF PERSONS AGAINST WHOM INDICTMENTS WERE FOUND FOR THE CRIME OF HIGH TREASON, BUT WHO ABSCONDED, AND ARE CALLED UPON TO SURRENDER THEMSELVES BY THE FIRST DAY OF FEBRUARY OR BE OUTLAWED

John Rolph, physician, M.P.P., Home District.
William Lyon M'kenzie, printer, Home District.
Silas Fletcher, yeoman, Home District.
Jacob Rymal, yeoman, Home District.
Richard Graham, yeoman, Home District.
Jeremiah Graham, yeoman, Home District.
John Mantack, yeoman, Home District.
Joseph Borden, yeoman, Home District.
Joshua Winn, yeoman, Home District.
David Gibson, surveyor and M.P.P., Home District.
Landon Wurtz, laborer, Home District.
James Marshall, storekeeper, Home District.
Alum Marr, yeoman, Home District.
Joseph Clarkson, yeoman, Home District.
Dudley Wilcox, yeoman, Home District.
Edmond Quirk, yeoman, Home District.
Thomas Brown, yeoman, Home District.
Levi Parsons, yeoman, Home District.
Jesse Loyd, yeoman, Home District.
Aaron Munshaw, yeoman, Home District.
Henry Stiles, yeoman, Home District.
William Fletcher, yeoman, Home District.
Daniel Fletcher, yeoman, Home District.
David M'Carty, yeoman, Home District.
Seth M'Carty, yeoman, Home District.
Nelson Gorham, yeoman, Home District.
Alexander M'Leod, yeoman, Home District.
Cornelius Willis, yeoman, Home District.
Erastus Clark, yeoman, Home District.
Charles Duncombe, M.P.P., London District.
James Dennis, yeoman, London District.
Eliakim Malcolm, yeoman, London District.
Peter Delong, yeoman, London District.
Orsimus B. Clark, merchant, London District.
Lyman Davis, laborer, London District.
Henry Fisher, yeoman, London District.
James Malcolm, yeoman, London District.
Pelham C. Teeple, yeoman, London District.
Norris Humphrey, merchant, London District.
Jesse Paulding, innkeeper, London District.
Joel P. Doan, tanner, London District.
Joshua G. Doan, tanner, London District.
John Talbot, gentleman, London District.
Samuel Edison, jun., innkeeper, London District.
Abraham Sutton, yeoman, London District.
Moses Chapman Nickerson, yeoman, London District.
George Lawton, yeoman, London District.
John Massacre, yeoman, London District.
Elisha Hall, yeoman, London District.
Solomon Hawes, yeoman, London District.
George Alexander Clark, merchant, Gore District.
John Vanarnam, innkeeper, Gore District.
Michael Marcellus Mills, merchant, Gore District.
George Washington Case, gentleman, Gore District.
Joseph Fletcher, yeoman, Gore District.
Angus M'Kenzie, yeoman, Gore District.
Alonzo Merriman, merchant, Niagara District.
Aaron Winchester, yeoman, Niagara District.
David Jennings, laborer, Niagara District.
Chester Jillet, laborer, Niagara District.
Thomas Lambert, laborer, Niagara District.

THE LIVES AND TIMES OF THE PATRIOTS

NUMERICAL ABSTRACT OF THE FOREGOING TABLE

Eastern District	—
Ottawa District	—
Johnstown District	8
Bathurst District	—
Prince Edward District	—
Midland District	75
Newcastle District	12
Home District	422
Niagara District	43
Gore District	90
Talbot District	—
London District	163
Western District	11
Persons who have absconded	61
Grand Total	885

APPENDIX H.

(1) NAVY ISLAND PROCLAMATION BY WILLIAM LYON MACKENZIE, CHAIRMAN PRO TEM. OF THE PROVINCIAL GOVERNMENT OF THE STATE OF UPPER CANADA

INHABITANTS OF UPPER CANADA!

For nearly fifty years has our country languished under the blighting influence of military despots, strangers from Europe, ruling us, not according to laws of our choice, but by the capricious dictates of their arbitrary power.

They have taxed us at their pleasure, robbed our exchequer, and carried off the proceeds to other lands—they have bribed and corrupted Ministers of the Gospel with the wealth raised by our industry—they have, in place of religious liberty, given Rectories and Clergy Reserves to a foreign priesthood, with spiritual power dangerous to our peace as a people—they have bestowed millions of our lands on a company of Europeans for a nominal consideration, and left them to fleece and impoverish our country—they have spurned our petitions, involved us in their wars, excited feelings of national and sectional animosity in counties, townships, and neighborhoods, and ruled us, as Ireland has been ruled, to the advantage of persons in other lands, and to the prostration of our energies as a people.

We are wearied of these oppressions, and resolved to throw off the yoke. Rise, Canadians! Rise as one man, and the glorious object of our wishes is accomplished.

Our intentions have been clearly stated to the world in the Declaration of Independence, adopted at Toronto on the 31st of July last, printed in the *Constitution, Correspondent and Advocate,* and the *Liberal,* which important paper was drawn up by Dr. John Rolph and myself, signed by the Central Committee, received the sanction of a large majority of the people of the Province, west of Port Hope and Cobourg, and is well known to be in accordance with the feelings and sentiments of nine-tenths of the people of this State.

We have planted the Standard of Liberty in Canada, for the attainment of the following objects:

Perpetual Peace, founded on a government of equal rights to all, secured by a written constitution, sanctioned by yourselves in a convention to be called as early as circumstances will permit.

Civil and Religious Liberty, in its fullest extent, that in all laws made, or to be made, every person be bound alike—neither shall any tenure, estate, charter, birth, or place confer any exemption from the ordinary course of legal proceedings and responsibilities whereunto others are subjected.

The Abolition of Hereditary Honors, of the laws of Entail and Primogeniture, and of hosts of pensioners who devour our substance.

A Legislature, composed of a Senate and Assembly chosen by the people.

An Executive, to be composed of a Governor and other officers elected by the public voice.

A Judiciary, to be chosen by the Governor and Senate, and composed of the most learned, honorable, and trustworthy of our citizens. The laws to be rendered cheap and expeditious.

A Free Trial by Jury—Sheriffs chosen by you, and not to hold office, as now, at the pleasure of our tyrants. The freedom of the press. Alas for it, now! The free presses in the Canadas are trampled down by the hand of arbitrary power.

The Vote by Ballot—free and peaceful township elections.

The people to elect their Court of Request Commissioners and Justices of the Peace—and also their Militia Officers, in all cases whatsoever.

Freedom of Trade—every man to be allowed to buy at the cheapest market, and sell at the dearest.

No man to be compelled to give military service, unless it be his choice.

Ample funds to be reserved from the vast natural resources of our country to secure the blessings of education to every citizen.

A frugal and economical Government, in order that the people may be prosperous and free from difficulty.

An end forever to the wearisome prayers, supplications, and mockeries attendant upon our connection with the lordlings of the Colonial Office, Downing Street, London.

The opening of the St. Lawrence to the trade of the world, so that the largest ships might pass up to Lake Superior, and the distribution of the wild lands of the country to the industry, capital, skill, and enterprise of worthy men of all nations.

For the attainment of these important objects, the patriots now in arms under the Standard of Liberty, on NAVY ISLAND, U. C., have established a Provisional Government of which the members are as follows, (with two other distinguished gentlemen, whose names there are powerful reasons for withholding from public view,) viz:

WILLIAM L. MACKENZIE, *Chairman, pro tem.*

Nelson Gorham,
Samuel Lount,
Silas Fletcher,
Jesse Lloyd,
Thomas Darling,
Adam Graham,

John Hawk,
Jacob Rymall,
William H. Doyle,
A. G. W. G. Van Egmond,
Charles Duncombe.

We have procured the important aid of General Van Rensselaer of Albany, of Colonel Sutherland, Colonel Van Egmond, and other military men of experience; and the citizens of Buffalo, to their eternal honor be it ever remembered, have proved to us the enduring principles of the Revolution of 1776, by supplying us with provisions, money, arms, ammunition, artillery, and volunteers; and vast numbers are floating to the standard under which, heaven willing, emancipation will be speedily won for a new and gallant nation hitherto held in Egyptian thraldom by the aristocracy of England.

BRAVE CANADIANS! Hasten to join that standard, and to make common cause with your fellow citizens now in arms in the Home, London, and Western Districts. The opportunity of the absence of the hired red coats of Europe is favorable to our emancipation. And short sighted is that man who does not now see that, although his apathy may protract the contest, it must end in *Independence*—freedom from European thraldom for ever!

Until Independence is won, trade and industry will be dormant, houses and lands will be unsaleable, merchants will be embarrassed, and farmers and mechanics harassed and troubled; that point once gained, the prospect is fair and cheering, a long day of prosperity may be ours.

The reverses in the Home District were owing, First, to accident, which revealed our design to our tyrants, and prevented a surprise; and Second, to the want of artillery. Three thousand five hundred men came and went, but we had no arms for one in twelve of them, nor could we procure them in the country.

Three hundred acres of the best of the public lands will be freely bestowed upon any volunteer, who shall assist personally in bringing to a conclusion the glorious struggle in which our youthful country is now engaged against the enemies of freedom all the world over.

Ten millions of these lands, fair and fertile, will, I trust, be speedily at our disposal, with the other vast resources of a country more extensive and rich in natural treasures than the United Kingdom or Old France.

Citizens! Soldiers of Liberty! Friends of Equal Rights! Let no man suffer in his property, person, or estate—let us pass through Canada, not to retaliate on others for our estates ravaged, our friends in dungeons, our homes burnt, our wheat and barns burnt, and our horses and cattle carried off; but let us show the praiseworthy example of protecting the houses, the homes, and the families of those who are in arms against their country and against the liberties of this continent. We will disclaim and severely punish all aggressions upon private property, and consider those as our enemies who may burn or destroy the smallest hut in Canada, unless necessity compel any one to do so in any cause for self-defence.

Whereas, at a time when the King and Parliament of Great Britain had solemnly agreed to redress the grievances of the people, Sir Francis Bond Head was sent out to this country with promises of conciliation and justice—and whereas, the said Head hath violated his oath of office as a Governor, trampled upon every vestige of our rights and privileges, bribed and corrupted the local Legislature, interfered with the freedom of elections, intimidated the freeholders, declared our country not entitled to the blessings of British freedom, prostrated openly the right of trial by jury, placed in office the most obsequious, treacherous, and unworthy of our population—and sought to rule Upper Canada by the mere force of his arbitrary power; imprisoned Dr. Morrison, Mr. Parker, and many others of our most respected citizens; banishing in the most cruel manner the highly respected Speaker of our late House of Assembly, the Honorable Mr. Bidwell, and causing the expatriation of that universally beloved and well tried eminent patriot, Dr. John Rolph, because they had made common cause with our injured people, and setting a vast price on the heads of several, as if they were guilty persons—for which crimes and misdemeanors he is deserving of being put upon his trial before the country—I do therefore hereby offer a reward of £500 for his apprehension, so that he may be dealt with as may appertain to justice.

In Lower Canada, divine providence has blessed the arms of the Sons of Liberty—a whole people are there manfully struggling for that freedom

APPENDIX 259

without which property is but a phantom, and life scarce worth having a gift of. General Girard is at the head of fifteen thousand determined democrats.

The friends of freedom in Upper Canada have continued to act in strong and regular concert with Mr. Papineau and the Lower Canada Patriots—and it is a pleasing reflection that between us and the ocean a population of six hundred thousand souls are now in arms, resolved to be free.

The tidings that worthy patriots are in arms is spreading through the Union, and the men who were oppressed in England, Ireland, Scotland, and the continent are flocking to our standard.

We must be successful!

I had the honour to address nearly three thousand of the citizens of Buffalo, two days ago, in the theatre. The friendship and sympathy they expressed is honorable to the great and flourishing Republic.

I am personally authorized to make known to you that from the moment that Sir Francis Bond Head declined to state in writing the objects he had in view, in sending a flag of truce to our camp in Toronto, the message once declined, our esteemed fellow citizen, Dr. John Rolph, openly announced his concurrence in the measures, and now decidedly approves of the stand we are taking in behalf of our beloved country, which will never be his until it be free and independent.

CANADIANS! My confidence in you is as strong and powerful, in this our day of trial and difficulty, as when, many years ago, in the zeal and ardor of youth, I appeared among you, the humble advocate of your rights and liberties. I need not remind you of the sufferings and persecutions I have endured for your sakes—the losses I have sustained—the risks I have run. Had I ten lives I would cheerfully give them up to procure freedom to the country of my children, of my early and disinterested choice. Let us act together; and warmed by the hope of success in a patriotic course, be able to repeat in the language so often happily quoted by Ireland's champion,

> The nations are fallen and thou still art young,
> Thy sun is but rising when others have set;
> And though Slavery's cloud o'er thy morning hath hung,
> The full tide of Freedom shall beam round thee yet.

Militia men of 1812! Will ye again rally round the standard of our tyrants! I can scarce believe it possible. Upper Canada Loyalists, what has been the recompense of your long tried and devoted attachment to England's Aristocracy? Obloquy and contempt.

Verily we have learnt in the school of experience, and are prepared to profit by the lessons of the past. Compare the great and flourishing nation of the United States with our divided and distracted land, and think what we also might have been, as brave, independent lords of the soil. Leave, then, Sir Francis Bond Head's defence to the miserable serfs dependent on his bounty, and to the last hour of your lives the proud remembrance will be yours—"We also were the deliverers of our country."

Navy Island, December 13, 1837.

(2) LIST OF MEN AT NAVY ISLAND.

(Lindsey Papers, University of Toronto Library, in trust.)

[The following list of Navy Island recruits is preceded in the Lindsey Papers by a confusing summary of the number of officers, men, and equipment, such as muskets, cartridges, cartridge boxes, swords, pistols, axes, shovels, saws, powder, and powder horns. The whole is headed 'Liberty Island. Copy of Reports handed in January 6th, 1838.' The material is not in its original form, but is a copy in female handwriting, possibly that of Mrs. Charles Lindsey. Enrolment under aliases and difficulties of decipherment probably explain the omission of a few known to have served on Navy Island. It is obvious that numerous errors are due to the copyist, but the material is presented exactly as it appears.]

MUSIC FOR PATRIOTIC ARMY

Wm. J. Taylor	Drum Major	Drums	4
Martin Cone	Fifer	Bass "	1
Philemon Webb	Ditto	Fifes	5
Anson Doolittle	"	Bugles	2
Benj.n Depew	"	Muskets	11
D. R. Thompson	"	Cartridges	110
Wm. M. Mer	Bugler	Boxes	11
Hyram. Ingram	Drummer	Swords	3
Peter Vrooman	Ditto		
Geo Roberts	"		
Alfred Gatfield	Bass Drum		

INFANTRY COMPANY A

Capt. Robt. M. Harper	3 Sargant Arthur Hughs	
1 Lieut Mathew Hayes	4 " Wm. Mihan	
2 " Henry Gardiner	5 " Geo. Turner	
3 " Walter Haskill	1 Corporal Patrick Garrihan	
1 Ensign Wm. Sherman	2 " Chas. N. Russell	
1 Sargant Wm. Patten	3 " Thomas Boyle	
2 Sargant Geo. W. Hall	4 " Geo. Vugal	
Joseph Bedford	H. Blozer	Wm. Lawrence
Nelson Sheddon	E. Hancock	Lewis Wood
Wm. H. Fox	T. Case	Comfort Bork
Dan'l B. Clark	J. Stephens	Chas Senter
Harrison Govins	Geo. Miller	Isac Wetherington
A. Jessup	John Devine	25 privates
P. Morton	B. Warner	14 officers
Jenks	E. Parens	
C. T. Baird	D. E. Williams	—
J. G. Frank	Geo. Joyes	39

INFANTRY COMPANY B

Capt. Lester Hoadley	3 Sargant James Clark	
1 Lieut Chas Newberry	4 " Richard Ward	
2 " Andrew Smith	1 Corp'l Green J. Shaw	
3 " Allen Murry	2 " James Arnold	
Ensign Wm. A. Chase	3 " John Kitrage	
Sargant Stephen Bishop	4 " David B. Logan	
2 Sargant Enoch W. Reynolds		
Thomas Leecus	Calvin M. Corbin	John Collons
Thomas Harrison	Isaac Mason	
Seneca W. Baker	Solomon Wright	Parsons) Head quarter
Wm. Kendall	Lotrop L. Goodwin	)
Wm. Kelly	Chester Losey	Jakes) on Guard
Lyman Walker	Joseph Hall	
Wm. Brewer	Geo. How	13 officers
Wm. Butt	James Deforrest	23 privates
Orletus Thari	Sardious How	—
Victor Perham	Rawson Bradley	34

Report of Companys this 3rd day of January 1838.

COMPANY C INFANTRY

Capt James C. Bacon	1 Sargant Samuel Ishum	
1 Lieut Benj.m Wait	2 " John Wilson	
2 " Elexander Toll	1 Corporal Wm. Clark	
3 " John M. Huffman	2 " Josiah Bugdon	
Edward Huffman	John McCormick	Wm Billings
Jonahan Stevens	John Brown	S. E. C. Forsyth
John Thompson	Philip Jackson	John Aim
Eve Tingley	John Abraham	Albert Morriss
Lemuel Scott	Abram George	John Taylor

APPENDIX 261

Stephen Carl
John Akins
Joseph Fletcher
Henry Gleason
James McNair

Joseph Herrings
Patrick Graham
James Watson
John Gwinup
Henry Van Rurin

Peter Squire
8 officers
26 Privates
—
34 Total

COMPANY D INFANTRY

arrived on Island Dec 25th 1838
Capt. James Krake
1 Lieut James Mitchell
2 " J. Taylor
1 Sargant Robt. D. Winn
2 " Arthur Reynolds

3 Sargant Patrick Burns
4 " Wm Dennis
1 Corp'l Peter Doran
2 " Wm Mitchell
3 " Anthony Fevere
4 " Wm Mitchell

S. L. Oney
John Gill
Alfred Wilcox
Ewin Wallace
Dan'l Hull
Wm Dan
Wm Williams
Wm Clinton
Henry Compton
James Hayes
Henry Nicols

Lyman Dout
Alexander Dewgaw
Francis Lepoint
Solomon Dennison
Antony Goody
John Fallick
Henry Williams
Patrick Burger
Peter Brevere
Nicholas Gregory
Wm Johnson

Pearl Washburn
James Murphy
Robt. Stout
Henry Sumnirz
Baker A. Rollington

11 officers
27 Privates
—
38 Total

1ST RIFLE COMPANY

Capt. Wm S. Burnham

1 Lieut Wm. McGuire
2 " Asa Daniels
1 Sargant Cratin Allen

2 Sargant James Cooper
1 Corp'l Thomas Clark
2 " James Vannater

Jessie Corner
Abraham Davis
Martin Tubbs
Justice Fish
John Fish
John
Chas. Branch
Abraham Tanner
David D. Cambell
Wm Tice
Thos. McGregor
Wm Johnson
John Wilson
Edward G. Willard
Reuben Cooper
Mathew Smith
Wm. Carrol
Mathias Taytor

James H. Wilson
Thomas B. Howton
Asahel R. Willard
Asahel Nichols
Lorenso D. Wood
Benj.m Lett
Comfort T. Bork
Isaac Lacy
John Daneils
Jonathan Jewel
James Tyler
Stephen Wilson
Nathan Lesure
Samuel Robbinson
David South
Wm. Fingerton, Jun.
Asa H. Kent
Jarvis Henderson

James Lindon
Martin Whiting
Chas Hulbert
S. Cloud
John Van Roncins
John Griffin
Chas. Shelby
E. Haywood
Edward Haywood
Joseph Pettit
Mathew Wade
Parker Hosmer

48 Private
7 Officers
—
55

Trumpets
Cans't Rowder [sic]
Musket Raks
Blankets
Sword
Powder horn
Jack Plain
Hammers
Priming wires
Fowling Piece

2 Robert Davison
2 John Ford
200 Geo Forbs
13 Sam'l Seargwill
4 Lyman W. Manley
1 Consider Button
1 Dewit. Clinton Grynman
2 Thos. D. Soggs
50 Reid L. Barnum
1 Enoch Wood

Elisha B. Warren
Jesse Derickson
Alex. McComb
Sam'l. Corbed
Daniel Bowker
Sam'l Glover
Moses Parsons
Numan Ducker
Phillander Roberts

The above is an inventory of Camp House No. 1
Chas. G. Irish, Jr. Qtr. Master Sgt.
In the command of the same R. M. Harper
Dec. 26th 1837. Lieutenant

Retn of Clock Pedlar
Cap. John Shelden
Privates
Thos. Hammond

Ingram Golden
Names of Volunteers Jny 5
Elias Mason
Allen Stiles

Wm. Cooper
Wm. Keyser

262 THE LIVES AND TIMES OF THE PATRIOTS

Rifles	55	List of Officers	Sargant. Major John Faejan
Compy A.	89	Conl J. S. Vreeland	202
" B.	36	Lieut Col. H. C. Seward	6
" C.	34	Major Sam'l B. Chase	
" D.	38	Adj'tant John Letts	208
	202	Quarter Mast. Chas. G. Irish Jr.	W. Wallace, Esq.

Return of Company A
Officers. 2 Sargants
) Leonard Marley
) Ira Dutton
) T. S. Phillips
) Henry Jackson
2 Corporals) Wm Warren
Privates 22 Ambrose B. Gillum
Muskets 20 Wm Cooper
Cartridge Bxes. 19 H B Boss
Cartridges 198 S. K. Camp
Belts 16 Paul Berry
Axes 4 Thos. Graham
Saws 3 Arms &
Shovels 4 4 Muskets
Flints 24 4 C. Boxes & Belts
Fifes 3 10 Cartridges
Names of Volunteers Jny 4th Cannen
Hamilton Henry 12 Cartridges
Willis Dowe 11 Clock
Jesse. I. Moore 12 of Buttons
Hiram F. Sickles 1 Hairn Sack
Peter F. Boss 1 Fine Pan
Benjamin Hunt 4 Blankets
Richard Teasdale 1 Kettle
S. B. Lyon 1 Knife
Sam'l Gucy 2 Tin pan

2 Cups
Isaac Humphrey
Thomas Obryan
Peter Dason
Hammond Kimble
David Kimble
Stephens Edmonds
Shedrick Finch
Dyer Stout
Peter Jourden
Leonard Lovetwell
Silas J. Corbin
T. Taylor
C. Bennell
Lucius Lincoln
Peter Nichols. Boatman
  Native of Sweden
Volunteers
Otis Glynny Ogdensburg.
        7 Jany
Wm Merkham, Upholsterer,
Mr. Lawson, Upholsterer,
  Walnut St.

Volunteers for Navy Is.
Jany 5
Deogeno Mackenzie
Patrick Mountain
Henry Mahony
Earl Arwoord
E. T. Dayden
Elias Brewer
Charles Seile
Elonzer White
Cha.
Sylvester P. Grumman

List of Articles Received
  on Navy Is: Jany 6th
  1838

9 Swords
4 Muskets
1 Keg of Powder
2 Large Cheeses
50 Pair of Socks
2 Pair of Pantaloons
1 Over Coat

24 Blankets
1 Horse Pistol
5 Pair of Boots
1 Pair of Shoes
6 Comforters
6 Pair of Mittens
3 Canisters of Powder
A quantity of Bread and
  Butter
A quantity of Beans
        McNaughton

A boat Cargo

Names of Volunteers

Thos. J. Sutherland
Leonard P. Crairy
W. P. Love
Jas. Evans
R. M. Harper
Stephen Eldridge
N. Gorham
S. Chandler
J. A. Cooper
J. S. Vrolomd
T. J. Sawton
Moses Evans
L. T. Bush
Wm. Mihan

J. G. Hopper
David Churchill
Caleb P. Fullerton
George Brady
S. E. C. Forsythe
Eber Cole
John H. Badgley
Alexander Davidson
Allen Wilcox
Thos. McGregor
Craton Allen
J. S. Chamberlain
I. Dart
A. B. Spencar
A. R. Galloway
E. R. Grey

D. L. Br.
Peter Pfanner
Jacob. Bergtold
Orlin Oatman
Joseph Willey
Wm. B. Howard
T. Ingman
Sam'l Bouchuup
Wm Bill
Wm Deales
Thos. McBath
Abram Davis
F. D. Tonsley
Henry. Doherty
Wm Davis
John Cocerin

The following are the officers of Company D. of Rochester

S. B. Chase, Capt
John Fagan. pt Lieu
Amos Van Brumt 2d Dv
Elijah Taylor Orderly
James Kraik 2d Sergs.

J. C. Mitchell 3d do.
John Mills
Ezra Horton 1st Corporal
William Dennis 2nd do.
Patrick Burns 3d.

T. Barnard
E. Leftaney
Wilnam Clinton
Wellington Rice

APPENDIX 263

Sam'l B. Chase, Capt.

John Danolds	Philip Moldoon	Williams Williams
Pearl Washburn	Anthony Ourdy	James Harp
Arron Warren	Henry Nichols	William Dun
(John McIntyre)	Francis Lapoon	Henry Williams
John Sears	Zebulun Lence	All annexed and were en-
Charles Fitzgerald	Patrick Bulyer	rolled on 23rd inst 1837.
Nicholas Gregory	James Baker	S. B. Chase, Capt.

APPENDIX I.

NAVY ISLAND CORRESPONDENCE.

(Lindsey Papers.)

(1)

Rushville, Yates Co. N Y

January 9th 1838

Gen. R. Van Rensselaer

Dr. Sir

I send from here this day a snug box containing thirty six sets of Cartridge boxes all made in the most substantial manner and in complete order for actual service—a donation to the brave Patriots under your command on Navy Island with the sincere wish that they may contribute to the complete success of your Gallant little Army in the Holy Cause in which they are engaged they are addressed to J. L. H. Fort Schlosser, Niagara Co. N. Y. care of J. Bassett, Rochester. As it would not only violate the law of our country, but also expose them to seisure by the U. S. Authorities, to address them to you, or to Navy Island, I adopted the above method and advise you thereof that you may take measure, to get hold of them on their arrival at Schlosser.

While I am writing I will also say that I have in my possession a brass Six Pounder mounted and in first rate order a most Capital piece and just the thing to stir up the Cold Blooded Royalist, with which ere this would have been upon Navy Island and myself with it but for the almost impassable state of the road,—My plans were arranged to have left here a week since but delayed from day to day in hope of an improvement instead of which it has constantly been growing worse and it is now so late and from all the information we get we learn that your plan is soon to make a debut to Canada I have my fears whether I shall be able to get there in season to be of any service to you and I have determined now to wait until I hear from you on the Subject which I hope to do by return of mail.

If the article spoken of will be wanted I will deliver it to you personally within five days after the receipt of your letter—. At any rate favour me with an answer and oblidge

Your old Friend

J. L. Hosford

Of Course any thing received by me will be strictly confidential

(2)

> Dr. Bancraft
> Col. Blackman
> Maj. Peck
> Maj. Green
> Esy. Page

Are entitled to the courtesy of Th: J. Sutherland. Gen.l Van Rensselaer will on his behalf extend such courtesy to each of them as may be consistent with the interest of our cause.

> Th: J. Sutherland.

(3)

Genl. Rensselaer.

Let me introduce to you our friend, Maj. S. C. Hawley—who is preparing a body of men for the Patriot cause—Whatever attention you shew him will be thankfully recei.d—

> I am yours
>
> Van Rensselaer
>
> Thursday.

(4)

> Schlosser Jany 6th 1838

Dear Sir

I am Desirous of having an interview with my husband on Navy Island and would Beg Leave to come and see him and have the Privilege to return back again in so doing you will confer a great favor to a Lonely woman I wish to give me an answer soon as possible as I am in waiting.

> E. Farnsworth

(5)

Gen Vanneslaer

> Sir Mrs Sutton Sends you a basket of Cakes and wishes them to be divided amongst the different camps
>
> > Yours Respec
> >
> > Wm Sutton

N B
> if the basket is not wanted let it be returned for to be filled and sent over again
>
> > W Sutton

APPENDIX 265

(6)

Gen Rensselaer

We send you 3 Coach Loads to night of good fellows—with arms and fourteen (14) Kegs of Powder—under the charge of Mr Chase of whom we give you a line the other day, and Major I. Williams of our Artillery —they are both fine fellows. If you can take our friend Chase about your person—I think he would do you good service. If possible keep our Rochester boys together—pay some attention to them and we will be able to recruit the corps—and make it a good and active body—shall probably send more the first of the week.

I am yours

Van R

R R V Rensselaer   [apparently in Mackenzie's
Rochester   handwriting]

(7)

Albany December 30th 1837

Dear Sir

You'll please excuse the liberty I take in addressing. I should like to enter as one of you company. Yet their may be obsticles in way. I am a Civil Engineer by profession. I should set off to morrow if I had where with to goe. If you should pay my expenses I will leap for joy. I may be of some to you as to drawing plans & sketches of positions &c.

An answer immediately will much oblidge

Yours respectfully

Redmond Hastings.

Gen Van Rensselaer

(8)

Buffalo 21 December 1837

Hble Wm. L. Mackenzie

Dear Sir

Permit me to take the liberty of introducing to you, Mr. Sidney Malthrop, an eminent artist of this city. His object in visiting you at Navy Island is for the purpose (with your permission) of taking your likeness. Many of your disinterested & warm friends here, are most anxious to possess a correct likeness of one, who had so honorably distinguished himself in the political arena, & in a peculiar degree contributed to sever those unholy ties, which a tyrannical and an oppressive Government have imposed upon the people of the provinces of upper and lower Canada. With best wishes for your final and compleat success,

    I remain Dr Sir with great respect,
      Your faithful & hum Servt
        J. O. Meara

P. S. Conscious of the bravery intrepidity of your estimable Commander, General Vanransellar & Col. Sutherland little doubt can be entertained of your ultimate success.

        J. O. M.

(9)

    an Inventory of Provisions etc Consumed of
    the Property Mrs Learned on Navy Island
    By the Volunteers of Buffalo etc To Wit

```
"  - 2 Barrels Pork    -   -   -   at $18   $36.00
"  -12. Bush—Potatoes  -   -   at 3/-        4.50
"  -   Barrel of Sour Crout  -  -   -        5.00
"      1 Bush of Peas  -   -   -    8/-      1.00
"      2 lbs. of YH. Tea   -   -    8 -      2.00
"      3 lbs. " Sugar  -   -   -    1/-       .38
```

The 3 Cows 2 Calves and Oxen 12 hogs the Wheat has been Wasted & The Cattle she wishes to have Privilege of Removing from the island with Your Permission She farther wishes you to Consider that it is taking the Only Subsistence from her Large family which in the absence of her husband Makes it Peculiarly Distressing She furthermore Wishes Me Say that as Soon As Practicable She Wishes to Remove on to Grand Island the Remains of this Property Cows & Cattle and to allow Several Men from Grand island to Come for the Same.

Grand island 19th Dec 1837   for Mrs. Learned
            E. H. Learned

[On the back of this letter is the following notation in Mackenzie's handwriting: Learned's claim for damages on Navy Isl^{d.} pd $20]

APPENDIX J.

THE PELEE RAID.

(1) STATEMENT OF JOHN McINTYRE.
(Lindsey Papers.)

Certificate. Burning of the Caroline. Samuel Wood the Traitor.

To the Editor of the *Gazette.*

Rochester, April 15, 1840.

Sir:—I was one of Capt. Chase's Company, on Navy Island, and taken prisoner at the battle of Point au Pelee Island. Since then I have been two years and some days in the British Prisons of Canada, with enough of cruel usage, a trial for my life, and at length restored to liberty. While at Fort Henry Governor Arthur sent down and offered life and freedom to any two prisoners who would be prevailed on to swear that the Caroline Steamer was actually engaged by the Patriots, and that she conveyed men

APPENDIX 267

arms and ammunition to Navy Island. All refused liberty on such terms, except one Samuel Wood, ship carpenter of, and who has recently returned towards, New York. He swore what the government desired, and after turning Queen's evidence against myself and four comrades, was restored to his country. I was examined by Col. Dundas, the Commander at Fort Henry, very minutely, but I told him I knew nothing of the Caroline, further than being on the island when she arrived there. We saved a voyage to Botany Bay, because, altho' indicted for being found in arms and in league with British subjects, they were unable to prove that there was more than one slave of Victoria along with us. His name was Wm. Carl, Chandler's servant, New Brunswick.

John McIntyre.

(2) THE ST. THOMAS CAVALRY, 1838.
(From C. O. Ermatinger, *The Talbot Regime*, 356.)
Captain James Ermatinger

John Bostwick
J. K. Woodward, Paymaster
Bark Rapelje
Daniel Marlatt
William Drake
John Thayer
Thomas Bobier
Richard Evans
John Sells
John Meek
James Meek
Thomas Meek
William Meek
Henry Bostwick
George W. Coll
Mr. Garrett, Port Stanley
R. Tomlinson, Port Stanley
Thomas Parish (killed at Pt. Pelee)
John Conrod
Frederick Huntley
George Smith, Five Stakes
Henry Finch, Aylmer, Flagbearer
Mr. Duck, Morpeth
Captain Julius Airey, Port Talbot
Thomas Backus

Robert Short
Peter Wilson
Jepthah Wilson
William Silcox
Henry Harris
John Couse
Mr. Marten
Mr. Richardson
Mr. Bell
Mr. Walker
Daniel Berdan
Frank Wade
Dr. Brydges
Montgomery
Benjamin Lloyd
Turvill
Dr. Stevens
Basset or Best, Port Stanley
Henry Ellis
Henry Bostwick
Dr. Mackenzie, Surgeon
Samuel Williams
Thomas Davidson
Henry Wilcox
John Pearce

APPENDIX K.
LOUNT AND MATTHEWS.

(1) THE REVEREND JOHN RYERSON'S ACCOUNT OF THE EXECUTIONS.
(John Ryerson to Egerton Ryerson, April 12, 1838, in Sissons, *Egerton Ryerson, His Life and Times*, I 445-8.)

At eight oclock today, thursday, the 12th, Lount & Matthews were executed. The gallows was erected just between the goal & courthouse. Very few persons present, except the military & the ruff scruff of the city.

268   THE LIVES AND TIMES OF THE PATRIOTS

The general feeling is in total opposition to the execution of these men. At their execution they manifested very good composure. Sheriff Jarvis burst into tears when he entered the room to prepare them for execution. They said to him very calmly, '*Mr. Jarvis, do your duty. We are prepared to meet death & our judge.*' They then, both of them, *put their arms around his neck & kissed him.* They were then prepared for the execution, they walked to the gallows with intire composure & firmness of step. Mr. Richardson walked along side of Lount & Br. Beatty along side of Matthews. They ascended the scaffold & knelt down on the *drop*, the rope was fastened to their necks while they were on their knees. Mr. Richardson engaged in prayer & when he came to that part of the Lord's Prayer, 'Forgive us our trespasses as we forgive them that trespass against us', the drop fell.

(2) THE GRAVES AND MONUMENTS.

It is said that the relatives of the executed men were refused permission to give them Christian burial in St. James' Cemetery, and consequently interred the bodies in the York General or Strangers' Burying Ground—more commonly called Potter's Field—located immediately north-west of the Bloor-Yonge intersection. There they remained over twenty-one years, but on November 28, 1859, were removed to the Toronto Necropolis by William Lyon Mackenzie, George Lount—brother of Samuel—and Charles W. and William Lount, his sons, and nephews of the Rebellion leader. The bodies lie in one grave, number 19, section C, located at the western end of the cemetery, near Sumach Street. The first monument over the grave was a small plain tablet of white marble with the simple inscription:

SAMUEL LOUNT
PETER MATTHEWS.

This tablet rests on the plot, near the monument.

In 1893 a larger memorial was raised, the committee in charge being Thomas W. Anderson, Charles Durand, and William Doel. It was unveiled on June 28, 1893, at 2 p.m. The monument is of gray granite, some fifteen feet high, and broken at the top to indicate that their lives were cut off. It carries the following inscription:

'This monument is erected to the memory of Samuel Lount, late of Holland Landing, County of York, Born 24th Sept., 1791, Died 12th April, 1838, and of Peter Matthews, late of Pickering, County Ontario, Born 1786, Died 12th April, 1838.

'Erected by their friends and sympathizers, A.D. 1893.

'Samuel Lount was the eldest son of the late Gabriel Lount, an Englishman who emigrated to Pennsylvania in the middle of the 18th century, and of Philadelphia Hughes, his wife, a Quakeress. He emigrated to Upper Canada and settled near Newmarket, in the County of York, in 1811. In 1834 he was elected to represent the County of Simcoe in the Upper Canada Legislature and served two years. In 1836 he became a candidate again but was defeated by corrupt practices used by his political opponents. A petition of 8,000 people asked for a reprieve which was refused. He lived a Patriot, and died for popular rights.

'Peter Matthews was the son of Peter Matthews, Senr., a U. E. Loyalist who fought for the British side in the American Revolutionary War and at its close settled with his wife and family in the Township of

Pickering in the then County of York. Peter Matthews, the son, belonged to Brock Volunteers during the war of 1812 to 1815 and fought in various battles in Upper Canada of that war. He was known and respected as an honest and prosperous farmer, always ready to do his duty to his adopted country, and died as he lived—a Patriot.'

[Mackenzie's *Caroline Almanack*, 40, says: 'Capt. Matthews left a widow and fifteen fine children, and Colonel Lount a widow and seven children.' The Lounts shortly afterwards removed to the Western States, where Mrs. Lount lived to old age, dying about 1882. No likeness of either Lount or Matthews is known to exist. Correspondence in the Lindsey Papers indicates that Mackenzie and the Lounts attempted to secure a likeness by opening his coffin on the occasion of the removal of the bodies from Potter's Field, but it proved entirely impossible. Among trivialities connected with the removal of the bodies is Durand's statement that Thomas Anderson, who had fought at Montgomery's and escaped to the United States, 'carried for fifty years one of Lount's teeth on his watch-chain, removed from his body in 1859'. (Durand, *Reminiscences*, 459-60.)]

(3) EDWARD THELLER'S BIOGRAPHICAL NOTICE OF LOUNT.

[From E. A. Theller, *Canada in 1837-8*, I, 233-4. These paragraphs rank among the best of a writer whose work is generally lacking in quality; and it was admitted even by Lount's political enemies that they convey a just estimate of the man.]

Samuel Lount was born in the state of Pennsylvania, and had lived there until he emigrated into Upper Canada, when he was twenty-two or twenty-three years of age. Entering that province, he located himself at Lake Simcoe, then a wilderness, where by industry and frugality he amassed a large property. To the many poor settlers who came from Europe and obtained grants of lands from the government he was a friend and adviser, and in cases of necessity their wants were supplied from his purse or his granaries. Many is the time, said some of our fellow-prisoners, that we have seen him, after the toils of the day were over, leave his home to carry provisions for miles through the pathless forest to the shanty of some poor and destitute settler, who with wife and family were rendered by want and sickness utterly destitute. Those acquainted with the history of new settlements need not be told how often those who have been accustomed to better days are obliged to embark in a new career of life, the duties of which they are totally ignorant and wholly unfitted for, nor how often sickness is engendered by their great bodily exertions, by neglect and deprivation.

In a country like that in which Mr. Lount was settled, the inhabitants resided far apart, and consisted generally of old, worn, and superannuated British officers, who, at the close of the war, pitched their tents, for the last time, in the wilderness. The sums which they obtained from the sale of their half-pay, almost expended in the transportation of their little families before arriving on the lands assigned them by government—unfitted, from their former pursuits, to bear the drudgery their new course of life required, it was frequently the case that before they could raise any thing from their lands they became perfectly destitute of the necessaries of subsistence. Too proud to seek assistance, they would starve rather than communicate their situation; but in Lount, their generous neighbour, they found one quick to discover and prompt in affording relief, and he would minister to their wants with such delicacy that the most sensitive would experience a pleasure rather than the pang of wounded pride.

(4) BIOGRAPHY OF SAMUEL LOUNT WRITTEN BY MACKENZIE.

(Lindsey Papers.)

Samuel and George Lount were sons of an English gentleman of liberal politics, who accompanied his friend, Dr. Joseph Priestley, to America after the Birmingham riots. Like the learned doctor, too, they were unitarians. Never did I meet with a man more regardless of place or office than Samuel Lount.

When Head, on the advice of Sullivan and the high church and landjobbing party, suddenly dissolved the 12th parliament, and resolved to adopt the very corrupt and outrageous course which Lord Durham has so ably described, Mr. Lount again offered himself as a candidate in opposition to the chief justice's brother, with a seeming certainty of success. But on the day of election he found the whole space round the hustings filled by a drunken and infuriated mob of government retainers, armed with knives and dirks, and evidently prepared to shed blood. Mr. Lount acted exactly as Lafontaine did afterwards at Terrebonne—he stated that to prevent personal injury to his friends and neighbors, he would protest and abandon the contest—and he did so. [Incomplete.]

(5) BIOGRAPHY OF PETER MATTHEWS WRITTEN BY MACKENZIE.

(Lindsey Papers.)

Capt. Peter Matthews was a jolly, hale, cheerful, cherry-cheeked farmer of Pickering, who lived on his own land, cultivated his own estate, and was the father of fifteen children, who beseeched the Sullivans, the Drapers, and the Robinsons in vain for that mercy to their father which they themselves must yet implore from a just God. Capt. M. had fought bravely for the King of England in the war of 1813, was a man of unstained reputation, well beloved by his neighbors, unassuming, modest in his deportment, a baptist, unfriendly to high church ascendancy, a true patriot, and indignant at the treacherous, fraudulent conduct of the detestable junto who, in 1837, governed Canada. I often got his vote for a seat in the legislature and always his approbation.

(6) LETTER OF MRS. SAMUEL LOUNT TO WILLIAM LYON MACKENZIE.

(Lindsey Papers.)

Utica Dec 8th 1838

Dear Friend:

I have been perusing a piece in one of your papers taken from the Christian Advocate [Guardian] well known to be a paper of little truth by every one acquainted it or its Proprieter stating that my Husband should have spoken very much against you which me and my family know to be false and I am persuaded you was acquainted with Mr. Lount years enough to think otherwise he even taught his family to respect Mr. Mackenzie as one of the most honest and honorable man he ever met with. I was with him the last three days of his life. Instead of berating his friends he prayed for their success as well as his Country Freedom and believed Canada could not long remain in the power of such merciless wretches who murdered its inhabitants for their love of Liberty.

APPENDIX 271

But he forgave his enemies and prayed they might Repent of their wickedness although he considered himself unjustly put to death by them and wished me never to ask life of his enemies. But my anxiety would not allow me to leave the least undone that was in my Power to do towards saving his life therefore I appeared before Sir Arthur in behalf of my Husband as before stated, his answer was if your Husband is as well prepared to die as represented, perhaps he will never will be again as well prepared if reprieved now and I do not think he can be prepared to die without bringing other guilty men to justice as the Council thinks he knows of many which I think if he would do mercy would be shown to him and I wish you would return direct to the Jail and tell him this from me, He made me several other answers which is not stated here, I lately been on a visit to Canada and found the tories determined to retain the Property from me and my Fatherless Children, I have ever wished to see you since I crossed the Lines as I could tell you more than I could write. Please Give my Love to Mrs. Mackenzie and family—I wish you to direct the Papers which you are so kind in sending me to Utica P. O. Shelby Town Macomb County, Michigan and Oblige your Friend.

Elizabeth Lount

Mr. W. L. Mackenzie.

(7) MISCELLANEOUS ITEMS IN THE LINDSEY PAPERS AND ELSEWHERE.

Mackenzie was assembling material in 1849 for 'The Canadian Tragedy' —a projected pamphlet upon the execution (see illustration of his title page, facing page 131). The 'Lount and Matthews' package in the Lindsey Papers consequently contains a large number of clippings and notes which he planned to use. One is entitled 'Lount's Last Day', and indicates some of his last visitors, preparations for the execution, etc. Another scrap of paper states that Robert Baldwin 'took $60 from Mrs. Lount, thro' her friends, for the very little he did for her husb.^{d}, & that little he did reluctantly.' The following note, also in Mackenzie's handwriting, elaborates somewhat Baldwin's policy in defending the Patriot prisoners:

Mr. John Carey states, Augt. 3, 1850, That R. Bald^{in} was Counsel for J. Montgmry; ... also for Lount & Matthews... He advised them to plead guilty. Arthur told Mrs. Lount that if Lount had pleaded not guilty his char^r st^d so high am'g the people, that the jurors cou^d have recom^d him to mercy, & he cou^d, in oppos^n to his Council, have st the case home.

In accordance with his outline of contents on the proposed title page, Mackenzie planned to use information apparently obtained from some of those whose duty it was to place the bodies of the executed men in rough wooden boxes and draw them in carts to the Potter's Field. He earlier published certain of these gruesome details in his *Caroline Almanack*, 40-1, of which the following provides sufficient illustration: 'Two ruffians seized the end of the rope and dragged the mangled corpse along the ground into the jail yard' with the comment, 'This is the way every damned rebel deserves to be used.'

The effects of the arrest and execution of Lount upon his family are given in detail in William R. Lount's letter to Mackenzie, Lindsey Papers. The Reverend John Ryerson stated that 'Lount's daughter, a young woman, was present when her father was condemned; it had such an effect on her that she went home & *died* directly. O!! these are melancholy times'.

APPENDIX L.
THE SHORT HILLS RAID.

(1) DISPOSITION OF THE PRISONERS.

Thirty-nine men and two women were arrested during the Short Hills raid, most for participation but a few for rendering assistance; the two women were members of the Wilson household and were apparently not held. The following list has been obtained by a collation of the 'Register of Prisoners' entering Toronto jail, the official list in *Imperial Blue Books*, XI, and other sources, for no one is entirely correct—if accuracy is possible when many of the prisoners were themselves inconsistent in the spelling of their names. The first twenty-three were removed to Toronto jail over the Fourth of July, returning to Niagara on the fourteenth to stand trial. It may be assumed that the rest were also removed temporarily to Toronto and placed in the Garrison or the Legislative Council Chamber.

E indicates executed, T transported.

Freeman Brady
Robert Kelly
Eber Rice
David Taylor
TSamuel Chandler
Abraham Clarke
Solomon Kemp
TJohn Grant
TJohn J. McNulty
TWilliam Reynolds
Loran Hedger
Street Chase
EJames Morreau
TNorman Mallory
TGeorge Cooley
Murdock McFadden
TLinus W. Miller
George Buck
TGarret Van Camp
TJames Gemmell

TJames Waggoner
Edward Seymour
TAlexander McLeod
TBenjamin Wait
Alexander Brady
Erastus Warner
Stephen Hart
James Doan
William Whitson
John W. Brown
TJohn Vernon
William Yerks
Samuel D. Haslip
Charles Malcolm
George Malcolm
Neal Brown
Clarke Bowers
Duncan Willson
TJacob R. Beemer

Of those whose sentence was commuted to transportation, Taylor, a Canadian, died at Fort Henry (see Miller, *Notes of an Exile*, 102-5), and Warner was not sent, probably because he had tuberculosis; while Reynolds was released in England (see chapter XIX). Brown and McFadden were sentenced to three years in Kingston penitentiary but were bailed a year later; Buck, originally sentenced to death, had his sentence commuted to three years' imprisonment; while the rest were either acquitted upon trial or released after a period in jail. Doan and Hart turned Queen's evidence, and the case against them was consequently dropped.

(2) LETTER OF ERASTUS WARNER TO MRS. PERMELIA WARNER, PORT HOPE.
(In the possession of his great-niece, Miss Loy Neads, Fort Frances, Ontario.)

Fort Henry—Oct 23—1838

Dear Mother—I embrace this oppertunity of conveying these few ill composed lines to you. Astating to you that I am well at Preasant and

APPENDIX 273

am sonserly wishing that those few lines will find you all enjoying the same state of health but I am in great want of clothing and money at presant as my clothes is all to pieces and Also I require money to get such things as is necessary for to live on such as tea and other articles but we live mutch better than in Niagara for we have a large room and good beds and our keeper is much more agreeable than those at Niagara therefore I have no fault to find for we are well yoused the clothes which I am in want of most is shirts and shoes and socks, and a coat for perhaps we will be removed very shortly and if it is possible to get these things I would be very happy indeed and nothing more at present therefore I must conclude with sending my sensere love to you all and best respects to all inquiring friends.

Erastus Warner.

(3) LETTER OF MARIA WAIT TO MRS. PERMELIA WARNER, PORT HOPE.
(In the possession of Miss Loy Neads, Fort Frances, Ontario.)

Kingston Nov. 9th 1838

Dear Maddam

I came down here to see Mr Wait, and just happened to be in time to see them all removed it is thought by some that they will not go farther than Quebeck but the sherif told me that they would be sent on to England immediately, yet I hope for something better there was 23 prisoners sent away from here. Your son was one of them but they seemed nothing daunted and went off in the best of spirits. this is a consolation to us to know that they beare their affliction with becoming fortitude for great is the affliction indeed to them and their friends that are left behind to mourn their loss but we must bear up and trust that kind heaven may have something better in store for us. I have written to you by your sons request as he wished you to know that he had gone.

I remain dear maddam
Yours truly
Maria Wait

(4) WARRANT ISSUED TO CAPTAIN MORTON OF THE *Captain Ross*.
(From Miller, *Notes of an Exile*, 131-2.)

[Two named in the warrant were not sent. Hills died and Walrath escaped before their sentence could be carried out. See note 3, p. 182, *supra*.]

PROVINCE OF LOWER CANADA, (Seal) J. COLBORNE.

VICTORIA, by the grace of God, of the United Kingdom of Great Britain and Ireland Queen, Defender of the Faith, &c., &c.,

To Digby B. Morton, Master of the barque, Captain Ross,—

Whereas, under and by virtue of a certain warrant of his Excellency, Sir George Arthur, K. C. H., Lieutenant Governor of our province of Upper Canada, and Major General commanding our forces therein, bearing date under his hand and seal of office at Toronto, in the said province of Upper Canada, the fifth day of November in the present year of our

Lord, one thousand eight hundred and thirty-eight, and in the second year of our reign, Ara Anderson, James Brown, Randall Wixon, William Alves, Robert Walker, Leonard Watson, John Goldsbury Parker, Finlay Malcolm, Paul Bedford, Horatio Hills, Charles P. Walroth, James Gemmel, John Grant, John James McNulty, Samuel Chandler, Benjamin Wait, Alexander McLeod, James Waggoner, Garret Van Camp, John Vernon and Jacob Beemer, severally indicted and convicted in due course of law in the courts of the said province of Upper Canada of the crime of high treason,—and Linus Wilson Miller, George Cooley, William Reynolds and Norman Mallory, in like manner severally indicted and convicted of felony—and Edwin Merrit in like manner indicted and convicted of the crime of murder, to all of which said persons and convicts our gracious pardon hath been extended upon condition nevertheless that they and each of them be transported and remain transported to our penal colony of Van Dieman's Land, for and during the period named in the patents of pardon so as aforesaid granted to the said convicts, and each of them: and whereas, the said several persons and convicts, are by and under a warrant in that behalf of his Excellency, Sir John Colborne, our administrator of the government, of our said province of Lower Canada, in that behalf, are now in the custody of our sherif of the district of Quebec, in our said province of Lower Canada, in order to their transportation as aforesaid: and whereas, we being willing that the bodies of the said . . . [the names repeated] . . . and of each and every of them now in our common gaol of our district of Quebec, should be directly delivered to you to be transported to Van Dieman's Land, being one of our penal settlements and foreign possessions, we have by our writ in that behalf, addressed to our said sherif, lately commanded our said sherif that he should deliver the said . . . [the names repeated] . . . and each and every of them, to your custody without delay, to be transported as aforesaid. We therefore command you receive the said . . . [the names repeated] . . . and each and every of them from our said sherif of our said district of Quebec, and that you do forthwith transport and convey or cause to be transported and conveyed the said . . . [the names repeated] . . . and each and every of them, to such part of the United Kingdom of Great Britain and Ireland, called England, as to us may seem fit, to the end that the said . . . [the names repeated] . . . may be thence again transported to our penal colony of Van Dieman's Land, according to the condition in our aforesaid pardons severally and respectively in that behalf contained, and that you do there deliver the bodies of the said . . . [the names repeated] . . . and the body of each and every of them, into the custody of such person or persons as may be lawfully authorised to receive the same.

In testimony whereof, we have caused these our letters to be made patent and the Great Seal of our said province of Lower Canada to be hereunto affixed.

Witness, our trusty and well-beloved Sir John Colborne, Knight Grand Cross of the most honorable military order of the Bath, and of the Royal Hanoverian Guelphic Order, Commander in Chief of our forces in the province of Lower Canada, &c., &c., &c.

At our government house in our city of Montreal, in our said province of Lower Canada, the seventeenth day of November, in the year of our Lord one thousand eight hundred and thirty-eight, and in the second year of her Majesty's reign.

By command,   D. DALY, Secretary of the Province.

APPENDIX 275

(5) LETTER OF FOX MAULE TO JOSEPH HUME CONCERNING CONDITIONS ON THE *York* HULK.

(From Wait, *Letters from Van Dieman's Land,* 218-9.)

HOME SECRETARY'S OFFICE,

February 10, 1839.

My Dear Sir:

I am directed by the Secretary of State, to return you the letter written and signed by the convict Wait, in behalf of his companions, purporting to give you a true account of their situation on board of the York hulk. I accompany it with some remarks I was desired to make, which, it is hoped, will convince you that his sufferings are not as great as he represents.

I have written to the Officer on board the hulk, and find they occupy the ward we directed they should be placed in; it is the same from which the boys were taken a month or two ago, when they were sent to the penitentiary at Rye, on the isle of Wight; and excepting the late alterations of the weather, I do not see why it is not as habitable for its present, as for its former occupants. He complains of the two preliminary processes of cutting off the hair, and assuming prison dress.

The reason assigned for the first is, to prevent the generating of vermin, which every means must be used to guard against in a community like the hulks; and I do not anticipate it being done in an 'inhuman manner.' The assumption of prison dress is, to afford a corresponding chance of detection, in an attempt to escape, when on shore at work.

As to the coldness of the ward they inhabit, I am told that a hanging stove was allowed them during the greatest severity of the weather.

And the provisions supplied them, is the same in quantity and quality, furnished to thousands of prisoners before them, by the government, without complaint; and several years experience, and the united opinions of various physicians, have taught us that it is perfectly wholesome, and sufficient for the actual necessities of any man, notwithstanding the assertion of the convict Wait, and his fellow convicts, to the contrary.

There were no orders issued from this office for a difference of treatment from the *other* felons, except that, by their own request, they were to be kept separate from them, and not to be sent out to work. Wait may be assured, that his letters, when written with such an independent spirit, and in such a tone of presumption, cannot pass unheeded.

When you have perused this letter, please return it, with whatever pertinent remarks may occur to you. And I am directed to say, you will do well to abstain from receiving the convict Wait's complaints of ill treatment, when in the custody of the officers of our government, for he is a cunning, designing fellow, and his associate convicts are his dupes.

I am, Sir, your obd't

Humble serv't,

(Signed) FOX MAULE,

Under Secretary of State.

Joseph Hume, Esq., M.P.

276   THE LIVES AND TIMES OF THE PATRIOTS

APPENDIX M.

THE ST. CLAIR RAIDS.

The following were arrested in the Western District at the time of, or shortly after, the raids along the St. Clair in June, 1838, though not all of them were participants. T indicates transported.

<table>
<tr><td>tHorace Cooley</td><td>Lambert Beaubien</td></tr>
<tr><td>Charles Bourman</td><td>Malcolm Burnham</td></tr>
<tr><td>Louis Burnham</td><td>James Coll</td></tr>
<tr><td>Orlando Boyington</td><td>Isaac Phillips</td></tr>
<tr><td>Henry B. Nugent</td><td>William Herrington</td></tr>
<tr><td>Reuben Markham</td><td></td></tr>
</table>

Bourman and Herrington were held for some months longer than the rest, who were discharged on bail in September. Cooley proceeded in 1839 to Van Diemen's Land with the Prescott and Windsor prisoners on the *Buffalo* (see chapter XIX). He is not, however, referred to as a St. Clair prisoner but included by the writers of the Patriot narratives as from the Short Hills, being apparently confused with George Cooley. There is no record that either of them ever left Van Diemen's Land.

APPENDIX N.

DOCUMENTS RELATIVE TO THE INVASION AT PRESCOTT.

(1) DANIEL HEUSTIS'S LIST OF PARTICIPANTS.
(Narrative, 62-6.)

[In the following list are placed in parantheses all names in the official list which are essentially different from the spelling given by Heustis. E indicates executed, T signifies transported to Van Diemen's Land, and * denotes those not in the official list of prisoners as recorded in Enclosure 4, Sir George Arthur to Lord Glenelg, February 5, 1839.]

On the morning of the 13th, when the battle first commenced, we had only 186 men. Four of these ran away without fighting at all. Five others, who had fought gallantly, made their escape previous to our capture. Their names were Junah Woodruff, William Hathaway, Benjamin Fulton, —— Tracy, and a Polander, whose name I cannot give. The following is a list of those killed and taken prisoners, numbering 177:

Names	Age	Residence
Samuel Austin	21	Alexandria, Jefferson County
Charles Allen	24	Scriba, Oswego County
T David Allen	87	Volney, Oswego County
* Philip Alger	—	Salina, Onondaga County
E Dorethus Abbey	48	Pamelia, Jefferson County
E Duncan Anderson	48	Lyme, Jefferson County
T Orlin Blodget	19	Philadelphia, Jefferson County
T John Bradley	28	Sackett's Harbor, Jefferson County
T Thomas Baker	47	Hannibal, Cayuga County
T John Berry	42	Oswego, Oswego County
T Chauncey Bugby	22	Lyme, Jefferson County
Hiram Barlow	19	Morristown, St. Lawrence County
Charles Brown	20	Hastings, Oswego County
John Brewster	19	Henderson, Jefferson County
T George T. Brown	23	Evans' Mills, Jefferson County
Rouse Bennett	19	Norway, Herkimer County
George Blonden (Blondeau)	21	Lower Canada
Ernest Barance (Berends)	40	Native of Poland
John Bromley	38	Depeauville, Jefferson County
Nelson Butterfield	22	Philadelphia, Jefferson County
Charles E. Brown	24	Brownsville, Jefferson County
E Christopher Buckley	30	Salina, Onondaga County

APPENDIX

	Names	Age	Residence
*	Hiram Colton	21	Philadelphia, Jefferson County
	Philip Coonrod (Conrod)	21	Salina, Onondaga County
T	Lysander Curtis	35	Ogdensburgh, St. Lawrence County
T	Robert G. Collins	32	Ogdensburgh, St. Lawrence County
	Eli Clark	61	Oswego, Oswego County
	Charles F. Crossman	19	Watertown, Jefferson County
	Paschal Carpenter (Cervanter)	20	Leroy, Jefferson County
T	John Cronkhite	29	Alexandria, Jefferson County
	Calvin S. Clark	19	Fort Covington, Franklin County
	Peter Cranker (Cronker)	23	Orleans, Jefferson County
T	Hugh Calhoun	35	Salina, Onondaga County
*	Truman Chipman	44	Upper Canada
	Nathan Coffin	27	Liverpool, Onondaga County
	Levi Chipman	45	Upper Canada
	James Cummings	40	Orleans, Jefferson County
T	Leonard Delano (Delino)	26	Watertown, Jefferson County
	Joseph Drumma (Drummond)	22	Salina, Onondaga County
	David Defield	28	Salina, Onondaga County
	Joseph Dodge	28	Salina, Onondaga County
T	Moses A. Dutcher	23	Brownsville, Jefferson County
	William Denio	21	Leroy, Jefferson County
T	Luther Darby	48	Watertown, Jefferson County
T	Aaron Dresser	24	Alexandria, Jefferson County
	Rensselaer Drake	23	Salina, Onondaga County
	John Elmore	19	Leroy, Jefferson County
*	Selah Evans	35	Leroy, Jefferson County
	Adam Empy	40	Rossee, St. Lawrence County
T	Edom Fellows	23	Dexter, Jefferson County
T	Michael Fraer	23	Clay, Onondaga County
	Edmund Foster	22	Alexandria, Jefferson County
*	Lorenzo E. Finney	21	Watertown, Jefferson County
T	William Gates	24	Lyme, Jefferson County
T	Emanuel Garrison	26	Brownsville, Jefferson County
T	Gideon A. Goodrich	43	Salina, Onondaga County
T	Nelson Griggs	28	Salina, Onondaga County
T	Jerry Griggs	21	Salina, Onondaga County
T	John Gilman	38	Brownsville, Jefferson County
	David Gould	24	Alexandria, Jefferson County
	Cornelius Goodrich	18	Salina, Onondaga County
	Francis Ganyo (Gaynion)	18	Lower Canada
*	John Graves	25	Cosmopolitan
E	Daniel George	28	Lyme, Jefferson County
T	Daniel D. Heustis	32	Watertown, Jefferson County
	Charles Haris (Horey)	22	Lyme, Jefferson County
	Edmund Holmes	24	Plattsburg, Clinton County
T	Garret Hicks	45	Alexandria, Jefferson County
	Hiram Hall	17	Orleans, Jefferson County
T	David House (Howth)	26	Alexandria, Jefferson County
*	Jacob Herald	—	France
	Moses Haynes	20	Salina, Onondaga County
T	James Inglish (Inglis)	28	Adams, Jefferson County
	Henry Johnson (Jantzer)	29	New York City
	John M. Jones	35	Philadelphia, Jefferson County
	George Kimball (Kimbalt)	20	Brownsville, Jefferson County
	Hirman Kenney (Kinney)	20	Palermo, Oswego County
T	Joseph Lefore (Leforte)	29	Lyme, Jefferson County
T	Daniel Liscomb (Liscum)	40	Lyme, Jefferson County
	Samuel Livingston	40	Lisbon, St. Lawrence County
	Joseph Lee	21	Palermo, Oswego County
T	Andrew Leeper	44	Lyme, Jefferson County
T	Hiram Loop	25	Scruple, Onondaga County
	Samuel Laraby	35	Rossee, St. Lawrence County
	Paul Lamear	—	Ogdensburgh, St. Lawrence County
E	Sylvester A. Lawton	28	Lyme, Jefferson County
E	Leman L. Leach (alias Lewis)	40	Salina, Onondaga County
	Oliver Lawton	22	Saratoga, Saratoga County
	Peter Myer (Meyer)	20	Salina, Onondaga County
	Sebastian Myer (Meyers)	20	Rochester, Munroe County
T	Calvin Matthews (Mathers)	25	Lysander, Onondaga County
T	Andrew Moore (More)	26	Adams, Jefferson County
	Justus Merriam (Miriam)	18	Brownsville, Jefferson County
T	Jehiel H. Martin	32	Oswego, Oswego County
	Phares Miller	18	Leroy, Jefferson County
T	John Morrisset	20	Lower Canada
T	Chauncey Matthews (Mathers)	25	Liverpool, Onondaga County
T	Foster Martin	34	Antwerp, Jefferson County
	Frederick Milow	—	Germany
	Oster Myer	30	Poland
	Alonzo Mayatt	18	Lower Canada

	Names	Age	Residence
	Joseph Norris	26	Rossee, St. Lawrence County
	Lawrence O'Reiley (Riley)	46	Lyme, Jefferson County
T	Alson Owen	27	Palermo, Oswego County
	Benjamin Obrey	18	Madrid, St. Lawrence County
*	Oliver Obrey	21	Madrid, St. Lawrence County
	William O'Neil	42	Alexandria, Jefferson County
	John Okonskie (O'Koinski)	32	Poland
	Jacob Putman	24	Palermo, Oswego County
T	Asa Priest	45	Auburn, Cayuga County
*	Gayus Powers	24	Brownsville, Jefferson County
T	Ira Poiley (Polly)	22	Lyme, Jefferson County
	Levi Putman	24	Lyme, Jefferson County
	Lawton S. Peck	20	Brownsville, Jefferson County
T	Jacob Paddock	18	Salina, Onondaga County
T	James Pierce	22	Orleans, Jefferson County
	Ethel Penny	19	Lyme, Jefferson County
	James Phillips	38	Ogdensburgh, St. Lawrence County
E	Joel Peeler	41	Rutland, Jefferson County
E	Russel Phelps	38	Lyme, Jefferson County
	Timothy Rawson (Rosin)	24	Alexandria, Jefferson County
T	William Reynolds	19	Orleans, Jefferson County
T	Asa H. Richardson	24	Upper Canada
*	Edgar Rogers	18	Watertown, Jefferson County
	Andrew Richardson	28	Rossee, St. Lawrence County
T	Solomon Reynolds	33	Queensbury, Warren County
*	Orson Rogers	19	Philadelphia, Jefferson County
	Lysander Root	27	Sackett's Harbor, Jefferson County
*	Charles Rogers	—	Philadelphia, Jefferson County
*	Baptiste Raza	20	Montreal, L. Canada
	Charles Smith	21	Lyme, Jefferson County
T	John G. Swansberg (Swanberg)	28	Alexandria, Jefferson County
	Price Senter	18	Perry, Genesee County
T	Hiram Sharp	25	Salina, Onondaga County
	Andrew Smith	21	Orleans, Jefferson County
	William Stebbins	18	Brownsville, Jefferson County
	James L. Snow	20	Hastings, Oswego County
T	Henry Shew	28	Philadelphia, Jefferson County
T	Orin W. Smith	32	Orleans, Jefferson County
T	Joseph W. Stewart	25	Waynesburg, Mifflin County, Penn.
T	Thomas Stockton	40	Rutland, Jefferson County
	William D. Sweet (Swete)	19	Alexandria, Jefferson County
	— Savoy	44	Lewisburg, Lewis County
E	Sylvanus Sweet (Swete)	21	Alexandria, Jefferson County
	Oliver Tucker	22	Rutland, Jefferson County
T	Joseph Thompson	26	Lyme, Jefferson County
	Abner B. Townsend	19	Philadelphia, Jefferson County
	Samuel Tibbetts (Tibbett)	25	Salina, Onondaga County
	John Thompson	27	Madrid, St. Lawrence County
	Nelson Truax	20	Antwerp, Jefferson County
*	John Thompson	24	Morristown, St. Lawrence County
T	Giles Thomas	27	Salina, Onondaga County
	George Venamber (Van Amber)	23	Alexandria, Jefferson County
	Charles Vanwermer	21	Ellisburg, Lewis County
	Tenike Venalstine	30	Salina, Onondaga County
	Martin Vanslike (Van Slyke)	23	Watertown, Jefferson County
	Hunter C. Vaughn (Vaughan)	21	Sackett's Harbor, Jefferson County
E	Nicholas A. S. Von Schoultz	43	Salina, Onondaga County
	Charles Wilson	23	Lyme, Jefferson County
T	Stephen S. Wright	25	Denmark, Lewis County
T	Nathan Whiting	45	Liverpool, Onondaga County
	Charles Woodruff	21	Salina, Onondaga County
	Joseph Wagner	24	Salina, Onondaga County
T	Riley Whitney	28	Leroy, Jefferson County
	Simeon Webster	21	Salina, Onondaga County
	William Wolcot (Woolcott)	20	Clay, Onondaga County
	Jeremiah Winegar	59	Brownsville, Jefferson County
	Sampson A. Wiley	20	Watertown, Jefferson County
T	Edward A. Wilson	27	Ogdensburgh, St. Lawrence County
	Henry E. Wilkey (Hosea Wilkie)	20	Orleans, Jefferson County
T	Samuel Washburn	23	Oswego, Oswego County
T	Bemis Woodbury	22	Auburn, Cayuga County
T	Patrick White	25	Lower Canada
	Monroe Wheelock	23	Watertown, Jefferson County
	Lorenzo West	26	Salina, Onondaga County
	Alexander Wright	21	Ogdensburgh, St. Lawrence County
E	Martin Woodruff	34	Salina, Onondaga County

The following-named persons, included in the foregoing list, were killed at Windmill Point: Nelson Butterfield, Charles E. Brown, Nathan Coffin, Rensselaer Drake,

APPENDIX 279

Adam Empy, Edmund Foster, Moses Haynes, Samuel Laraby, Paul Lamear, Oster Myer, Benjamin Obrey, James Phillips, Leonard Root, —— Savoy, Tenike Venalstine, Lorenzo West, Alexander Wright—17.
Wounded, and died in the hospital: John Bromley, Frederick Millow, Monroe Wheelock—3.
Wounded, but not mortally: Philip Alger, Ernest Barance, Hiram Colton, Leonard Delano, Selah Evans, Lorenzo E. Finney, Jacob Herald, George Kimball, Andrew Moore, John Morrisset, Oliver Obrey, John Okonskie, Orson Rogers, Giles Thomas, Stephen S. Wright, William Wolcot, Bemis Woodbury—17.
I account for the 182 men engaged in the battle of Prescott as follows: Killed, 17; wounded and afterwards died, 3; escaped before the surrender, 5; executed 11; pardoned, 64; discharged without a trial, 22; transported in the *Buffalo*, 60; total 182.

(2) ESCAPE OF N. WILLIAMS AFTER THE BATTLE OF WINDMILL POINT.

[The following account was reprinted in the Toronto *Mirror*, February 8, 1839, from the *Fort Ontario Aurora*. Williams is not listed by Heustis (see appendix N (1), *supra*), but he may have enlisted under a pseudonym. His companions, Snow and Brown, were captured.]

ESCAPE FROM U. CANADA.

Central Square, Dec. 21, 1838.

Mr. Dickinson:—After considerable delay occasioned by ill health, I embrace the opportunity of communicating to the public the particulars of my escape from Wind Mill Point on the evening of the 16th November last. In the Narrative of the Expedition I had occasion to observe that about sunset we were ordered to lay down our arms and march out and surrender ourselves to the enemy. But contrary to our expectations, even this unhappy alternative was not granted us. No sooner had we marched out and called for quarters than a brisk fire was opened upon us, and several of our men severely wounded. Being then ordered to retreat into the Mill, our men readily acquiesced with the exception of four or five of us, among whom were James L. Snow, Chas. S. Brown, and myself, besides two others whose names I do not know.

Instead of again retreating into the mill we repaired to a stone house, which was nearer and afforded a more immediate asylum than the Mill. The main body of the enemy had now marched down within about 5 rods of us, and, as we supposed, would soon assail our building and make us indiscriminate subjects of an inhuman massacre. Our situation at this time was emphatically a critical one. Between an undisputed submission to such a fate and a resolute defence of ourselves, we, in the ultimate, saw little or no difference. However, we soon resolved upon the latter, and then our lives, if thus taken, should be at the price of blood. Having a pair of pistols I presented them to my companion and seized a musket myself; we stationed ourselves at the door prepared to meet our unhappy fate. But contrary to our anticipations we were not molested, but were left to the entire control of the house. Having waited about the space of half an hour, whilst in the meantime the attention of the enemy was directed to the mill, I suggested to my companions the propriety of leaving the house and retreating to the bank of the river where we might secrete ourselves in a pine grove which was situated in the rear of the mill. Accordingly we abandoned our first position and concealed ourselves as well as possible in the grove, about six rods from the main body of our men. About 6 o'clock P.M. our men were taken prisoners and our buildings with the exception of the Mill set on fire. A search was then made in the grove for any one who might thus far have escaped. To the discharge of this task several of the militia were appointed who with their lights commenced a vigilant search in the vicinity of our concealment. Having approached within about two rods of us, I beckoned to my companions, J. L. Snow and C. S. Brown, to follow me. My desire was then to pass up the river about half a mile, get beyond the main body of the enemy, and cross the road at that point. We had not proceeded far before I recognized my companions some distance in the rear, apparently making little effort to follow me; having no time to lose I did not return to urge them on, but hastened onward as fast as possible. I resolved to try the advantage of stratagem. I then resolved to ascend the bank of the river, gain possession of the road and feign journeying to Prescott—but no sooner had I gained possession of the road than I was discovered by the sentinel in the rear and bid to stop. However of this I took no notice but travelled on as though nothing had happened, till accosted the second time, attended with a threat that if I did not stop 'he would shoot me down'. Having now got the distance of several rods from the sentinel and having a better opportunity to cross the road and fields, I resolved to make the best of the opportunity which presented. Accordingly I started at the height of my speed, being fired upon by the sentinel and given chase by 3 of the militia, who also discharged their fusils, though without any effect upon me. The pursuit was continued about forty rods and ended only by a precipitation of myself into a 'mud-hole', which I did not discover till it had been encountered. Knowing that my pursuers were near, I resolved to remain in this situation a few minutes and await the result. As I hoped, my followers came up and without stopping or paying me any attention, like the ancient High Priest, 'passed by on the other side'. After passing the distance of a few rods I recovered myself, retraced my steps a short distance, and then repaired to the fields, leaving my pursuers to follow a different direction. Consequently I sought a direction directly from the river and into the country more remote from the Patriot excitement. Having gained the fields I continued my journey through the most unfrequented part of the country till I had travelled several miles from the river. Feeling a good deal fatigued I repaired to a small barn, where I purposed to remain thro' the night and subsequent day; but from the intense coldness of the night I was obliged to abandon the idea and proceed on my journey. My intention was at this time to gain the river, and if possible to cross to the American shore; but on approaching the river my previous conjectures were confirmed by the discovery of a guard upon the river, which rendered any attempt to cross at that time imprudent. I then retraced my steps into the country, hardly knowing whether to remain in the forest or repair to some dwelling and call for entertainment. However, on discovering a house at some distance in the field, I resolved to repair to it and seek protection; accordingly I approached the romantic spot and after rapping at the door gained admission. Although the characteristics of extreme poverty were everywhere to be recognized, yet the kindness and hospitality with which I was entertained contributed more to the happiness of my situation than all the luxuries of affluence & wealth.

To my friend and benefactor riches were a stranger, yet the frank, open, and expressive features of his countenance plainly indicated that he was neither a stranger to happiness or the more exalted feelings of our nature. To such a person had Providence directed me for protection. And to him I made known my situation, whilst his every feature bespoke an anxiety for my welfare as I rehearsed my adventurous tale. The wife was engaged at the same time in preparing what little their scanty means afforded for my supper. However, it was enough, although their kindness was wont to bestow a more palatable meal, but it was the best their circumstances afforded, and with this I was conducted to the chamber where a pallet of straw was prepared for my acceptance, on which I couched for the remainder of the night. Having remained in this situation through the night and subsequent day, I was advised about eleven o'clock P.M. to continue my journey to the river, obtain a boat, and escape to the American shore. After receiving the watch word which would be required by the guard, I proceeded to the river in accordance with the advice of my benefactor. On reaching the river I commenced a search for a boat, but here I found my ingenuity again brought to a test as the inhabitants had taken the precaution of withdrawing them from the river. But committing my case to the care of Providence, I resolved to risk myself upon the strength of means within my reach. After considerable search, for the want of more suitable materials I was compelled to make use of some rails which I placed on the river, of which I constructed a raft on which by the assistance of a stake for a paddle I effected a landing on the American shore after a pleasant voyage of about two hours. A shrewd friend has since remarked that the most despisable thing in the whole affair was the smuggling of a few rails from the Canada side over to the American shore; but taking the first cost into consideration, the expense of importation, &c., I can assure him that I have not yet had reason to lament the undertaking.

I cannot in justice to my own feelings and to true merit close this narrative without mentioning in particular the names of a few among the many who on my return bestowed upon me every attention which my situation demanded. Having lost my trunk and clothing through the kindness of Dr. Sherman of Ogdensburg. [sic.] To Mr. King and Mr. Daniels of the same place I must return my sincere thanks, as well as several others whose names I must omit. The name of Dr. Dewey, Mr. Pratt, and Mr. Fletcher of Antwerp, Mr. Simons and Turner of Watertown, and Capt. Waugh of Sacket's Harbor I have reasons to remember with sentiments of esteem and lasting gratitude. Such, kind reader, is the hasty account of my escape from a place and scenes which will ever be remembered with the most painful regret.

Yours truly,
N. WILLIAMS.

(3) THE CHARGE AGAINST STEPHEN S. WRIGHT.

For the said Stephen S. Wright, on the 12th day of November, and on divers other days between that day and the sixteenth day of November, in the second year of the reign of our Sovereign Lady Victoria, by the grace of God, of the United Kingdom of Great Britain and Ireland, Queen, defender of the faith, with forces and arms, at the township of Augusta, in the District of Johnstown and Province of Upper Canada, being a citizen of a foreign State at peace with the United Kingdom of Great Britain and Ireland, that is to say the United States of America, having joined himself to several subjects of our said Lady the Queen, who were there, and there unlawfully and traitorously in arms against our said Lady the Queen, the said Stephen S. Wright, with the said subjects of her said majesty, so unlawfully and traitorously in arms as aforesaid, did then and there, armed with guns and bayonets and other warlike weapons, feloniously kill and slay divers of her said Majesty's loyal subjects, contrary to the statute in such cases made and provided, and against the peace of our said

282 THE LIVES AND TIMES OF THE PATRIOTS

Lady the Queen, her Crown and dignity. You are hereby notified that the foregoing is a copy of the charge preferred against you, and upon which you will be tried before the Militia General Court-Martial, assembled at Fort Henry, in the Midland District, on Monday, the 22nd of December, 1838. You will forward to me the names of any witnesses you desire to have summoned for your defence. Dated 21st of December, 1838.

WM. H. DRAPER,

Advocate-General.

(4) THE TRIAL OF VON SCHOULTZ.

Proceedings of a Militia General Court Martial holden at Fort Henry, at Kingston, for the trial of Nils Szoltevcky Von Schoultz, on Monday the 26th of November, 1838.

(Public Archives of Canada.)

[The following statement by Von Schoultz is given as 'the prisoner's acknowledgement to a paper already drawn and signed.' The statement was prepared by Magistrate George Baker and stated that 'voluntarily and without reluctance, . . he read it over and said that one line in it was incorrect, and so much as he requested was struck out. The remainder he said was the truth.' 'Burgh' in the document is a misspelling of 'Birge'.]

Neils Szoltevki Von Schoultz a Pole aged thirty one years. In Eighteen hundred and thirty six Came to the United States—is a Chemist: resided in Selina heard of the new Government of Canada for the first time about the beginning of November—was told by a Society in Salina that if he went to Ogdensburg to General Burgh of the Patriot army he should have particulars. Accordingly embarked at Oswego in the United States Steamer on Sunday the eleventh of November: landed the following morning below Prescott—designed to land at Ogdensburg. The General put the boat in the river and directed them to land on the Canada side; that he would meet them—was never sworn into the service—never regularly joined the Patriot Army: left Oswego to see the General (Burgh) before finally joining— his father was a major in the regiment of Cracows, and was killed; after which the present Von Schoultz got his rank of Major in the Polish Army—Never received pay in the Patriot service: saw Bill Johnson when he brought provisions and ammunition: Johnson brought the three pieces of artillery on Monday morning. General Burgh was to have the command but never appeared: Burgh is from Cassanovia in the State of New York—Johnson left when he landed the artillery: on Monday evening when the general had not appeared the prisoner undertook to lead the party back to the American shore—on Tuesday their adjutant came over and said that Schooners were coming to their assistance and to take them off—the adjutant immediately returned—on Tuesday seven or eight were killed and fourteen or fifteen wounded. Mr. Stone a merchant in Salina first introduced this informant to the Patriots: does not know the name of the Patriot leader at Salina: brought two of his countrymen with him, who joined at Oswego; was told that the Upper Canadians would all join them: about one hundred and eighty landed below Prescott—on Monday night informant sent a man floating on a plank to have boats sent from the American shore to take them over—the man never returned. When he embarked at Oswego he knew that a great many men were on board

APPENDIX 283

with the same intention as himself: paid his passage money (twelve shillings and six pence)—two or three hundred passengers in all—saw some of them pay the passage-money—Burgh, when he came to the schooner left Ogdensburgh in a small steam boat; on the night of Wednesday no relief came to them. Johnson attempted to come over with small boats, but was defeated. On Thursday night a steam boat came over near the shore, but put off again without landing any thing or taking away the wounded; does not know her name. Was told to make a landing in Canada and that forces would join them, and that the British regulars would also come over to the Patriots—on Monday night he first took the Command to withdraw the party from below Prescott. Since that time he was sometimes called Captain and sometimes General. No man from the Canada shore joined them after landing: understood that all the men in the schooners and steamboat were Americans: did not know of any British subjects being among them: never was in Canada before: did not know of any assistance being given by the American Government—In the Attack the British fired first: procured the flag used by him at Salina: it was given to him by Mr. Stone to be handed to General Burgh. Never swore any men into the service—

(Signed)   S. Von Schoultz.

acknowledged before
me 27th Nov. 1838.
(Signed) G. Baker J. P.

The prisoner addressed the Court to the following effect—

When I found we had no medical stores for the wounded I was willing to give them up. On Friday evening when Colonel Fraser sent in a flag to remove the dead I met him and told him that I would give up the British wounded as I had no means of taking care of them and we had already given up all the bedding and every comfort we could for their accommodation. I merely state this to show that there was no inhumanity shewn to the wounded.

As regards the maltreatment of Captain Johnston's body—I tried to get away the body but the fire was such that I could not. Two men were wounded in the attempt. I put a sentinel to shoot the hogs that might approach the body and he fired to keep them off. This may shew that I had no concern in mutilating his body—I have no witnesses to call.

(5) BIOGRAPHY OF VON SCHOULTZ BY WARREN GREEN, SALINA (SYRACUSE).

(From a letter, December 28, 1838, to the *Syracuse Standard.*)

Niles Gustaf Schobtewiskii Von Schoultz was of Swedish descent, a Pole by birth, and of noble extraction. He had just finished an education, which versed him deep in the Sciences, both useful and ornamental, and had acquired the highest literary honors of the principal and most celebrated Universities of Northern Europe, when he found himself engaged in that sanguinary and unequal contest between Poland and Russia, the unhappy termination of which lost to himself a country, and to that unfortunate country everything but a name. As he was extremely modest in his pretensions, I have seldom heard him revert to personal achievements incidental to events so memorable, and then only under circumstances of the highest excitement. But I have learnt from these occasional departures from self-reserve, and incontestibly from other sources, that the important part he enacted was brilliant with heroic adventures and hair-breadth escapes, the bare recital of which is calculated to enchain and captivate the most casual listener. Certain it is, he signalized himself amid a host of heroes, for his rise was sudden, from the comparative obscurity of the scholar to the very responsible command of a colonel.

In that sanguinary and decisive struggle before the walls of Warsaw, his father and a brother fell martyrs to the sacred cause of liberty. His mother and a sister fled in the disguise of peasants, but were taken and banished to Russia, and are now confined to a space of ten miles square of that Empire. Himself gashed and scarred with wounds, but covered with imperishable glory—a fugitive wandering from country to country—friends and fortune lost, despoiled of home and kindred, with a constitutioned much impaired, he finally effected a landing on our shores, commonly denominated "the home of the brave and the land of the free." He evidently has been a traveller, as is to be inferred by his own declarations, as well as from rich stores of information he has acquired from actual observation. Sweden, Denmark, Finland, Lapland, Norway, Germany, Holland, Austria, Italy, Switzerland, France, Spain, Portugal, England, and finally America have been the theatre of his travels, and he had not only acquired a general geographical knowledge of them all but an intimate acquaintance with the habits, manners and customs of their inhabitants. I have heard him dwell long and eloquently on these, to me, novel and interesting topics—of Polar snows, and Italian skies, and of burning African suns—he had served beneath the scorching rays of the latter, and dwelt under the benign influence of the former—of Florence, its statuary, its picture galleries, and above all, of the urbanity and hospitality of its inhabitants, he was ecstatic in praise. He spoke eight different dialects, but, at the time of his arrival here, he had only an imperfect knowledge of our own. His contiguity to, and his father's interest in the celebrated mines of Cracow, led him to an intimate knowledge of the manufacture of our principal and staple article, salt. Thrown upon his own resources, in a land of strangers, divested of every vestige of property but a few valuable family relics, he cast about him with his usual energy for means of a livelihood, and these considerations brought him to the Onondaga salines in the fall of 1836. Here he fitted up a small laboratory —made his experiments—became confirmed in the truth of his own theory, and succeeded in convincing at least one individual of the practicability and utility of his improvement. In short he proceeded to Washington— obtained Letters Patent—visited and analyzed the principal springs in Virginia—made the most favorable impressions wherever he extended his business or acquaintance, and finally returned here according to promise, and put two of our furnaces in operation on his plan *successfully*. While here, he listened to the current report of Patriot suffering, of the oppressors and the oppressed, of a vast population, seven-tenths of which waited the coming of the liberators with open and extended arms. His sympathizing soul was fired at the thought of again being permitted to strike for freedom—his enthusiastic recklessness of danger led him into its very vortex, and he has perished—ignominiously perished.

On a review of the sparkling incidents of his brief and romantic career, I still think on him as the creature of a high wrought fancy rather than of sober reality—like a meteor of uncommon brilliancy, which has suddenly illumined the path of my dull existence, and as suddenly disappeared for ever.

APPENDIX 285

(6) DISPOSITION OF THE PRISONERS TAKEN AT WINDMILL POINT.

The following members of the Prescott expedition gave Queen's evidence against their fellow-prisoners: Jean Baptiste Raza, Alonzo Mayatt, Laurent Melhit (a boy of fourteen), Levi Chipman, and John Graves.

Those executed were as follows:

December   8—Nils S. Von Schoultz.
December 12—Dorrephus Abbey and Daniel George.
December 19—Martin Woodruff.
December 22—Joel Peeler and Sylvanus Sweet.
January   4—Christopher Buckley, Sylvester Lawton, Russell Phelps, and Duncan Anderson.
February 11—Leman L. Leach (alias Beach and Lewis).

Particulars concerning these men and their executions may be found in the narratives of Heustis, Lyon, and Gates, in Mackenzie's *Caroline Almanack*, and to a lesser extent in the contemporary press. The official list of those executed (Public Archives of Canada, S Series, Rebellion Papers, Court Martial 1838-1840) omits the name of Leach, but there is no doubt of his execution. Possibly it was delayed by investigation of his earlier Patriot activities, for he not only participated, probably under an assumed name, in the destruction of the *Sir Robert Peel*, but 'acted the part of a guerilla and was back and forth along the lines'. (Syracuse *Sunday Herald*, November 16, 1884.) The same newspaper states that a meeting was held in the Onondaga County Court House and plans made to raise a monument to Von Schoultz, Woodruff, and Buckley. Nothing came of the plan, however, and the only memorial was the naming of a street after Buckley in Salina (Syracuse); nor does it appear that the bodies of any of the executed men were claimed by relatives or friends, unless that of George was taken to Watertown by his widow. Last letters of Von Schoultz, Abbey, and Lawton are given in Lyon, 52-63.

The disposition of the other prisoners was based upon their age and prominence in the raid. Available official documents are alone insufficient indication of those transported, for some last-minute changes were made. State Book L, p. 460, Public Archives of Canada, gives the names of 64 men whose death sentence was commuted to transportation for life. The following five, however, were not sent to Van Diemen's Land: Laurence Reilly (Riley, O'Reiley), aged 46; Eli Clarke, aged 61; John M. Jones, aged 35; Oliver Lawton, aged 22; and David Defield, aged 28. Of these the first two may have been excused because they were older than most of those transported, and Lawton because he was slightly younger. Defield, however, was a special case. He is reported to have been on Navy Island, but in spite of his extensive Patriot activities he was eventually released because his mother, wife of a tavern-keeper, saved Colonel Fitzgibbon from capture by American troops at Lundy's Lane in the War of 1812. (See Bonnycastle, *Canada and the Canadians*, I 260.) Lawton and Jones were possibly released for giving information, for they were freed at the same time as the other informers (see the list of eleven in the Toronto *Mirror*, August 9, 1839, quoting the Kingston *Upper Canada Herald*). One man omitted from the official list, Jacob Paddock, was sent to Van Diemen's Land, making a total of sixty, as given in Heustis's and other lists. Of the remaining prisoners, most under 21, the *Commodore Barry* carried twenty-two to Sackett's Harbor on April 8, 1839, and thirty-seven more on April 27. As may be seen from the information in Heustis's list (appendix N (1),

286   THE LIVES AND TIMES OF THE PATRIOTS

supra,), the informers and a few others were not reported in the official list of prisoners, but they were held until the summer of 1839.

APPENDIX O.

DOCUMENTS RELATIVE TO THE BATTLE OF WINDSOR.

(1) OFFICIAL LIST OF PRISONERS AND THEIR DISPOSITION.

(See Enclosure 5 in Sir George Arthur to Lord Glenelg, February 5, 1839.)

[E indicates those executed, and T those transported to Van Diemen's Land. Supplementary information has been added from Thomas Sutherland's *Loose Leaves* and Daniel Heustis's *Narrative*. An additional prisoner, Daniel Sweetman, is known to have given Queen's evidence at the trial of Goodrich. If the name is not an alias, it is possible that one or two others have been omitted, though four informers—Barber, Bartlet, M'Dougall, and Putnam—are included. See also p. 150, *supra*.]

	Name	Age	Place of Birth or Residence
	Israel G. Attwood	18	Jefferson, New York
T	James M. Aitcheson	28	London, U.C.
E	Daniel D. Bedford	27	Hope Township, U.C.
	William Bartlet	31	New York State
T	Henry V. Barnum	25	Charlotteville, U.C., and Ypsilanti, Michigan
	Sidney Barber	35	Connecticut
E	Albert Clark	21	New Hampshire
	Oliver Crandell	41	New York State and Cleveland
E	Cornelius Cunningham	32	Vermont and Beachville, U.C.
E	Joshua G. Doan	—	Sugar Loaf, U.C.
T	James D. Fero	25	Long Point, U.C., and Ypsilanti
T	John S. Gutridge	30	Cayuga County, N.Y., and Cleveland
	Joseph Grasson	19	London District
	Harrison P. Goodrich	—	Vermont
	Joseph Horton	15	Vermont and Buffalo
	Ezra Horton	16	Vermont and Buffalo
	David Hay	18	Scotland and Cleveland
	Cornelius Higgins	17	Vermont
	William Jones	29	New York State
	Daniel Kennedy	20	New York State
E	Hiram B. Lynn	26	Ann Arbor, Michigan
	Stephen Meadon	20	Albany
	Orin J. Maybee	—	
	David M'Dougall	25	Scotland
T	Michael Morin (Murray)	31	Lockport
T	Robert Marsh	25	Detroit
T	William Nottage	38	Halifax, N.S., and Amherst, Ohio
E	Amos Perley (Thomas Purley)	—	St. John, New Brunswick
	George Putnam	—	London District
	Charles Read	17	England and Cleveland
T	Samuel Snow	38	Strongsville, Ohio
T	Elizur Stevens	27	Lebanon, New York
T	Alvin B. Sweet	22	Windfield, New York
T	Chauncey Sheldon	57	Utica, Michigan
T	John Spragge	23	Amherst, Ohio
T	Riley M. Stewart	31	Avon, Ohio
T	John H. Simmonds (Simons)	28	Lockport and Buffalo
T	John B. Tyrrell	24	St. Thomas, U.C.
	Abraham Tiffany	48	Albany
	Truman Woodbury	—	Lockport
	Robert Whitney	—	New York State and Cleveland
T	John C. Williams	38	Vermont and Rochester
T	Elijah C. Woodman	42	London, U.C.
T	James P. Williams	24	Cleveland

(2) LETTER OF J. G. DOAN TO HIS WIFE JUST PRIOR TO HIS EXECUTION.

['The following pathetic letter has been published, of recent years, by Mr. William Harrison, of Bayfield. It is addressed to "Mrs. Fanny Done, at Mr. Buscerk's, London," and is said to have been found in the sleigh of Mr. John Davidson, then of Port Stanley, who had overtaken a lady on the road (possibly the wife of the condemned man) and driven her into London, and it may be surmised that she dropped the letter before alighting.' (C. O. Ermatinger, *The Talbot Regime*, 297-8.) As Judge Ermatinger points out, the date '1837' must be in error for '1839'.]

London, 27th January, 1837.

Dear Wife,—

I am at this moment confined in the cell from which I am to go to the scaffold. I received my sentence to-day, and am to be executed on the sixth of February. I am permitted to see you to-morrow, any time after ten o'clock in the morning, as may suit you best. I wish you to think of such questions as you wish to ask me, as I do not know how long you will be permitted to stay. Think as little of my unhappy fate as you can, as from the love you bear to me and have ever evinced, I know too well how it must affect you. I wish you to inform my father and brother of my sentence as soon as possible. I must say good-bye for the night, and may God protect you and my dear child, and give you fortitude to meet that coming event with that Christian grace and fortitude which is the gift of Him, our Lord, who created us. That this may be the case is the prayer of your affectionate husband,

JOSHUA G. DONE.

(3) ADDRESS PREPARED BY AMOS PERLEY TO DELIVER FROM THE SCAFFOLD.

(From Charles S. Buck's unpublished 'Old Sparta and Its Neighbourhood.' The Address and two of Perley's letters to Captain C. S. Perley, a loyalist relative, are in the possession of Mrs. W. K. Cole, Sparta.)

Citizens and Soldiers:

You are assembled here to witness the execution of the sentence of death upon two of your fellow creatures, and whatever cause led to the conviction of them, it involves a serious and all important question that should receive your careful and earnest consideration; whether it is consistent with the laws of God and the dictates of true humanity to take that which you cannot give or in accordance with the true spirit of Christianity. This is an important subject of enquiry, and has long been doubted by many of the more thinking and Christian citizens of Europe and America.

The Cause that led me to my present unhappy fate was the false and wicked misrepresentations of your own citizens. A conviction of this should rest on the minds of the disaffected and disloyal, if there be any present, and speak in a voice of thunder to them to beware of committing the same sin. To such I would say, you can accomplish the object for which you are contending much sooner by reform than by revolution, and correct the abuses of which you complain by petitioning, and through the ballot-box, and restore peace once more to your now unhappy country, with all its attendant blessings and ever-varying charms.

The universal extension of human liberty and religious freedom is a subject that has brought the mind and talent of the great and good of all ages to its aid and defence, and its consummation is a thing to be devoutly hoped for. By pursuing such a course as humanity and charity may point out to you, you may expect to enjoy all the blessings of freedom.

Canadians: You have a country vast in extent, and having all the facilities of agriculture and commerce of the most favored clime. You have connecting chains of rivers and lakes which are navigable the whole length of your territory, connecting with the Atlantic, which is a source of wealth and commerce seldom met with in any country, and by pursuing a mild and persuasive course, you will soon see the olive branch of Peace flourishing in your soil and the Tree of Liberty taking root therein.

Roll on majestic source of wealth and happiness, and may the inhabitants of your shores soon enjoy liberty and happiness! May the voice of your country soon call you, her sons, together to celebrate the anniversary of her redemption. May the unstained and bloodless banner of Liberty be soon unrolled, and its standard planted on her thousand hills. May the gates of her temples be thrown open, their roofs echo the anthem, the holy fire be kindled upon her altars, and its incense fill the heavens. May the call go forth to the congregation of her children, and obedient to her summons may they meet together to commemorate her triumphs, and celebrate her coming fame. May she call them into her presence with the glad song of deliverance, and the sweet music of Peace. May they enter her courts, not following in the train of a conqueror but surrounded by the angel bands of civil and religious virtue. May you bind her brows not with garlands dipped in blood wantonly shed, but with green and fadeless laurels of ancient renown. May you kneel at her shrine, not to fill her ears with the praises of a hero, not to imprecate vengeance upon the head of an enemy, but to contemplate and draw inspiration again from the memories of her departed patriarchs, and to offer up the tribute of hearts filled with thanksgiving and gratitude.

The cause of human liberty is rapidly progressing and may the time soon come when her pillars shall rest on the remotest corners of the earth. Then shall volumes of incense incessantly arise from altars inscribed to liberty, when the whole human family shall unitedly worship in her sacred temple, and offer up their sacrifices to the Great Author.

God prosper the cause of Liberty, Fraternity, and Brotherly Love.

Amos Perley.

(4) THE EXECUTIONS.

The following were hanged in London:

January 7—Hiram B. Lynn.
January 11—Daniel D. Bedford.
January 14—Albert Clark.
February 4—Cornelius Cunningham.
February 6—Joshua G. Doan and Amos Perley.

Doan had been prominent in the Duncombe rising but had escaped. Bedford had spent six months in jail at the same time, but upon petitioning he was pardoned on providing security to keep the peace for three years. Numerous statements, letters, and reports of the executions are to be found in the contemporary press, the Public Archives of Canada, and in private possession in the vicinity of the homes of those hanged. The diary of the Reverend William Proudfoot, Presbyterian clergyman of London, whose nephew, James Aitcheson, was among those transported, comments on the events. Describing the hanging of Lynn, he notes on January 8

APPENDIX 289

that only 200 were present, though 'the Tories, who were big with hope that hanging rebels would be a very popular measure, expected 5,000 spectators'. On the twenty-first he wrote:
'What a savage set of beings these loyalists must be! Now what satisfaction can it give to any man to see a man hanged; who but a devil would derive any satisfaction from such a scene? It is necessary, forsooth, to satisfy their bloodthirsty souls by shedding blood... God pity us if we be under the Tories—these ogres whose appetites for blood must be satisfied'.

Bedford was buried in the Friends' Burying Ground, North Norwich; Doan and Perley in the Friends' Burying Ground, Sparta; while the bodies of the others do not appear to have been claimed.

(5) THE EPITAPH ON THE TOMBSTONE OF SURGEON HUME.

[Surgeon Hume, who was killed during the Battle of Windsor, was buried in the old churchyard at Sandwich. The following epitaph on his tombstone is said to have been written by Colonel John Prince, the leader of the Canadian militia engaged at Windsor.]

SACRED

To the Memory of

JOHN JAMES HUME, ESQRE. M. D.

Staff Assistant Surgeon

who was inhumanly murdered and his body afterwards brutally mangled by a gang of armed ruffians from the United States

Styling themselves

"PATRIOTS",

who committed this cowardly and shameful outrage on the morning of the 4th December, 1838: having intercepted the deceased while proceeding to render professional assistance to her Majesty's gallant Militia engaged at Windsor, U. C., in repelling the incursion of this rebel

crew more properly styled

PIRATES.

APPENDIX P.

DOCUMENTS RELATIVE TO THE RETURN OF THE STATE PRISONERS FROM VAN DIEMEN'S LAND.

(1) LETTER OF STEPHEN WRIGHT AND AARON DRESSER TO THE NEW YORK *Tribune.*

New-York, February 17th, 1844.

To the Editors of The Tribune:

The undersigned were engaged with Col. Von Schoultz in the affair of the Windmill, near Prescott, in November, 1838. They were tried by a militia court-martial at Kingston, Canada, and sentenced to death, but sent to Van Dieman's Land as convicts; where, after a residence of nearly four years, they were forgiven and allowed to return to their native country by Sir John Franklin, the British governor.

On our voyage out we doubled the Cape of Good Hope; on our voyage home we doubled Cape Horn—performing in all a journey of upward of thirty thousand miles, and sailing once at least round the world.

As there are fifty-four of our comrades who were under Von Schoultz still in captivity, we think it a duty to them and their relatives to offer the public an account of their present circumstances, so far as the same are known to us.

To do this in the most satisfactory manner we here name them severally. They are all in tolerable health except Thomas Stockton, who is in a consumption. Severe treatment and other causes, which it would only excite unkind feelings for us to dwell upon, have made great inroads upon many constitutions once very strong; and should it be the pleasure of the British Government to release them, seeing that it is on the most friendly terms with ours, and perfect peace prevailing on this continent, their wives, sisters, parents, and other relatives may expect to meet with men broken down, care-worn, or in many, if not in most cases, friends who have painfully endured a very heavy, and, as some think, most unmerited bondage.

There names are: David Allen, Orlin Blodgett, George T. Brown, Robert G. Collins, Luther Darby, William Gates, John Morrisset, James Pearce, Joseph Thomson, John Berry, Chauncey Bugby, Patrick White, Thomas Baker, John Cronkhite, John Thomas, Nathan Whiting, Riley Whitney, Edward A. Wilson, Samuel Washburn, Bemis Woodbury, John Bradley, James Inglish, Joseph Lafore, Daniel Liscomb, Hiram Loop, Calvin and Chauncey Matthews, Andrew Moore, Jehiel H. Martin, Hugh Calhoun, Leonard Delano, Moses A. Dutcher, Elon Fellowes, Michael Frier, Manuel Garrison, Gideon A. Goodrich, Nelson and Jeremiah Griggs, John Gillman, Daniel D. Heustis, Garret Hicks, David House, Hiram Sharp, Henry Shew, Orin W. Smith, Joseph W. Stewart, Foster Martin, Ira Polly, Jacob Paddock, William and Solomon Reynolds, Asa H. Richardson, and John G. Swansburgh. Also T. Stockton, who is in ill health.

The following Prescott prisoners are dead: Anson Owen, Asa Priest, Lysander Curtis, John Stuart of Ohio, William Nottage, and Andrew Leaper.

The above are nearly all Americans. The Prisoners from Windsor and the Short Hills, partly Canadian and partly from the United States, are in tolerable health, except Robert Marsh, who is consumptive. Their names are, Chauncey Sheldon, Elijah C. Woodman, Michael Murray, John H. Simmons, Alvin B. Sweet, Simeon Goodrich, James M. Acheson, Elijah Stevens, John C. Williams, Samuel Snow, Riley M. Stewart, John Sprague, John B. Tyrrell, James DeWitt Fero, Henry V. Barnum, John Varnum, James Waggoner, Norman Mallory, Horace Cooley, John Grant, Lynus W. Miller (student at law), and Joseph Stewart.

Of these, L. W. Miller and Joseph Stewart are at Port Arthur, a place of additional punishment. They attempted to recover their freedom, and suffer accordingly.

The prisoners were in hopes that when President Tyler and Mr. Webster concluded the late Treaty with Britain through Lord Ashburton, and when Canada got a new constitution, their hard fate would be remembered; but no one of these on the island knows of any steps taken for a release. Mr. Everett, our minister at London, told us he was doing what

APPENDIX 291

he could for his unhappy countrymen, but thought it was very doubtful whether they would be allowed again to see their native land. We were five months on the passage from Van Dieman's Land to London, and Mr. Everett got us a ship to New-York.

We say it with truth and sincerity, that we would not of *choice* pass the rest of our lives on Van Dieman's Land if the whole island were given to us in freehold as a gift; and as there can be no fear that our unfortunate friends who remain there will ever again desire to interfere with Canada, we would entreat the generous and humane to exert themselves to procure their release. We have not to complain of unusual harshness toward ourselves, and yet both of us have often wished to be relieved by death from the horrid bondage entailed on those who were situated as we were. To be obliged to drag out an existence in such a convict colony and among such a population is in itself a punishment severe beyond our power to describe.

Several parties, in all about one thousand five hundred men, were placed last May under proper officers by the governor for the purpose of securing four criminals guilty of murder, &c. We were in one of these parties by whom the criminals were secured; and this and general good conduct procured several persons their liberty, among whom we two were fortunate to be included.

Morrisset, Murry, and Lafore are, we think, from Lower Canada.

We can speak more decidedly as to our comrades from Prescott, Windsort, and the Short Hills, above named, because when we got our freedom, we visited most of them, though scattered through the interior of the country following their several trades or occupations. One of us, Aaron Dresser, resides in Alexandria, Jefferson county—the other, Stephen S. Wright, lives in Denmark, Lewis county, both in New-York State. We will be happy to reply to any post-paid letters from the relatives of our comrades, and to give them any further information in our power.

AARON DRESSER,
STEPHEN S. WRIGHT.

[A number of errors occur in the above letter: (1) Joseph Stewart, a Prescott prisoner, is included also in the Windsor and Short Hills list; (2) In the list of dead, John Stuart was a Windsor prisoner officially known as James P. Williams; (3) William Nottage in the same list was a Windsor prisoner; (4) Three Short Hills men who died—McNulty, Van Camp, and McLeod—and three others who had escaped—Wait, Gemmell, and Chandler —are omitted from the list; (5) George Cooley and Jacob Beemer, of the Short Hills, are also omitted; (6) John Varnum is an error for John Vernon; (7) Horace Cooley was a St. Clair prisoner, not Short Hills. Allowing for these mistakes, the entire 92 exiles are accounted for.]

(2) LETTER OF EDWARD EVERETT, UNITED STATES AMBASSADOR TO GREAT BRITAIN, TO DANIEL D. HEUSTIS, DECEMBER 5, 1846.

[When he wrote the letter Mr. Everett was President of Harvard College. It is reprinted from Heustis's *Narrative*, 161-3.]

Cambridge, 5th Dec., 1846.

Dear Sir: I will now endeavor to comply with your request to be furnished with some account of the steps taken by me to procure the liberation of the American citizens who were transported to Van Dieman's Land for having taken part in the movement in Canada in 1838. My official correspondence on this subject was quite voluminous, but the following is the substance, and will, I suppose, answer your purpose.

Among the papers which I found awaiting me in London on my arrival there in November, 1841, were petitions for the release of one or two of the Americans in Van Dieman's Land, with private letters requesting me to interfere in their behalf. These documents were transmitted to me through the Department of State, but it was left wholly to my discretion what use I should make of them. The relations between the two countries at that time were not favorable to any movement for the release of the prisoners. I bore their case, however, constantly in mind, and occasionally mentioned it informally to Lord Aberdeen. While Lord Ashburton was at Washington in 1842 our government requested his good offices in this matter; and after the ratification of the treaty some correspondence on the subject took place between Mr. Webster and Mr. Fox. Having noticed this correspondence in the American papers, I took occasion early in December to call the attention of the British Minister to the subject more particularly than I had felt authorized to do before; and he assured me he was willing, whenever his government granted an amnesty to the Canadians implicated, that it should be extended to the citizens of the United States. This seemed to me all that could be reasonably asked; but a good deal of delay took place before the measure was decided on.

In the meantime Messrs. Wright and Dresser, two of the Americans concerned, had been pardoned in consequence of some services rendered to the local magistracy. They called upon me in London on the 26th of December, 1843, and I am glad to learn from you that they were pleased with their reception and that they reached home in safety.

In the month of January, 1844, information having reached our government that a general amnesty had been granted to the Canadians, I was directed to bring the case of our countrymen informally to the consideration of Lord Aberdeen. He told me that no such comprehensive measure had been adopted, but that the Governor-General had been clothed with a large discretion to grant a pardon to all such individuals as might, by themselves or through their friends, petition for it, provided there were no aggravating circumstances against them; and he renewed his promise that, as far as depended on him, the same course should be pursued toward American citizens. Lord Stanley also, the Colonial Minister, gave me the same assurance. The application was to be forwarded through the Department of State to the American Minister in London. I immediately presented the only application in proper form which was then in my hands. It was in favour of Mr. David Allen and was promptly granted. I of course gave our government immediate intelligence of these events, and also wrote to the friends of some of the individuals concerned, letting them know what was necessary to be done.

As soon as the information could take effect in the United States, petitions began to be forwarded to me by the Department in considerable numbers. Ten were received at once, in April, 1844, and seventeen in the month of May following. Your case was one of the seventeen. It was on the 31st of May that I wrote the letter to Mr. Hathaway, our Consul at Hobart Town, of which he spoke to you. In this letter I gave him a list of those who had been pardoned, twenty-eight in number, in addition to Messrs. Wright and Dresser, and I informed him of the willingness of the British Government to pardon all whose friends applied. Commiserating the condition of those who might not have parents or other relations to take an interest in their release, I requested Mr. Hathaway, 'if he heard of any poor fellow that had no friends, to let me know his name, &c., and I would endeavour to get him pardoned'. Mr. Hathaway's answer did not reach me till May, 1845. It contained a list of a considerable number still in Van Dieman's Land, but I had already obtained the pardon of most of them.

I find by a dispatch of the 29th October, 1844, that forty-one in the whole had at that time been pardoned, and on subsequent applications seventeen were added to the number. I send you a list of the whole, but I am inclined to think one or two individuals are given twice, under names somewhat varied.

I suggested to the Department the propriety of making some provision to aid those thus liberated in their return, as there might be cases where without such assistance it would be impossible for them to get home. I was led to make this suggestion by the difficulty experienced by Messrs. Wright and Dresser, although provided with a free passage to London by the British colonial government. The Secretary of State decided, with great regret, that there was no appropriation from which such aid could be legally given.

I was led on this as on some other occasions to lament that no fund is placed at the disposal of our foreign ministers for the relief of distressed countrymen, and no discretion allowed in the application of the contingent fund of the legation for that purpose. So far is this from being the case, that having once expended £13. 18. 2 for the defence of an American seaman on trial for his life, whose friendless case had been represented to me by the chaplain of Newgate, that charge was disallowed in the settlement of my accounts since my return, although I have reason to think my interference saved the man's life.

In reference to an expression in the warrant for your pardon, that it took place 'in consideration of some circumstances which had been humbly represented' to the Queen, you express your belief that some personal application may have been made by me in your favor. Such, however, is not the case. The words quoted by you are probably words of an official form in all warrants for pardon. The usages of the British government would not permit a foreign minister, under ordinary circumstances, to make a personal application to the Sovereign on a matter of business; nor was there in this case any occasion for it. As soon as the ministry made up their minds to pardon the Canadians, every application which I made in favour of an American was granted as soon as it could pass through the forms of office. If there was any casual delay I always found it easy to hasten a decision by dropping a hint in the proper quarter. The most friendly disposition was manifested throughout by Lord Aberdeen and Lord Stanley. It was my practice when an application was forwarded to me from the Department of State to address a note to the Foreign Office as soon as it could be prepared, frequently the same day. I think I can say that no American had a day added to his captivity by my neglect.

I took an interest in the fate of yourself and your associates because I had reason to think you were mostly young men who had been led by false representations of the state of things in Canada to suppose that the movement in 1838 resembled the revolutionary war in the United States. Several, as I perceived from the memorials in their favor, had left aged parents or other relatives at home in great affliction. I had also formed, besides, a very unfavourable opinion of Van Dieman's Land as a school of moral improvement.

If any further information in my power to furnish is desired by you I shall be happy to afford it; in the meantime I remain, very truly,

Your well-wisher,
EDWARD EVERETT.

Mr. Daniel D. Heustis.

(3) LIST OF AMERICAN CITIZENS PARDONED ON APPLICATION OF MR. EVERETT.

(Enclosed in the foregoing letter to Daniel Heustis.)

David Allen, Thomas Baker, Henry V. Barnum, John Berry, George T. Brown, Chauncey Bugby, Robert G. Collins, John Cronkhite, Luther Darby, Leonard Delano, Moses A. Dutcher, Elon Fellows, James DeWitt Fero, Michael Fraer, Emmanuel Garrison, William Gates, John Gilman, George S. Goodrich, Gideon A. Goodrich, Jerry Griggs, Nelson J. Griggs, John S. Guttridge, Daniel D. Heustis, Garrett Hicks, David House, Daniel Liscomb, Hiram Loop, Norman Mallory, Robert Marsh, Jehiel H. Martin, Linus W. Miller, Benjamin Mott, Samuel Newcome, Jacob Paddock, James Pierce, Ira Polley, Solomon Reynolds, Riley M. Stewart, Hiram Sharp, Chauncey Sheldon, Henry Shew, Orin W. Smith, Samuel Snow, Elizur Stevens, Joseph Stewart, Thomas Stockton, John G. Swansberg, Alvin B. Sweet, John Thomas, Joseph Thompson, Samuel Washburn, Nathan Whiting, Riley Whitney, James P. Williams, John C. Williams, Edward A. Wilson, Bemis Woodbury, Elijah C. Woodman—58.

[Thomas Stockton died before notice of his pardon reached him. Benjamin Mott and Samuel Newcome are apparently the two names referred to by Mr. Everett as aliases, so that fifty-six prisoners were actually pardoned through his good offices. Orrin Smith's parchment pardon is reproduced facing page 243, and printed herewith, appendix P (5).]

(4) PARDON OF STEPHEN S. WRIGHT BY SIR JOHN FRANKLIN.

(From Wright's Narrative in Lyon, *Narrative and Recollections of Van Dieman's Land, during a Three Years' Captivity of Stephen S. Wright*, 33-4.)

[Stephen Wright and Aaron Dresser were pardoned in 1843 for effecting the capture of bush-rangers.]

By His Excellency, Sir John Franklin, Knight Commander of the Royal Hanoverian Guelphic Order, Knight of the Greek Order of the Redeemer, and a Captain in Her Majesty's Royal Navy, Lieutenant Governor of the Island of Van Dieman's Land and its dependencies.

Whereas Stephen Smith Wright, who arrived at Hobart Town by the ship Buffalo in the year 1840, under a sentence of transportation for life, passed upon him at the Province of Upper Canada in the year 1838, hath, by his good conduct and behavior during his residence in this island, appeared to me, the said Lieutenant Governor, to be a fit object for the extension to him of an absolute remission of his sentence: Now, therefore, in consideration of the premises, I, the Lieutenant Governor aforesaid, by virtue of the powers and authorities in me in his behalf vested, do, by this instrument, absolutely remit all the residue or remainder of the time or term of transportation yet to come or unexpired, of or under

APPENDIX 295

the said sentence so passed upon the said Stephen Smith Wright, as aforesaid, and the same is hereby remitted accordingly.

Register E.
Folio 28.

L. S. In testimony whereof I have hereunto set my hand, and caused also the seal of Van Dieman's land and its dependencies to be hereunto affixed, at Hobart Town, in Van Dieman's Land, aforesaid, this twenty-second day of June, in the year of our Lord one thousand eight hundred and forty-three.

(Signed) JOHN FRANKLIN.

J. E. RIETENO, Colonial Secretary, and Register.

(5) PARDON OF ORRIN SMITH BY SIR EARDLEY WILMOT.

(From the original in the possession of Mr. J. Donald Garnsey, Clayton, N.Y.)

VAN DIEMENS LAND

To all to whom these presents shall come—I Sir John Eardley Eardley Wilmot Baronet Lieutenant Governor of the Island of Van Diemens Land and its Dependencies— send Greeting.

Whereas by Her Majestys Royal Warrant under the Sign Manual bearing date in Buckingham Palace the Ninth day of May one thousand eight hundred and forty four countersigned by one of Her Majestys Secretaries of State and addressed to the Lieutenant Governor of the Island of Van Diemens Land for the time being Her Majesty the Queen was pleased in consideration of some circumstances humbly represented to Her to extend Her Grace and Mercy unto Orrin W. Smith who was tried at a Court Martial in Upper Canada and convicted of feloniously invading the Province of Upper Canada and sentenced to Death which sentence was commuted to transportation for Life and to grant him Her free pardon for his said crime. Now know ye that I the said Sir John Eardley Eardley Wilmot Baronet Lieutenant Governor of the Island of Van Diemens Land and its Dependencies have received Her Majestys Warrant and do hereby certify and declare that the said Orrin W. Smith hath and ought to enjoy Her Majestys free pardon for the said Crime whereof he was convicted as aforesaid. And I do hereby discharge the said Orrin W. Smith from all custody in respect of his said sentence and transportation.

In testimony whereof I have hereunto set my hand and caused the Seal of the Island of Van Diemens Land to be hereunto affixed.

Dated at Hobart Town this Fifth day of December in the year of Our Lord one thousand eight hundred and forty four.

By His Excellencys Command
J. E. RIETENO
Colonial Secretary.

(Signed) J. EARDLEY WILMOT.

296   THE LIVES AND TIMES OF THE PATRIOTS

[On the back of the parchment pardon is the following description of Smith, taken on the deck of the prison-ship *Buffalo* upon arrival at Van Diemen's Land.]

PERSONAL DESCRIPTION OF ORRIN W. SMITH.

Trade Farm Labourer
Height Five feet Six Inches
Age Thirty Two Years
Complexion Sallow
Head Round
Hair Dark Brown
Whiskers Reddish
Visage Dark

Forehead High
Eyebrows Sandy
Eyes Grey
Mouth Wide
Chin Round
Native Place Vermont
Remarks Bald—wears Wig

(6) LETTER OF LINUS W. MILLER TO THE NEW YORK *Express.*

To the Editors of the N. Y. Express:

Gentlemen—Having once more set foot on the shore of my native land after a painful exile of many years, I hasten to perform a promise which I made to my unfortunate comrades on taking leave of them in Van Dieman's Land in Sept. last—to make their situation known in a country under whose institutions they claim a birthright, and which I trust they have in no wise disgraced.

Most of them through the kind intercession of the American Government had been pardoned when I left, and I have every reason to hope that *all* are now *free*. Yet after many long years of physical and mental suffering, the extent and intensity of which no language can describe, these men are set at liberty in the PENAL COLONY of a foreign land 16,000 miles from home, without any means of returning to their friends and the country which they still remember and venerate as their own. Many of them are in want of proper food and clothing. They are willing and anxious to labor, but owing to the distressed state of the colony are seldom able to find employment. An American vessel rarely touches at Hobartown, and then only serving to remind them of home.

It ought to be borne in mind that while they have been suffering in exile, many of the principal leaders who were instrumental in getting up the rebellion have been rewarded by the British Government with places of honor and trust in Canada. It also appears from the best legal advice which can be obtained in V. D. L. that the detention of the whole party, since the moment of their first landing, has been an illegal assumption of power on the part of the local authorities; and an action for damages is now pending in the Supreme Court of that colony, the heads of which have shown a disposition, as far as possible, to delay its issue. I will add that the conduct of the party has generally been such as to gain them the respect and esteem of the most respectable inhabitants of the colony, not excepting those in authority.

Under those circumstances may I not hope that means may be taken to hasten their return? They already feel very thankful to the Government of their own country for its intercession in their behalf in respect of their pardon. Can there be any impropriety in that Government's assisting them home where they will have an opportunity of expressing their gratitude; and may I not hope, gentlemen, that you will use your influence in forwarding so charitable an object? The following is a list of the names of those who were in Van Dieman's Land on the 25th of September:

Joseph Stewart	John Berry
Solomon Reynolds	Chancey Matthews
Elijah C. Woodman	Calvin Mathers
Orlan Blodgit	Andrew Moore
Ash H. Richardson	Wm. Reynolds
Hugh Calhoun	Jos. Leforte
Henry Shew	John Brodley
Thos. Baker	Moses A. Dutcher
John C. Williams	R. M. Stewart
Henry V. Barnhum	Horace Cooley
G. B. Cooley	Norman Mallory
J. S. Gutteridge	Jas. Waggoner
Michael Fraer	John Vernon
Robert G. Colling	James M. Aitcherson

The three last were tried as British subjects.

Twenty-seven left in January, 1845, in the U. S. whaling vessel "Steiglitz" for the Sandwich Islands, where they arrived safe—but there was no United States vessels there homeward bound at that time.

12 have died, some of them, I am sorry to say, in consequence of the severity of their sufferings. Their names are

Alexander McLeod	John McNulty
G. Van Camp	J. P. Williams
Asa Priest	Andrew Leper
L. Curtis	F. Martin
Wm. Notage	John Simmons
Alson Owen	Thos. Stockton,

I am, gentlemen, yours, etc.,

L. W. MILLER.

New York, January 28.

[The letter was reprinted in the Buffalo *Morning Express* of February 4, 1846, with the following comment:

'Our Government has manifested a criminal indifference towards these unfortunate Exiles. They were deluded into Canada, it is true, but their offence was not such and one as should have shut them out from the sympathy of their country. A vessel should be despatched to bring them home. They have expiated, too severely, the error which consigned them to many years of banishment and suffering.']

APPENDIX Q.

EXTENSION OF AMNESTY TO EXILED LEADERS IN THE UNITED STATES.

Patent of Pardon to David Gibson, late of the Township of York, attainted of High Treason. Recorded 9th June 1843.

(From a photographic copy in the possession of Mr. T. Wilbur Best, Toronto.)

Victoria by the Grace of God of the United Kingdom of Great Britain and Ireland, Queen, Defender of the Faith, &c., &c., &c.

To all to whom these Presents shall come, Greeting.

Whereas heretofore in our Court of Oyer and Terminer and Gaol Delivery for the Home District of Our Province of Upper Canada, for cognizance of certain of High Treason and Treasonable Practices committed within that Province—before the Honorable John Beverley Robinson, then being Our Chief Justice of Our Court known by the Style of the Court of King's Bench for the Province of Upper Canada, and one of the Justices assigned in and by Our Commission dated at Toronto the Second day of February in the first year of Our Reign and issued under and by virtue of a certain Act of the Parliament of the said Province of Upper Canada, passed in the first year of Our Reign, intituled "An Act to pro-"vide for the more effectual and impartial Trial of Persons charged with "Treason and Treasonable Practices committed in this Province",—and others his Associates in Our said Commission, appointed and named, an Indictment was found by the Grand Jury at and before the said Court of Oyer and Terminer and Gaol Delivery against David Gibson, then late of the Township of York, in the Home District, Land Surveyor, for High Treason, and thereupon a Warrant was duly issued to Our Sheriff of the said Home District commanding him that he should take the said David Gibson, and him safely keep, so that he might have him by his body to answer to the said Indictment and to be further dealt with according to law, to which said Warrant Our said Sheriff returned that the said David Gibson was not to be found in his District, whereupon such proceedings were had in pursuance of the Provisions of a certain Act of the Parliament of Upper Canada, passed in the first year of Our Reign, intituled "An Act "to provide for the more speedy attainder of persons indicted for High "Treason who have fled from this Province, or remain concealed therein "to escape from Justice," that afterward in and in Michaelmas Term in the Fourth Year of Our Reign it was ordered by the Consideration and judgment of our said Court of King's Bench for the Province of Upper Canada, that Judgement of Attainder against the said David Gibson should be entered of Record, whereby and by force of the said last mentioned Act the said David Gibson stood and was adjudged attainted of the crime of High Treason and became liable to suffer as a person attainted of High Treason by the Laws of the Land ought to suffer and forfeit. Now know Ye that We, on taking the premises into our Royal Consideration for divers good causes Us thereunto moving, of Our Special Grace have pardoned, remitted, and released, and by these Our Letters Patent do pardon, remit, and release the said David Gibson of and from his said offence, the Attainder aforesaid, and all and every forfeiture and punishment whatsoever which may or might be inflicted on him the said David Gibson for or by reason of the said High Treason, Indictment and Attainder from the day of the date of these Presents.

In testimony whereof We have caused these Our Letters to be made Patent and the Great Seal of our said Province to be hereunto affixed. Witness Our Right Trusty and Well Beloved Sir Charles Theophilus Metcalfe, Bart G.C.B., one of Our Most Honorable Privy Council, Governor General of British North America, and Captain General and Governor in Chief in and over Our Provinces of Canada, Nova Scotia, New Brunswick and the Island of Prince Edward and Vice Admiral of the same, &c. &c. &c. at Kingston, this thirtieth day of May, in the Year of our Lord one thousand eight hundred and forty three and in the Sixth Year of Our Reign.

INDEX

A

Abbey, Colonel Dorrephus, 134, 140 fn.
Aberdeen, Lord, 219.
Aitcheson, James, 213 fn., 230 fn.
Alexander, Sir James, 153 fn., 160-1.
Allan, A. G., 38.
Allen, David, 219, 223.
Alves, William, 21, 192, 202 fn., 207 fn., 232 fn.
Alway, Robert, 52, 54 fn.
American Revolutionary War, 7, 17 fn., 71, 106.
Anderson, Captain Anthony, 15, 16, 17, 18 fn., 34.
Anderson, David, 50, 54, 90.
Anderson, Duncan, 140 fn.
Anderson, Ira, 202 fn.
Anderson, Colonel John, 118 fn., 119, 232 fn.
Anderson, Robert, 50.
Anderson, William, 159.
Anderson, Colonel, 35.
Armour, Robert, 38, 39, 41.
Armstrong, John, 13 fn.
Armstrong, Thomas, 13 fn.
Arnold, Richard, 79, 80.
Arthur, Sir George, 53 fn., 80 fn., 104-6, 108, 110, 112, 151 fn., 157, 165 fn., 172 fn., 174-5, 182 fn., 186 fn., 187, 188 fn., 194 fn., 197, 210, 216 fn., 232.
Ash, Joseph, jr., 168, 169, 170, 173.
Ash, Joseph, sr., 168, 169, 170, 173.
Ashburton, Lord, 189.
Asher, William, 23.
Askin, Colonel J. B., 50, 79 fn.

B

Bâby, Charles, 4 fn., 146.
Bâby, Francis, 145, 147.
Bâby, Lieutenant W. L., 91.
Bacon, Colonel, 96, 97.
Baker, Thomas, 230 fn.
Baker, William, 167, 168, 170, 173.
Baldwin, Robert, 6, 19, 66 fn., 236.
Barber, Sidney, 150.
Barclay, George, 230 fn.
Barnum, Henry, 223 fn.
Bartlett, William, 150.
Beach, Captain, 141.
Beakes, N., 72 fn.
Bedford, Daniel, 150 fn.
Bedford, Paul, 202 fn.
Beebe, Nelson, 83, 86.
Beemer, Jacob, 106, 107, 110, 182, 183, 200, 202 fn., 203 fn., 207, 213 fn., 229.
Beemer, Joseph, 48, 203 fn.
Berry, John, 229-30.
Bidwell, Marshall S., 7, 9, 13 fn., 19, 26, 34 fn., 62, 73, 206, 231, 240, 241 fn.
Bierce, General L. V., 132, 133, 143, 146, 150, 186.
Birge, General John W., 13 fn., 133, 134, 140, 160, 161, 186.
Blake, Edward, 236, 241.
Blodget, Orlin, 230 fn.
Bonnycastle, Sir Richard, 77 fn., 83 fn., 149 fn., 155 fn., 159, 166 fn., 175, 179, 191 fn.
Bostwick, Colonel John, 50.
Boswell, Captain J. C., 170.
Boulton, D'Arcy, 169, 170, 172, 173.
Boulton, Hon. George S., 34, 37, 42, 169.
Boulton, Attorney-General H. J., 4, 8, 23.
Bradley, John, 229.
Bradley, Colonel, 99.
Bradshaw, Amos, 230 fn.

Brady, General Hugh, 95, 102, 113.
Brady, John, 170.
Brady, Moses, 104.
Brady, Philip, 103 fn.
Bridgeford, David, 114.
Broderick, Captain, 146.
Brodieau, Francis, 187.
Brophy, Stephen, 91 fn., 115 fn., 116, 117, 118 fn.
Brougham, Lord, 129, 152, 203.
Brown, George, 226, 236, 237.
Brown, James, 202 fn.
Brown, John, 110 fn.
Brown, Thomas Storrow, 13.
Browne, Captain, 100, 101.
Browne, John, 230 fn.
Buck, Roe, 38, 39, 40, 41, 42.
Buckley, Captain Christopher, 133, 140 fn.
Bugbee, Chauncey, 227.
Burnham, Hon. Zacheus, 34, 37, 39 fn.
Bush, J. C., 173.

C

Chisholm, Colonel John, 31.
Chrysler, James, 59.
Clark, Benjamin, 169, 170.
Clark, Captain Charles, 37, 170.
Clark, Orsimus, 49.
Clinton, George, 72 fn.
Clutier, Francis, 91 fn.
Colborne, Sir John, 5, 125, 187.
Collins, Francis, 2 fn.
Collins, Robert, 230 fn.
Comfort, William, 30, 61.
Conant, Daniel, 68.
Conger, Captain, 37.
Conklin, Seth, 77 fn.
Cook, Ephraim, 182 fn., 230 fn.
Cook, Robert, 111 fn.
Cooley, George, 202 fn., 209, 229.
Cooley, Horace, 113, 198 fn., 214, 229.
Coon, Peter, 47, 48.
Copland, William, 18, 30 fn., 52.
Covert, Lieutenant H., 41.
Cowall, Captain, 35.
Crew, William, 114.
Cronkhite, John, 223 fn.
Crysler, Colonel John, 135.
Culver, Theron, 91 fn., 123 fn., 125, 126 fn., 128.
Cummings, James, 105.
Cunningham, Colonel Cornelius, 147-50.
Curtis, Lysander, 213 fn.
Calcutt, Captain, 87.
Calhoun, Hugh, 229.
Campbell, John, 10.
Carfrae, Major, 24.
Carl, William, 103 fn.
Carmichael, Hugh, 19.
Carmon, Edward, 230 fn.
Carrier, J. B., 127, 128.
Carroll, William, 102, 103 fn.
Case, Colonel G. W., 104.
Chalmers, Colonel, 30.
Chandler, Samuel, 32, 84, 103 fn., 104-7, 110, 113, 200, 202 fn., 206, 209-10, 221-2.
Chase, Abner, 54.
Chase, Benjamin, 229.
Chase, Walter, 54, 90, 117, 118 fn.
Chatterton, Lieutenant R. D., 40, 41, 170.

D

Dafoe, David, 176.
Darby, Luther, 223 fn., 225.
Darling, Thomas, 73, 74 fn.
Davis, Asa, 62.
Davis, Captain E. Wingate, 133 fn.

INDEX

Davis, George, 91 fn.
Dean, John, 198 fn.
De Grassi, Charlotte, 18 fn.
De Grassi, Cornelia, 18 fn.
Delaney, Garret, 49.
Delano, Leonard, 223 fn., 225.
Delong, Albert, 49.
Demande, Antoine, 147.
Denham, Lord, 207.
Dennis, James, 48.
De Witt, John H., 175.
Dickens, Charles, 77 fn.
Dickson, Elizabeth, 64.
Doan, James W., 107.
Doan, Joel, 54.
Doan, Joshua Gillam, 50, 54, 147, 150 fn., 180, 231 fn.
Dodd, Captain, 95, 96.
Dodge, Colonel W. W., 91, 93, 123, 125-30.
Doel, John, 13 fn., 192.
Doel, Rev. John, 13 fn., 115, 191-2.
Doherty, Bernard, 80.
Doyle, W., 11, 73.
Draper, William H., 105, 141, 171, 230.
Dresser, Aaron, 136, 218, 222-3.
Drew, Captain Andrew, 78, 79, 80-5.
Drolet, Charles, 126, 128, 129.
Duffield, Betty, 118 fn.
Duncan, John, 66, 67 fn.
Duncombe, Dr. Charles, 21, 46-56, 58, 72, 73, 75, 81, 91, 95, 104, 105, 111 fn., 147, 182 fn., 231.
Dundas, Colonel, 137.
Dunn, John H., 6.
Durand, Charles, 60, 61, 192, 193, 196 fn., 230 fn., 232.
Durand, Mrs. Charles, 60, 61.
Durfee, Amos, 81, 189.
Durham, Lord, 93, 107, 110, 157, 164, 174, 187, 189, 203, 206, 238, 241.
Dutcher, Moses, 229, 230 fn.
Dutcher, W. A., 13.

E

Early, Allen, 160.
Edmondson, William, 15.
Elgin, Lord, 236 fn., 238.
Elliot, Colonel W., 151 fn.
Elliott, John, 9 fn., 13 fn.
Ellis, E. D., 188.
Elmsley, Lieutenant, 81 fn., 113.
Elton, Luther, 230 fn.
Emigh, King, 49.
Emmons, Uriah, 230 fn.
Ermatinger, Captain James, 101.
Evans, Captain, 40.
Everett, Edward, 219 fn., 223 fn., 229, 230 fn.
Everett, Obed, 64.

F

Farrow, John, 160.
Fellows, Elon, 217, 223 fn.
Fero, James, 219, 223 fn., 225.
Finlaison, C. S., 81 fn,
Finlay, John, 48.
Fisher, Henry, 50, 54.
Fitzgibbon, Colonel James, 16, 17, 21-9.
Fletcher, Silas, 11, 22, 29, 30, 63, 73, 75, 154, 180, 232 fn.
Forward, Marshal, 159 fn.
Foster, Solomon, 135.
Fothergill, Charles, 2 fn., 40 fn.
Fowell, Lieutenant, 135.
Fox, Captain, 100, 101.
Fraser, Michael, 230 fn.
Frank, John, 164.
Franklin, Sir John, 209 et seq.
Fraser, James, 60.
Fraser, Colonel R. D., 156 fn., 157.
Frey, Samuel C., 158, 159 fn.
Fry, Elizabeth, 206.

G

Ganthier, Constant, 147.
Garrison, Emmanuel, 227.
Garron, Marshal, 74.
Garrow, N., 161.
Gates, William, 136, 197-8, 199 fn., 210 et seq., 225 fn., 227, 230 fn.
George, Daniel, 134, 136, 140 fn.
Gemmell, James, 202 fn., 207, 214, 221-2.
Gibson, Captain David, 10, 15, 16, 18, 20, 22, 26, 30, 67, 77, 181, 231.
Gillet, Captain, 88.
Gillet, Reynolds, 188.
Gilman, John, 223 fn.
Ghent, David, 30 fn.
Glenelg, Lord, 6, 9, 34 fn., 36, 52 fn., 53 fn., 62 fn., 75 fn., 79 fn., 104, 110, 129, 151 fn., 186 fn.
Goodrich, Gideon, 146, 147, 223 fn., 224.
Gorham, Nelson, 11, 49, 63, 73-82, 231-2.
Gould, Joseph, 21, 25.
Gourlay, Robert, 1, 2 fn.
Gowan, Lieutenant-Colonel Ogle, 135.
Graham, Adam, 73.
Graham, Lieutenant, 78.
Grant, John, 108, 202 fn., 204 fn., 206-7, 214, 223 fn., 224, 225.
Grant, Peter, 193 fn.
Gray, Amelia, 114.
Green, Rev. Anson, 57, 141.
Green, Jack, 54 fn.
Green, Warren, 140.
Grey, Earl, 233.
Griggs, Jerry, 223 fn.
Griggs, Nelson, 223.
Guttridge, John, 229, 230 fn.
Gymer, William, 25 fn., 114.

H

Hagerman, Attorney-General C. A., 60 fn.
Haight, Ephraim, 54.
Haling, John, 230 fn.
Hall, Elisha, 54.
Ham, Colonel, 39.
Hamilton, Alexander, 54 fn., 110.
Hammil, John, 182 fn.
Handy, General Henry S., 88, 89, 92, 112, 143.
Harmon, John H., 150.
Harrison, President William H., 161.
Hart, George, 171.
Hart, Samuel P., 8, 166-73.
Harvell, Colonel, 145, 149, 188.
Hastings, Howland, 151 fn.
Hathaway, John, 64.
Hathaway, American Consul, 223 fn.
Hawk, John, 18 fn., 49, 73.
Hayes, Matthew, 85.
Head, Sir Edmund, 6 fn.
Head, Sir Francis Bond, 1-27, 32 fn., 34, 36, 43-7, 50, 52, 57, 62-3, 74-5, 79 fn., 81, 85, 92, 103 fn., 114, 122 fn., 183, 234 fn., 241.
Heath, Cornet, 107.
Henderson, James, 20 fn.
Henry, George, 112.
Henry, Robert, 168, 170.
Henry, Thomas, 40 fn.
Herman, John, 155 fn.
Heustis, Daniel D., 134 fn., 135 fn., 168 fn., 180-1, 197, 198 fn., 206, 211 et seq., 219 fn., 223, 225-6.
Heward, C. R., 4 fn.

INDEX

Hicks, Garret, 219, 227.
Higgins, Cornelius, 195.
Highland, William, 198 fn.
Hill, A. B., 159 fn., 178 fn., 185.
Hill, Thomas, 193 fn.
Hills, Horatio, 182 fn.
Hoadley, Major Lester, 102.
Hogan, John Sheridan, 189 fn.
Holmes, Samuel, 102.
Holsenburgh, George, 155 fn.
Horne, Dr. R. C., 18, 19, 20 fn.
House, David, 223 fn., 225.
Hull, Henry, 91 fn., 123 fn., 125-8.
Hume, Dr. John, 141 fn., 146.
Hume, Joseph, 203.
Hunt, Frank, 47 fn.
Hunt, Jedediah, 148-50.
Hunt, John W., 24 fn.
Hunter, Henry, 159 fn.
Hunter, James, 159 fn.
Hunter, Dr. James, 11, 39-42, 132.
Hunter, 126, 127.
Hunters' Lodge, 56, 121, 132-53, 178-90.
Hyslop, Squire, 64.

I

Inglish (English), James, 229.
Ingersoll, James, 23 fn.

J

Jackson, President Andrew, 48, 184.
Jackson, Philip, 102, 103 fn.
Jacques, Lewis, 48.
James, A. B., 160.
Jarvis, Samuel P., 4 fn., 19, 24.
Jarvis, William, 20, 166 fn.
Jennings, David, 108.
Jillet, Chester, 108.
Johnson, Lieutenant, 141.
Johnston, Kate, 160-1.
Johnston, William, 84, 98, 105 fn., 132, 135 fn., 140, 153-163, 172, 186, 188.
Jones, Adjutant, 95, 96.
Jones, Judge Jonas, 8, 23, 63 fn., 170, 173, 183.

K

Kavanagh, James, 20 fn.
Kelley, Jacob, 49.
Kelly, John, 47.
Kemp, Solomon, 106, 108.
Kennedy, Edward, 64, 65, 66, 118 fn.
Kennedy, Edward, *alias* Molson, 167-74.
Kerr, Captain, 50.
Ketchum, Jesse, 115 fn., 206.
Ketchum, William, 16, 114, 115.
King, Rt. Hon. W. L. Mackenzie, 233 fn.
Kingsmill, Colonel, 41.
Kirby, Colonel, 32.

L

Lambert, Thomas, 108.
Lang, Captain, 90.
Lang, Colonel, 183.
Laurier, Sir Wilfrid, 241 fn.
Lawton, George, 54.
Lawton, Sylvester, 140 fn.
Leach, Leman, *alias* Lewis, 140 fn.
Leader, Alvan, 111 fn.
Learned, E. H., 73.
Leavitt, William H., 159 fn.
Lee, Nathan, 158, 159 fn.
Leeper, Andrew, 213 fn.
Lefore, Joseph, 230 fn.
Lemprière, General T. J., 216.
Lenoux, Louis, 91 fn.
Leonard, Elijah, 59.

Lesslie, James, 61.
Lesslie, John, 2.
Lesslie, William, 13 fn., 61.
Lett, Lieutenant Benjamin, 84, 97, 153, 163-177.
Lindsey, Mrs. Charles, 233, 236.
Linfoot, John, 15, 22, 25 fn., 114.
Liscombe, Daniel, 227.
Lloyd, Jesse, 11, 12, 30, 63, 73.
Loop, Hiram, 230 fn.
Lossing, Solomon, 52.
Lount, Samuel, 11, 12, 15, 16, 18, 19, 20, 22, 25, 29, 30, 56 fn., 63-6, 73, 85, 115, 122-3, 144, 164, 181, 187-8, 196 fn., 231, 239.
Lount, Mrs. Samuel, 15, 182 fn.
Lount, William R., 66 fn., 108, 144, 166 fn.
Luce, Alfred, 8.
Luddington, Major, 187.
Lynn, Hiram B., 150 fn.
Lyon, Caleb, 151 fn., 222 fn.
Lyons, John, 4 fn.

M

McAfee, Captain Samuel, 32.
McBane, Major, 137.
McCarrick, William, 103 fn.
McCartan, Thomas, 102.
McCormack, William, 99, 101.
McCormick, Lieutenant Sheppard, 80, 167.
McCrae, John, 97.
Macdonald, Sir John, 62 fn.
McDonald, Lieutenant, 36, 38, 41.
McDonnell, Colonel Alexander, 35, 58.
Macdonnell, Captain George, 135.
McDonnell, Colonel, 31.
McDougall, David, 150.
M'Dougall, Peter, 4 fn.
Mace, Isaac, 102.
McGrath, Captain, 23.
McGuire, William, 47, 48.
McIntyre, John, 102, 103 fn.
Mack, Andrew, 188.
McKenny, Richard, 111.
Mackenzie, Dr. A. K., 182 fn., 189 fn.
Mackenzie, Diogenes, 102, 103 fn.
Mackenzie, Kenneth, 170.
Mackenzie, William Lyon, 1-33, 38, 46, 47, 49, 50, 57, 58, 60, 61, 62, 63, 64, 71-86, 89, 102, 108, 111 fn., 114, 122 fn., 123, 124, 130 fn., 132, 145 fn., 155 fn., 163, 164, 166 fn., 167, 172, 174 fn., 178, 179, 180, 181, 182 fn., 183, 185, 186, 187, 188, 189 fn., 193 fn., 206, 222, 231-41.
Mackenzie, Mrs. W. L., 2, 84, 85, 181.
McKinney, Colonel, 96.
McKinstry, D. C., 188.
Mackintosh, John, 13 fn., 236.
McKyes, Captain, 37.
McLean, Captain, 21.
McLean, Judge, 23, 34.
McLeod, Alexander (Loyalist), 106, 113, 201-2, 209, 231 fn.
McLeod, Alexander (Patriot), 78, 81 fn., 82 fn., 189, 200, 209.
McLeod, General Donald, 94-98, 102, 105, 106, 107, 113, 139, 156 fn., 158, 159 fn., 164, 180, 187.
MacNab, Sir Allan, 17 fn., 21, 22, 24, 49, 50, 51, 52, 53, 54, 58, 59, 65, 75, 78, 79, 80 fn., 84, 159, 175 fn., 183, 184 fn., 197.
McNulty, John J., 108, 202 fn., 209.
M'Swain, Roderick, 157.
Maitland, Colonel John, 96, 99, 100, 101.
Maitland, Sir Peregrine, 4, 234 fn.

INDEX

Mallory, Norman, 108, 202 fn., 209, 230.
Mallory, Captain, 59.
Malcolm, Charles, 47 fn.
Malcolm, Eliakim, 47-9, 52-4.
Malcolm, Finlay, sr., 47 fn., 52.
Malcolm, Finlay, jr., 47 fn., 202 fn.
Malcolm, George, 47 fn.
Malcolm, Isaac B., 47.
Malcolm, James, 47 fn., 50.
Malcolm, John, 47 fn.
Malcolm, Norman, 47 fn.
Malcolm, Peter, 47 fn., 182 fn.
Mantack, John, 15.
Marcy, Governor, 80, 156 fn., 158, 159 fn.
Marr, John, 118 fn.
Marsh, David O., 195.
Marsh, Robert, 82, 83, 147, 148, 150, 194-9, 216-7, 223, 224, 225.
Marsh, Thomas, 37 fn.
Martin, Foster, 213 fn.
Martin, Jehiel, 227.
Martin, John, 155 fn.
Mason, Governor Stevens, 88.
Masonic Lodge, 46, 179, 221, 222, 228.
Matthews, Calvin, 229.
Matthews (Mathers), Chauncey, 229.
Matthews, Captain Peter, 11, 22, 23, 38 fn., 42, 56 fn., 66, 67, 115, 122, 123, 144, 181, 187, 188, 196 fn., 239.
Melbourne, Lord, 129, 152.
Menzies, George, 65, 85.
Meredith, Sergeant H. H., 39.
Merriman, Alonzo, 108 fn.
Merritt, William H., sr., 23 fn., 206.
Metcalfe, Sir Charles, 231.
Miller, Edwin, 102.
Miller, Henry, 175.
Miller, Linus W., 105, 107, 108, 109, 110, 113, 181, 182, 183, 197 fn., 202 fn., 204, 206-8, 209 fn., 213 *et seq.*, 223 fn., 226, 230 fn.
Miller, Phares, 133.
Miller, Stephen, 146.
Miller, Colonel W. R., 187.
Mills, John, 13 fn.
Mills, Michael M., 183.
Mills, Samuel, 54.
Mitchell, Captain, 226.
Monroe, President James, 82 fn.
Montgomery, John, 15, 25, 114-20, 166-7, 231-2, 233, 236.
Moodie, Lieutenant-Colonel Robert, 17, 18, 28 fn., 34, 236.
Moodie, Captain, 200.
Moon, Henry J., 167-78.
Morden, Gilbert, 117, 118 fn., 232 fn.
Morin, Michael, 214.
Morreau, Colonel James, 56 fn., 104, 105, 106, 107, 109, 110, 114, 199.
Morrisette, John, 223.
Morrison, Dr. Thomas D., 9 fn., 13, 14, 15, 21, 22, 61, 63, 73, 231, 240.
Murphy, Major, 58.
Murray, (Morin), Michael, 226.
Myers, Isaac, 103 fn.
Myers, Jacob W., 173.
Myers, P. Hamilton, 160 fn.

N

Nelles, William, 65.
Nelson, Dr. Wolfred, 178 fn.
Nickles, William, 159 fn.
Nightengale, Thomas, 16.
Normandy, Lord, 152, 188 fn., 206.
Norton, Lewis, 230 fn.
Nottage, William, 213 fn.

O

O'Grady, Rev. W. J., 6.
O'Hara, Colonel, 24.

Orange Lodge, 10, 46, 59 fn., 115, 163, 166, 192, 237.
Orgen, John, 115.
Oswald, James, 50.
Overholt, Abraham, 106.
Overholt, Martin, 106, 200.
Owen, Alson, 213 fn., 217.

P

Paddock, Jacob, 214, 230 fn.
Papineau, Louis Joseph, 12.
Parish, Thomas, 101, 102.
Parker, Chauncey, 91.
Parker, John G., 117, 118, 125 fn., 201-4
Parker, R. G., 123 fn., 124-5, 128, 151.
Parson, Timothy, 13 fn., 76.
Partridge, Abram, 91 fn., 124, 128.
Patridge, James, 60 fn.
Paulding, Jesse, 54.
Pearce, James, 227.
Peeler, Joel, 140 fn.
Perley, Amos, 146, 150 fn.
Perley, Colonel Charles, 51.
Perry, Charles, 38, 39.
Perry, Peter, 13 fn.
Pew, Benjamin, 91 fn., 123 fn.
Phelps, Russel, 140 fn.
Phillips, James, 158, 159 fn.
Pockard, John, 155 fn.
Polly, Ira, 223 fn.
Potts, James, 159 fn.
Powell, John, 8, 17, 34, 166 fn.
Price, J. Hervey, 13, 16, 19, 29, 63, 236.
Priest, Asa, 199.
Prince, Colonel John, 88, 92, 93, 145-6, 150-1, 235, 237.
Purdy, William, 36, 58.
Putnam, General, 145, 188.
Putnam, George, 55, 150.

R

Radcliff, Colonel Thomas, 89, 90, 91.
Read, Wilson, 118 fn.
Rebellion Losses Act, 119, 238.
REGIMENTS:
  Brady Guards, 150.
  Cavan Volunteers, 40.
  Clapp's Volunteers, 99 fn.
  Cobourg Rifles, 36, 79.
  Coldstream Guards, 126, 129.
  Cramahe Militia, 37.
  Doan's Spartan Rangers, 50.
  Dundas Militia, 135, 141.
  Durham Cavalry, 42.
  Glengarry Militia, 135, 141, 202.
  Grenville Militia, 94 fn., 135, 141.
  Haldimand Militia, 37.
  Huron Militia, 43 fn.
  Kent Militia, 91.
  Northumberland Militia, 35.
  Ohio Militia, 102.
  Port Hope Rifles, 41.
  Queen's Royal Borderers, 34 fn.
  St. Thomas Cavalry, 99-102, 121.
  1st Battalion Incorporated Militia, 175.
  9th Provincial Battalion, 135.
  15th Regiment of Foot, 85.
  32nd Regiment, 96, 99, 100, 102, 180.
  34th Regiment, 146.
  83rd Regiment, 96, 99, 118, 137, 138, 141, 198.
Reid, John, 29, 64.
Reid, Robert, 35.
Reid, Colonel, 163.
Reynolds, Nelson G., 173.
Reynolds, Solomon, 230 fn.
Reynolds, William, 214, 229.
Reynolds, William (*alias* David Deal), 105, 202 fn., 204 fn., 206, 207.

INDEX 303

Rice, Eber, 106.
Rich, Captain, 60.
Richardson, Asa, 229.
Richardson, Charles, 4 fn.
Richardson, Rev. James, 122, 196.
Ridout, George, 22.
Roaf, Rev. John, 196 fn.
Robbins, Francis, 230 fn.
Robbins, William, 159 fn., 160.
Roberts, Commissary-General, 210.
Robinson, John, 230 fn.
Robinson, J., 44.
Robinson, Chief Justice John Beverley, 6, 8, 18, 60 fn., 61, 144, 193.
Robinson, Thomas, 144.
Robinson (Robertson), 159 fn.
Roebuck, John A., 203.
Rogers, Captain James, 41.
Rogers, Robert, 37 fn., 39, 44 fn.
Rolph, Dr. John, 6, 8, 9 fn., 13-16, 18 fn., 19, 21, 34 fn., 46, 61-3, 71, 73, 84, 98, 180, 231, 234 fn., 237, 240.
Rouse, George, 48.
Rummerfeldt, John, 230 fn.
Russell, Lord John, 203, 206.
Ruttan, Charles, 170.
Ruttan, H. J., 34, 37, 41, 171.
Ryan, 17 fn.
Ryerson, Rev. Egerton, 7, 9, 12, 34 fn., 57, 115 fn., 122 fn., 240 fn.
Ryerson, Rev. John, 63 fn., 196 fn.
Ryerson, Rev. William, 192.
Rymal, Jacob, 31, 73.

S

Sackrider, Abraham, 47, 48.
St. Augustin, Francis, 91 fn.
Sandom, Captain, 135, 136.
Saunders, Corporal, 42.
Scanlon, Hugh, 158 fn., 159 fn., 183.
Scott, Colin, 230 fn.
Scott, C. C., 230 fn.
Scott, Enos, 111.
Scott, John (Job), 111.
Scott, Dr. Thomas, 158.
Scott, General, 84, 85, 97, 186.
Seward, Governor William H., 176, 226.
Seward, Colonel, 99, 102.
Seymour, Edward, 106-8.
Sharp, Hiram, 227.
Sharpe, William, 20.
Sheldon, Chauncey, 213, 223 fn.
Shell, F., 25.
Shenich, Mrs., 55.
Shepard, Jacob, 63-4.
Shepard, Joseph, 17, 29.
Shepard, Michael, 118 fn.
Shepard, Thomas, 118 fn.
Sherwood, Henry, 4 fn.
Shew, Henry, 229.
SHIPS:
 Alliance, 89.
 Anne, 54 fn., 88, 118, 121, 124, 126 fn., 193 fn.
 Areta, 222.
 Barcelona, 84.
 Belle, 227.
 Brockville, 139.
 British North America, 202.
 Buffalo, 148, 198-9, 210, 213-4.
 Canton, 207-8, 224.
 Captain Ross, 202-3, 205 fn., 209.
 Caroline, 44 fn., 78-82, 86, 88, 156, 159, 167, 178, 180, 184, 185.
 Champlain, 143, 150.
 Charlotte of Oswego, 134, 135.
 Charlotte of Toronto, 134.
 Cobourg, 135-7, 201, 207 fn.
 Commodore Barrie, 115, 123, 175.
 Constitution, 74.
 Dragon, 202.
 Dolphin, 207.
 Edward Everett, 226.
 Eliza Ann, 227.
 Erie, 92, 94, 150.
 Experiment, 110 fn., 135, 137, 227.
 Express, 171.
 Fama, 225.
 Fame, 226.
 Fame, whaler, 226.
 Geo. Strong, 90, 92.
 Gerard, 188.
 Governor Marcy, 113.
 Gratiot, 113.
 Great Britain, 176.
 Guernsey, 167, 168, 171, 175.
 Industry, 67-69.
 Isabella, 215.
 Kingston, 227.
 King William, 198.
 Levant, 224.
 Leviathan hulk, 204-5.
 McComb, 89.
 Marquis of Hastings, 205, 206 fn., 209.
 Meteor, 204.
 Neptune, 201.
 New England, 85.
 Oneida, 157.
 Oswego, 159.
 Paul Pry, 135, 137.
 Queen Victoria, 135, 137.
 Red Jacket, 105.
 St. George, 44 fn., 157, 200.
 Samuel Robertson, 216.
 Sir Robert Peel, 98, 105 fn., 132, 156, 157, 158, 159 fn., 161, 164, 181, 184, 185, 207 fn.
 Sons of Commerce, 226.
 Steiglitz, 223-4.
 Telegraph, 160, 185.
 Thames, 144.
 Transit, 18, 62.
 Traveller, 35, 172, 188.
 United States, 134, 135, 188.
 Volunteer, 233.
 Wellington, 207 fn.
 William IV., 137.
 York hulk, 205 fn., 204-5, 207, 210.
 Young Eagle, 228-9.
Simmons, John, 213 fn.
Smart, Major, 37.
Smith, A., 187.
Smith, Charles, 136.
Smith, Nathaniel, 91 fn., 123 fn.
Smith, Orrin, 213 fn., 223 fn., 225.
Smith, Robert, 158, 159 fn., 160.
Smith, Stephen, 182 fn.
Smith, William, 159 fn.
Snider, Elias, 49.
Snider, William, 114.
Snow, Samuel, 147, 180, 197, 212 *et seq.*, 223, 224.
Sparke, Captain, 145.
Spenser, G., 63 fn.
Spragge, Aaron, 26 fn.
Sprague, Foster, 169, 171.
Sprague, John, 230 fn.
Staples, John D., 230 fn.
Stevens, Cutting G., 104.
Stevens, Elizur, 223 fn., 224.
Stevens, Samuel, 173.
Stevens, American Ambassador, 207 fn.
Stewart, Captain Hugh, 17 fn., 25 fn.
Stewart, James, 171.
Stewart, General J. B., 187.
Stewart, John, 118 fn.
Stewart, Joseph, 214-6, 230 fn.

INDEX

Stewart, Riley, 230 fn.
Stiles, Edgar, 20 fn.
Stockdale, William, 118.
Stockton, Thomas, 213 fn., 223 fn.
Stores, Ebenezer B., 155 fn.
Strachan, Rev. John, 6, 8, 18 fn., 24.
Strachan, Colonel, 90.
Strickland, Colonel Samuel, 35.
Sullivan, John, 144, 146.
Summers, James, 188.
Sumner, Bailiff, 111.
Sutherland, General Thomas J., 71-4, 89, 90, 92-4, 123, 151, 186 fn.
Sutherland, Captain, 188.
Sutter, Captain, 225.
Swanberg, John G., 223 fn.
Sweet, Alvin, 223 fn.
Sweet, Sylvanus, 140 fn., 195.
Sweetman, Daniel, 150.
Symonds, Thomas, 102.

T

Talbot, Colonel Thomas, 47.
Tarr, John, 159 fn.
Taschereau, T. T., 128.
Taylor, 167, 169.
Thayer, Squire, 91 fn., 123 fn., 159 fn.
Theller, General Edward Alexander, 54 fn., 88-91, 93-4, 117, 121-131, 188.
Thomas, John, 223, 225-6.
Thompson, David, 65.
Thompson, Joseph, 223 fn., 225.
Thompson, Samuel, 22, 26-7, 30 fn.
Thompson, Major, 51.
Thompson, 149-50.
Thorpe, Judge Thomas, 2 fn.
Tidey, J. A., 201.
Tiffany, Abraham, 75 fn., 150.
Tilden, Charles, 55, 56.
Toles, Nathan, 148.
Tompkins, Caleb, 49.
Toucy, Riley, 160.
Town, Nathan, 182 fn.
Townshend, Colonel H. D., 96, 107.
Tracy, Thomas, 118 fn.
Traill, Mrs. Catharine, 35, 86.
Treaty of Washington, 189.
Tremaine, Jonathan, 170.
Truax, Nelson, 134 fn., 135 fn., 141 fn.
Trull, Jesse, 40 fn.
Tufford, John, 48, 182 fn.
Turnacliff, Jonathan, 160.
Tyler, A., 226 fn.
Tyler, President John, 189.
Tyrrell, John, 213 fn., 223.

U

Union, Act of, 203 fn.
Ussher, Captain Edgeworth, 164, 175.
Ussher, Captain, 175 fn.

V

Van Buren, President Martin, 86, 161, 184, 185.
Van Camp, Garret, 108, 202 fn., 209.
Van Clute, John, 160.
Van Egmond, Colonel Anthony, 8, 21-2, 29, 63, 73, 111 fn., 192.
Van Egmond, Edouard, 63 fn.
Van Rensselaer, Captain Henry, 100, 102.
Van Rensselaer, General Rensselaer, 71-4, 82-4, 89 fn., 102, 154-5, 183, 187.
Vernon, John, 202 fn., 209, 230 fn.
Von Schoultz, Colonel Nils Szoltevcky, 133, 134, 135, 137, 139, 140, 141, 153, 188.
Vreeland, General, 94, 95.

W

Waggoner, James, 105, 202 fn., 209, 229.
Wait, Major Benjamin, 53, 54, 102, 108, 110, 181, 200-10, 216 fn., 221-2.
Wait, Mrs. B., 23 fn., 110 fn., 181, 199-201, 206, 210, 221 fn.
Walker, Robert, 202 fn.
Walrath, Charles, 182 fn.
Walsh, Sergeant Frederick, 144.
Walsh, Patrick, 159 fn.
Warner, Benjamin, 102.
Warner, Chester, 158, 159 fn.
Warner, Erastus, 110.
Warner, Seth D., 158, 159 fn.
Warren, Benjamin, 163.
Warren, Captain, 36, 38, 39, 41, 42, 79.
Warren, R., 111.
Washburn, Samuel, 230 fn.
Washington, President George, 241.
Watson, Joseph, 230 fn.
Watson, Leonard, 118, 201-2.
Watson, Peter, 118 fn.
Webb, William, 182 fn.
Weir, Lieutenant, 141 fn.
Weller, William, 34.
Wellington, Duke of, 152.
Wells, William B., 158, 159 fn.
White, Patrick, 229.
Whitehead, Colonel, 111.
Whiting, Nathan, 223 fn., 225.
Whitney, Riley, 219, 227.
Wideman, Captain Ludovick, 11, 25, 26.
Wilcox, Absalom, 29.
Wilcox, Allan, 30, 31.
Wilcox, Ebenezer, 111 fn.
Wilcox, Samuel, 151 fn.
Wilcox, Colonel, 95, 96.
Wiley, Sampson, 133.
Wilkins, Peter, 167, 168, 170, 171, 173.
Willard, Luther B., 188.
Willcocks, Joseph, 2 fn.
Williams, James P., 213 fn.
Williams, John C., 230 fn.
Williams, N., 139.
Williams, Robert H., 172, 173.
Williams, Samuel, 91, 101.
Williams, Captain, 37.
Williams, Colonel, 37.
Wilmot, Sir Eardley, 216.
Wilson, Ebenezer, 159 fn.
Wilson, Edward, 223 fn.
Wilson, Henry, 168, 170.
Wilson, Dr. John, 54, 105-6, 110-11, 182-3.
Wilson, Lewis, 105.
Wilson, William, 192.
Wilson, Captain, 60.
Winchester, Aaron, 106, 108.
Winnegar, Jeremiah, 140.
Wixon, Asa, 230 fn.
Wixon, Randal, 200, 202 fn.
Wood, James, 102, 103 fn.
Wood, Captain, 198.
Woodbury, Bemis, 223 fn.
Woodman, Elijah, 59, 195-6, 213, 221 fn., 228-9.
Woodruff, Colonel Martin, 133-4, 140 fn.
Woods, Judge R. S., 51 fn., 80 fn., 222.
Woodward, Lieutenant, 55 fn.
Worth, Colonel, 136, 137.
Wright, Henry, 20.
Wright, Stephen, 137, 142, 197, 212 *et seq.*, 222-3.
Wrigley, S. F., 81.
Wyatt, Surveyor-General, 2 fn.

Y

Yeigh, Adam, 48.
Yeigh, Captain Jacob, 49, 54.
Young, Captain Selah, 223-4.
Young, Colonel, 137.

CANADIAN UNIVERSITY PAPERBOOKS

Related titles in the series

2. *The Fur Trade in Canada* by Harold Adams Innis,
10. *The Birth of Western Canada* by G. F. G. Stanley,

12. *Between the Red and the Rockies* by Grant MacEwan,

14. *The Life and Times of Confederation, 1864–1867* by Peter B. Waite,
16. *The Great Migration* by Edwin C. Guillet,
20. *Testament of My Childhood* by Robert de Roquebrune, translated from the French by Felix Walter,
30. *Pioneer Days in Upper Canada* by Edwin C. Guillet,
36. *The Englishwoman in America* by Isabella Lucy Bird,

40. *Toronto during the French Régime: A History of the Toronto Region from Brulé to Simcoe, 1615–1793* by Percy J. Robinson,

47. *Pioneer Travel* by Edwin C. Guillet,
53. *The Incredible War of 1812* by J. Mackay Hitsman,

73. *Pioneer Arts and Crafts* by Edwin C. Guillet,

www.ingramcontent.com/pod-product-compliance
Lightning Source LLC
Chambersburg PA
CBHW031405290426

44110CB00011B/265